East-West European Economic Interaction

The Vienna Institute for Comparative Economic Studies organises a series of international workshops concerned with problems of East-West European economic interaction, guided by an International Steering Committee consisting of:

The present volume is based on Workshop Session X held in Florence 22–24 September 1986.

Workshop Papers so far published:

Vol. 1–4 A list of these titles can be obtained and copies can be ordered from The Vienna Institute for Comparitive Economic Studies, P.O. Box 87, A-1103 Vienna, Austria. The remaining volumes are available from Macmillan. Series Editor: Philipp Rieger, Chairman of the Workshop
Vol. 5 East and West in the Energy Squeeze (1980)
Vol. 6 East-South-West: Economic Interactions between Three Worlds (1981)
Vol. 7 Regional Integration in East and West (1983)
Vol. 8 East-West Trade and Finance in the World Economy (1985)
Vol. 9 Industrial Policies and Structural Change (1986)
Vol. 10 Macroeconomic Management and the Enterprise in East and West (1988)

Macroeconomic Management and the Enterprise in East and West

Edited by Christopher T. Saunders

M in association with
THE VIENNA INSTITUTE
FOR COMPARATIVE ECONOMIC STUDIES

Director: Univ. Doz. Dr. G. Fink

First published 1988

Published by
THE MACMILLAN PRESS LTD
Houndmills, Basingstoke, Hampshire RG21 2XS
and London
Companies and representatives
throughout the world

Printed in Great Britain by
Richard Clay Ltd, Bungay, Suffolk

British Library Cataloguing in Publication Data
Macroeconomic management and the enterprise
in East and West: Workshop papers. —
(East-West European economic interaction; 10)
1. Macroeconomics policies
I. Saunders, Christopher, *1907-* II. Series
339
ISBN 0–333–40475–0

Preface

In view of the revolutionary changes in the world economy during the past decades, the Workshop's Steering Committee suggested that the session should be devoted to an analysis of the economic steering mechanisms and instruments obtaining in both systems, at the macro- as well as the micro-level.

The relative certainties of postwar economic development and policies disappeared at about the same time in the market economies of the West as in the more sheltered centrally planned economies. Economic strategies and policy instruments, evolved and successfully applied during the high-growth period of the 1950s and 1960s, proved of diminishing and doubtful value in times of rapid change and mounting uncertainties. Unprecedented fluctuations in exchange rates after the breakdown of the world monetary system established at Bretton Woods; the violent oil-price increases enforced by the OPEC-cartel resulting in periods of stagflation; substantial changes in raw material prices and industrial structures; all made the economic tasks confronting governments in the industrial West, i.e. the provision of stable macro-economic conditions for the countries' enterprises, increasingly difficult. Government policies no longer provided reliable orientations for the business strategies of firms. They had to evolve more flexible methods in order to respond quickly to new and unforeseen developments at home and abroad.

Rival economic doctrines added to the uncertainties of the world environment and have thrown doubt on the viability of many of the techniques employed in the past. Confidence, for example in the reliability of macro-economic forecasting as the basis for policy action, has been greatly impaired. The dramatic slowdown in the growth rates of the economies of the industrial West seems to signal the end of a historically unique epoch of unfettered growth.

At about the same time in the 1970s a pronounced slowing down in the growth performance of the centrally planned economies set in. The highly centralised planned economy of the USSR, for instance, had reached the highest growth rates in the 1950s. The USSR's real growth, still substantial in the closing 1960s, came to near stagnation towards the late 1970s and early 1980s - witness Mr. Gorbatchov. The management model of administrative planning, widely adopted in the CMEA countries, evolved by an extensive development strategy, relying on ample resources of labour, raw materials and energy inputs, was reaching the limits of its growth potential and could no longer satisfy the need of industrially more advanced societies. The need became obvious for far-reaching reforms and a restructuring of the entire system. This implies the transition from predominantly administrative forms of management to the use of economic guiding instruments. In this process the establishment of wholly self-supporting enterprises operating largely under market conditions are allotted key roles.

In the contributions of authors both from the East and the West the need to decentralise both strategic planning and current operations features quite strongly. This shift from "top-down" to "bottom-up" decision-making, nascent already for a long time, has many implications for both governmental and business methods, affecting both macro-economic steering techniques and the policy strategies of capitalist corporations as well as of socialist enterprises. It must be recognised, however: there are no simple solutions; and the debate is continuing in both systems.

* * *

The Tenth Workshop, from which this book derives, was held in Florence on 22-24 September 1986. The Vienna Institute is greatly indebted to the Associazione Italiana per lo Studio dei Sistemi Economici Comparati for its assistance and hospitality, and also to the Cassa di Risparmi e Depositi di Prato for its financial sponsorship.

In organising the Workshop, the WIIW has been assisted by the international Steering Committee. The Tenth Workshop war arranged and competently conducted by the Institute's secretariat under the responsibility of the Director, Dr. Gerhard Fink, and Mrs. Gerlinde Schöfbeck. In this they had the loyal cooperation of the Fondazione di Ricerche e Studi Internazionali di Firenze - especially of Prof. Alberto Tripiccione - and of Prof. Giangiacomo Nardozzi, as well as of Ms. Mila Biagotti and Ms. Sabina Vivarelli.

The papers and discussions have again been edited with accustomed skill by Prof. C.T. Saunders, assisted by Fred Prager. The typesetting and page make-up were efficiently carried out by Mrs. Renate Garbacz and Mr. Michael Esterházy and the index was prepared with care by Mrs. Audrey Bamber. We are grateful, as always, for the valuable cooperation of Mr. T.M. Farmiloe of the Macmillan Press Ltd.

Philipp Rieger
Chairman of the Workshop

This session of the Workshop on East-West European Economic Interaction has been jointly promoted by The Vienna Institute for Comparative Economic Studies and by the Italian *Associazione per lo Studio dei Sistemi Economici Comparati* (ASSEC). The Italian Association was founded two years ago and we hope, with this meeting, to develop further contacts with the Vienna Institute. As a member of ASSEC, I was asked to organise the present session of the Workshop. In this task I was able to enlist the *Fondazione di Ricerche e Studi Internazionali* for coping with all organisational problems. The Fondazione is a non-profit body whose main activity is to arrange, in association with the Ministry of Foreign Affairs (represented by Min.L.M. Fontana Giusti), courses and seminars for Italian and foreign diplomats. By providing hospitality to the participants in the Florence session of the workshop, the Fondazione and its Director, Prof. Alberto Tripiccione, made their contribution to the mutual understanding of the economic and institutional features of the various countries represented. But we owe this hospitality not only to the goodwill of the Fondazione but also to the financial support of the *Cassa di Risparmio e Depositi di Prato*. I wish to thank the President and the Board of Directors of this bank for their generous support.

Prof. Giangiacomo Nardozzi
Director

Istituto di Economia
University of Florence

TABLE OF CONTENTS

Christopher Saunders
Editor's introduction 1

PART I - PROSPECTS FOR THE WORLD ECONOMY

Chapter 1: Oleg Bogomolov
An overall view to West and East 19

Chapter 2: Lawrence R. Klein and *Daniel L. Bond*
The medium-term outlook for the world economy and the implications for East-West economic relations 33

Chapter 3: Józef Pajestka
Global shifts and their impact on national policies 47

Comments on Part I: *Gerhard Fink* 59
Andrea Boltho 61
Peter Beck 64

PART II - TWO NATIONAL EXAMPLES

Chapter 4: Norbert Kloten
Recent experience with macroeconomic policy in the Federal Republic of Germany 65

Chapter 5: Hans Seidel
Austria's macro-economic policies in the last decade 91

PART III - POLICIES FOR EXTERNAL ECONOMIC RELATIONS

Chapter 6: József Bognár
Decision-making and instruments for socialist foreign trade 101

Chapter 7: Wolfgang Heinrichs
Growth and the foreign balance: experience and problems of the German Democratic Republic 111

Chapter 8: Peter Sydow
Intensive development as an instrument for export-led growth in the German Democratic Republic 123

Chapter 9: Henri Bourguinat
The European Monetary System: first lessons and new challenges 133

Chapter 10: Dominick Salvatore
The new protectionism with nontariff instruments 155

Chapter 11: Paul Marer
Comparing the foreign economic strategies of market and centrally planned economies 183

Comments on Part II & III: *Márton Tardos* 217
Domenico Nuti 219
Fritz Breuss 223
Ante Čičin-Šain 225
Aleksander Lukaszewicz 228

PART IV - THE MANAGEMENT OF ENTERPRISE STRATEGIES

Chapter 12: Jan Lipiński
Problems of controlling markets and resource allocation in conditions of excess demand: the Polish case 231

Chapter 13: Jadranko Bendeković and *Ivan Teodorović*
Investment decision-making in Yugoslavia 255

Chapter 14: Aleksander Kraus
Strategic planning and innovation in a Yugoslav self-management enterprise: Metalservis 269

Chapter 15: László Horváth
Marketing and innovation strategy in a major Hungarian enterprise: Taurus 279

Chapter 16: Peter Beck
Recent developments in planning and decision-taking in large corporations 295

Chapter 17: Wilhelm Rall
Strategic planning in a changing competitive environment 315

Comments on Part IV:
Josef Kreuter 330
Hans-Jürgen Wagener 337
Peter Beck 351
László Horváth 353
Jan Lipiński 354

APPENDIX

Richard F Kaufman
Economic trends and defence burdens in the United States and the Soviet Union 357

LIST OF PARTICIPANTS 363

INDEX 367

EDITOR'S INTRODUCTION

Christopher Saunders[1)]

Policy makers and their advisers, whether in government or in enterprises, whether in market or socialist economies, and whether their interest lies in macro- or microeconomics, have been forced by the turbulent environment of the last 10-15 years to reconsider the aims and methods of their strategic thinking and the instruments with which strategies can be executed. How changes of direction have been accomplished- in some cases failed to be carried through - is the main theme of this book. The authors, many with long experience of strategic planning as operators or as analysts or in both capacities, discuss the lessons to be learnt for forward-looking policy making.

Fast economic growth in earlier decades furnished what now appears (in retrospect) to have been a relatively favourable environment for formulating strategies with the aid of rather confident forecasting and econometric analysis, at both macroeconomic and enterprise levels. In the West, it was widely held, for example, that governments would take action to prevent serious unemployment and would have both the will and the ability to maintain macroeconomic stability. These assumptions proved illusory. At the microeconomic level, managements had to look for ways of coping with new uncertainties about the circumstances in which they would need to operate and compete. Although a considerable academic literature exists, framed mostly in rather abstract terms, on solutions for the problems of decision-making under uncertainty, application in practice presents all the difficulties of combining strategy with flexible adaptation to unforeseen shifts in circumstances.

In the socialist economies, the new conditions created a somewhat different set of problems: in particular, the need to aim at a deeper and more effective incorporation in the world economy. Ways needed to be found to stimulate enterprises, by devolution of responsibilities and a balanced use of market forces, to respond to the macroeconomic objectives of intensive, outward-oriented growth and technical progress, while continuing to improve living standards and social welfare. Although systemic differences naturally affect strategic priorities, the book brings out interesting similarities between Eastern and Western enterprise managements in the ways in which they approach the problems of business strategies.

---

1) Science Policy Research Unit, University of Sussex, Brighton, UK

Common to contributions from both East and West is recognition of the need for a global rather than a purely national approach, on the part of both governments and enterprise managements, to creative thinking and creative action for making full use of the rapidly changing conditions for economic and social progress.

Plan of the book

The book falls into four Parts - necessarily with some overlapping of the topics treated.

Part I provides, as background, three overall assessments of the state and prospects of the world economy.

Part II contains case studies of the development of macroeconomic policy-making in the Federal Republic of Germany and Austria.

Part III discusses the foreign trade policies of three countries; the European Monetary system; the "new protectionism"; and a comparison of foreign economic strategies in market and socialist economies.

Part IV comprises six chapters dealing mainly with enterprise strategies in East and West.

In what follows, a summary is attempted of some points emerging from the chapters, together with selected comments from participants in the workshop where the contributions were originally presented; contributors were able to revise their views before publication. The material was completed in spring 1987.

Part I - Prospects for the world economy (Chh. 1-3)

The first three chapters provide rather contrasting approaches. Bogomolov *(Ch. 1) stresses the problems faced by the West in reviving economic growth and reports on the reforms being undertaken in the East.* Klein and Bond *(Ch. 2), using an econometric model, project a more hopeful medium-term future for the West, if with qualifications, while noting some impediments to stable growth in the East.* Pajestka *(Ch. 3) strongly criticises traditional ways of interpreting trends in the world economy and proposes more meaningful methods of global analysis.*

Bogomolov begins by warning against complacency in assessing the prospects for early recovery of economic growth in the West. He stresses two unresolved problems of indebtedness. On one side is the paradox of the US - the world's leading power - becoming a major debtor: the Federal Government as a result of cumulated budget deficits, and the economy as a whole as a result of cumulated deficits on the current balance of payments. Military expenditure, he notes, has played a large part in the build-up of these (interconnected) loads of debt. (In an Appendix at the end of this book, *Kaufmann* contributes a paper comparing, tentatively, defence expenditure in the US and the USSR with their respective levels of national income - an exercise fraught with familiar statistical difficulties.) The massive inflow of international capital into the US to finance the deficit, in *Bogomolov*'s view, could have been better used for more productive investment. On the other side, world development has been held back by the inability of many Third World countries, additionally hampered by Western protectionism, to service in full the debts acquired in earlier years. The debt has become a "delayed-action mine" threatening the world economy. And the expected benefits from the collapse of oil prices have failed to emerge.

He turns next to the radical efforts being made in the USSR and other socialist countries to evolve an "integrated conception of a new economic mechanism" which, on the macro-economic level, will give greater authority to the state in solving key problems while, at the micro level, giving more independence to enterprises. But he stresses that success depends on changing people's attitudes to their work as much as on the wider adoption of new technologies.

A more sanguine, and more quantitative, view of medium-term prospects is taken by *Klein* and *Bond* (Ch. 2), derived from the Wharton-Link world forecasting model. They pay particular attention to the far-reaching consequences of developments in the oil and energy markets. Other key variables include the rise and fall of the dollar's exchange rate, the decline of inflation and the beginning of a fall in interest rates. Each factor has both helpful and damaging effects but, in the authors' view, "in every case the good outweighs the bad side in its effects on world averages". On what could be regarded as moderately optimistic assumptions about the key variables, the model (on what is described as the "base-line scenario") projects recovery of world output and trade without serious inflation. The picture, as the authors say, looks "deceptively calm and peaceful". But the growth rate of 3 per cent a year in North America and Western Europe would not substantially reduce unemployment; many commodity prices are likely to remain depressed (although oil prices are expected to rise gradually from $ 15 a barrel); prospects for developing nations are uncertain; the large imbalances in world trade should be reduced, but only slowly; the international debt problems should be alleviated, but will not vanish without very fundamental adjustments. Moreover, the scenario is qualified: thus an uncontrolled collapse of the dollar could lead to a capital flight from the US forcing a rise in US interest rates and a US recession with world-wide consequences.

In the East European economies, *Klein* and *Bond* suggest, conditions have become rather more favourable. The most difficult adjustments of their international debts have been negotiated: except in Poland, the worst of the debt crises has been passed and credit ratings have greatly improved. But, even with new credits and imports from the West, the accumulated shortfall of investments in the 1980s may well impede the desired technical modernisation. The future of energy supplies and prices may become crucial. The USSR is looking for a rise in oil prices to recover the serious loss of hard currency revenues. Low oil prices, the authors suggest, could lead the USSR to put heavy pressure on the other CMEA countries to improve the range and quality of their exports to the USSR, as well as to repay their debts, if energy supplies to these countries are to continue at current levels.

Pajestka (Ch. 3) suggests that the usual ways of economic analysis and projection - essentially synthetic aggregations of relationships between traditional variables (output, trade, investment etc.) - cannot be regarded as genuinely "global models". Global thinking should, rather, look for the "logic of change" to be found in the behaviour and objectives of the decision-making economic and political organisations, including governments. Thus history should be viewed in terms of series of cycles - actions, leading to reactions, leading to new situations. The theoretical background is the concept of relations between the "centre" (the major capitalist economies) and the "periphery". Such an approach can reveal the forces building up to those unexpected transformations which the more familiar economic models - and the social scientists and politicians - fail to foresee.

On this interpretation of the international experience of the last two or three decades, OPEC's price-raising move was an initiatory action opening a new phase in global development and intended to impose a redistribution of world income in favour of poorer countries in general. What followed, *Pajestka* suggests, was a reaction by the "centre" taking the form first of the stagflation of the late 1970s and secondly of the longer-term efforts to save energy and develope alternative sources. He advances, tentatively, the proposition that this reaction might even be interpreted as a conscious strategy to counteract the intended redistribution of world income. Whether deliberate or not - he leaves the question open - the reaction was effective in reducing energy use; it also led to the second OPEC action - and to the subsequent collapse of the oil market. However, the resulting turbulence had some potentially positive results, such as the hopes aroused by the UN Declaration on the New International Economic Order. True, these hopes were disappointed and were replaced by a new solidarity among the industrial powers - a "partisan global policy". But the author still holds out a hope that the new situation could lead to a wider application of rationality in international policy-making, inducing national policy-makers to reflect on the global consequences of their actions.

Commenting on Part I, *Boltho* and *Fink* both take a somewhat sceptical view of the relative optimism of the projections by *Klein* and *Bond* for Western recovery. *Fink* finds *Bogomolov*'s assessment for the West more realistic; he also feels that the problems of the East European debts are likely to be more persistent than *Klein/Bond* seem to expect, and is less confident than *Bogomolov* about the progress of economic reform in the USSR. Both *Boltho* and *Fink* question *Pajestka*'s "Machiavellian" interpretation of the West's reaction to OPEC. On the same issue, *Beck* disputes the implication that OPEC was in fact an effective cartel; OPEC lost control and the violent price fluctuations were basically the result of world market forces.

Part II - National macroeconomic strategies: the Federal Republic of Germany and Austria (Chh. 4 and 5)

Two authors of considerable experience reflect on policy developments in two countries generally regarded as post-war success stories for their relatively smooth economic progress within a framework of popular consensus. Both authors show, however, that the disturbances of the last decade or two have uncovered a certain fragility in the two systems in responding to less favourable circumstances.

Kloten (Ch. 4) recounts the strengths, until the late 1960s, and subsequent weaknesses of the macroeconomic policies pursued in the FRG. The original post-war concepts, loosely inspired by the Keynesian approach, codified in the Stability and Growth Act of 1967 and influenced by the Advisory Council of Economic Experts (of which the author was once chairman), worked well in the 1950s and 1960s. A reasonable consensus was established between the major political parties on the Social Market Economy and the machinery of "concerted action". The main function of macro-policy was seen to be the fostering of a favourable climate for the creative micro-activities of the private sector.

But after the 1960s, the development was more troubled. Official guidelines were disputed; industrial conflicts reappeared; growth slowed down, unemployment rose alarmingly; inflation began to be seen as a threat. While external influences obviously played a part, *Kloten* lays stress on domestic weaknesses, especially the inappropriately-timed growth of public expenditure financed by both tax increases and a growing public debt. Disillusion with demand management weakened the principle of concerted action and the machinery of the Stability and Growth Act "degenerated more and more into an empty shell". Policy then shifted towards monetary instruments combined with consolidation of the public finances: this approach of the Christian Democrat/Free Democrat coalition of 1982 was, in the author's view, "undoubtedly the right principle to adopt".

Kloten then suggests criteria for the future conduct of macro-policy. One of his conclusions from the FRG's experience is that "policy must not demand too much of the public sector". In particular, budgetary policy should so far as possible be relieved of its counter-cyclical function and oriented towards the medium-term. This should, in his view, help to stabilise the economy. The use of official forecasts should be limited, but government should provide clear and consistent information for guidance. For the FRG, "it is probably monetary policy which best meets the criteria".

There are some parallels in the account given by *Seidel* (Ch. 5) of the evolution of socio-economic policy in Austria. Until the early 1980s the guiding influence was the system of ideas sometimes described as "Austro-Keynesianism" - a label given, rather doubtfully, to the corporatist network of institutions for economic management through dialogue between the interest groups (business, labour and farmers). The aims, and degree of success, of this characteristically Austrian system can be compared with those of the rather less institutionalised machinery of the FRG. Until OPEC I, the Austrian economy succeeded better than some others in maintaining growth, relatively low unemployment, low inflation and a tolerable balance of payments with a policy-mix including control of incomes and prices and demand management by budgetary and monetary instruments. Even after OPEC I, Austria proved for some time relatively shock-resistant, but could not wholly escape the consequences of the increasing international integration of the economy. After OPEC II, efforts to ride the storm alone, by expansionary policies, led to a threatening rise in the public debt and to some (although only moderate) rise in unemployment.

In *Seidel*'s view, the main lessons to be learnt - lessons now being absorbed - are: (i) although Austro-Keynesianism, in one sense, is said to be fading out, yet its basic teaching about macroeconomic policies remains valid, if difficult to apply in a small trade-dependent country; (ii) such policies, appropriate for smoothing-out short-term fluctuations, are less appropriate for persistent periods of recession; (iii) unemployment (about 5 per cent at present) can be kept relatively low by reducing labour supply (early retirement, shorter hours, limits on immigration); (iv) most important, more attention must be given to the long-standing structural weakness of Austrian industry, notably its excessive concentration on traditional basic industries; in this last respect, the system of consensus between interest groups, despite its many virtues, can impede the radical changes required.

Part III - Policies for external economic relations (Chh. 6-11)

The first three chapters in this Part discuss the experience and prospects of Hungary and the German Democratic Republic in seeking to develope new macro- and micro-strategies oriented towards intensive growth, technical progress and competitiveness in world trade. Two following chapters deal with developments in international policy - the European Monetary System as a move towards integration within the EC, and, by contrast, the new wave of protectionism. The last chapter is a comparative assessment of external economic strategies in East and West.

Drawing on close acquaintance of the evolution of Hungarian policies, *Bognár* (Ch. 6) emphasises that the opening-up of the socialist economies represents - like the whole process of economic reform - a new and creative phase in the history of the socialist economic system; this strategic shift has reached a point of no return - it is a "new model replacing the old one". He is concerned, particularly, with the acute political and administrative problems of reconciling the divergent interest groups which exist in socialist (as in capitalist) societies. One such problem is divergence between the "micro-interests" of enterprises and the "macro-interest" of the state. Since the reforms, the ability of enterprises to engage in autonomous activities means that an increasingly complex function of the central authorities is that of linking enterprise interests with overall economic policy. Especially important are the central policies for expansion of foreign trade. But foreign trade policies cannot be insulated in separate compartments from domestic policies.

Bognár discusses in more detail the application of these principles to the essential functions of the banking system, which carries much of the load of operating the "economic" instruments which in Hungary have largely superseded administrative regulation of enterprises. Thus it may be desirable to curb the interest of enterprises in pushing exports to "easy" markets, or exports which yield an unsatisfactory balance of hard currency revenue over hard currency inputs. To promote the macro-economic interest, the instruments of central policy must be applied continuously, and not only in the formation of five-year plans. "The real economic results are produced by the micro-sphere; the task in the macro-sphere is rather to create the economic conditions promoting success".

The experience and policies of the German Democratic Republic are discussed by *Heinrichs* (Ch. 7) and *Sydow* (Ch. 8). Both authors lay stress on the new process of intensive development which began in the early 1980s, replacing the extensive form of growth of earlier phases. The macroeconomic policy, expressed in the plan for 1986-1990, is aimed at output growth of 4.5-5.0 per cent a year, based upon modernisation and rationalisation of industry and agriculture. The objective, related to both economic and social concerns, is to improve international competitiveness and overcome external constraints on growth by renovation of the productive apparatus and thereby to raise living standards and promote social welfare. By responding to the challenge of the "scientific and technological revolution", the GDR can hope to take its place among the leading industrial nations. This of course involves full use of the opportunities for specialisation and cooperation within the CMEA and also for adapting the pattern of East-West relations to the needs of the 1990s.

Both authors make a special point of the need for more efficient use of all inputs - labour, materials, energy, capital equipment - as well as the need for improving the technical and marketable quality of output to meet world standards (raising the ratio of national income produced to productive consumption - a ratio which increased for the first time in the early 1980s). Because the GDR depends on imports for a large proportion of primary inputs and equipment, *Heinrichs* draws particular attention to the opportunities for saving hard currency food imports by technical and managerial improvement in agriculture, especially in cereals. In general, the concept of intensive development calls not only for expansion of exports but also for rational and cost-effective planning of imports. To create incentives for raising quality standards, *Heinrichs* observes that new systems of price regulation are being tested providing premium prices and profits for innovatory products, together with penalties for continued sale of obsolete goods.

On the organisation of scientific and technological progress, *Sydow* stresses the strengthening of the links between the research institutes and the industrial combines by contractual relationships gearing basic research to the practical long-term needs of the economy. He lists the priorities on which allocation of state funds for R & D should be concentrated; these include not only the familiar areas of high technology, but also high-value consumer goods, modern construction methods, health and environmental protection and new solutions for public transport - reinforcing the combination of social with economic aims. As *Sydow* puts it, in socialist production relations "the human person is an active factor whose all-round development is the focus of all efforts".

With *Bourguinat* (Ch. 9) we move back to Western Europe. He assesses the performance of the European Monetary System (EMS) as an international policy initiative; EMS springs from the European Economic Community but differs from other EC institutions in that not all EC countries are members (notably the UK has hitherto hesitated to join). The author asks first whether the EMS has succeeded in its original purpose of moderating short-term fluctuations in members' exchange rates. Measures of variance in intra-EMS rates do indeed show greater stability than the variance in important non-EMS countries' rates (dollar, sterling, yen). The second, longer-term, purpose was to reinforce the integration of member economies through mutual trade. Evidence of success in this respect is less certain; the rate of trade diversion within the EC slowed down and there was no marked growth of cross-border integration between EC firms. From *Bourguinat*'s review, it may be concluded that the circumstances of the time frustrated full achievement of the EMS objective of creating a more favourable climate for integration and growth.

Bourguinat goes on to consider possibilities of expanding the functions of EMS. He takes the view that UK membership would benefit the group as a whole by enlarging the basket of currencies on which the European Currency Unit (the ECU) is based; it would benefit the UK by imposing a certain discipline on economic policy. However, he recognises that the effort to stabilise exchange rates among countries subject to differing inflationary pressures could lead to divergent and volatile interest rates; as an international currency, sterling would need a wider margin of exchange rate variation than other member currencies. But if the UK remains outside, the "hegemony" of the Deutschemark within EMS - indeed within Western Europe - would be strengthened.

The author considers the future of EMS, and the ECU, as a step towards a more widely used European currency. Its use is already increasing, although only very slowly, for commercial and financial transactions, but there are serious obstacles to further expansion (including continued controls over international capital movements).

Throughout the post-war years, the official foreign trade policies of the Western industrial countries have been geared to the multilateral and non-discriminatory liberalisation of trade through the successive GATT rounds. But, as *Salvatore* (Ch. 10) points out, the disturbing counterpart during the last decade has been the growth of a multitude of non-tariff barriers (NTBs). "New protectionism" in the form of NTBs today represents "the most serious threat to the post-war trading system and world welfare", despite the efforts in GATT to establish codes for their use. The author distinguishes between: "explicit" NTBs (import quotas, "voluntary export restraints", anti-dumping measures etc.) for which the GATT codes provide and which are at least documented and measurable; and "implicit" NTBs (subsidies, agricultural supports, discriminatory public procurement, hygienic and other quality standards and a variety of administrative regulations). It is these implicit barriers - difficult to identify or measure - which in the author's view are the potentially most dangerous and insidious threat to the world trade system.

Salvatore summarises such data as exist on the growth and extent of NTBs and analyses their causes and consequences. He points to the somewhat ambivalent attitudes of governments which recognise their obligations to the GATT rules and commitments to a liberal trade regime, but are unable to resist the pressures for protection, often coming from politically powerful producing interests. Such pressures come from both the "sunrise" and "sunset" industries and influence the shape of industrial policies. A statistical analysis of US data shows, as might be expected, that the volume of producer demands for protection varies inversely with the ups and downs of the business cycle; renewed expansion could reverse the protectionist drift.

Meanwhile, *Salvatore* points out, one of the most prominent forms of NTBs - the voluntary export restraint - tends to be preferred to tariffs by the exporting country against which they are directed. Quantitative limitation of exports can yield higher prices and profits to the exporter instead of yielding - as tariffs do - tax revenue to the importing nation.

A wide-ranging paper by *Marer* (Ch. 11) compares foreign trade strategies not only in the industrial West and the socialist countries but also in a number of developing countries. Within each of these three groups there are important differences between nations in the degree of "openness" of policy. He assesses openness in foreign trade, in foreign direct investment and in integration in the international financial system. Doubting the validity of such commonly used measures as the ratio of foreign trade to national income - which in any case tends to be correlated with a country's size, natural resources etc. - he insists that "openness" should be assessed in the light of the economic system, the industrial structure, the level of development and other specific circumstances of the economy studied. Moreover any assessment should be based on actual behaviour - the outcome - rather than on examination of policy declarations.

As a rough approximation, *Marer* classifies countries in three groups:
- the "open economies" of the Western industrial countries and the East Asian NICs; despite many continuing exceptions (especially in agricultural trade), basically open strategies have prevailed, determined by well-established competitiveness;
- the "inward-oriented" economies of most developing countries other than some NICs; import-substitution policies are frequently accompanied by extensive state ownership;

- the "extremely inward-oriented" economies, consisting of all CMEA countries and a few developing nations.

In the socialist countries, *Marer* suggests, the earlier drive for industrialisation, pushed through by import-substitution strategies, was replaced in some by the "growth-via-debt" policy of foreign borrowing to finance technical and export-oriented modernisation, but without much success. He concludes that the reforms and changes of direction so far introduced are far too limited to achieve their purpose of promoting international competitiveness. More "fundamental reforms" are needed and must include much more freedom for decision-makers in the enterprises to pursue profit, drastic reforms of the price structure to reflect market forces, elimination of many monopolistic organisations including the foreign trade monopolies, and realistic exchange rates. Protectionism, whether open or disguised, whether in planned or in market economies, is a major obstacle to the economic and social progress at which policy-makers aim; typically, indeed, it leads in *Marer*'s opinion to "outcomes the opposite of those intended".

The papers in Parts II and III give rise to a number of comments and criticisms. *Tardos* (from Hungary) calls attention to the relative economic success of the three German-speaking countries - the FRG (Ch. 4), Austria (Ch. 5) and the GDR (Chh. 7 and 8). This leads him to suggest that more attention should be paid to the "non-economic" or "social anthropology" approach in explaining national performance. On the economic aspects, he believes that the FRG could benefit from some central coordination of policies; in the GDR, while the hierarchical structure is largely accepted because of German social attitudes, the combines have not solved the problems of harmonising supply with demand. *Nuti* (from Italy) expresses some doubts about *Kloten*'s (Ch. 4) conclusions from FRG experience.

Breuss (from Austria), while reinforcing *Salvatore*'s (Ch. 10) stress on the perils of growing protectionism, suggests that the GATT system is too much dominated by the big countries and blocs; some form of compensation is needed to offset the weak bargaining power of the smaller economies, and of the Third World. *Čičin-Šain* (from Yugoslavia) feels, like *Marer*, that successful pursuit of outward-looking policies by the socialist countries will need much more substantial systemic change than is generally appreciated. By contrast, *Lukaszewicz* (from Poland) holds that *Marer*'s (Ch. 11) criticism of socialist countries' import-substitution policies underestimates the social objectives and political factors which underlie their overall economic strategies. Moreover, he feels, *Marer* fails to appreciate either the progress already made in reform or the obstacles due to the politicisation of international economic relations.

Part IV - The management of enterprise strategies (Chh. 12-17)

In Part IV we pass from the macro to the micro. The six chapters deal mainly with changes in the methods of strategic planning in enterprises, both in East and West. One element, naturally more significant in socialist systems, is the way in which enterprise policies are influenced by, and influence, the policies of the central governments. This interaction is discussed by Lipiński *(Ch. 12) for Poland and by* Bendeković and Teodorović *(Ch. 13) for Yugoslavia (it also arises in* Bognár's *(Ch. 6) discussion of Hungary). In the next two chapters,* Kraus *(Ch. 14) recounts the experience of an expanding self-managing enterprise in Yugoslavia and* Horváth *(Ch. 15) deals similarly with a Hungarian state-owned enterprise, both writing from their own managerial experience. Also drawing on much personal experience,* Beck *(Ch. 16) and* Rall *(Ch. 17) consider the new problems of strategic planning in large Western corporations.*

Lipiński (Ch. 12) analyses the problems of recovery from the *Polish* crisis. The reforms introduced in 1982 - autonomy and self-financing of enterprises, subject, in principle, only to central regulation by "economic" instruments - were originally expected to lead to the increasing play of market mechanisms as coordinators of economic activities. These expectations have not yet been realised. The reason is the continuing state of excess demand for scarce resources which frustrates enterprises from responding either to market demand or to meeting their own needs for modernisation. Thus although the reforms have certainly not been abandoned, their implementation has had to be restricted by reviving administrative measures for resource allocation and prices. Allocations of materials, finance etc. are based on preferential supplies to certain "protected" activities - at the expense of the rest who of course have to fill the gaps, where they can, by "well-known informal processes".

While the ideal solution is of course expansion of supplies, *Lipiński* doubts whether balanced markets can be achieved by 1990. He discusses some possible methods of reducing imbalances by price policies even at existing levels of supply. For *consumer goods,* one method could be to reduce real incomes by raising prices without compensation in pay. To this course he objects that consumers on the whole prefer queuing for scarce goods at affordable prices to ample supplies at prices beyond their reach. An alternative could be to restrain incomes by taxing enterprises which pay out wage increases above some norm; that, he feels, would be impossible to enforce. A more reasonable course in consumer markets, he suggests, would be to keep down the prices, if necessary by subsidies, of those goods for which price increases are most likely to provoke pay demands, offset by compensating increases in prices of other goods. Differential rates of turnover tax might also help.

On *capital goods*, he notes the excessive propensity to invest which characterised planners and enterprises in the 1970s. Although that tendency has been forced to give way to rather more cautious behaviour, excess demand persists - partly because of "privileged" public projects. More consistent application of the principle of adjusting prices to the "world price" (in hard currencies) could offer some relief. Allowing prices to be determined by bargaining between enterprises has had to be replaced by controls aimed at putting pressure on costs and waste; but the controls still tend to be based on the "cost-plus" principle which is impossible to monitor effectively. A better administrative solution might be to set ceilings on price increases (related to foreign trade prices where relevant) for the average prices of groups of commodities rather than for individual goods, covering all enterprises concerned. But *Lipiński* recognises, in conclusion, that the measures discussed can do no more than alleviate the consequences of the shortage economy.

Changes in investment planning in *Yugoslavia* are reviewed by *Bendeković* and *Teodorović* (Ch. 13). Allocation of investment funds, at the heart of any system of development planning, has moved from the "top-down" central controls of the early post-war years with the progressive decentralisation of authority associated with the self-management system. The present system dates from 1974 and its aim is to provide a mechanism for "coordinating decisions made on the basis of market signals". The big issue throughout has been the excessive pressure on investment funds arising not only from the self-managing enterprises but also from the republican and local authorities. A priority system has been established to rank proposals initiated by enterprises and other organisations (from the "bottom-up"). Except for projects which enterprises can finance from their own funds (about half the total) and a small amount funded by government grants, the machinery for allocation is run mainly by the banks. The familiar difficulty is to establish rational criteria for project evaluation by which enterprises must justify their proposals and the banks choose between them. The admitted misdirection of limited investment funds in the past has been due to a variety of pressures. But one reason has been the lack, at all levels, of sufficient professional expertise to make competent project evaluations. So an important improvement now being undertaken is the establishment of training centres to build up a corpus of people, in the enterprises and the banks, and as consultants, capable of applying nation-wide criteria which take account of financial feasibility as well as of the government's economic and social policies.

The record of Yugoslav investment problems is followed by *Kraus* (Ch. 14) with a lively account, based on his own involvement, of the recent expansion strategy of a prominent *Yugoslav* self-managing enterprise - Metalservis (MS). The firm originally suffered, in the author's view, from a certain "inertness and a relatively quiet life", limiting its business to storage and wholesale trade for the domestic market. In 1977 a new management team branched out into a number of new activities, helped by the relaxing of much administrative regulation and control. Expansion and diversification called for an influx of young and well-qualified managerial staff - which was achieved over a period frankly described by the author as "tempestuous". The self-management framework meant that at each stage the workforce had to be convinced of the need for continuous development, involving the setting aside of funds from current income. Expansion took the form of a modern warehouse complex with the latest storage technologies and computerised processes. The firms also moved into retailing, foreign trade and joint ventures and established new port facilities. The need for in-house R & D was met by taking over an existing research institute. The author stresses the importance of an effective marketing operation in a competitive situation.

On the relation between macro and micro policies, *Kraus* feels that the central planning system in Yugoslavia "is not of great help to us. We must often take decisions by relying more and more on our own strategic observation and assessments". The major aim of MS has been to introduce a responsible and entrepreneurial spirit in a society where this spirit was not well developed.

A detailed account of the formation of long-term strategy in one of the largest state-owned *Hungarian* enterprises (Taurus, manufacturer of rubber products) is given by *Horváth* (Ch. 15), previously general manager. While learning from the planning practice of Western corporations, the Taurus planners were pioneers of long-term enterprise planning within the Hungarian New Economic Mechanism. *Horváth* describes the process of planning - up to the year 2000 - as beginning with the setting out of several variants, taking into account, *inter alia:* the overall development of the national economy (using the official long-term macro-plan, which he regards as providing useful information but which is not a compulsory basis for enterprise strategies); and the expected evolution of supply and demand in the world rubber industry. Recognising that Taurus, a modest producer in an industry dominated by a few Western multinationals, could not hope to compete successfully in all products, the plan provides for specialisation in a few products for which the firm is most competitive. Some other products were, in principle, to be regarded as dispensable.

Out of 128 possible combinations of projections for a few quantifiable variables, two were selected as bases for the "accepted economic strategy" of the enterprise. *Horváth* insists, however, that the strategy must be treated as flexible, adaptable to changing circumstances. Like *Kraus* in the previous chapter, he stresses the importance of marketing (Taurus has had the right to conduct its own foreign trade since 1981) and particularly of integrating innovation into the marketing system.

On strategic planning in large Western corporations, *Beck* (Ch. 16) draws from his own experience two major lessons. First, strategists have moved away from "scientific" quantitative forecasting to a more judgemental approach. He attributes this change in part to the uncertainties and complexities of the future state of the world, but in part, too, to a certain disillusion resulting from forecasts which failed to come true (of which he gives examples). Mathematical models, he writes, can be useful "but only when used for research and not for prediction". Secondly, the organisation of strategic decision-making is changing. Earlier, the operations of all branches of large and diversified corporations tended to be determined by a corporate plan based on the work of a central planning unit; "managers away from the centre saw themselves more and more as administrators of other people's plans".

For the formation of successful enterprise strategies, *Beck* proposes certain principles: (i) the organisation of planning must be decentralised, bringing to bear the experience and views of on-line managers as well as the expertise of the professional planners; (ii) the process is thus one of interaction between the centre and the operating units; (iii) the planners at each level should concentrate less on predicting the future and more on understanding the forces that will mould the future - in particular picking out areas which demand future-oriented decisions; (iv) managers at every level must have a clear grasp of the major aims of the corporation; (v) thus line-managers should not only be their own planners but also leaders enthusing their own units. *Beck* recognises that this "multi-level planning" raises many problems of achieving mutual trust between delegator and delegatee.

Finally, plans must be regarded as flexible, in the sense that managements must be prepared to change direction when the unexpected occurs. So alternative scenarios should be studied throughout the preparation of the strategy. It is very rarely that the planning process yields a single optimal plan of action which should, or could, be pursued through every shift of fortune.

In many ways, *Rall* (Ch. 17) takes much the same line as *Beck* about the changing process of enterprise planning, agreeing that managements are moving away from mechanical forecasting and "have to learn the art of coping with uncertainty and instability" in the firm's environment. However, he adds to *Beck*'s call for flexibility the thought that adapting to circumstances can also mean an "aggressive" approach, prepared to exploit external changes - which could be described as "creating the future". Further, *Rall* agrees with *Beck* in insisting that the initiative in strategy-making is shifting from the centre to line-management - although top management remains the final decision-maker and the central planning unit retains the job of grasping the "structure and dynamics of a business".

The author illustrates these points by two practical examples of the variety of decision-making processes. One example is an automobile manufacturer, in an industry technically mature but highly volatile and internationally competitive. Strategic thinking requires in the first place good knowledge of the market and of competitors, in order to identify the company's comparative advantages in terms of international trade theory. The second example is a company making equipment for factory automation. To capture a fair share of the growing market is the key not merely to success but even to survival. A realistic grasp of the company's potential for "globalisation" is essential. Common to both examples is what *Rall* describes as the passage from "strategic planning to strategic management".

The papers in Part IV evoke extensive comments especially from *Kreuter* (from Czechoslovakia) and *Wagener* (from the Netherlands).

Kreuter agrees that strategic planning in socialist enterprises has some similarities with capitalist practices and that the inherent problems of dialogue and trust between the centre and the operating units are common to both systems. But he also feels that the systemic differences are important: uncertainties and risks, although no longer so easily transferable to the centre as they were before, seem more manageable in socialist planning. He suggests that the success of the Hungarian Taurus group, as described by *Horváth*, may owe something to its rather well protected market - a suggestion denied by *Horváth* in a rejoinder. *Kreuter* criticises *Lipiński*'s somewhat pessimistic view of the possibilities of an early radical solution of the excess demand situation in Poland: could not a consistent policy free more resources?

Doubts about the similarities between planning in socialist and capitalist firms are expressed by *Wagener;* especially because socialist enterprises mostly operate in a sellers' market, the differences are decisive. He asks, further, what is meant by the "autonomy" of a socialist enterprise? Where do property rights reside? Who bears the risks in the last resort? Are there not problems in defining the appropriate unit for decision-making? *Wagener* goes on to review the more fundamental question of whether central planning can create an environment stable enough to allow enterprises to execute rational strategic plans. He draws some lessons from the experience of Poland and Yugoslavia as presented by *Lipiński*, *Bendeković/Teodorović* and *Kraus*. Among other things, he is sceptical of the view that "money illusion" explains Polish consumers' egalitarian preference for queues over high prices; in a rejoinder, *Lipiński* defends the reasonableness of this preference. *Wagener* also thinks that *Lipiński*'s proposal to curb wage claims by low prices for essentials, although appearing reasonable, seems to represent a return to traditional socialist controls. In general, *Wagener* sees the outlook for Poland as sombre unless public confidence can remove the socio-political constraints on more hopeful policies. In his rejoinder, *Lipiński* agrees that more radical changes are necessary, including more use of monetary and fiscal instruments, but believes that such measures could not have their full effect for 6-7 years at least.

On Yugoslavia, *Wagener* suggests that over-investment may be due in part to a conflict of pressures under the self-management system: managers press for investment while workers' primary interest is in their own pay; in the end both groups get their way - at the cost of inflation. Both Poland and Yugoslavia, in *Wagener*'s view, suffer rom inability of the governments to impose either effective administrative control or effective financial and budgetary discipline.

On a different issue, *Beck*, observing the general stress on high technologies, warns that the most important use of modern technologies is not in generating new industries but in technical modernisation throughout the economy - including the old-established sectors.

PART I - PROSPECTS FOR THE WORLD ECONOMY

Chapter 1

AN OVERALL VIEW TO WEST AND EAST

Oleg Bogomolov[1)]

There are many reasons for supposing that both the world economy and international politics are on the verge of major changes. This makes it difficult to forecast the progress of events, the more so because our mental attitudes are to a great extent governed by old ideas. Thus, most Western economists expected the depreciation of the US dollar, and the drop of oil prices, to bring about a significant revival of the Western economy. This forecast still fails to be justified by events; indeed there are many symptoms of short run weakness.

It is evident that the development of the world economy is increasingly affected by factors whose significance we cannot fully appreciate. Among them, special attention should be paid to the repercussions of the arms race. Not only are enormous resources (according to some estimates, up to $ 970 bn in 1984 prices, or about 6 per cent of the gross product of the entire world[2)] annually withdrawn from the economic turnover and spent for non-productive purposes; this in itself limits the possibilities for social and economic progress, to say nothing of a growing threat of thermonuclear conflict capable of annihilating human civilisation. But the arms race also undermines the world economy, because existing international financial mechanisms enable the US to cover a considerable part of their military expenditures at the expense of the credit resources of the rest of the world.

1.1 Impact of US borrowing on the world economy

According to estimates of experts independent of the US government, the Strategic Defence Initiative (SDI) might cost more than $ 1,000 bn and this spending will be financed, to a considerable extent, by Europe (such is the opinion of Wassily Leontief, an American economist) in the

---

1) Academician; Director, Institute for the Socialist World Economy, Academy of Sciences of the USSR, Moscow

2) Journal of Commerce, 23 July 1986

same way as Europe financed the Vietnam war at one time.[3] Armament expenditures lays a heavy burden on the US budget, reflected in the rising public debt. In 1984-85, the Federal budget deficit was $ 212 bn having tripled over the previous five years. For 1985-86, the figure may be even higher[4]. From 1980 to 1986 the US public debt doubled to an astronomic figure of about $ 2,000 bn. The servicing of this debt amounts to $ 143 bn. in 1985-86 and will increase, according to estimates by the Budget Commission of the US Congress, to $ 214 bn. in 1989, which will further complicate the problem of budget balance. Government borrowings absorb the major portion of American savings which in different conditions, could find productive use as business investments.

Defence spending, public debt servicing, plus expenditures on some other secondary items of the budget (except social security) will constitute about 17 per cent of the US GDP in 1987.[5] The US economy could not bear such a load without capital inflow from abroad.

Indeed, half the US budget deficit is financed by capital inflow - over $ 100 bn in 1985. According to data of the US Department of Commerce, published on June 24, 1986, American deposits abroad increased in 1985 by $ 52.2 bn, while foreign deposits in the US rose by $ 166 bn.[6] The difference represents a net capital inflow to the US, encouraged by high interest rates on bank deposits and government bonds, as well as by the overvaluation of the dollar. In 1980, interest rates reached the unprecedented level of 21.5 per cent; by the end of 1984 they fell to 10.75 per cent and by mid-1986 to 8.5 per cent - which is still abnormal at present rates of inflation (1.5 per cent in the US). The exchange rate of the dollar fell heavily in 1985 and 1986 especially in relation to the Japanese yen and the FRG mark (the trade-weighted rate fell by about 25 per cent from early 1985 to mid-1986). One cannot say that the long-standing artificial overevaluation of the dollar has yet been corrected. The dollar has not become substantially cheaper in relation to the currencies of Canada, Taiwan, Hong-Kong.

Foreign capital flows into the US, since profits on investments there are much higher than in many other Western countries. Besides, new US rules exempt foreign investors from taxation of their dividends. However, high interest rates, instability of the oil market, and the forthcoming

---

3) Nouvelle Observateur, 27 June and 3 July 1986

4) The Situation in the World, Worldwatch, Washington DC, 1986

5) David Stockman, Der Triumph der Politik, Bertelsmann Verlag, München, 1986, p. 437

6) United Press International, 24 June 1986

tax reforms in the US do not encourage businessmen to invest in fixed capital. They frequently prefer to invest in banks and securities, which results in slowing down economic growth.

The overvalued dollar made US imports less expensive and reduced the competitiveness of US exports. In addition to the technological lag in modernising a number of industries, this gives rise to the increasing deficit on the US trade and payment balances. The deficit on current account more than doubled in 1984 compared with 1983 and rose to nearly $ 120 bn., in 1985; in 1986 it reached $ 140 bn.

The richest country in the world has become an international debtor. Different views may be held about the implications for the world economy of this new debtor status of the US. In the opinion of the US President, this gives no reason for anxiety, but merely demonstrates the strength of the American economy since it attracts foreign investors. Independent economists, however, find the situation dangerous. The US entered 1986 with a net foreign indebtedness of over $ 100 bn. and by 1989 this figure may amount to $ 600 bn. which would necessitate $ 60 bn. of annual debt servicing payments - a sum equal to the output of 1.5 mn. workers. The most optimistic forecasts envisage that improvement could be expected only when the debt falls to $ 400 bn.

Professor Lester C. Thurow, in an article titled "The 20's and 30's can happen again", writes: "Since the world's wealthiest nation has never been the world's largest debtor, and since the world's reserve currency has never been held by a debtor nation, no one knows the thickness of the financial ice upon which the world is skating".[7] If, for some reason, foreign investors decide to get rid of their American securities, this might force a considerable new increase in the US interest rates- which would result in an economic depression.

The suggestion that the US recovery and import boom, while favouring European and Japanese exports, would encourage an economic upturn in Western Europe and Japan failed to come true. Developments in 1985 and 1986 point to aggravated difficulties. Growth rates of GDP in the US, the FRG and Japan in 1986 have fallen far short of official forecasts of 4 per cent, and little improvement is expected in 1987.[8] Many economists take the view that GDP growth in these countries will continue slack until new stimuli are applied.

Now the US find that the role of locomotive for the world economy should be taken by Western Europe and Japan, since American companies

---

7) New York Times, 22 January 1986

8) Newsweek, 30 June 1986, p. 41; Time, 28 July 1986

need a sharp increase in demand for their goods from overseas. But in present conditions this task is not so simple.

Because of high interest rates in the US, West European banks are also bound to maintain high rates so as to limit capital outflow. But in fact it is investment in fixed capital that is limited, not the capital outflow. Fixed capital investment remains sluggish. The active trade and payment balances of Japan, the FRG, and some other European economies mean a untilateral outflow of resources from these countries, narrowing the opportunities for investment in their own fixed assets. The higher exchange rates for the currencies of these countries against the dollar weaken incentives for the development of their export industries. For example, in Japan stagnation is observed not only in ship-building, metallurgy and construction, but also threatens electronics manufacturers. Many West European politicians and economists find that the low pace of development and high level of unemployment (10.8 per cent of the labour force of the EEC countries in 1986 against 11.1 per cent in 1985[9]) are caused to a great extent by the international economic situation and, in particular, by the pumping of capital into the US. The gap in growth rates of output and employment between Western Europe and the US during recent years is explained by specific features of the international financial mechanisms rather than by weakening of European competitiveness (although that weakening is a part of the explanation).

1.2 Effects on the Third World

If such financial mechanisms long prevail, an explosion with profound consequences for all countries of the world is inevitable. Especially dangerous in these conditions is the enormous indebtedness of developing countries, which by the end of 1985 approached $ 1,000 bn., necessitating $ 135 bn. for debt servicing ($ 74 bn. in interest and $ 61 bn. in debt repayment). For five years already, debt servicing has been absorbing 25 per cent of the export revenues of Third World countries (30 per cent in Africa and 40 per cent in Latin America[10]). The capacity of developing countries to pay is rather questionable. Their current account deficits in 1983 were estimated at $ 50-60 bn (including about $ 20 bn. in the OPEC countries). They were slightly reduced in 1985, but still remain very significant.

To attain a positive balance, the developing countries must escape from the difficult economic situation in which they find themselves due

---

9) Associated Press, 21 July 1986

10) Combat pour la Paix, February 1986

to recession in the industrialised West, must ensure high rates of economic growth, and increase output of export goods - of manufactures in the first place. This requires a simultaneous increase in imports of machinery and equipment, spare parts and materials for maintenance and development of their own industries. But the burden of debt servicing forces cuts in imports. And they cannot increase exports in the proportions required. In 1985 the volume of exports of developing countries declined by 0.5 per cent with substantially unchanged imports, while their terms of trade worsened by 2 per cent. In the region where the lion's share of the external debt is concentrated - Latin America - countries face a reduced physical volume of both exports and imports. Even the petroleum-exporting countries have found themselves in the red - their exports in 1985 fell by more than 6 per cent, although the main impact of the fall in oil prices came only in 1986.[11)] The developing countries lose many billions of dollars through worsened terms of trade, since raw materials and fuels exported by them become cheaper in relation to the value of their imports. Furthermore, high interest rates caused a capital outflow from a number of major debtor countries. The inflow of external resources to the developing countries gave way to an outflow, narrowing still further the limited possibilities for their economic growth. In 1984-1985 the net outflow of resources from these countries is estimated at $ 14.5-16.5 bn.[12)]

The indebtedness of the developing countries is a delayed-action mine for the whole world economy. While the economic backwardness and dependence of Third World countries, the weakness of their export base and the unequal character of their relations with Western industrial centres persist, this mine cannot be defused. The solution of the problem of indebtedness of developing countries, as well as of a number of other countries including socialist states, is further complicated by protectionist measures. Protectionism takes on global proportions and more sophisticated forms (including the "voluntary" export restrictions).

The US and other developed states endeavour, by means of protectionist measures, to fence off certain branches of their economies from foreign competition - namely those branches which, because of insufficient technological progress or short-sighted economic policies, have found themselves in difficulties. As historical experience shows, protection may be justified when it serves to protect a newly created industry, but has no excuse

---

11) OECD Economic Outlook, May 1986

12) "Economic situation in capitalist and developing countries. Review for 1985 and beginning of 1986". Annex to the magazine Mirovaya Ekonomika i Mezhdunarodnyje Otnoshenija, Moscow, 1986, p. 22

when the problem lies in the market of financially and industrially strong economies.

Protectionism and any discriminatory measures taken by some Western countries in trade with developing and socialist countries hinder the recovery of the world economy and progress in East-West relations. Especially intolerable is the use of trade sanctions and technological embargoes as political leverage against other countries. In imposing more severe restrictions on external economic exchanges, the US and West European countries might lose their markets. Meanwhile, it is difficult to maintain business activity without expanding trade in all areas.

The prospects for revival of the world economy, and for alleviation of the acute problems, are closely related to the expansion of domestic consumption in the leading countries of the West. But there are many obstacles in the way, including uncertainty about the future which restrains businessmen both in Western Europe and Japan from a resolute intensification of their investment activity. This is also true of the United States. Yet governments do not rush to apply appropriate stimulants. The growth of demand in the world market is hampered by a whole number of factors already mentioned: the need to reduce the US budget deficit and the US payments deficit which forces import cuts; the limited financial capacities of developing and socialist countries; growing protectionism, etc. After a considerable increase in 1984, world trade growth slowed down in volume in 1985 to less than 4 per cent.[13)]

A powerful impetus is needed to revitalise the world economy, to liberate the vast resources available for technical modernisation of a number of old industries in Western countries, for accelerating industrialisation of developing states, and for the fight against starvation, poverty and unemployment. In the opinion of the UN Development Planning Committee, to overcome their economic difficulties the developing countries need doubled annual inflow of external resources to reach $ 80 bn. by 1990.[14)] The Baker plan, had it been implemented, would not save the situation. The scheme to convert banks' claims for loans to developing countries into stocks and securities will obviously have only limited effectiveness and will not eliminate the debt crisis. Besides, it is a dubious prescription from the standpoint of the national independence and sovereignty of developing countries. Hence, one should not expect recovery of the world economy to come from growth of import demand of the Third World.

---

13) UN/ECE, Economic Survey of Europe in 1985-86, pp. 3 and 152

14) Financial Times, 19 June 1986

The oil price drop is not likely, either, to give such an impetus, although in the long run lower energy prices should be favourable for economic growth in energy-importing countries - first of all West European counties, US and Japan. However, in the short run lower oil prices create considerable difficulties in adapting the economy to the new situation. Such difficulties are experienced, for example, by the energy sector of the American economy, and by the oil and other industries of Britain, Norway and the Netherlands.

Of course, the drop in oil prices, pulling down prices for other energy sources, reflects a new situation in the world economy: an absolute reduction of oil production in the world by 11 per cent as compared to the maximum level of 1979[15)], accumulation of vast strategic oil reserves, technological advances in energy saving, the crisis of the OPEC and its weakened influence in the world petroleum market.

According to forecasts of the International Energy Agency, (June 1986), the annual growth in energy consumption in the OECD countries up to 1990 is estimated at 1.9 per cent, and for the following decade at 1.4 per cent a year, with the share of oil tending to fall. The annual demand for oil of the OECD countries might increase in 1986-1990, on the IEA estimates, only by 70 mn. t.[16)]

It may be expected that the oil price will be stabilised, through OPEC efforts, but on a level at most half the previous maximum. All this means that the drastic reduction of the export revenues of oil-extracting countries and, hence, of their demand for imported goods, is of a long-term character. The OPEC countries' export income fell from $ 282 bn. in 1981 to $ 147 bn. in 1985. The indebtedness of poor OPEC countries, such as Algeria, Indonesia, Iran and Iraq, has considerably increased, and the debt crisis has been aggravated in Mexico.

The new situation in the world economy has also worsened the external balances of the socialist countries which suffered substantial foreign exchange losses due to falling prices for oil, petroleum products and other energy sources - resulting in import cuts and further difficulties in repayment of foreign debts. The dollar devaluation has also increased their foreign debt, since the share of non-dollar currencies in the indebtedness is rather high, as is the share of trade in these currencies.

---

15) Glückauf, No. 5, 6 March 1986

16) BIKI, 8 July 1986

In short, the repercussions of the drop in oil prices on the world economy are contradictory enough; and in view of the growing interdependence of countries one can hardly be sure that the final balance will come out with a positive sign.

1.3 Prospects and policies in the socialist world

The socialist world can contribute to activating the world economy. However, the opportunities should not be overestimated; East-West relations account for merely 3-4 per cent of the total volume of world trade, so that their influence on global economic processes is not great. But, on the other hand, the essential dependence of these relations on the generally unstable economy and foreign trade of the West should be taken into account, as should the asymmetry in the significance of these relations for economic development of the partners. During recent years, the industrially developed capitalist states accounted for 26-30 per cent of the foreign trade of socialist countries. For West European countries, the share of trade relations with the socialist world is very much less but cannot be neglected in view of both economic and political considerations.

The economic development of the CMEA member countries, although to some extent influenced by global economic processes, is nevertheless governed by its own laws and faces different problems. Because of annual and medium-term plans, the rhythm of development of these countries is more reliable and stable than in Western market economies. While in Western Europe the annual growth of gross domestic product in 1984 and 1985 was about 2.2-2.3 per cent, in the European CMEA countries it was about 3.5-3.6 per cent.[17] The Soviet Union and some other CMEA countries managed to arrest the decline of economic growth rates observed at the end of the 1970s and early 1980s. At present they set as their strategic task the acceleration of their development, by improvement of management of the national economy, by speeding-up scientific and technological advance, by structural changes in industry and other measures. By better use of existing resources, by better production organisation and stronger labour discipline, and by more effective incentives, these countries can considerably improve their economic efficiency.

The Soviet Union has entered a period of radical changes both in the economy and in many other spheres of social life. The economic strategy elaborated by the 27th Congress of the CPSU calls on the society to achieve the highest world indicators of productivity of social labour and

---

17) "Economic situation in capitalist and developing countries", op. cit., p. 35. Data on CMEA countries from author's calculations

scientific and technological progress in the foreseable future. It is proposed to double the national income by the end of this century and to double the production potential with qualitative restructuring. In the same period, it is intended to increase labour productivity by a factor of 2.3-2.5, to reduce the energy-intensity of national income by 30 per cent and halve its metal-intensity. The annual average growth of the national income employed for consumption and accumulation will be increased from 3.1 per cent in 1981-1985 to 3.5-4.0 per cent in 1986-1990 and to about 5 per cent later.[18)]

The country must decisively put an end to unfavourable trends in the development of the economy, instil a stronger dynamism, and open broad opportunities for the initiative and creative activity of the people. Quite naturally, the feasibility and reality of such a task may be questioned, as may be the reserves and leverage available to the State for its accomplishment. The scale of the objectives set may arouse a certain scepticism (as is evidenced by comments in the West), the more so since unrealistic targets were put forward in the past.

Of course, if one projects into the future the growth rates and trends of development characteristic of the last five years, and if one assumes that the existing methods of economic management cannot be radically changed, then the figures cited may indeed seem to represent a superhuman task. However, the strategy of acceleration adopted in the USSR rests upon a calculation of resources available, and on an assessment (very careful) of the effects of restructuring both the technological basis and the system of socio-economic relations. It also stems from the study and critical reassessment of our own and international experience in accelerating the growth rate.

1.4 Technical progress and economic reform

A major impact can come from more intensive development of science and technology and, first of all, from their application in the economy. The Soviet strategy of acceleration relies mainly on this factor, especially with a view to long-term prospects. The object is a shift to novel machinery and technology which would result in a jump in the productivity of socialist labour and in the quality of the products; the purpose is also restructuring in accordance with trends in world technological and economic progress, and rearrangement of the production structure on both the macro- and micro-levels. This necessitates a well thought-out scientific and technological strategy, and a balanced structural policy. Experience in the USSR, as

---

18) Documents of the 27th Congress of the CPSU, Moscow, 1986, pp. 268, 273-274, 277

well as in a number of other socialist countries, shows that miscalculations in this area are too costly for the national economy; therefore better quality of state planning and of major investment policy decisions is of the utmost importance.

In the USSR, for example, programmes have been elaborated envisaging a radical renovation of the entire machine-building complex, occupation of leading positions in such areas as informatics and electronics, automation and robotisation of production, biotechnology and new structural materials.

Technical modernisation of the economy and its restructuring are capable, as calculations confirm, of ensuring a considerable future growth of the productivity of socialist labour, of national income, and of fully covering the associated costs. Moreover, opportunities for new investments are greatly broadened. But capital for the modernisation and rearrangement of the structure is needed right now, although the amount is rather limited because of slow and mainly extensive development in the past. For this reason, all other growth factors have to be activated. These are, first of all, those that require no new large investments or additional manpower. At the same time, it is important to improve the efficiency of the available investment resources, directing them primarily to renovation and modernisation of existing production facilities, rather than to new constructions; and to take measures for saving resources and energy, rather than for expansion of the production of raw materials and fuels, though it is impossible to manage without such expansion. All this, of course, is closely connected with the setting of new priorities in state planning.

The key instrument in the strategy of acceleration, in the first stage of its implementation while shortage of resources is still felt, is, of course, a radical reform of the economic mechanism and the mobilisation, through this reform and by social and political measures, of the creative energy and activity of the nation. A full use of the vast growth reserves concealed in man himself - his knowledge, qualification, honest and interested attitude to the job - is another important factor in the reform. The search for optimal forms and methods of planning in present conditions, as well as for effective social inventives, has been going on in the Soviet Union for some years; but the time has now come to formulate and implement, on the basis of national and international experience, an integrated conception of a new economic mechanism. This must ensure a greater authority of the centre in solving key problems of economic and social development simultaneously with enlarged economic independence of enterprises, research-production associations, inter-industrial science-technology complexes and local authorities. In doing so, management from the centre will be effected to a greater extent by economic, not administrative, compulsion and by shifting industrial enterprises and collective and state farms onto genuine economic self-support encouraging them to take independent decisions, responsibilities and risks and to demonstrate socialist enterprise.

The reform of the economic mechanism in accordance with these concepts is inseparable from a corresponding rearrangement of the entire system of social relations so as to involve, in the acceleration process, the broad masses of people, the working teams - indeed every citizen- to improve discipline and order. A further development of socialist democracy in the transition to the intensive model of growth has also become an economic imperative.

Today one can hardly quantify the dynamic gains for the Soviet economy from the introduction of a more flexible and refined mechanism of economic management. It is even more difficult to measure the effects to be derived from a changed attitude of people to their work, and from successive realisation of the principles of socialist justice. But it can be assumed that these effects are as important, or even more important, levers of acceleration as new machinery and technology.

Most CMEA member countries, as can be seen from their draft plans for 1986-1990, schedule insignificant increase in growth rates. The GNP growth rates for all European CMEA countries (excluding USSR) during this period are expected to be 3-4 per cent. These countries lay special emphasis on restoring a balanced development of the economy and its external relations and qualitative rather than quantitative parameters of development. They also envisage an expansion of investment activity, and a gradual rise in the share of accumulation, in the national income in those countries where it has been noticeably reduced during recent years. In future, growing effects of modernisation and improvement of the economic structure will create even stronger dynamics of development in the CMEA countries.

During recent years, China has been playing a rapidly increasing role in the entire world economy and in its socialist part. China is distinguished from other great powers by the highest rate of economic growth. In 1981-1985 the annual average growth rate of national income was 9.8 per cent, of industrial output 10.7 per cent, and of agricultural production 11.4 per cent. Equally dynamic were China's external economic relations. The sources of this rapid growth lie in the profound and positive transformation of the social life of the nation, and in the economic reform, started in the countryside and now covering industry and all other spheres of the economy. Of course, the process of restructuring in China is not free from socio-economic costs and aggravation of certain contradictions. In particular, inflation tendencies appeared, the social differentiation of the population became more strongly pronounced, the raw material and fuel base of industry is lagging behind, and a large deficit in the payments balance is emerging. All this makes the leadership adjust economic policy, restraining investment activity and growth rates so as to prevent the economy from "overheating".

Meanwhile, the level of economic development of the country still remains very low. But China with its one billion population and vast natural resources has an immense growth potential. Severe lessons from the past have enriched the experience of management of such a big power and have helped to control the course of economic and social policies. This diminishes the probability of major economic miscalculations in the future and allows a prediction of at least a doubling, and quite possibly, even a tripling, of the national income by the end of this century. The economy will acquire a still more open character: the People's Republic of China will become a major world exporter and importer of a wide range of commodities.

In the economic policies of the USSR, of other CMEA countries and of China the expansion of international economic cooperation is regarded as an important factor for accelerating technological progress and growth rates. In the first place, the CMEA countries are taking steps to intensify their mutual relations and to derive greater benefits from them. They approved a plan of action and started to execute the Comprehensive Programme of Scientific and Technological Progress to the Year 2000. Now much depends on finding efficient economic mechanisms for cooperation, carrying out appropriate reforms in this field as well.

1.5 The role of East-West relations

These countries also seek ways to activate business cooperation with developing states and with countries of the West. Progress in control of armaments and reduction of the arsenals of nuclear and conventional arms could give a new impetus to East-West economic relations and promote the recovery of the world economy as a whole.

During the early 1970s, CMEA countries' trade with the West was particularly dynamic; in the second half it substantially slowed down, while in the early 1980s growth turned to stagnation. But a revival in East-West trade is now observed. How sound is it? From the purely economic standpoint, East-West business has substantial unused possibilities for development on both sides. With amelioration of the political climate, a growth of the share of the West in the foreign trade of CMEA countries cannot be excluded.

Though CMEA countries have managed to improve their external balance with the West and to control their hard-currency indebtedness, many other urgent problems of business interaction still await solution; in particular, the commodity structure of the trade exchanges must be improved. In exports to the West from CMEA, raw materials, fuels and foodstuffs still account for more than 75 per cent while finished goods make up about 25 per cent including some 7 per cent for machinery and equipment. The prospects of trade expansion depend on improvement of this structure.

In strengthening their joint economic and technological potential, the CMEA countries do not seek, as has been repeatedly stated, to fence themselves off from other countries of the world in science and technology. It is quite clear that exchanges and contacts in this and many other areas are objectively indispensable. The CMEA countries merely intend to ensure their invulnerability in the most vital fields of scientific and technological progress.

The switching of CMEA economies onto the path of intensive development will expand their export and import potentialities, including East-West relations, and will change the structure of both demand and supply. The CMEA countries will seek to improve the efficiency of their imports through more extensive buying of systems of machines and production lines for modernising the machine-building, industrial and agricultural infrastructure, the light and food industries and the application of industrial technologies to agriculture. Promising, also, is the construction of "turnkey" enterprises in these countries with the assistance of Western companies, including small and medium-size ones, especially on a product-buyback basis. The CMEA countries are aware of the need to find new forms of interaction. In particular, the opportunities for joint ventures are being studied. The experience of the formation of special economic zones for the activity of foreign and mixed companies in the territory of socialist countries is also attractive.

The CMEA countries call for improvement of world economic relations by strictly observing the principles of equality and respect of each other's interests, and by denial of discrimination and of the use of trade as a means of political pressure. We must join together to find optimal solutions for regulating the economic life of the world community, for creating favourable conditions for trade exchanges, for better structures of world production and trade, for rational utilisation of resources of raw materials and energy, and for protection of the environment. It would be useful to elaborate an effective reform of the international monetary system, to legalise and normalise relations between the CMEA and the European Community, and to provide measures for building mutual confidence in the economic sphere.

Business cooperation with socialist states developing their economies on the basis of five-year plans and long-term programmes can bring stability and greater durability into the external economic relations of Western, especially European, countries.

Chapter 2

THE MEDIUM-TERM OUTLOOK FOR THE WORLD ECONOMY AND THE IMPLICATIONS FOR EAST-WEST ECONOMIC RELATIONS

Lawrence R. Klein[1]
Daniel L. Bond[2]

2.1 The environment

Background factors for the world economic environment have rarely looked so favourable as they do now. Energy prices are now following the laws of supply and demand, which are more understandable than the somewhat arbitrary decisions of OPEC. The US dollar has depreciated from its unusually high value in early 1985. Interest rates have been falling in many countries and inflation has been brought under control in most, if not all, parts of the world. None of these momentous economic events is an unqualified positive factor in the outlook, but in every case the good outweighs the bad side in its effect on world averages.

Obviously some countries or regions which are important oil producers and exporters are experiencing a setback because of low and falling oil prices, but if we concluded that the world economy suffered a significant setback in 1973-75 and 1979-80, when oil prices rose so markedly, then it is reasonable to conclude now that the world, as a whole, will benefit when prices come down. The reasoning is not completely symmetrical, however, because some major exporters are now heavily burdened with international debt, which was not the case in 1973, when the energy terms of trade began to change. Apart from the altered conditions for such countries as Mexico, Venezuela, Nigeria and Indonesia, the gains for energy consumers all over the world outweigh the losses for producers. Simulations of the Wharton World Model and of Project LINK indicate that a drop in oil prices of $ 10 per barrel makes for an improvement in world GDP by about 1.0 per cent[3]. It is also remarkable that the

---

1) Professor, University of Pennsylvania, Philadelphia

2) Wharton Econometric Forecasting Associates, Inc., Washington DC

3) The Wharton/LINK model projections in this paper were compiled in late 1986. For an explanation and more detail of the baseline scenario, and an earlier version, see D. Bond & L. Klein in C. Saunders (ed), East-West Trade and Finance in the World Economy, London, Macmillan, 1985, Ch. 1 (Session VIII of the present series of Workshops).

NOTE: This paper was drafted during summer 1986, and revised in February 1987 making use of later statistical information and of points raised by commentators.

tendency towards lower inflation rates that began in 1981 coincided with a levelling off of oil prices and was helped by their decline in later years. In fact, we have had the unusual experience of decreases in the major price indexes of a few industrial countries during some months of 1986, just after the break in oil prices.

Economists had difficulty in predicting the course of exchange rates after the abandonment of fixed parities in 1969. The ascendancy of the US dollar after 1980 was puzzling, not in its initial phase, which was a natural reaction to the return of the US current account to balance, but in its magnitude and prolongation after 1983. Economic analysis indicated that the dollar would eventually have to depreciate, but the timing posed a problem. After a sharp speculative run-up in early 1985, the dollar finally did recede. Its fall has been monitored and urged along by the joint actions of the finance ministers of major industrial nations who met in New York on September 22, 1985. According to the Wharton and LINK forecast, the dollar will still decline during the next few years. It is not that the decline does so much all by itself for the good of the world economy, but a gradual and steady decline that is accompanied by falling interest rates can be quite beneficial. This is the scenario of the "soft landing", and its contribution to world economic performance is shown in *Table 2.1*.

Table 2.1

Estimated effects of a dollar depreciation[a]

Deviations from baseline scenario

	1986	1987	1988	1989	1990
World trade volume	–0.1	0.4	0.5	0.9	1.1
World GDP (real)[b]	0.02	0.05	0.07	0.09	0.14
OECD inflation[c]	–0.4	–0.6	–0.8	–0.6	–0.4

[a] US dollar depreciates below baseline path by 10 % in 1986, 15 % in 1987, and 20 % in 1988-90.

[b] Deviations for trade volume and GDP are measured as percentage deviations from yearly *levels* in Baseline Scenario.

[c] Deviations for OECD inflation are measured as differences in percentage rates of price change (inflation). They are *percentage points*.

The opposite of the soft-landing case, which is currently unfolding, is the "crash landing" case - a capital flight from the US and probably a rise in interest rates to attract capital for financing the American fiscal deficit. The capital flight could be caused by a loss of confidence on the part of foreign investors in the quality of dollar-denominated financial assets. The crash landing scenario would generate an American and a world recession. This is not part of the baseline outlook, but it cannot be ruled out of consideration.

Table 2.2

Selected world economic indicators
(Percent change)

	1986	1987	1988	1989	1990
World trade volume growth	3.0	3.3	4.4	3.2	2.5
World GDP growth	2.4	2.7	2.9	2.7	2.1
of which –					
OECD countries	2.5	2.7	2.8	2.4	1.4
Developing countries	0.9	2.4	3.4	3.5	4.0
Centrally planned economies	3.5	2.8	3.0	3.1	2.9
OECD inflation	3.0	3.4	4.2	4.7	4.8

Source: Wharton World Model forecast of December 1986.

The decline of the dollar benefits US exports and restrains imports. This happens with a time-lag. That is precisely what happened when the dollar fell in 1977-78; by 1979-80, the export-import balance improved enough to bring the current account back to equilibrium. If the US benefits by the dollar depreciation, some trading partners must lose exports and gain imports. The world benefits if the US coasts in towards a soft landing and especially if the offsets in current balances occur in Japan and West Germany. The latter development is more uncertain unless there are additional economic changes, in particular, stronger tendencies towards *domestic* economic recovery in Japan and West Germany.

The declines in interest rates that have occurred in many industrial countries, together with the fall of the dollar, are beneficial. In the US, interest-sensitive activities in housing and durable goods purchases are already responding nicely and should continue to do so. The forecast calls for a business investment expansion, and that event is eagerly awaited. Western European and Japanese investment should also respond to the lower pattern of interest rates. This is the second stage of the expansion that should allow the improvement in the economic environment.

The US is a net debtor, and lower interest rates contribute to the improvement of the current account, as well as to the servicing of domestic debt, which can help to reduce the fiscal deficit - a serious economic handicap for the US. The developing countries are also significant beneficiaries of lower interest rates because many of them have heavy burdens of debt servicing. Lower interest costs help to mitigate, but do not completely offset, the losses of export earnings that are being experienced by the oil exporting countries in the Third World; some oil exporting countries are net creditors in the world economy, and they lose portfolio returns when interest rates decline.

Uncontrolled inflation can be destabilising, and that is reason enough to want to see it eradicated. Japan, Western Europe, the US, and Canada dealt successfully with inflation, bringing it down from ranges of 20-30 per cent to 5-10 per cent or even lower. These gains, however, had their counterpart costs, namely in the distressing rise of unemployment throughout the OECD countries. Also, the conquering of inflation has not been uniform. There are still serious pockets of inflation in Southern Europe and in the Third World; but now that this phase of economic adjustment is largely behind us, the world economy is poised for recovery, and some recovery is already taking place.

2.2 Prospects for East-West Trade

Several changes in the outlook for the world economy are likely to have significant impacts on the external economic relations of the Soviet and East European economies. The most important of these is the decline in world oil prices. The depreciation of the dollar, growth in world trade, lower commodity prices and interest rates, and the continued liquidity of world capital markets will also play a role.

As was pointed out above, one positive effect of lower oil prices is the accompanying increase in aggregate world growth and trade, particularly in Western Europe and Japan. This is expected to increase the demand for the Soviet and East European exports in general, and manufactured goods in particular. The expectation is that the terms of trade will continue to shift in favour of manufactured goods exporters, which is additional good news for most of the East European countries.

While the continued depression of non-fuel commodity prices will have a negative impact on Soviet and East European exports, this will be partly counter-balanced by the expected weakness in grain prices. With the region's net grain imports expected to remain in the range of 20 to 30 million metric tons a year through the rest of the 1980s, the forecast for a continuation of grain prices at 50 to 70 per cent of 1980 levels will make a major contribution to reducing the cost of agricultural imports for the Soviet Union and most of the East European countries.

The continuing decline in the value of the dollar will have a negative effect on the Soviet Union. Roughly half of the Soviet Union's hard-currency earnings come from oil exports, the prices of which are set in dollars. However, most Soviet hard-currency imports are in non-dollar-based prices - with the exception of grain imports which amount to about one-fourth of the total. The decline in the value of the dollar relative to West European currencies and the yen will cause an additional deterioration in the Soviet Union's terms of trade with non-socialist countries. The East European economies will be less affected by the dollar's decline, as most of their hard-currency trade - exports as well as imports - is transacted in West European currencies.

Interest rates are expected to stay at relatively low levels (LIBOR in the 7 to 8 per cent range) throughout the forecast period, largely due to the dampening of inflation brought about by continued low oil prices. This will substantially reduce the burden of interest payments for the more heavily indebted countries such as Poland, Hungary, and Yugoslavia.

Finally, it appears that the Soviet Union and most East European countries are likely to continue to be well received on international capital markets. After shying away from most East European countries during the first half of the 1980s, Western lenders now appear eager to lend to these countries (Poland being the exception). According to OECD statistics, these countries obtained $ 4.2 billion in 1985 through international medium- and long-term financing, 55 per cent more than the amount borrowed in 1984, and about five times that of 1983.

The credit ratings of the Soviet Union and East European countries improved dramatically compared with previous years. This was reflected in the terms that they were able to obtain on their loans, which become increasingly more favourable over the past two years. The fact that a sizeable portion of the funds borrowed in 1985 has been used to refinance old debt (and to build up reserves for East Germany, Hungary and Bulgaria) means that their ratings will probably continue to improve.

One regional factor that could have an important effect on East-West trade over the coming years will be the repayment of East European debts to the Soviet Union. Based on rough estimates from data on rouble trade and service balances over the period 1960-84, the rouble debt of Eastern Europe (excluding Yugoslavia) to the Soviet Union amounted to approximately 13 billion roubles in 1985. Although we do not know the repayment terms of this debt, a number of indications suggest that the Soviet Union wants most countries in the regain to repay their rouble debts by 1990. (Poland is apparently being given additional time.) This repayment process appears to have begun in 1985, as the Soviet trade surplus with these countries declined by about 800 million roubles.

Most of the above developments appear favourable for an expansion of East-West trade over the next few years. The one change in the global economy that threatens such an expansion is the recent decline in world energy prices.

2.3 Impact of lower oil prices on East-West relations

The expected continued weakness in world oil prices will have a major impact on the Soviet and East European economies and on their economic relations with the West. (In Wharton's "baseline" forecast, the average dollar price of crude oil is assumed to drop by roughly 50 per cent in 1986 relative to the average price in 1985. This would put the average transaction price of a barrel of crude oil at less than $ 15, where it is expected to stay through mid-1987. The forecast calls for oil prices then to increase gradually over the period 1987-91 at an average annual rate of 12 per cent, i.e., about 6 per cent faster than the expected increase in overall world trade prices.)

Since the Soviet Union is a net oil exporter, while the East European countries are net oil importers, the basic effect of a decline in world oil trade prices should be to worsen the trade balance of the former and improve the trade balances of the latter. While there are a number of important complicating factors in the analysis, particularly as regards the impact on the East European economies, this is basically what we expect to happen over the medium-term.

It is estimated that the Soviet Union loses $ 550 million in hard-currency export revenues for each one-dollar drop in the price of oil. About half of Soviet oil exports have gone to CMEA countries in recent years, with most of the rest being sold outside the CMEA at world market prices. In 1985 the Soviet Union exported an estimated 3.4 million barrels a day of crude and products, 8 per cent less than in 1984. It appears that the Soviets were making a major push to get production back to the level of 12 million b/d in 1986, so that the expected quantity of exports in that year was 3.5-3.6 million b/d.

The East European countries (including Yugoslavia) import over two million b/d of oil each year, mostly crude, 70 per cent of it from the Soviet Union. They also export about 450,000 b/d of oil each year, almost all in the form of products sold in Western Europe. In recent years Eastern Europe has earned roughly 15-20 per cent of its hard currency from the export of crude oil and products. Whether the region can maintain this trade with lower oil prices, and how profitable it will be, depends on the trade arrangements they negotiate with the Soviet Union and other crude suppliers.

However, on balance, a decline in oil prices should help Eastern Europe considerably. The degree of the impact is difficult to tell, as it is complicated by the disparity in price-setting between intra-CMEA trade and trade with other countries. Unless world oil prices go even lower, it is unlikely that East European importers would find it cheaper to switch to non-Soviet oil supplies for most of their crude. (While th nominal price that East European countries paid for Soviet oil in 1985 was an estimated 25 roubles per barrel -or $ 30/barrel at official exchange rates - it is likely that the real cost was closer to $ 15 to $ 20 a barrel.) There are other reasons why East European countries are not likely to switch to free-market oil: most of their refining capacity is designed for Soviet crude; they would probably not want to risk losing preferential access to Soviet supplies if world prices went up again; and they would have to allocate hard currency to pay for this oil, or find oil exporters willing to take their goods in barter.

However, it should be stressed that even if the price that Eastern Europe pays for Soviet oil is approaching or exceeding world oil prices, the region will soon benefit substantially from the recent decline in world prices. According to the Wharton forecast for world oil prices and exchange rates, the price of a barrel of Soviet oil in Transferable Roubles (TR) should rise by only a couple of percentage points in 1986, after which the price will drop by 30 per cent in 1987 and fall to 10 TR/barrel by 1990. (This assumes that the value of the TR in dollars will move in step with changes in the value of a weighted basket of Euro-currencies relative to the dollar.)

It seems most likely that the Soviet Union will continue to give high priority to production and export of oil, with exports to Eastern Europe remaining at roughly the same levels as in 1985. Exports to the West are likely to stay either at 1985 levels, or climb back to 1984 levels if the Soviets are able to increase production or reduce domestic consumption.

This is a "conservative reaction" in that the Soviet authorities expected to continue to handle their oil trade in much the same way as over the past few years, for several reasons. With the great uncertainty in the oil markets, the Soviet authorities will naturally be cautious about making any change that could have long-term implications. Also, given their large hard-currency reserves and access to Western credits, they are probably not under any great pressure to change their trading policy immediately. This conservatism is reinforced by the Soviets' own view that oil prices will go up again in the near future. It now appears that the USSR is cooperating with OPEC in order to achieve their mutual goal of higher oil prices.

The implication of this forecast is that there will be a sharp decrease in Soviet hard-currency oil export revenues. The exact amount of the drop would depend on the success of the Soviet effort to increase the share of products in their oil trade. It will also depend on the pricing arrangements (such as netback agreements) that they might negotiate.[4)]

The Soviets will probably try to compensate for the fall in hard-currency oil export revenues in other ways. They are likely to increase exports of other goods, sell gold, and borrow. However, it is unlikely that the Soviet Union can increase non-oil exports quickly. The second most important hard-currency earner is natural gas sold to Western Europe. Soviet natural gas sales to Western Europe are expected almost to double in volume during the current Plan period (going from 32 billion cubic meters in 1985 to 60 bcm in 1990). But gas prices will go down if oil prices remain depressed since this gas is sold under oil price-indexed contracts. (The Soviet gas price formulas established with West European buyers are in general based on crude oil import prices, domestic petroleum product prices and prices of domestic energy substitutes in Western Europe. Prices are probably recalculated on a monthly basis, using an average of prices for the previous nine to twelve months.)

The Soviet Union could also increase exports of other raw materials and manufactured goods. But the aggregate impact of even a successful effort would not be large since almost two-third of Soviet hard-currency earnings come from oil, gas or gold sales. (Since the Soviets would not want to increase gold sales enough to drive prices down, they would probably not be able to realize more than $ 2 to $ 3 billion from gold sales in any one year.)

In 1985 the Soviet Union was able to borrow more than $ 1.5 billion on the Western syndicated-loan market, all at excellent terms. It is likely that the Soviets will continue to use such financing to help to compensate for future shortfalls in export earnings. However, the Soviets will be

---

4) The Soviet Union could protect its hard-currency revenues by reducing the amount of oil it sells to Eastern Europe for roubles. It could then sell this oil on other world markets, or allow East Europe to buy some of it for hard-currency.

There are some real problem with this scenario. First, if the reduction in oil supplies reduces the ability or willingness of Eastern Europe to produce the "hard" goods that the Soviets expect from these countries, this could leave the Soviets in the same position as if they reduced imports from the West.

Second, if the East European countries paid for additional Soviet oil in dollars, they would have to increase their trade surpluses with the West or increase their hard-currency indebtedness, neither of which are easy or attractive options. Instead of buying more Soviet oil for dollars, they could buy oil on world markets - but they face the same problems in terms of payment.

Even from the Soviet perspective, this is not a particularly inviting strategy. They are sure to face an intense reaction from the East Europeans if they renege on their trade agreements. The increase in revenue from the diverted oil would probably make up for only part of the decline caused by the drop in oil prices. Furthermore, they would disturb their relationship with the members of OPEC by putting more oil on an already overloaded world market.

areful not to go too heavily into debt, and they are likely to cease orrowing if lending terms deteriorate.

Obviously, the Soviets will be faced with the prospect of having ɔ reduce imports from the West if oil prices remain low and if they o not increase their oil exports to the West. If the Soviets are forced ɔ cut back on imports from the West, it is likely that they will seek ubstitutes in Eastern Europe. While East European technology may lag ehind that of the West, in certain areas it is superior to Soviet technology. 'hus the Soviets are likely to put pressure on Eastern Europe to supply etter quality goods that can be substitutes for imports from the West. 'his will be most important in the case of machinery and equipment mbodying more sophisticated technology.

The key question is whether or not Eastern Europe can supply goods ı sufficient quantity and quality to meet Soviet needs. Already the Soviet Jnion is taking two-thirds of all capital goods exported by Eastern Europe ɔ CMEA countries. Furthermore, machinery and equipment account for ıree-fifths of East European exports to the Soviet Union.

It will probably be difficult for most East European countries substantially ɔ increase machinery exports to the Soviet Union. Domestic capacity limited, and they need to maintain their current levels of exports to ıe West if they are to be able to service their debts. In addition, there as been a significant reduction in investment in the region over the ıst few years, which has left these economies with an ageing and depleted apital stock, and a pent-up domestic demand for capital goods.

The Soviet Union's pressure on Eastern Europe is likely to be intense. t the CMEA summit in 1984, the Soviets made clear that their continued ıpply of energy to the region depended upon Eastern Europe supplying ıe USSR with high quality goods, embodying technology at world standards. 'he Soviet Union has also made it clear that East European countries vith the exception of Poland) would have to reduce their bilateral trade eficits, and start paying off the rouble debts accumulated over the past ecade. The drop in oil prices is simply adding greater urgency to the ɔviet demands.

Nevertheless, Eastern Europe will benefit from lower oil prices over ıe next few years. Taking the volumes of East European (excluding Yugoslavia) il imports from the Soviet Union projected in the baseline forecast (roughly 3 million barrels/day), and applying our estimates of TR prices, the ımulative cost of these imports over the period 1986-1991 would be 3 billion roubles. This compares with a cost of 73 billion roubles if we se a constant (1985) price of 25 TR/barrel. Although this calculation approximate - no distinction is made between crude and product prices, ıd it is assumed that all oil is priced on the basis of a five-year moving average of world prices, translated at the TR/$ rate of each year - th difference of 30 billion roubles is twice the estimated 1985 value of th region's entire rouble debt to the Soviet Union.

If our forecast of the general trend in world oil prices proves correc the reduced cost of imports of Soviet oil should make it possible fc the East Europeans to achieve the trade surpluses they need to pay of their Soviet debts without increasing the quantity of their exports o cutting their imports. This expected improvement in East European term of trade vis-à-vis the Soviet Union may also take much of the pressur off their own economies, facilitating the required quality improvemen in East European exports.

2.3 The forecast for 1986-1991

World trade has suffered a slump. Oil and commodity trade has bee seriously depressed, but all goods have experienced the slowdown. Whe the US grew so strongly in 1984 and imported manufactures at a ve high rate, many other countries benefitted by export growth, but the was a great slowdown in 1985. For all but the centrally planned economie 1986 has turned out to be slightly weaker than 1985. After 1986, it expected that world trade volume will expand by about 2.5 or 4.5 p cent per year. Associated with this moderate but steady rate of trac growth, there should be a corresponding steady recovery of output. Wor GDP is expected to be on a path of 2.5 to 3 per cent growth, with 198 a year in which more strengths come together and reinforce one another.

In particular, Western Europe has shown slightly more recove strength in 1986, thus helping the US to improve its trade performanc The developing areas of the Pacific have recovered more vigorously, t virtue of export expansion with currency values tied to a falling dolla Japan, on the other hand, has been restrained by a strong yen appreciatio They are seeking more domestic growth, but the response has not bee strong enough to overcome weaker export performance. Oddly enoug Japan continues to earn a great deal of foreign exchange, even thou the volume of exports measured in constant yen has performed poorly.

China, viewed as a Pacific nation, should also be outstanding, principa because she is instituting economic reforms, which have been quite e pansionary. The second largest country in this area of the world, aft China, is India. Steady progress at rates between 4 and 5 per cent annual are much smaller than China's, but they are equally impressive. Th are being achieved in a more favourable environment in respect of inflati and balance of payments stability.

Elsewhere in the Third World, prospects are mixed. Some Latin Americ countries are prepared to grow vigorously, but Mexico is once again ecession, dealing with its severe debt crisis. The Middle East is upset)y internal conflict and weak oil markets. These are enough to hold back xpansion in that area. As for Africa, with its chronic state of depression, here are no immediate signs of a breakout.

Overall, developing countries are expected to grow by a percen-age point or more above the world average. However, against this seemingly uperior performance, we must place their 1 to 2 per cent higher rate f population expansion.

The Soviet Union and most of the East European countries are planning or significantly more rapid growth in 1986-90 than was either planned r achieved over the last five years. Some objective reasons merit this ptimism. The economic situation at the start of the new Plan period ppears more favourable for most East European countries than it did efore the last Plan period. At that time, it was already becoming apparent hat a substantial adjustment of East European external accounts was eeded to cope with the mounting debts. Now that the most difficult djustments have been made, most East European planners are expecting he debt-servicing burden to lessen over the next few years.

One problem in meeting the growth targets that a number of the ast European economies will face for the next five years, is suggested y the declines in investment that occurred during 1981-85. This has aused a sharp slowdown in the modernisation and replacement of capital tock in these countries, which could make it difficult for them to realise ne volumes and quality of production targeted. It will also affect their oreign trade performance, especially in manufactures, where the lack f modernisation is making their exports less competitive on world markets. o compensate, the targeted rates of investment growth have been increased or the new Plan period.

Soviet hard-currency exports are projected to increase at an average nnual rate of 7 per cent, while the growth rate foreseen for East European xports is near the 8.9 per cent average annual rate of growth projected or Western imports. The East European countries are likely to allow considerably more rapid increase of imports in the second half of the 980s. This is expected to lead to a decline in East European hard-currency ade balances, with current trade surpluses changing into deficits after few years.

If the level of Soviet and East European indebtedness remains within ne limits projected, the real burden of debt servicing for these economies ill be reduced. Perhaps the single indicator that best reveals the burden f debt on an economy is the ratio of interest payments to exports. On nis basis, the interest burden lessens steadily throughout the entire orecast period. While the region is expected to be increasing its indebtedness over the next three years, this is a period when we expect interest rates to drop to a new low.

Hidden within the aggregate figures are the less optimistic projections for a few East European debtors. Debt-service burdens will remain especially heavy in Poland, Hungary and Yugoslavia. However, even for these countries we expect the burden to diminish considerably by the end of the decade. The only country for which we are predicting a substantial increase in debt-service is the Soviet Union. But because of the relatively low level of current indebtedness, the required increase in Soviet payments should not pose a serious problem.

2.4 Problems and issues

The results (*Table 2.2*) look deceptively calm and peaceful. They indicate stable recovery without inflation; they are manifestations of the soft landing case. But these broad aggregates cover up many problem areas, or simply fail to deal with some disturbing issues.

A world recession is probably going to be avoided. At worst, 198 turns out, in retrospect, to have been nothing more than a slowing of world recovery. The dollar and interest rate adjustments contribute a great deal to the smoothing of the course of the economy and to avoiding a significant downturn of the business cycle; but risks still exist. It is not only disparities of fortune among countries that give rise to world economic problems; there are also issues that ultimately affect all countries.

There is, first, the pressing problem of unemployment in Wester Europe and, to a lesser extent, in North America. Unemployment is als serious in many developing countries, but accurate statistics of its magnitud are not maintained. The overall growth rate of 3 per cent a year is simpl not strong enough to bring down unemployment. At least one more ful point of growth, on average, would be needed to have much immediat impact on unemployment; and even with that kind of expansion man structural problems in labour markets would not be resolved. Youth unemployment, in particular, would remain as a vexing problem.

The world recession of the early 1980s brought with it a depresse state of the main world commodity markets. There is oversupply in man agricultural commodities (even in the presence of African hunger!) and also in many industrial materials. Some material markets are feeling th pressure of weak business conditions, but others are going through a industrial transformation in which traditional commodities are being technologically displaced. The fall in the dollar should, in normal circumstances lead to rises of dollar-denominated commodity prices, but that is nc now happening.

Two other major problems are the large surpluses and deficits i the external balances of many countries. The most noteworthy cases of disequilibrium are the US deficit against the Japanese and West German surpluses. Dollar depreciation and harmonisation of domestic policies between countries may in the end lead to improvement, but at present the US deficit is so large and pervasive that it generates widespread demands for protectionist legislation that could lead to debilitating trade wars. A close watch is now being kept on movements of the dollar and on adjustments of trade balances to see whether enough improvement can be achieved to hold back the forces of protectionism.

Another serious imbalance in the world economy is the persistence of high indebtedness in some key countries. In Latin America, the worst problems are in Argentina, Brazil, Mexico, Venezuela, Peru, Bolivia, and Chile. The Philippines and Indonesia pose problems in the Far East. Nigeria is in trouble in Africa and Poland in Eastern Europe. These are only the most prominent cases; there are many others. Lower interest rates, higher commodity prices, and world growth can all help to alleviate the situation but some more fundamental adjustments will probably be needed. Meanwhile, the stability of the world's entire financial system is at stake.

The overall prospects for the developing countries are uncertain. Famine, debt burdens, sluggish growth (recession in some areas), and pockets of inflation are all problems. The developing countries must be allowed to participate in the general improvements in living standards if there is to be politico-economic stability in the world over the remainder of this century.

These problem areas all contribute to a significant downside risk for the consensus projection of the world economy. There are some upside risks, too. They are not problems, in the same sense as those already considered, but they are important issues, with some possible side-effects.

The global analysis presented here focusses mainly on the near-term recovery process. But for the long run the underlying growth trends will be dominant, and foremost in this area is the emergence of new technologies. The great transformations that are now taking place give rise to short-run problems of labour displacement, the phasing-in of new sectors, and the phasing-down of traditional sectors. That is why we find unemployment and excess capacity in steel, other metalworking industries, and in manufacturing at large. The principal upside risk in the consensus forecast arises if new investment is strong and large scale productivity gains are realised. The choices between work and leisure, spending and saving, unemployment and retraining, call for difficult decisions. In a sense, such decisions are already beinig made in both the OECD and CMEA countries. A few developing countries are also participating in the development of the new technologies and are not simply waiting to realise the benefits after they have been successfully demonstrated in the advanced countries. But vast differentials are apparent even between the countries actively engaged in developing the new technologies. The problem of technology transfer is important.

Automation, robotisation, and computerisation are clearly visible in the US, Japan, parts of Western Europe, and a few other countries. If the techniques now being developed become widely diffused throughout the world, then a fast growth scenario has a good chance of being achieved in the total world economy.

Technological progress has always been given a major role in Soviet and East European plans. However, it now appears to be the dominant theme, for several reasons. First, technological progress is seen as the major source of productivity increases and the key to growth. Second, the lag in the technological level of CMEA countries' products is hurting their trade with the rest of the world.

Each CMEA country has plans to strengthen its own technological capabilities. The general trend is to emphasise the need for linking scientific research more directly to the production process, since the weakest link in the system is the application of new technology.

However, most of these countries are too small to be able to rely on their own resources to develop the technology they need. Thus region-wide cooperation is also stressed in the plans. The "Comprehensive Programme for Scientific and Technological Cooperation" among the Soviet and East European countries serves as the blueprint for regional efforts to find ways to cooperate in this field, and it is referred to in each country's plan.

So far, the Comprehensive Programme and earlier cooperation agreements have not been as successful as their participants had hoped. Several basic impediments to integration - particularly the inadequacies of the price system and the lack of a regional convertible currency - have yet to be overcome. Only in areas such as computer technology, where the advantages of cooperation and specialisation far outweigh the disadvantages, has substantial progress been made on a region-wide basis. However, the pressures for improvement noted above, and the limited availability of hard currency with which to purchase Western technology, now make regional cooperation more attractive.

For the same reasons, a number of East European countries are attempting to increase the scope of industrial cooperation and joint ventures with Western companies. Recently, the Soviet Union has also indicated an interest in this area. It may be that recent changes in world economic conditions and perceptions will put new life into this form of East-West cooperation.

Chapter 3

GLOBAL SHIFTS AND THEIR IMPACT ON NATIONAL POLICIES

Józef Pajestka[1)]

3.1 Methods of global analysis

Economic literature subdivides its subject-matter into micro- and macro-economics: hence micro- and macro-theories, analyses, etc. Though macro-economics might be thought etymologically to refer to any broad approach to the subject, it has generally been understood to be concerned with *national* economy.

For some two decades, however, we have seen the emergence of *global* concerns: global thinking, and consideration of global economics. These notions are, indeed, slowly emerging in the current stream of economic thinking, particularly in connection with the various institutional and conceptual initiatives of the United Nations. The UN can justly be considered as having a built-in bias for international and global thinking.

We have had, of course, the notion of the "world economy". Is there any difference between the "world economy" and the "global economy"? Both terms can be and often are used as synonyms. It seems, however, that while the term "world economy" has been traditionally used to describe aggregate behaviour on the world scale, the term "global economy" might be used to imply, rather, a kind of organic entity of world processes. The term "global economy" would then be analogous to "national economy", which also denotes not just a mere aggregate but an economic organism, with certain laws of behaviour. Recent thinking tends towards this kind of terminological convention.

We have a relatively long experience in describing the world economic processes in quantitative terms, and in analysing the performance of the world economy. This experience has been built up mainly within the United Nations, which has also developed a unified system of statistical concepts and classifications for that purpose. Analysis of the type indicated, which can be called *survey-type,* are mostly descriptive, although not devoid of a certain explanatory value. They operate with aggregated data concerning:

- outputs (GDP, GNP, sectors, main commodities)
- capital investments (with some breakdown)

---

1) Professor, Polish Academy of Sciences, Warsaw

- international trade and financial flows
- various social indicators.

Time-series of such aggregated data are available for the world economy as a whole, for important country groupings, and also for many individual countries.

Descriptive analyses of this type can display: trends, up or down, in economic performance of the world economy; differentiation between trends for various country-groupings, and hence the facts about growing or diminishing discrepancies in socio-economic levels between the various country groups; behaviour of the factors influencing the development - capital investment, foreign trade, financial flows, structural change, and thus a certain explanation of the reasons for changing performance. If carried on continuously, the descriptive analyses can add up to better understanding of the processes of economic change within the global framework. One can also say that continuous description of economic developments on the world scale has certainly enriched knowledge of the processes affecting the economic environment of individual countries, helping them to have better understanding of the necessary premises for their own policies.

Description of some features and trends, though a necessary element for better understanding of socio-economic reality, is certainly not yet sufficient. Deeper explanatory insight is required for better anticipation of the most probable future changes, which is a condition *sine qua non* of more efficient development policy. The poor explanatory capability of survey-type analysis must be recognised. This has been largely understood, and has led to various attempts to improve this aspect of world economic analyses.

For a number of years experiments have been conducted in the application of economic models for analyses and projections of the world economy. These seem to have begun in the mid-1960s with the very aggregated models of the world economy built in the UN Secretariat, and used for projections for the Second UN Development Decade. (As far as my knowledge goes, they were based on a conceptual model of the "two gaps" - of savings/investment and of the balance of payments - developed by Chenery). More disaggregated projections were produced in the Second Report for the Club of Rome[2)] (Pestel and Mesarovic). A well-known, disaggregated projection was also prepared for the UN by Leontief.[3)] Continuous studies and projections are carried on in applying the global "Link" model (Klein).

---

2) M. Mesarovic & E. Pestel, Mankind at the Turning Point, New York, Dutton/Readers' Digest Press, 1974

3) United Nations, The Future of the World Economy, New York, 1977

Projection models are always based on some theoretical assumptions about the patterns of behaviour in the system considered. This is true also of global models, whether the theoretical assumptions are explicit or implied. There are also, however, global models not presented in the form of quantitative formulae but which may serve for diagnosing global processes. The best example here is the "centre-periphery" model of Raúl Prebisch. I do not intend to evaluate the whole experience of global models, quantitative or not. Suffice it to say that they demonstrate a certain progress in understanding the global processes: something can be learnt from global projections, and should not be neglected. I think, however, that comprehensive, disaggregated model projections, down to the country level, are not the only method for better understanding of global economic performance, or for better anticipation of the most probable future changes. We should try various methods, so long as they offer some promise of enriching our understanding of the global processes.

In what follows, I am going to apply a method somewhat different from those indicated above. It puts the main emphasis not on presentation of the trends of change, but rather on the "logic of change", and therefore not on the behaviour of economic variables, but on the behaviour of the various agents (and institutions), involved in the policy of change.

This methodological approach assumes that there are *agents influencing the global processes*, and, indeed, carrying on some kind of *global policy*. It would seem that this assumption reflects the real world of the present time. The behaviour of agents can also be displayed by describing certain *specific actions*, which may be a convenient way of describing and analysing the ongoing process of change on the global scale. The process can then be presented by the following scheme:

Situation$_0$
------->Action$_1$
------>Situation$_1$
------->Reaction$_2$------
---->Situation$_2$
-------->Action$_3$
------>Situation$_3$

No uniform description of situations or actions seems required or recommendable, since they are supposed to reflect the actual course of events. It is understandable that any description of global processes of the kind discussed must rely on some theoretical approach. My description and interpretation can be understood as based on a conceptual frame of the "centre-periphery" type. This defines particularly the choice of agents though, of course, I attach a greater role to identifying the real agents than to any general scheme.

I leave it to the reader to appraise the merits of this method. Let me say, however, that its merits depend on its explanatory capability. My method is not, of course, a substitute for other methods of global analysis (such as the types mentioned above) but rather a supplementary form of analysis.

3.2 Major shifts effected by OPEC's action

It is widely agreed that the 1970s opened a new era in global developments, being anything but a continuation of the post-war trends. The world economy entered a period of turbulence, in a confused search for new patterns. What happened was, of course, a result of forces and tendencies at work over a long period. They came to the fore, however, not by a continuous process but by way of unexpected changes. It must be said, *ex post*, that the power of vision of the social scientists, as well as of the politicians, was clearly too weak to foresee the coming changes. Policy, then, should have been aimed at catching up with events, at adjusting to them as quickly as possible. What we saw instead was policy-makers, taken by surprise, resorting to convulsive reactions rather than to conscious, purposeful action. This is not a universal criticism, but is still appropriate for a number of cases.

A first, major change came with the decision of OPEC to raise the price of oil. What followed was called the "energy crisis", though this is certainly a rather misleading term. What really happened was that a group of developing countries took a dramatic step to impose a new international distribution of income by raising the price of the most important commodity - oil, the source of energy on which contemporary civilisation relies most heavily. Reliance on oil proved so deep and universal, that it could not quickly be dispensed with, or replaced. That is why OPEC's action proved so effective.

The dramatic change came about in the context of global issues. The way was prepared by the new, and growing global awareness created by the reports of the Secretary General of the UN, U Thant, by the publications of the Club of Rome, and by a number of other studies of natural environment, world imbalances etc. It is important to note that:

(a) the OPEC action was intended to change dramatically the international distribution of income in favour of the developing countries, and really achieved that aim, gaining support from the solidarity of practically all the developing countries. Never before had this solidarity appeared in such strength on the global level;

(b) the action brought to the surface the two most critical global issues: the appalling socio-economic discrepancies dominating the world scene; and the most serious, indeed dangerous, potential resource limitation (energy).

It can, then, be said that the OPEC action had a historical dimension: it made manifest cumulative historical forces rendering change necessary, and it ushered in a new period of changed patterns. For the first time in human history the global issues came very strongly to the surface - not as mere intellectual arguments but as real forces - exercising a deep influence on interhuman relations on a global scale. They can be said to have created new challenges, which are here to stay with us and which must be met in one way or another.

In my view, it is not so much OPEC's action as the reaction to it that has had the deepest impact on the patterns of future global developments. World history has seen more radical changes in the terms of trade, involving international income distribution, without such wide repercussions. This time, however, it was much more - a real trial of strength on the global arena, against the background of historical forces making for change. This is why the OPEC action ushered in a new round of global processes.

3.3 A strategic response to the challenge

While it is widely agreed that the OPEC action started the turbulence of the 1970s, there is almost universal silence about the counteraction. Yet can one imagine that such a heavy blow, inflicting immediate losses on the major industrial powers, with the prospect of their continuation, met no counteraction? It is certainly not the major industrial powers which lack strategic vision in world economic relations, even though one should not exaggerate their capacities in that field. The silence on the side of politicians can well be understood, but why did the economists keep silence? I will have something to say on that subject later.

My proposition is that the OPEC challenge was in fact met with great efficiency by a strategic counteraction. This consisted principally in two measures:

- stagflation on a global scale,
- energy saving and opening up alternative energy sources.

The second of these could be expected to bring solutions only over a long period. Hence the particular role of stagflation as an immediate countermeasure.

As already noted, stagflation:

(a) by virtue of stagnation held back overall demand for energy, and

(b) by virtue of inflation, further upset the new price relations resulting from the OPEC action - in favour of the energy-importing industrial countries.

Whether the global stagflation was a consciously devised strategy or not, is not the important question. If it had not happened, it should had been invented. If anybody prefers to argue that it was not purposefully devised, but rather just a supportive reaction, I would have no strong opposing arguments. In any case, it can now be seen that stagflation proved an extremely efficient response, counteracting OPEC's action. Still, this was not understood, and still fails to be regarded as a way of understanding the global interaction. Maybe that is why we had the second oil price hike in 1979, followed by the deepest global economic recession of the early 1980s.

To sum up the experience of counteracting the OPEC action, the following evaluation seems justified:

(a) the strategic counteraction taken by the oil importing industrial countries proved most efficient in upsetting the price relations imposed by OPEC, i.e. in counteracting the intended income redistribution in favour of the developing countries;

(b) the counteraction proved, however, very painful. The cost consisted in the slow-down of economic growth, and, particularly because of the heavy depression of the early 1980s, in extensive human suffering as well as in economic repercussions - mass unemployment, inflation, etc.

(c) as regards the long-term global issues, it should be observed that the adjustment processes developed in a positive way, postponing the threatened limitations of energy supplies; society has become less energy-consuming and, therefore, a better balance has been gained between human civilisation and the ecosphere. (The change observed in this respect is still only marginal and no long-term conclusions can be drawn from it.)

(d) Another global issue - the glaring disproportions and inequalities between the various nations and races - has, however, become even more accentuated. One might comment that society once again proved better able to solve technological problems - a better balance between man and nature - than to solve the crucial problems in interhuman relations. This appraisal, although valid for the time being, suggests threats for the future.

3.4 Declaration on the NIEO and its failure

The 1970s were not only a period of global turbulence and global shifts. They were also, at least for some time, a period of great hopes in the capacity of the international community to organise global relationships in a more rational way. Those hopes took the shape of the declaration on the New International Economic Order (the NIEO) made by the UN General Assembly in 1975. Some other important documents were accepted, having the same aim - to reform international economic relations in the direction of greater global rationality and greater justice. Among the various actions discussed in this Chapter, the proclamation on the NIEO was the most official and comprehensive, and obtained the greatest publicity. All that has not added to its real effectiveness. Unilateral actions have had greater chances of success than the only multilateral action proclaimed by consensus in the highest UN forum.

It seems worth noting that the idea of the NIEO came after OPEC's successful action, and was based on the belief that solidarity of the Third World, and some economic leverage at its disposal (like OPEC), will usher in a new era of international economic relations in which patterns more beneficial for the developing countries can be established. NIEO was a great idea, but its impact on real life proved almost zero. *Ex post*, one can say that this could have been expected. Still, this international experience requires most serious reconsideration.

Despite all the hopes and importance attached to NIEO, there were just not sufficient forces to put it into effect. Proclaiming NIEO testified to the fact that the global economy needs some rationality and some guidance; and shows that this need is maturing in people's minds. The inability of the international community to implement it proved that the path from a great idea to reality is particularly difficult in this field. One cannot escape from the conclusion that beliefs in the feasibility of NIEO in the circumstances of the period proved over-credulous.

Lack of success of NIEO does not mean that it was a useless exercise. It was a first experiment, undertaken multilaterally, in institutionalising greater purposefulness and rationality in a global framework. The evolutionary process of civilisation found a substitute for it: the global policy executed by the main capitalist metropolis. This has proved more efficient, because it has had the support of the most powerful forces. This solution occupies the stage to-day. One may like it or not, but it is more important to understand it, because it plays a most crucial role in determining the global processes. I call the new solution - the substitute for NIEO- the "partisan global policy". Since it is a competitive solution, it is inimical to NIEO and to its origin.

3.5 Major institutional changes supporting the "Partisan Global Policy"

Before we analyse further developments in the recent global processes, it seems relevant to indicate certain changes taking place in the constitution of the major agents operating on the global scene, and creating a new fabric for the global economy.

It has been mentioned already that NIEO was born as a result of the spectacular growth of the solidarity, and apparent new economic power, of the Third World. In other words - using Raúl Prebisch's terminology- the "periphery" became more united and forceful as an agent of global processes. Much deeper changes have taken place, however, on the other side - the main capitalist "centre". In countering OPEC, the highly industrialised countries developed their own solidarity matching that of the Third World; one could argue indeed that the solidarity of the rich and powerful proved the more efficient, although I would not give that argument the greatest significance in historical perspective. It was not the solidarity of the rich which promoted a new global pattern. Of much greater import was a profound institutional change which had been going on for some time. It comprised two critical elements:

(a) the development of a network of transnational enterprises, dominating international trade, finance and the transfer of technology,

(b) the global monetary system which, after detachment from gold, became extremely manipulatory.

Transnational corporations have a longer history and nothing happened during the 1970s resembling any kind of "institutional reform". Yet, their growth in number and scope made a new pattern in the global economy. The international monetary system has also, at least formally, remained within the framework of the Bretton Woods agreement. The main change which came about - detachment of the US dollar from gold - was undertaken unilaterally, without involving any new international agreement. Thus the international monetary system does not seem to have been subject to any reform during the 1970s. It has been criticised as being "no system", and many voices have called for its reform. In fact, however, the international monetary system did acquire some new features.

While superficially, then, no deep reform of the international economy was visible, the real change in the two fields mentioned during the 1970s was most profound, and introduced a really new stage of development of global economic relations. This change was, in my view, incomparably more significant than that officially proclaimed and loudly publicised under the heading of the NIEO. Yet it has not been sufficiently appraised in economic literature.

The institutional change deeply modified the fabric of international economy in two important ways:

(a) the global economic system acquired new features allowing it to be guided (or manipulated) to a much greater extent than ever before. It is to be observed that the socialist countries, although outside the direct influence of the new guidance, felt the impact of the monetary system and of the activities of the transnational corporations more than in the past.

(b) The function of global guidance has fallen to the US, both because of the role of the dollar in the international monetary system and because of the role of transnational corporations operating within the scope of influence of the US authorities. Some authors point to a diminishing role of the US in the global economy, based on the share of foreign trade in the US, but ignore the institutional changes, which have increased the influence of the US in the global economy.

One might speculate that the modifications of the international fabric noted above, though potentially called for by institutional changes, were still latent and came about only during the confrontation with OPEC. In my view, the OPEC action only slightly accelerated the latent developments, working like a catalyst.

It is against the background described that there developed a system of guidance of global relations which I have called the "partisan global policy". It is this system which proved much more efficient than NIEO, which opposed NIEO and was indeed a substitute for it.

Theoretically one could visualise two alternative systems: one designed and managed multilaterally (such as those proposed by NIEO, or by the Development Decades of the UN); and a second, shaped by a leading country or a group of countries, working in the interests of the managing agents. As observed already, evolutionary processes brought about the second alternative. This solution became established and shaped the institutions, and some patterns of behaviour. It can be, of course, changed, but it is already developing its power of survival. Therefore any proposal for reinstating NIEO or anything similar must take into account the new international facts.

Understanding the agents operating on the global scene is most important for the analysis of global processes. The method applied here for this analysis, as explained earlier, is based on the institutional changes described above and on their consequences for global policy. This is, however, not the way in which the global processes are usually presented. The traditional but still dominant presentation relies on the existence of an open international market mechanism. It ignores, of course, what I called the "global policy". But that cannot be ignored if one wants to develop thinking relevant to reality. Ignoring the fact of global policy has led most economic analysts into failing (as mentioned above) to take into account the strategic response to the OPEC action. This failure continues to be seen in analyses of future global processes. Let me put forward the proposition that without reconsideration of the methodological premises, the economic analysts will be unable to display the global processes in a sufficiently relevant way.

3.6 Recession of the early 1980s and indebtedness

By continuing the previous argumentation, the fall in global economic performance of the early 1980s can be presented as a result of the strong reaction of the "centre" to the new OPEC action in 1979. Accepting this interpretation, one would have to state, however, that it was a genuine overreaction. The blow was extremely strong but therefore also efficient. OPEC received a knock, losing the drive of its energy supply, with the chance of regaining some of its former power receding into a rather distant future. Consequently the Third World's hopes for a build-up of economic power crumbled and its drive to implement the NIEO finally weakened. On the other hand, however, the cost of victory for the centre was terrible. It was a real Pyrrhic victory - with the deepest recession of the whole post-war period, and its painful social, economic and political consequences.

I am fully aware that many (if not most) economic analysts would reject the above interpretation of the recent recession. Let us therefore look deeper into its argumentation.

We must distinguish an originator of an action from a purposeful actor. It should not be difficult to agree on the originator of the deep fall in the world economy during the early 1980s and of the resulting shocks. A most knowledgeable judgement refers to "all of the post-1979 shocks that stemmed in considerable part from the unintended effects of the monetary, budgetary, and revenue policy choices made by US administrations".[4] In the language of the present paper, this would be expressed in the following form: the shocks stemmed from the partisan global policy of the main capitalist metropolis. Apart from terminology - which is not so important - the difference of opinion seems to be reduced to the judgement about whether the effects of the actions were "unintended" or whether they were consciously aimed at, or expected, as necessary side-effects. Judgements on that subject are coloured with emotions; e.g. the statement that the OPEC action was counteracted with great efficiency may sound very nice, while the statement that the downswing of economic

4) John Lewis, Development Strategies Reconsidered, Washington DC, Overseas Development Council, 1986, p. 28

activity was purposefully brought about does not sound so good.

I do not intend to define here precisely to what extent the global policy discussed was purposeful and how far it was unintended. Policy is usually both, and it is rather a question of degree than of "yes or no". More important is the proposition that the partisan global policy has been operating - well or badly, consciously or not fully intended- in this case. Its operation has become a "natural pattern" once the institutional change has taken shape. To speak of the "partisan global policy" is no indictment but a statement about the real course of affairs.

The global policy gave birth also to the indebtedness crisis. I am again not asserting that the indebtedness crisis was the result of full knowledge and intention. There are arguments however, for maintaining that without the new patterns of the global set-up, the indebtedness would not have reached its actual scale and shape. The origins of the international debt crisis lie in a conjuncture of international factors and of internal causes specific for each case. The former include:

- the "petrodollar recycling" originating from oil price increases after 1973,
- the dollar inflation,
- the unsound lending practices of many commercial banks,
- the increase in interest rates to unprecedented levels, originating in the US,
- the appreciation of the value of the US dollar,
- the deep 1981-83 world recession.

In evaluating the origins of the international debt crisis, one should not forget that throughout the second half of the 1970s, almost till 1982 (the August "Black Friday", the Mexican crisis), the severity of the debt crisis was not appreciated. Again the intellectual power of anticipation proved critically weak. This fact also demonstrates that what brought home the international debt crisis was the global recession of 1981-83. The recession, however, was initiated to a substantial degree by the global policy of the main industrial countries, particularly the US, which control the most efficient instruments of global policy.

We are accumulating, then, new experience of the partisan global policy. To the deep recession of the early 1980s and the international debt crisis, one should add the hunger crisis in Africa, the potential dangers of destabilisation in Latin America (because of indebtedness), and the ensuing political tensions in East-West relations. This summary record hardly gives reason for a favourable judgement.

From a distance, one might observe that the global policy discussed is really myopic and self-centered; it may change, by learning from reality. Can it, however, change its own patterns to such an extent that it is no longer "partisan" and in the long-term acquires features of a more universal rationality? I must leave this question open.

3.7 Lessons for national policies

To draw lessons for national policies from the experience of global turbulence of the 1970s and 1980s seems at present a very fashionable subject for economic debate. Without going into this subject in any depth, I can make a few observations.

In the debates, the various policy patterns are evaluated to find how they survived the global turbulence. That is correct. Evaluation on that basis is very often applied to the future. It implies, then, that the future will be similar to what we know of experience of the recent past. We have no ground for that assumption, which recalls the generals trying again and again to fight the last war in the different conditions of a new war. My view is that the "new war" in global affairs is going to be rather different from the recent past. We should, therefore, concentrate more on global developments, trying to see national policies in the light of expected future conditions rather than in the light of the past.

In the debates most of the old controversies appear to have been revived: import-saving versus export-oriented patterns, industry-led versus agriculture-led patterns, state-guided versus market oriented patterns, etc. Words of caution seem to be needed to protect thinking from simplistic alternatives, supposed to be universally valid, of the either-or type. In framing the strategy, nothing can replace many-sided and complex analysis. Recent historical experience has certainly not changed that.

COMMENTS ON PART I - PROSPECTS FOR THE WORLD ECONOMY

Gerhard Fink[1]

Reading *Klein* and *Bond* (Ch. 2), one can feel quite strongly the optimistic overtones: soft landing of the dollar and low oil prices may trigger accelerated growth in the OECD area. We all hope it will be like that. However, as *Bogomolov* (Ch. 1) puts it rightly, so far it has not happenned.

This is not to say that *Klein* and *Bond* have painted too bright a picture; they also give some weight to lasting disturbances in the world economy. But *Bogomolov*'s more pessimistic assessment sounds more realistic to me. I think that accelerated growth in the West did not emerge in 1986 because of the fall of the dollar and the drop in oil prices. This has brought new uncertainties causing high adjustment costs. In addition, it is far from clear how the dollar or the oil price may develop in the next few months, not to speak about the years to come. It may be hoped that the dollar and the oil price stabilise at present levels, but who can guarantee that the dollar will not move into the free-fall/crash landing scenario? Who can guarantee that the oil price may not fall further, or may go up again? Under such uncertainties and immense imbalances in the world economy, a significant acceleration of growth can hardly be expected. Economies mostly prosper if expectations are favourable and promise to remain so at least for some time. At present, expectations are far from being stable, and some (fall of the dollar) are quite unfavourable - at least for Europe and the NICs.

In contrast to *Klein* and *Bond*, I do not consider the East European debt crisis to be over. True, most of the East European countries have successfully adjusted, and reduced the level of the debt. But still many problems recur or are not solved: Poland still cannot service her debt, Romania and Yugoslavia have had to reschedule again, Hungary and Bulgaria will pretty soon have to cut back on imports from the West to keep debt under control, the hard currency surplus of the GDR may vanish this year, and the USSR suffers tremendous revenue losses in hard currency exports. We now look more soberly at the debt problems, but they are not completely solved.

I am substantially less optimistic about Soviet economic reform than *Bogomolov*. So far, the climate for discussing reform has changed in the USSR. But the measures taken hardly indicate a concept of reform: rather

1) Director, WIIW (The Vienna Institute for Comparative Economic Studies), Vienna

half-steps taken half-heartedly. It certainly will take several years before a reform concept can be developed in the USSR - and it will take several more years before a reform will be implemented.

Finally, let me turn to *Pajestka* (Ch. 3). It is difficult to do justice to this paper. Very subtle wording allows different interpretations of a number of passages. I will discuss what can be called the "background music" rather than the detail. First of all I am puzzled by the presentation of the oil price shocks in 1973 and 1979 as a success for developing countries in general. Such an approach leaves the non-OPEC developing countries which were hurt most by this action out of consideration. No consideration at all is given to the consequences of the oil price shock on all non-OPEC economies, including the industrialised West. Such a tremendous terms of trade loss necessarily leads to a severe struggle for income distribution within societies. Neither the entrepreneurs nor the wage earners want to lose income; but someone has to lose in such a situation.

Pajestka comes close to presenting the stagnation of the 1970s and the anti-inflation policies of the 1980s as hostile countermeasures by developed market economies against the "LDC-success" in shooting up the oil price. I have a different interpretation. In the accounting books of the enterprises the severe terms of trade loss materialised as increased costs of production. Since entrepreneurs want to maintain their incomes, they raised prices to maintain a "normal" level of profits. Workers usually react to price increases by demanding higher wages, because they also do not want to lose income. The consequences of this cost-inflation spiral were stagnant production because of the weak profitability expectations, but also inflation because of the cost increases. When the oil price shock was repeated, governments tried to avoid the economic policy mistakes made after the first oil shock and have concentrated first of all on suppressing inflation; but stagnation in most economies could not be avoided. Economic growth was faster in countries where a social consensus could be maintained (e.g. Austria, Japan) and where workers accepted a substantial part of the burden. In countries where a social consensus could not be maintained, workers had to be forced to accept that burden: unemployment was generated.

I think we can learn from the last fifteen years that unilateral, forceful action in favour of a single country, or group of countries, does more harm than good to the world economy. A strategy of stepwise improvements by negotiated action is much more promising - also for developing countries.

Andrea Boltho[1)]

Pajestka (Ch. 3) has provided a stimulating paper which analyses trends in the world economy over the last 10 to 15 years from a standpoint that goes beyond that of orthodox economics as traditionally viewed in the West. His main thesis is that there is a "logic of change" behind some of the trends we have witnessed and that, in particular, a "partisan global policy", basically influenced by the US, has tended to dominate the world economy. This is not necessarily new. Political scientists have long argued that power politics and economics interact and have often underlined the hegemonic role of the US in the post-war system. But *Pajestka* goes beyond such broad generalisations and puts forward specific instances of "global" policies. The most striking one is his analysis of the West's reaction to the two oil shocks. He sees a "strategic counteraction" at work here, centered, uncontroversially, on greater oil conservation and the development of alternative energy sources, but also, and more controversially, on stagflation. The latter is interpreted as at least a half-conscious attempt to weaken OPEC by reducing oil demand (*via* stagnation) and by eroding the terms of trade deterioration (*via* inflation).

There is a Machiavellian element in such a thesis and there may well be a sense in which Kissinger's actions in the mid-1970s may have at least partly fitted such an interpretation. But from there to argue that one of the main aims of the economic policies of a score of Western countries over the last decade was consciously, or unconsciously, to try to weaken OPEC, even at the cost of stagflation, is a step that, to me at least, seems far-fetched. It is very doubtful that inflation was a positive *objective* of any of the major economies, even though some (e.g. Italy or the UK) accommodated themselves to it in the later 1970s. Elsewhere, and in particular in West Germany and in Japan, inflation was seen very much as a major *obstacle* to renewed growth and this view became generalised after the second oil shock. It is true that stagnation, or at least a period of recession, was seen by many as indispensable; and the 1980-82 slowdown, in particular, was clearly engineered by economic policies. Yet it would seem too simple to interpret the austerity policies of this period as a (successful) attempt to curb OPEC's power. To most observers they would appear to have been dictated much more by internal rather than external considerations. First and foremost among them was precisely the control of inflation.

---

1) Magdalen College, University of Oxford

Going beyond this and trying to look at what *Pajestka* calls the "logic of change", it could be argued that the ultimate aim of these deflationary policies, particularly in Western Europe, was to curb trade union power, to diminish labour market rigidities, and to restore some of the old "rules of the game" of a market economy. The danger to the smooth functioning of the economic system was seen to come much more from longer-run and deeply entrenched trends in the welfare state, in falling profitability and in inflationary expectations that went back to the full employment days of the late 1960s, than from the sudden emergence of OPEC as a new force in the international arena.

Klein and *Bond* (Ch. 2) present a more orthodox view of the world economy up to the end of the decade. This view is strongly coloured by three major events that took place in the course of 1986 - falling oil prices, falling interest rates and falling values of the US dollar. Though two of these trends may have negative consequences for some countries, on balance their combination should be favourable for the world economy at large. As a result, and despite lingering uncertainties on external imbalances and LDC debt, the authors expect world trade to grow at 3.3 per cent per annum between 1986 and 1990 (as against only 2.2 per cent per annum between 1979 and 1986), and OECD output to expand at an average annual rate of some 2.4 percent (as against the previous cycle's 2.1 percent). Such developments, in turn, would have favourable consequences for the Third World and also for the prospects for East-West trade.

The evidence available (in autumn 1986) does not fully support the relative optimism of the paper. The growth of world output remains sluggish and many fear a continuation of the subdued economic conditions of 1985. To some extent this may be due to the long lags with which the trends isolated in the paper affect activity. In the short-run the fall in oil prices may actually have been deflationary (as, paradoxically, were the two earlier shocks), since it shifted income from a high absorbing area (OPEC) to a low absorbing area (the OECD countries). And the distribution of this income gain in the OECD area is heavily skewed towards corporations whose investment plans are depressed by generalised uncertainty on demand prospects. Similarly, the benefits to the US of dollar depreciation may take a long time to come through, the more so if the protracted period of overvaluation has actually destroyed manufacturing capacity or, at least, severely impaired the ability of the tradeable sector of the economy to respond to changes in demand. This, in turn, keeps alive American protectionist pressures. Finally, the fall in interest rates has gone *pari passu* with a declining rate of inflation so that (roughly calculated) real interest rates, in the autumn of 1986, are no lower, and in some cases may actually be higher, than 12 months earlier.

It can be hoped, however, that these various lags will eventually unwind and allow some improvement in the output and employment situation. But a more worrying aspect of the world economy at present, on which the authors are silent, is the prospect for the US budget deficit, now that the Gramm-Rudman legislation has been found to be unconstitutional. There is a clear danger that future Federal deficits will continue to be very large, thus raising expectations of impending recession and/or inflation and possibly frightening foreign investors away from the US capital market. This, in turn, could lead to a crash landing for the dollar. More broadly, the prospect of continuing dissaving by the US government suggests that the country as a whole may continue to dissave as well, i.e. run a current balance deficit for a prolonged period. While such action in the mid-1980s may have contributed to world economic stabilisation by providing a rapidly growing market for Third World exports, it would seem profoundly wrong that the richest economy of the world should continue, over the longer term, to crowd out poorer countries from international capital markets rather than transfer resources to them as it had done in the period after 1945.

Peter Beck[1)]

I wish to make two comments about oil-related matters. First, *Pajestka* (Ch. 3) implies that in the 1970s two major forces opposed each other - OPEC and the major industrialised powers, each taking concerted action against the other. In his view OPEC won a signal victory in 1973, the industrial powers counterattacked, but OPEC went into the attack again in 1979 and won a further price hike.

The reality was surely quite different. From its inception in 1960 until early 1983, OPEC never acted as a real cartel: it did not set or control the level of oil production of its members. It attempted to influence prices, but was able to do so only when market forces - international supply and demand - would allow. Thus 1973 saw a tightening supply situation and therefore ripe conditions for price increases. Between 1973 and 1979, one country - Saudi Arabia - was able to keep the supply/demand balance sufficiently tight to hold prices relatively stable in money terms, though not in real terms, but at the time Saudi Arabia did not seem to want that. In 1979 everyone lost control. The consumer countries panicked, prices rocketed upwards and all OPEC could do was to 'legitimise' one price hike after the other; it was certainly not in control. To stop the market-led fall in oil prices which began in 1981/82, OPEC finally established itself as a production-limiting carel, but this lasted only from 1983 until 1985 and did not stop the price slide. Thus international market forces - not OPEC, nor the industrial countries, nor, indeed, the major oil companies - have so far controlled the international price of oil.

This leads to a second comment. *Klein* and *Bond* (Ch. 2) mention a Wharton model's forecast of a steady rise of 12 percent a year in oil prices from 1987 to 1991, impyling a 1991 price of some $ 25 a barrel. Well, such a price could be possible, but not a steady increase to that level. There is at present no control mechanism which could deliver steady prices, never mind steady increases. Wild fluctuations are far more plausible. Even if $ 25 is right for 1991, the price could be nearer $ 10 in 1990 and nearer $ 40 in 1992 (or *vice versa*).

---

1) Chairman, Strategic Planning Society, London

PART II - TWO NATIONAL EXAMPLES

Chapter 4

RECENT EXPERIENCE WITH MACROECONOMIC POLICY IN THE FEDERAL REPUBLIC OF GERMANY

Norbert Kloten[1)]

Macroeconomic policy in the Federal Republic of Germany over the last few years cannot be explained without referring back to experience with the "Act to Promote Economic Stability and Growth" (1967) and all the other events forming the essence of the 1970s. To a large extent, today's actions not merely reflect the experiences of that time, but are also the result, as it were, of burdens imposed directly by decisions taken then. In the course of the past decade and a half there has been a major change of opinion as to what role an active macroeconomic policy should and can play. Instead of a far-reaching social consensus there are now fundamental differences between the views of the political parties and, to some extent, of those of social groupings. The common position in favour of a "social market economy" (*soziale Marktwirtschaft*) - CDU/CSU and, to a large extent, also FDP - or a "free economic order" - SPD - has changed to include a range of standpoints which suggests that the future will witness highly divergent developments depending on the composition of the political power structure. Yet when the Act first became law, everything seemed to be straightforward and - apparently - in accordance with well-established scientific views on macroeconomic processes.

4.1 New structures for policy-making in the "social market economy"

In the 1950s, and until the mid-1960s, there were no rules for coordination among the institutions setting the general conditions for overall economic development. There was no need and no intention to coordinate process-steering decisions; nor did such coordination appear in line with neo-liberal concepts, for on the one hand priority was given to regulatory policy (*Ordnungspolitik*) for reasons of principle and on the other hand it seemed sufficient that all official institutions should act in accordance with their specific tasks. However, theoretical reasoning and empirical observations paved the way for the idea of a target-oriented business

---

1) Board member of the Bundesbank, Stuttgart

cycle policy. The issue became more and more pressing; monetary policy was increasingly undermined by inflows of currencies from other countries; the influx of labour from East Germany ceased during the third post-war cycle as a result of the Berlin Wall; and the problem of safeguarding economic growth became an increasing focus of attention. The discussion surrounding the benefits of global process-steering was given impetus by the dispute between Erhard and Hallstein, the President of the EC Commission in Brussels, in the European Parliament in Strasbourg (November 1962) concerning medium-term forecasts and programmes which the Commission was promoting on the model of the French "planification" system.

These suggestions were not well received in the FRG and - as, so to speak, a moderate prophylactic alternative - on 14 August 1963 the German legislators set up the Council of Economic Experts (*Sachverständigenrat zur Begutachtung der gesamtwirtschaftlichen Entwicklung*) to facilitate opinion-forming on the part of all agents responsible for economic policy, as well as on the part of the public. The intention was that the Council should draw attention to undesirable trends and possible ways of avoiding them. The formation of such a council is without parallel: it is independent of the executive and has the right to hear the views of the responsible Federal Ministers and the President of the Bundesbank; its annual report, which has to be submitted to the Bundestag and Bundesrat on 15 November each year, and published simultaneously, must be commented upon by the Federal Government in its subsequent Annual Economic Report. The new advisory body quickly gained an excellent reputation.

The same basic considerations finally led to the "Act to Promote Economic Stability and Growth" *(Gesetz zur Förderung der Stabilität und des Wachstums der Wirtschaft)* of 8 June 1967. This Act, which at first did not include the term "growth" and which went through a number of drafts, was ultimately hailed by all parties represented in parliament, as well as by the social groups, as a milestone on the way to a rational economic policy. It was called "the basic law of process steering" in a market economy (Schlecht), a "Magna Charta" of modern business cycle policy (Neumark) and a "synthesis of the Keynesian message and the Freiburg imperative" (Schiller). The intention of the Act was indeed geared totally to the model of a market economy. This manifested itself in the absence of quantitative planning and any form of official process-direction, in the renunciation of any kind of intervention-oriented income policy, in the clear separation between business cycle policy and structural policy and in adherence to the role of competition. The Act immediately attracted worldwide attention as the most modern response of lawmakers to recent scientific findings. By means of prognostic guideline data, as well as partly compulsory and partly indicative and optional rules of conduct, it was intended to ensure that the actions of all governmental decision-makers and all social groups were appropriate to the given situation and directed towards the right targets. Changes in the Basic Law (*Grundgesetz*) and amendments to relevant Federal laws were intended to enable the State in particular to fulfil these requirements - not least by creating appropriate institutions such as the public authorities' Economic Policy Council *(Konjunkturrat der öffentlichen Hand)* and the public sector's Fiscal Planning Council *(Finanzplanungsrat)*, as well as by means of medium-term fiscal planning and by defining a range of public interests as "joint tasks" *(Gemeinschaftsaufgaben)* which are the joint responsibility of the Federal Government *(Bund)* and the States *(Länder)*. The "concerted action" (Article 3 (1) of the Stability and Growth Act) was designed to be the level of coordination for income policy decisions.

The underlying idea of the Act was that, in principle, general economic equilibrium, characterised by price level stability, a high level of employment, external balance and a continuous and appropriate rate of real growth (the set of targets laid down in Article 1 of the Stability and Growth Act), was "feasible". These targets are to some extent open to interpretation. Furthermore, they are in a specific relationship to one another, commonly called the "magic square". The assumption that appropriate macroeconomic policy can lead to the simultaneous achievement of all four targets means that the economy is considered capable of moving along a balanced path of growth, in both nominal and real terms, and at the same time achieving the stabilisation of overall economic development accompanied by stable prices. The rationale of this concept means that there do not have to be, at least in the medium-term, any "trade-offs" between the targets which could hinder the simultaneous achievement of certain goals - especially a relationship of the "Phillips-curve" type, which embodies the idea of a close connection between the level of employment and the inflation rate. The German point of view suggested the following conclusion: in the event of disequilibrium, the target that is violated the most, or seems to be in greatest danger of violation, always has priority, even if the then necessary use of appropriate macroeconomic policy instruments works against the other targets in the short term. In the meantime, however, the interrelationship between the targets has come to be seen in quite a different perspective. Price stability is considered as necessary for the realisation of optimal rates of growth and employment and of an income distribution which is based on individual productivity. In other words, inflation is regarded as one of the reasons for failure to reach the other global economic targets. Price stability is thus more than just a policy target; it is a fundamental prerequisite for stabilising economic development at a high level. It therefore does not make sense to tolerate inflation for the sake of possible expected gains in employment and growth. On the contrary, a consistent stabilisation policy seems to be a necessary (albeit not sufficient) condition for the success of macroeconomic policy. Seen in these terms, the target of price stability must in the long run be allocated a privileged position in the set of global economic targets.

The widespread reservations with regard to the inclusion of "growth" as one of the targets laid down in the Act were taken into account by introducing the formula "within the framework of a market economy" as a limiting system of reference for growth-oriented action. However, the reluctance to subsume "growth" in the list of global economic targets, and the resultant orientation of macroeconomic policy towards this goal, are understandable. From a market-oriented point of view, growth is the result of individual decisions of all the private and public-sector economic entities involved at the micro-level. Thus growth becomes an *ex-post* aggregate which is determined statistically. This position sees the economy as a process of trial and error and ascribes an extremely high risk to growth rate forecasts. What is even more important, however, it does not make any sense for economic policy to determine *ex-ante* rates of growth, as this might result in building-up a fixation on a particular policy. This could also divert attention from creating, at the micro-level, the conditions necessary for a maximum of economic dynamics in a environment of price stability. From an orthodox point of view, it is thus advisable to forego growth rate forecasts of any type, even in a conditional form, and even more in the sense of a clearly defined target rate which the public would interpret as binding. There was no lack of awareness of the problems involved. However, no real problems were foreseen at that time, since most politicians and economists believed that the targets of growth and employment could be realised if only overall economic development could be stabilised by limiting the upswings and downswings of the business cycle. Business-cycle oriented policies thus became the focal point of all stabilisation-policy tasks or, to put it another way: in the longer term, employment and growth were seen merely as reflecting the respective sizes of the real capital stock and the potential labour force. At the time, long-term forcecasts thus took into account only the expected factor supplies.

According to the intentions of the Stability and Growth Act, the task of stabilisation was to be fulfilled by means of anticyclical actions. This rule was especially binding for the public sector; the Act, in the form it took, was thus primarily a law regulating fiscal policy and was quite obviously based on the ideas of "Keynesian policy". All central, regional and local authorities, especially the Federal Government and the Länder, were given specific rules of action for the individual phases of the business cycle. In the field of monetary policy, the law-makers limited themselves to a few "complementary regulations"; monetary-policy actions otherwise seemed to be defined clearly enough in the Bundesbank Act *(Bundesbankgesetz)*.

In the field of income policy, reliance was essentially placed on reasonable behaviour on the part of both employers and employees. Hardly anything else would have been possible, because the Basic Law of the Federal Republic had granted freedom of association to the participants in the labour market, while the Collective Agreements Act *(Tarifvertragsgesetz)* of 9 April 1949 had given the trade unions and employers' associations autonomy in wage negotiations. The scope for State income policy had thus been very limited from the outset. In other words, the state had given the employers and employees, represented by their organisations, the major part of the responsibility for an important overall economic cost factor - the level of nominal (and - to some extent - real) wage costs - and, as a result, to a certain degree the responsibility for the level of profits (entrepreneurial income). However, this trust seemed well-founded, because the Act was specifically designed to limit, to put into perspective or even to eliminate those potential conflicts which may emanate from market processes. Global economic data for orientation purposes, supplied by the state, were intended not least to ensure that the choice and application of the economic-policy instruments used were appropriate to the given situation and targets in question and also to induce "reasonable" behaviour, compatible with the overall economic situation, on the part of all those involved. The mildest form of state income policy seemed sufficient for achieving these goals - the "concerted action" as a forum for discussion by all parties concerned.

Within the context of the tasks assigned by the Stability and Growth Act to the policy sectors involved, a policy for foreign trade and payments was required to ensure that the economy was "safeguarded against external influences" (although this is specified in only a somewhat vague form in Article 4 of the Act), in other words, to prevent stabilisation policy in the form of macroeconomic demand management from being undermined by influences originating abroad. Because of the extensive liberalisation of the movement of goods and capital, concern was focussed on inflows and outflows of international liquidity caused by the system itself (reflecting the international exchange rate system prevailing at that time, based on the Bretton Woods agreements) and representing a considerable threat to the stability-oriented monetary policy. The contribution of foreign trade and payments policy was thus essentially reduced to monetary-policy action, more specifically to exchange-rate measures directed towards external balance in the sense of a balance of payments equilibrium brought about by market forces. Such a balance can certainly be compatible with even sustained surpluses, and even with temporary deficits, in the current account.

4.2 The failings of economic management after the 1960s

In retrospect, it becomes obvious that the aim of stabilising overall economic development at a high level, in a stable monetary environment, was not reached. The predetermined targets were not hit, and intensification of the distributive struggle was not avoided. Furthermore, there was a major expansion of the public sector. This can easily be demonstrated. There is no need for direct comparisons between the target projections published in the annual reports (under Article 2 (1) of the Stability and Growth Act) and the actual values realised in those years; *Tables 4.1-4.3* of the Statistical Annex show the actual development clearly enough.

All in all, it is evident that deviations caused by business cycles have been increasingly replaced by undesired developments which persisted beyond the cycles. This is especially true of employment and growth. Unemployment became a permanent feature, while at the same time the rate of growth of the economy's production potential fell by half. In the field of monetary stabilisation, and with regard to safeguarding the economy against external influences, there were ups and downs. In the public sector, state activities in a broad range of fields expanded in the years through 1982. The ratio of public expenditure to the GNP rose from 39.1 per cent in 1970 to 49.8 per cent in 1982. Roughly half of this increase is due to the state's activities in the narrow sense and the other half to the social insurance sector. The burden imposed on the population by taxes and other charges, above all social security contributions, increased accordingly. However, this was by no means sufficient to finance public expenditure. The financial gap was closed by new state borrowing, which meant that the total outstanding public debt increased from DM 123.2 billion in 1970 to DM 606.0 billion in 1982 (Annex *Table 4.3*).

It is not easy to describe the reasons for these undesirable developments. The analysis has to take account of complex historical processes. Many factors, including exogenous influences such as the two oil price shocks, had an effect. In a somewhat simplified frame of reference, the main reasons can be listed:

(a) As a result of being oriented towards the different phases of a business cycle, any form of anticyclical policy crucially depends on "forecasts". Its success depends on early diagnosis of the need for action (it is sufficient for just one of the overall economic targets to be in jeopardy) and on immediate measures being applied to the extent required by the situation. A key role is thus played by the global economic guideline data obtained on the basis of overall economic forecasts and target projections. If these fail, any new set of global economic guideline data will soon be the subject of dispute. This is indeed what happened. From 1967 onwards the state's guideline data failed to fulfil the expectations placed upon them; the same holds true for the forecasts and target projections, even though the Federal Government, the Bundesbank and the Council of Economic Experts took great pains in this respect and their diagnoses and forecasts were of remarkable quality. However, they repeatedly ran against the limits imposed on any situation analysis by the very nature of the facts prevailing at the given time. This was soon bound to bring the policy of macroeconomic demand management into discredit. Especially after the events of 1969, the year of the booming economy, growing doubts were expressed about the official announcements; this led to interpretations of business-cycle data and proposals for alternative economic policies which were oriented towards specific interests and designed to further them. There was a growing reluctance to comply with the requirements of stabilisation policy and at the same time various groups set up their own departments staffed with forecasting specialists. In the late 1960s and early 1970s, the trade unions and industrial organisations were already trying to "appropriate" the state's instruments for their own purposes.

(b) The Stability and Growth Act was intended in particular to realise the advantages of an anticyclical fiscal policy without allowing possible disadvantages to emerge. This required above all that the Federal, Land and local authorities should be willing and able to act in a anticyclical manner. The Federal Government and the Länder were required in particular "to consider the needs of overall economic equilibrium in their economic and fiscal-policy measures" (Article 1 of the Stability and Growth Act). However, even the first stabilisation programmes already had considerable procyclical effects. This is the way things continued. The Federal government was, probably, the most willing to pursue anticyclical policies; the Länder were far less prepared to do so. The local authorities, which are likewise required to act in accordance with the targets set out in the Stability and Growth Act have in reality always acted differently ("free-rider" behaviour). The expected contribution of fiscal policy towards ironing out cyclical fluctuations and thus towards stabilisation of economic growth was already a subject of dispute when it proved impossible to cushion the "superboom" in 1969. This would have been the right time to use the taxation-policy instruments provided for in Articles 26/27 of the Act, but "the forces of society failed each other"

(Schiller). It was not until July 1970 that a tailor-made measure was introduced in the form of the "repayable anticyclical surtax" which in retrospect proved to have been inappropriate to the situation. Side-by-side with Federal government actions motivated by business-cycle considerations, the conflicts which the demand for anticyclical action created for other public authorities, with their traditional functions and special decision-making processes, led to many inconsistencies. In 1973, for example, a "stability loan" was issued in order to curb the excessive upswing of the economy, but at the same time all budget planning was directed towards expansion- and, what was even more important, allocative and redistributive goals were increasingly superimposed on the target of economic stability.

(c) The ten stabilisation programmes enacted between autumn 1974 and autumn 1978 were intended to boost business activity by providing demand stimuli, but also increasingly to strengthen the economy's growth potential and in addition to fulfil the demand for "social symmetry". Their main effects, however, were an increase in public service employment as well as heavy subsequent burdens on the budgets of the central, Länder and local authorities and on the social insurance institutions. The public sector was increasingly required to compensate for the lack of private demand by additional demand on the part of the State - although, as became obvious, it cannot do so. This fostered expansion of the state machinery and of the public debt, promoting the development of "structural" budget deficits. In the years that followed, medium-term fiscal planning became mere camouflage. At the same time there were growing collisions of interests between the various authorities, particularly between the interests of the Federal Government and the Länder. The "joint tasks" (*Gemeinschaftsaufgaben*), which were in reality intended to see them peacefully united in the realisation of joint projects, became a source of dispute, particularly where financing was concerned. The opposition parties used the Federal Council (*Bundesrat*) as a means of fighting the Federal Government and thus made this institution subject to the influence of political parties - which had not been the intention of the authors of the Basis Law.

(d) The scope for undesirable developments would have been far smaller if the legislature and executive had shown greater respect for the Act. However, there was a preference for tailor-made solutions. This was the case in July 1970 with the repayable anticyclical surtax, and also in May 1973 when, instead of applying Articles 26/27 of the Stability and Growth Act, a highly problematic investment tax was introduced. When the economic support programmes were activated from the autumn of 1974 onwards, it was no longer even asked what the Act prescribed for such a situation. Such actions impaired the Act's credibility; this tendency is reinforced by the fact that even today there is no implementing law as called for in Article 115 of the Basic Law or any connection between Article 115 and Article 109 (2) of the Basic Law.

(e) The expansion of the public sector partly originated from the idea, prevalent in the early 1970s, that the State had remained poor in an environment of wealth and had neglected its essential task of "providing the means to meet the basic needs of society", that social concerns had not been given sufficient attention and that many reforms were therefore long overdue. Together with demands for the correction of income distribution, this was the main reason for both a fiscal policy and an income policy designed "to test the economy to see what it could bear". Although this is not the fault of the Stability and Growth Act, the Act could not be used to check this trend. On the contrary, a succession of new stabilisation-policy programmes resulted in numerous forms of undesirable proliferation in the public sector itself. In this environment, the bureaucracy made use of its opportunities and expanded in an inflationary manner. This was fostered by the fact that politicians used the increased tax revenue during business cycle upswings (the built-in flexibility of income tax), especially before elections, for opportune increases in expenditure. In other words, fiscal policy was used more and more to attract votes - a development also supported by the opposition parties in parliament.

(f) The trade unions, which at the beginning (albeit reluctantly) had submitted to the overall economic necessities indicated by the guideline data, felt as early as 1969 that they had been cheated. Even in the face of a "profit explosion", the employers were not willing to grant additional productivity-oriented wage increases. The result was wildcat strikes (Hoesch steelworks in the autumn of 1969). The shock was a severe one; the initial willingness to adapt gave way to deep scepticism, especially because the industrial trade unions, as members of the German Trade Union Federation (DGB), were not prepared to accept any of the limitations required by the "concerted action". The distributive struggle became more intense, reaching its peak in 1974 when the trade unions tried to push through prophylactic wage increases to compensate for suspected losses in real income caused by the first oil price shock. In its role as employer in the public sector, the State itself fostered this development by submitting almost without resistance to trade union demands. The wage costs per unit of output rose rapidly and inflation increased. Confrontation with the limits set by monetary policy was unavoidable, with depressing effects on growth and employment. The tension between the parties on the labour market hardened. From 1978 onwards, the machinery of "concerted action", which had provided (albeit increasingly rarely) a useful forum for discussion - even though wages themselves were not debated - was in effect dead.

(g) The aim of safeguarding the economy against external influences was characterised from the outset by the fundamental disagreement between DM revaluations on the one hand and alternative actions on the other. With the Bretton Woods exchange rate system increasingly disintegrating, imbalances continued to exist well into the spring of 1973, which meant that one of the decisive conditions for the functioning of policy remained unfulfilled. Excessive inflows of foreign currency and the resultant immense increase in the banking sector's liquidity, as well as changes in the behaviour of credit institutions (in the form of more and more generally accepted recourse to loans on securities, a measure which is supposed to be reserved for exceptional situations), increasingly jeopardised control of events in the monetary field. In 1971 and 1972, for example, the volume of central bank money expanded by 12 and 13 per cent respectively, although between May and December 1971 it was possible to counteract the dangerous undermining of monetary policy by the courageous floating of the DM. At the beginning of 1972 the only remedy which could help was an emergency measure in the form of the "Cash Deposit Act" (*Bardepotgesetz*) - a form of foreign exchange control. However, this return to official monetary controls did not prove successful. It was only after the final collapse of the Bretton Woods system and the change to floating exchange rates - in Europe in the form of the "Snake" - that the central bank managed to regain control over the expansion in the monetary sector. The Bundesbank made use of its opportunities; however, it is still a matter of dispute whether the monetary-policy course adopted at that time was too severe and - since it continued well into 1974 - was maintained for too long. The restrictive monetary policy was not least a result of the increase in wages and prices caused by the second oil price shock of 1979. The trade unions, as well as employers and even the government itself, had obviously assumed that monetary policy would have no choice other than to follow a permissive course.

There was much debate as to whether "rational expectations" could perhaps have protected the economy against the harm which resulted. The answer was to set monetary targets.

4.3 The shift to monetary management and budgetary consolidation

Although the 1970s in particular witnessed numerous - often bold- attempts to bring about a change for the better, the Stability and Growth Act degenerated more and more into an empty shell. It was above all the institutional elements that survived, such as the public sector's Fiscal Planning Council (*Finanzplanungsrat*) and the public authorities' Economic Policy Council *(Konjunkturrat der öffentlichen Hand)* together with the instrument of medium-term fiscal planning which, however, consisted for many years more in wishful thinking than in serious budgetary estimates. Two conclusions emerge: even the best law cannot fulfil the expectations placed on it if the social forces fail each other, and in particular if political opportunism prevents compliance with the law. However, a law will also fail to produce the expected results if it reflects a global concept which involves over-ambitious conditions for success. Undesirable developments are unavoidable in both cases, and particularly if both apply at the same time. If such developments are dominant over a lengthy period, the result will be structural distortions in the economy which can be corrected only by many years of consistent political action.

By comparison, it is relatively easy for monetary policy to correct even high rates of inflation, provided that appropriate monetary measures are taken. More serious problems arise, however, from the direct consequences - the effects on growth and employment. This is especially true if, over a long period, entrepreneurial income - commonly called "profit" - comes off worst in the distributive struggle. Once optimism about expected rates of growth gives way to a basically pessimistic view (as happenned in the mid-1970s), and once equity ratios start to decline and at the same time the risks of creating new jobs and thus of boosting overall employment increase, there will inevitably be adverse effects on investment behaviour, on the labour market and, in the long run, on the rate of growth of the production potential; although this rate is in general a relatively stable macroeconomic variable, it nevertheless fell from an average of around 4.5 per cent a year in the 1960s (and early 1970s) to less than 1.5 per cent in the early 1980s. If there is investment at all in such circumstances, it is mostly directed towards rationalisation and thus increases unemployment, particularly if there is a growing demand for jobs at the same time. Such developments are reinforced if the public sector expands rapidly and the tax burden and social security costs increase excessively as well. Any attempt to reverse the trend in such conditions involves an immense task for stabilisation-policy; it also means that growing importance must be attached to supply-oriented measures, although this does not imply that the steering of global demand becomes unimportant. On the contrary, the two measures must be carefully coordinated. All in all, what is required in such circumstances is a strategy of "economic recovery" and "normalisation".

During the 1970s, many discerning observers, and to a growing extent also the Council of Economic Experts, were already arguing that the public sector and in particular the local authorities - but not only the local authorities - should be relieved as far as was warrantable of the obligation to operate on an anticyclical basis. A fiscal policy which essentially confines itself to fulfilling its task of "providing the means for meeting the basic needs of society" in the true sense of the term, but which does this in a consistent manner, is - it was maintained - at least better than measures which are intended to be anticyclical but which in the end have procyclical effects. There would then no longer be room for the "asymmetrical" action on the part of the public sector (credit-financed additional expenditure during a recession and full use of higher tax revenue during an upswing) which had been repeatedly observed in the past. The government could nevertheless still make its contribution to creating favourable conditions for growth, and to solving the problems of structural adjustment, provided that it designed the public expenditure structure accordingly.

This means, among other things, refraining from a mechanistic view of the economy, which interprets it as a system of interrelated aggregates capable of being regulated as desired by increasing or decreasing nominal demand, above all by government actions. Such a philosophy underestimates all the forces which operate at the micro-level of the markets and which in the long run determine the size of the macroeconomic aggregates in a free market economy. A lack of dynamic vigour in the private sector - whatever the reasons for it - cannot simply be offset by increased State spending, especially as the structure of State spending is, after all, "State-specific". Furthermore, the public sector is - as it turned out- embedded in a parallelogram of political forces. It would undoubtedly be asking too much of the "State" as an institution to expect it to be able to take decisions without considering the interests of the parties involved ("in splendid isolation", as Klaus-Dieter Arndt puts it).

There was also considerable disillusionment as regards the opportunities offered by income policy. It had become only too obvious that distribution ideologies, the influence of intra-organisational issues and of the political sphere, the options attached to forthcoming elections and many other factors - including exogenous shocks - carry far more weight than the usual guideline formulas such as "productivity-oriented wage policy", macro-economic guideline data or forums for discussion which, like the "concerted action", were designed to provide coordination. What is more important is a stabilisation policy which limits the scope for income policy in a clear and foreseeable manner.

From 1975 onwards, the Bundesbank - in agreement with the Federal Government - endeavoured to achieve this in its own way. In December 1974 it decided, on the basis of experience during the first half of the year, that in future neither the political decision-makers nor the social groups should have any doubts regarding the direction of monetary policy. This was to be achieved by public announcement of a monetary target defining the development of the central bank money stock (currency held by non-banks plus required minimum reserves on banks' domestic liabilities calculated at constant reserve ratios, based on January 1974) over the following calendar year. There were a number of changes in the technique used: first a current rate from December to December, then a year-on-year rate of change (from 1976 onwards) and finally a current rate yet again (from 1979 onwards) but now between fourth quarter and fourth quarter (from 1980 onwards), combined with a target zone or range (used for the first time in 1979).

The monetary targets, which are adopted and published in December of each year for the following year (*Diagrams 4.1 (a)* and *(b)* in the Annex), are essentially geared to the medium-term (Annex *Table 4.4*). Despite criticism on particular points, the concept as such is today no longer a subject of debate (moreover, the system was soon also adopted abroad). It is unanimously agreed that the Bundesbank's new monetary strategy was on the whole successful. There has not yet been a single year in which it was necessary to revise the target, even though things did not always develop as desired. The greatest deviations occurred in the years 1978 and 1986, periods which witnessed strong revaluations of the DM with respect to the dollar and fairly intense international pressure on the Federal Republic to assume the role of "locomotive". In all other years, monetary measures were mainly directed towards the domestic economy, even though - as in February 1981 when a "special 12 per cent Lombard advance" was introduced - account was still taken of external economic influences.

Fiscal policy-makers also had to draw conclusions from experience. The Federal Government, Länder and local authorities are now following a course which in the FRG is termed a "policy of consolidation". There was no alternative to this policy at the beginning of the 1980s and there is still none today. The reason is simple. The expansion of the budgets of all levels of government and of the quasi-governmental institutions (especially the social insurance institutions), together with the resultant increased burden of taxes and social security contributions and - probably even more important - the financial deficits of the public authorities (from 1979 far in excess of the budgetary estimates), gave people the feeling that fiscal policy was getting out of control. Confidence in the soundness of public finances was fading. Each time additional funds were granted for economic support programmes, this gave rise to the fear that in the end the only consequence would be a further increase in the burden of taxes and contributions. By claiming an enormous share of the real GNP, resulting in heavy tax and contribution burdens, the public sector was also increasingly paralysing economic forces. The system was hindering efficiency and the social security network had long since grown out of proportion. In 1982 even the SPD/FDP government could no longer escape the need to consolidate finances and thus reduce the increased "structural" deficit, despite the fact that such a policy was in no way in line with its philosophy of fiscal policy. Consolidation started at a bad time in the business cycle, coinciding with a period of recession when the public sector should really have provided an expansionary stimulus. However, all enthusiasm for new economic support programmes was obviously gone.

The new coalition, formed by the Christian Democrats and the Free Democrats, identified itself with the task of consolidation as soon as it took office in the autumn of 1982. "Consolidation" has thus become the principal characteristic of fiscal policy in the Federal Republic over the past few years. This was without a doubt the right principle to adopt. In the given circumstances, additional public expenditure to support economic activity - although repeatedly demanded - would have increased neither private households' propensity to consume nor entrepreneurs' propensity to invest. However, there was good reason to believe that a consistent policy of consolidation would build up confidence. This turned out to be true, even though the measure of success achieved did not come up to expectations. In particular, it has not proved possible to cut back on subsidies, which had grown wildly in every sector - indeed, new ones were granted instead. It was nevertheless possible - which is in itself quite remarkable - to limit increases in public authority expenditure to around 3 per cent a year for several years. As the nominal GNP grew more rapidly at the same time, and was bound to be reflected in tax revenues, it proved possible to reduce the very excessive financial deficits relatively quickly (Annex *Table 4.5*). This, however, was aided by the transfer of very high Bundesbank profits to the Federal Government.

From the very beginning, the Federal Minister of Finance had linked the reduction of the "structural" deficit with the intention of thereby creating scope for tax cuts, even though the aim was initially to compensate only for the additional burdens resulting from hidden tax increases caused by progressive rates of direct tax. Two stages were planned. The first step, which has already been realised (1986), mainly served social policy goals (child allowance and basic allowance), while the second step in 1988 will substantially lower marginal tax rates. All this is intended to pave the way for a major tax reform in 1989. Only when all this has been accomplished can the consolidation policy be called successful in the sense of reducing the ratio of public expenditure to GNP and - to a small extent - the taxation ratio. Success can be achieved only if "quantitative" consolidation is accompanied by "qualitative" consolidation - that is, by reforming the revenue and expenditure structures.

4.4 Lessons from experience

In the light of all these experiences of macroeconomic policy over the past one and a half decades, one central question emerges: what lessons must be drawn for the concept and execution of this policy? On the basis of systematic criteria, the task is to find the stabilisation-policy strategy that will reduce the risks outlined on as broad a scale as possible and which for this very reason has a high likelihood of success. Such a strategy for minimising potential conflicts must fulfil the following conditions in particular:

- It must be characterised by a comparatively limited use of forecasts and thus at the same time offer the best guarantee that the guideline data for economic policy will be correct.
- It must not demand too much of the public sector. This means that it must so far as possible release fiscal policy from its anticyclical task so that it can in principle be neutral with respect to the business cycle. Fiscal policy can thus be oriented towards the medium-term and can be better controlled from the political point of view.
- Monetary policy should be steady and predictable and not subject to harmful political constraints or be used as a substitute for other fields of policy.
- Monetary and fiscal policy should give clear guidelines to the parties on the labour market. In this way the parties cannot escape responsibility for the important macroeconomic aggregate represented by labour costs (or for the pay structure and the contractual organisation of the labour market). At the same time, income policy must work towards appropriate long-term forms of coordination between the interests of the parties on the labour market and ensure that they

are kept in contact with each other at all times.

- It must ensure that the economy is safeguarded against external influences without recourse to official controls.

The stabilisation strategy which is most likely to fulfil all these requirements will be one that is oriented towards the medium-term; as far as possible, therefore, it should forego systematic anticyclical actions. The production potential, embodying the production possibilities in an economy, is particularly suitable for use as a central indicator. The question may remain open whether the forecast (most likely) rate of growth of the production potential for the coming year alone will suffice or whether this rate should itself be seen as a medium-term target; the latter could make sense if there were a sustained slowing-down of economic growth affecting the rate of increase of the production potential. Such a medium-term orientation in itself has a stabilising effect on the economy and in principle implies only a comparatively small need for macroeconomic forecasts and short-term action. This in no way precludes the possibility of a flexible response to unforeseen events such as exogenous shocks.

The medium-term orientation must be viewed as the central element of a comprehensive stabilisation concept which for its part includes both supply and demand components and compatibility between the regulatory and process-steering decisions of economic policy. Such a strategy can be reduced to a relatively small number of basic process-steering rules. This should not be misunderstood as meaning rules in the monetarist sense, which are characterised by monolithic inflexibility. In modern democracies, moreover, the political decision-makers - both parliaments and executive organs - would not and indeed could not accept such rules. Notwithstanding forms of built-in flexibility, macroeconomic decisions are in the end taken on a discretionary basis, even for a medium-term orientation. However, they should not be taken on an *ad hoc* basis - meaning arbitrarily and without guidance - but instead systematically geared to the global concept, irrespective of whether this is codified in legal form (as in the Stability and Growth Act).

In a market economy, however, it is the principal task of the legislature and executive to direct economic activity by providing a clear and consistent framework of basic data. In the Federal Republic, it has also proved effective to respect the rights of the parties on the labour market as laid down in the Basic Law and in the laws regulating the labour market. The same holds true of the special status granted by the legislature to the Bundesbank. It has become apparent, too, that autonomous advisory bodies made up of independent experts (without party affiliations), as well as independent economic research institutes, can help to make the political decision-making process more objective.

It is difficult in a market economy to draw the line between the public (State) sector and the private sector. There is no clear-cut dividing line; in the early 1980s, however, there was general agreement in the Federal Republic that the public sector - the Federal, Land and local authorities and, to an even greater extent, the quasi-governmental institutions - had expanded far beyond any such line. The motto formerly propagated by the Social Democrats and in particular by Karl Schiller - as much of a market economy (private sector) as possible, as much State (public sector) as necessary - basically assigns the burden of proof to the State.

In the Federal Republic, it is probably monetary policy which best fulfils the criteria set out. Fiscal policy still has a very long way to go, with a need for quantitative and qualitative consolidation accompanied by reduction of the ratio of public expenditure to GNP. Although there are unmistakable signs of a recovery in the public sector, there has proved to be a considerable amount of resistance. In income policy, the years of recession have paved the way for "normalising" income distribution. However, the conflicting interests of labour and capital remain a reality, as do the diverging positions within their organisations. These cannot be reconciled by appeals for a social consensus or by forms of "economic democracy", something which is being increasingly propounded again today. The only solution is to give all parties an insight into economic processes and - even more important - to ensure a broad distribution of wealth in the long-term, in particular allowing employees to hold a share of the productive assets. However, there is little to suggest that in the foreseeable future there will be a breakthrough in policy relating to the creation and distribution of wealth or with regard to the key aspects of a basic agreement. Foreign trade and payments policy, as well as the ways of safeguarding the economy against external influences, are increasingly being taken out of the hands of the country itself. Limits are imposed by the ties created by membership of the European Community, the European Monetary System and international institutions such as the International Monetary Fund. Many of the developments now emerging will probably make the task of safeguarding the national economy more difficult. This is true of new moves towards monetary integration in Europe, as well as of the arguments in favour of target zones for exchange rates and the use of "basic indicators" or "concerted actions" at an international level.

The overall success of macroeconomic policy depends on a large number of factors. I have endeavoured to illustrate this with reference to the Federal Republic of Germany. In the final analysis, however, the success of such a policy will be determined by the overall conditions prevailing in a country and above all by the willingness of society as a whole, and of the parties and social groups making up this society, to identify themselves with a free social and economic order and to accept its rules.

Table 4.1

Development of the "magic square" of targeted variables: Federal Republic of Germany, 1967-1986

	Price developments			Economic growth rates			Unemployment	Foreign trade and payments		
	Cost of living index for all households	Index of producer prices of industrial products	GNP deflator	GNP at constant prices	Production potential at constant prices	Utilization of production potential in %	Unemployment rate in %	Balance of foreign trade and services	Balance on current account	Change in the Bundesbank's net external assets
	Changes from previous year in %							billions of DM		
1967	1.6	–0.7	1.4	–0.1	3.3	93.6	2.1	17.3	10.0	–0.1
1968	1.6	–0.7	1.8	5.8	3.1	95.9	1.5	19.8	11.9	7.0
1969	1.9	1.8	3.5	7.5	3.6	99.4	0.8	17.6	7.5	–14.4
1970	3.6	5.0	7.3	5.0	4.6	100.0	0.7	14.1	3.2	22.7
1971	5.1	4.3	7.7	3.0	4.5	98.4	0.8	15.5	2.8	11.0
1972	5.6	2.7	5.6	4.2	4.4	98.3	1.1	18.5	2.7	15.2
1973	6.9	6.6	6.0	4.7	3.9	99.1	1.2	29.1	12.4	16.1
1974	6.9	13.4	6.9	0.2	2.8	96.6	2.5	43.4	26.6	–9.1
1975	5.9	4.6	6.7	–1.4	2.0	93.2	4.7	28.9	10.0	3.3
1976	4.4	3.8	3.3	5.6	2.3	96.0	4.6	29.1	9.9	1.3
1977	3.6	2.7	3.8	2.7	2.3	96.6	4.5	29.5	9.5	2.6
1978	2.7	1.1	3.8	3.3	2.6	96.9	4.3	37.3	18.1	12.2
1979	4.2	4.8	3.7	4.0	2.5	98.5	3.7	11.1	–11.0	–7.3
1980	5.4	7.5	4.8	1.5	2.6	97.3	3.7	–3.0	–28.5	–25.7
1981	6.3	7.8	4.2	0.0	2.1	95.5	5.3	14.7	–11.7	1.3
1982	5.3	5.8	4.7	–1.0	1.8	93.2	7.6	37.5	9.9	2.7
1983	3.3	1.5	3.2	1.5	1.4	93.3	9.3	36.9	10.6	–1.6
1984	2.4	2.9	1.9	3.0	1.7	94.2	9.3	50.3	19.9	–1.0
1985	2.2	2.3	2.1	2.4	1.4	95.4	9.4	72.7	38.9	–1.3
1986[a)]	–0.2	–3.0	3.1	2.5	1.8	96.1	9.0	107.3	77.9	2.8

[a)] provisional

Sources: Federal Statistical Office, Deutsche Bundesbank, Council of Economic Experts

The development of wages and salaries, productivity, labour costs per unit produced and factor income distribution: FRG 1967–1986

Year	Wages and salaries per employee	Labour productivity[a]	Labour costs per unit produced[b]	Real Wages according to Council of Economic experts[c]	Wage ratio adjusted[d] in %
	Changes from previous year in %				
1967	3.4	3.3	0.0	−1.7	62.9
1968	6.1	5.5	1.2	−2.0	61.2
1969	9.2	5.8	3.4	2.6	61.4
1970	15.3	3.8	11.7	3.3	62.9
1971	11.3	2.3	9.3	1.1	63.7
1972	9.2	4.5	5.2	−0.4	63.6
1973	11.2	4.0	7.9	1.1	64.2
1974	10.9	1.6	9.7	1.7	66.0
1975	6.4	1.3	5.9	−1.5	66.1
1976	6.9	6.3	1.4	−1.9	64.4
1977	6.9	3.1	3.4	−0.3	64.5
1978	5.4	2.3	3.3	−0.5	63.6
1979	5.7	2.7	3.1	0.0	63.4
1980	6.7	0.3	10.7	2.4	64.9
1981	4.9	0.9	4.3	0.0	65.6
1982	4.1	1.1	3.1	−1.6	65.2
1983	3.2	3.0	0.7	−2.5	63.5
1984[e]	2.9	2.6	0.7	−1.0	62.5
1985[e]	2.9	1.9	1.2	−1.5	61.6
1986	3.9[e]	1.6[f]	2.5[f]	−0.9[f]	60.4[f]

[a] GDP in 1980 prices per member of the labour force

[b] $\frac{\text{Gross income per employee}}{\text{GDP in 1980 prices per member of the labour force}}$

[c] The Council of Economic Experts estimates the influence of wage development on the sales-costs ratio in industry as a whole according to changes in Real Wages; this does not change if labour costs per unit produced as a proportion of sales prices less other factor costs per unit, stay constant

[d] Adjusted by the share of employees in the labour force, 1960

[e] Provisional

[f] Estimated value

Sources: Deutsche Bundesbank, Council of Economic Experts

Table 4.3

Gross national product and public finance: FRG 1967-1986

	1967-70	1970-80	1981	1982	1983	1984	1985	1986[a]
				Changes in %				
Nominal GNP	+36.9	+119.8	+4.0	+3.4	+5.1	+5.0	+4.8	+5.6
Real GNP (in 1980 prices)	+19.4	+31.0	−0.0	−1.0	+1.8	+3.0	+2.5	+2.5
Expenditure of Federal, Land and local authorities	+37.7	+159.9	+6.4	+3.7	+1.4	+2.5	+3.4	+4.0
Revenue of Federal, Land and local authorities	+39.9	+140.4	+3.1	+5.6	+4.6	+4.5	+4.9	+3.5
Of which, taxes	+37.9	+136.7	+1.5	+2.3	+4.7	+4.6	+5.4	+4.1
Debts of public authorities[b]	+18.0	+274.1	+15.9	+13.5	+9.7	+6.8	+6.3	+5.9
Expenditure by wage and salary earners' pension insurance funds	+34.1	+177.7	+5.2	+6.5	+2.0	+6.1	+2.4	
Expenditure on benefits by statutory health insurance funds	+29.8	+260.4	+7.3	+0.5	+3.5	+7.9	+5.0	+5.4 (Jan.-Sept.)
Expenditure of Bundesanstalt für Arbeit	+23.2	+454.8	+9.9	+18.5	−2.2	−9.2	+0.3	+7.1

(continued)

Table 4.3 (continued)

Figures for individual years	1967	1970	1975	1980	1982	1983	1984	1985	1986
					in billion DM				
Debts of public authorities[b]	104.4	123.2	253.1	460.9	606.0	664.9	710.2	754.7	799.5
Net borrowing by public authorities[b]	13.0	6.5	53.6	53.8	68.6	56.2	49.8	40.5	44.5
					Ratios in %				
Ratio of public expenditure to GNP (wider sense)[c]	39.2	39.1	49.5	48.6	49.8	48.6	48.2	47.4	46.3
Ratio of public expenditure to GNP (narrow sense)[d]	27.7	27.9	33.4	32.8	33.2	32.1	31.6	31.1	30.4
Levies ratio[e]	37.8	39.3	43.8	45.6	46.6	46.1	46.2	46.3	45.6
Taxation ratio[f]	23.8	24.0	24.7	25.7	24.7	24.7	24.9	24.0	24.4
Social security contribution ratio[g]	11.4	12.5	16.2	16.7	17.8	17.3	17.3	17.3	16.9

[a] Provisional

[b] Federal Government, Länder Governments, local authorities, Equalisation of Burdens Fund and ERP Special Fund

[c] Expenditure by the state as % of nominal GNP

[d] Expenditure by the central, Land and local authorities as % of nominal GNP

[e] Taxes, social security contributions, charges and other ordinary state revenue as % of nominal GNP

[f] Taxes as % of nominal GNP

[g] Social security contributions as % of nominal GNP

Sources: Federal Statistical Office, Deutsche Bundesbank, Federal Ministry for Labour and Social Affairs, Federal Ministry of Finance, Council of Economic Experts.

Table 4.4

Monetary Target Calculation at the Deutsche Bundesbank

The monetary target is estimated from each year's targeted economic development, as expected by the Deutsche Bundesbank. Up to 1984 the following variables had been taken into account:

a) The expected growth of the production potential
b) The desired change in the utilisation of the production potential
c) The "unavoidable" rise in prices
d) The expected development of the "velocity of circulation" of money

Since 1984 was a year of practically stable prices the inclusion of an "unavoidable" rise in prices was no longer necessary.

Example: Derivation of the monetary target for 1986[a]

Assumptions:		
– Real rate of growth of the production potential:	+2.5 %	
– Increase in the general price level, measured by the GNP deflator:	+2%	
Nominal rate of growth of the production potential:	+4.5 %	
Monetary targets:		
Yearly average increased in the central bank money stock:	+4.5 %	
Current rate 4th quarter 1985 to 4th quarter 1986:	+4.0	– 4.5 %
"Corridor" (range)	+3.5	– 5.5 %

[a] There have been no adjustments for changes in the utilisation of the production potential and in the "velocity of circulation" as purely business cycle-induced changes in utilisation of production potential correspond with changes in the "velocity of circulation" and no trend in money-holdings is in evidence.

Table 4.5

Financial net position, net borrowing and structural deficits of the Federal, Land and local authorities: FRG: 1974–1986

	1974	1975	1976	1977	1978	1979	1980	1981	1982	1983	1984	1985	1986[a]
Financial net position[b] in billions of DM	−27.26	−63.85	−48.03	−31.18	−39.62	−46.57	−57.07	−75.65	−69.94	−55.29	−46.06	−38.96	−46.0
in % of GNP	−2.8	−6.2	−4.3	−2.6	−3.1	−3.3	−3.8	−4.9	−4.4	−3.3	−2.6	−2.1	−2.4
Net borrowing[b] in billions of DM	22.5	53.6	46.7	31.7	40.6	43.4	53.8	69.6	68.2	56.2	49.8	40.5	44.5
Structural deficit as defined by the Council of Economic Experts	10.2	22.6	14.6	−1.9	11.4	26.6	36.7	38.0	28.0	17.0	4.0	1.5	0

[a] Provisional

[b] The financial net position and the net borrowing usually do not coincide because the financial net position also includes movements of reserves and some budget deficits which will be covered by budgetary expenditures at a later time.

Sources: Council of Economic Experts, Federal Ministry of Finance, Deutsche Bundesbank

Diagram 4.1 (a)

Central Bank money stock[a], growth and targets: Fed. Rep. Germany 1975–1978

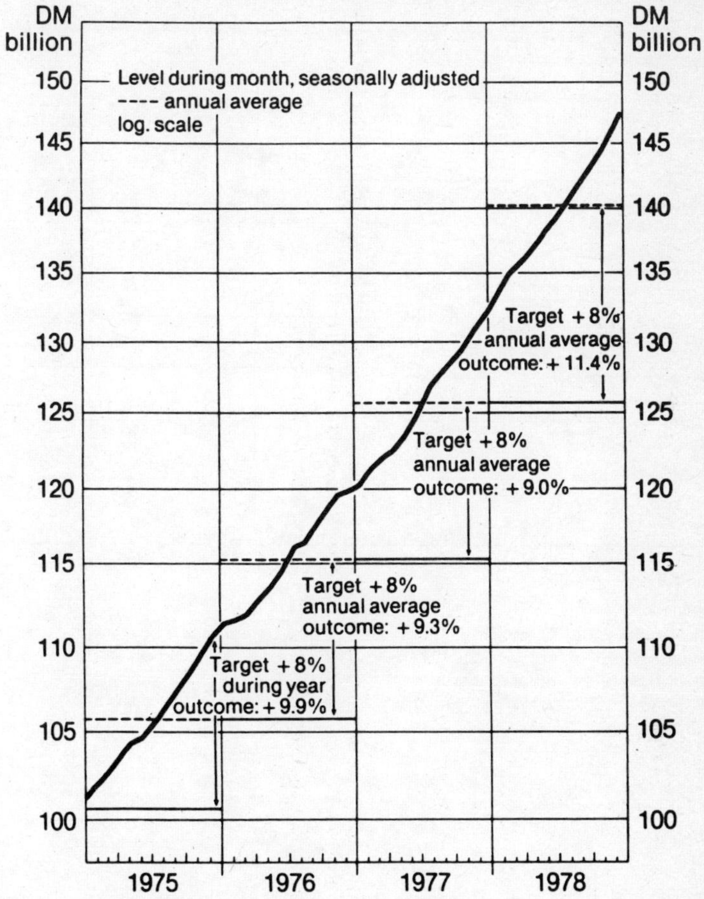

[a]Currency in circulation (including the bank's cash balances of domestic notes and coins) plus required reserves on domestic liabilities (calculated at constant reserve ratios, base: January 1974).

Diagram 4.1 (b)

Central Bank money stock[a], growth and targets : Fed. Rep. Germany 1979–1987

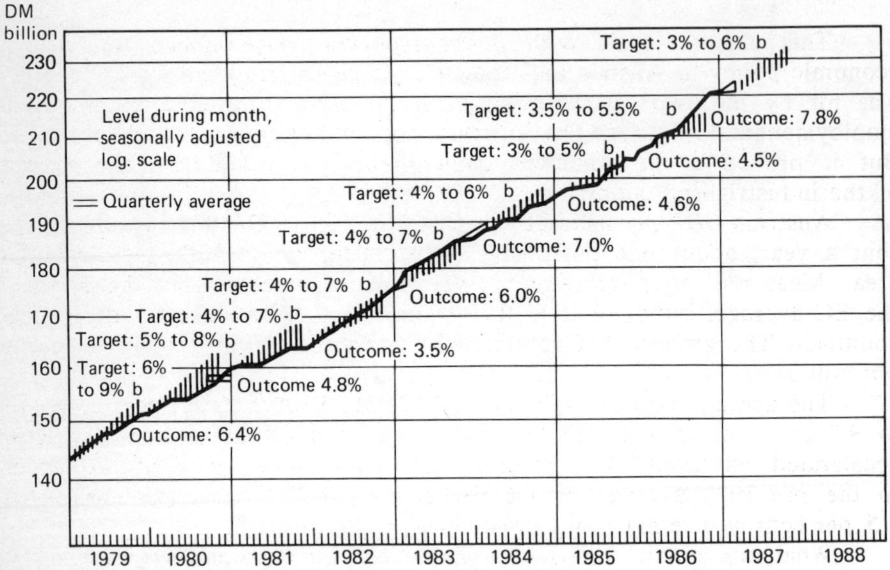

[a]Currency in circulation (excluding the banks' cash balances of domestic notes and coins, which from March 1978 are deductible from the minimum reserves) plus required reserves on domestic liabilities (calculated at constant reserve ratios, base: January 1974). - [b]Between the fourth quarter of the preceding year and the fourth quarter of the current year.

Chapter 5

AUSTRIA'S MACRO-ECONOMIC POLICIES IN THE LAST DECADE

Hans Seidel[1)]

This chapter deals with *macro-economic performance* and macro-economic *policy* in Austria in 1973-1985. In this period the world economy was hit by the two oil price surges with devastating effects on output, employment and inflation. The Austrian economy, of course, was no exception. But it proved to be somewhat more *shock resistant* than the average of the industrialised countries.

Austrian *GDP per head* at constant prices in 1973-1985 rose by 2.5 per cent a year, about one percentage point faster than in the whole OECD area. Measured at purchasing power parities, income per head equals the EC average, although it is still lower than in the richest industrialised countries. The growth differential diminished somewhat during the period but still exists.

The average rate of *inflation* in 1973-1985 was 5.7 per cent compared to 9.8 per cent in the OECD area. After each oil price surge, inflation accelerated but could be brought back after some years of adjustment to the pre-1973 average of 3.5 per cent. (In 1986 inflation declined to 1.5 per cent as a temporary consequence of the oil price fall.)

What for many Austrians seems most important, *unemployment* up to the early 1980s could be kept at 2 per cent of the labour force. It has risen since to 4.8 per cent but is still less than half the Western European average. In *performance indexes* which combine different macro-economic variables, Austria ranks high among the industrialised countries, usually second only to Japan.

5.1 "Austro-Keynesianism"

Some experts claim that the relatively good economic performance, especially up to the end of the 1970s, was at least partly the result of a macro-economic policy labelled *"Austro-Keynesianism"*. There is no generally agreed definition of Austro-Keynesianism. Dr. Kreisky, the former Chancellor of Austria, said Austro-Keynesianism has as much to do with Keynes as Austro-Marxism with Marx, namely nothing. In a narrow sense, Austro-Keynesianism stands for a macro-economic policy mix, with a somewhat unorthodox assignment of policy instruments to economic goals.

---

1) Professor, Institut für Höhere Studien, Vienna

In the whole post-war period, inflation was regarded as mainly a result of cost pressures and of the price-setting behaviour of firms. Therefore a comprehensive and institutionalised *incomes policy* was designed to keep inflation low in conditions of full employment. As early as 1957 a Commission for Prices and Wages was set up by the social partners, controlling price and wages on a voluntary basis. Partly as a result of the price-wage policy adopted, the Austrian economy was characterised by a *"fixed-price* and *quantity-flexible"* regime. The Austrian National Bank was expected to accommodate the level of prices and production determined by market forces and the cooperative actions of the social partners. (This "banking-school" version of the role of the central bank was presented and defended by the President of the National Bank as late as 1981.) Restrictive monetary measures should be limited to situations when the economy was clearly overheated. Even then specific actions in overheated sectors were preferred to non-discriminating actions curbing total demand.

Given this background, it seemed self evident that the first oil price shock should be interpreted both as cost inflation and demand deflation. To tackle both problems two different instruments were needed. The Austrian policy makers used incomes policy and exchange rate policy (the so-called hard-currency-option) to contain inflation. And they applied an expansionary fiscal and monetary policy to fight the deep recession in the mid-1970s and to keep unemployment low. This *double-track* strategy seemed a better way to absorb the supply shocks from the oil price surges than fighting inflation by a non-accommodating monetary policy and shifting the responsibility for the resulting unemployment to (nominal or real) wage rigidity.

Against the Austrian policy-mix three objections might be raised and indeed have been raised:

a) Incomes policy does not work
b) an expansionary monetary and fiscal policy worsens the balance of payments
c) demand management, even if successful in the short run, impairs economic growth in the medium term because it conceals structural defects and delays adjustments.

The failures and achievements of Austria's economic policy can conveniently be discussed under these three heads.

5.2 Incomes policy

In Austria, by contrast with most other industrialised countries, an institutionalised incomes policy has been operated for three decades.

This incomes policy is based on an *neo-corporatist socio-economic structure.* In all studies of "neo-corporatism" Austria ranks high, usually first among the industrialised nations. The institutions of the Austrian socio-economic system cannot be described adequately here. But a few remarks seem appropriate to indicate the interrelationship between the institutional set-up and the choice of macro-economic strategies.

Austria has developed an unusually extensive and highly centralised system for the representation of economic interests, both on a compulsory and on a voluntary basis. The large organisations representing business, agriculture and labour, have been working together and with the government since World War II in many fields of common interest. In some periods the *social partners* practically determined the economic policy of the government. One of the main subjects of cooperation was, and is, price and wage policy. This cooperation is based on what might be called a basic consensus among the social partners about the social and economic order, the main economic goals and the distribution of incomes.

To implement the *price and wage policy* of the social partners the Commission for Prices and Wages was set up in 1957, mainly on a voluntary basis. The Commission has three subcommittees, one for wages, one for prices and a Council for socio-economic affairs. Claims for higher wages and prices have to be brought to the respective subcommittees. They decide whether an intended price increase is justified or if it is the proper time to start wage negotiations.

More important than the institutional set-up are the practical results. The social partners in Austria are so convinced of the advantages of their cooperation that they did not give much attention to formulating and testing hypotheses about actual price-wage behaviour. After all, the mere fact that in Austria there are practically no strikes, seems to justify the existing corporate system. The main criticisms came from foreign experts. Branson suspected that incomes policy will work only so long as absorption is higher than domestic output.[2] Flanagan diagnoses a breakdown of the traditional wage equations.[3] But actually the Austrian system of incomes policy functioned surprisingly well in the stormy years under consideration.

The main requirement for wage policy in the last 15 years has been *wage flexibility* in both real and nominal terms. Real wages had to adjust

---

2) William H. Branson, "Commentary" in Sven Arndt (ed.), The Political Economy of Austria, Washington DC and London, American Enterprise Institute, 1982

3) R.J. Flanagan, D.W. Soskice and L. Ulman, Unionism, Economic Stabilization and Incomes Policies, Washington DC, The Brookings Institution, 1983

to deterioration in the terms of trade and to the decline of productivity growth. And the required real wage moderation had to be brought about by nominal wage moderation rather than by inflation in order to keep the Austrian economy competitive at the chosen exchange rate.

By and large these two requirements were met. The annual rate of increase of nominal wages declined in one decade from 11 to 5 per cent. Real wages were stagnant at the beginning of the 1980s as against an annual increase of more than 4 per cent ten years before. And what seems most important: wage moderation would be achieved with a relatively low rate of unemployment. In estimates of the traditional Phillips curves, unemployment has a relatively high negative coefficient and wages adjust rapidly enough to changes in productivity trends.

As regards *international competitiveness:* after the first oil price shock, the increase in labour costs could not be reduced as fast as the nominal exchange rate rose. The real appreciation of the Schilling helped to absorb the nominal and real shock caused by the first oil price surge. After 1978, however, international cost competitiveness improved more or less steadily up to 1985. (Some deterioration probably occurred in 1986 because of the sharp decline of the US dollar.)

5.3 Balance of payments constraints

It is well known that a small country launching expansionary policies is liable to run into *balance of payments difficulties.* In the last decade much larger countries, such as West Germany, France and to a certain degree even the United States, experienced external constraints when they allowed or induced domestic demand to expand faster than it was expanding abroad. Therefore it was no surprise that after OPEC I the Austrian foreign balance on current account should have deteriorated rapidly. This just indicated that the anticyclical policy in Austria was more effective than similar efforts abroad. (In fact, after the short recession of 1975, domestic demand rose at the same rate as before OPEC I).

The vulnerability of the balance of payments was enhanced by the *hard currency policy.* From the early 1970s the Austrian authorities have tied the external value of the Austrian Schilling to the Deutschemark. The exchange rate was used primarily (and in my view correctly) as an instrument to curb inflation and not as an instrument to balance the foreign account at a given level of capacity utilisation.

Austria could, for a time, afford external deficits because its net *foreign debt* was insignificant and the recycling of the petro-dollars facilitated debt-financing.

Moreover the above-average growth rate, and the relatively high rate of investment, seemed to guarantee a smooth debt service and gave

Austria access to the international capital markets at relatively low costs. (In fact, Austria's foreign debt is almost exclusively denominated in Swiss francs and DM).

Nevertheless, the speed with which the balance of payments deteriorated in the mid-1970s gave rise to some concern and created doubts whether the hard currency option could be maintained. Some shift towards a balance of payments-oriented policy was thus called for. In the course of 1977, domestic demand was restricted somewhat and by 1978 higher rates of value added tax for luxury goods (especially for cars) reduced its import content. This was not regarded as a fundamental change in policy, but rather as a question of timing and magnitudes. The measures taken prevented a further deterioration of the trade deficit. The remaining deficit was called "structural". To attain equilibrium, the structure of production and demand had to be adjusted to the higher energy prices.

Two years later, in 1979, balance of payments pressures again emerged; this time the *capital balance* was the troublemaker. Austria's monetary authorities were accustomed to keep nominal interest rates, both short and long term, relatively stable. This was possible because the financial markets were regulated and only loosely connected with international markets. When oil prices started climbing again in 1979, and interest rates rose worldwide, the Austrian policy-makers, in accordance with their intention to stabilise costs (and interest rates were regarded mainly as a cost), tried to keep interest rates low. But this time they failed because the growing internationalisation of the banking system allowed interest rate arbitrage on a substantial scale. Heavy losses of exchange reserves forced the monetary authorities to give up their cheap money policy within a few months.

Goods and financial markets by the end of the 1970s became internationally integrated to an extent that left little scope for manoeuvre: that was the lesson the Austrian policy makers had to learn. This does not mean that the volume of money, the level of prices and interest rates became literally exogenous at the given exchange rate, as economic theory assumes for small open economies. Prices in Austria are still stickier than abroad. For example, petrol prices since the beginning of 1986 have receded in Austria much more slowly than in Germany or Switzerland. And money market rates for some months in 1985 had to be 2 points higher than in Germany in order to induce a substantial import of short-term capital. (The high correlation between changes in money market rates in the two countries since 1979 seems to be more a result of monetary policies than of market forces.) But market imperfections are not a very reliable basis for a consistent macro-economic strategy.

5.4 The fading out of Austro-Keynesianism

By and large, Austria's economic policy-makers have learned their lesson. When after OPEC II the world economy tumbled into a prolonged recession the Austrian authorities again tried to "lean against the wind". The budget deficit was allowed to increase to an unprecedented level, and monetary policy was eased. But the anticyclical policy operated on a much more moderate scale than after OPEC I. This can easily be demonstrated by comparing the 3 year periods 1974-1977 and 1980-1983. The structural deficit of general government, as a percentage of GDP, rose in the first period by 3.5 points and in the second period only by 0.6 points. The supply of money after OPEC I accommodated the high rate of inflation, while after OPEC II the monetary authorities allowed only a declining rate of inflation. In real terms, M1 rose in the first 3 year period by 9 per cent, but in the second period only by 2 per cent. (*Table 5.1*).

Table 5.1

Demand management and macro-economic performance after OPEC I and OPEC II

	1974-1977	1980-1983
	% increase over 3 years	
Structural government budget deficit (% of GDP)[a]	+3.5	+0.6
M1 in real terms	+9.2	+1.9
Real domestic demand	+11.2	+0.2
Foreign balance on current account (% of GDP)[a]	-2.4	+2.3
GDP	+8.7	+3.0
Employment	+0.6	-2.5
Rate of unemployment %[a]	+0.5	+2.6

[a] Change in % points

At least partly as a result of the differing strength and determination of the anticyclical policies, domestic demand in the first period grew by only 11 per cent and stagnated in the second period. In the recession after OPEC I the foreign balance on current account turned into a considerable deficit; in the recession after OPEC II the current balance was brought into equilibrium: output grew faster than domestic demand.

Since the beginning of the worldwide recovery in 1983, demand management has lost its previous dominating role. Monetary policy is designed to keep the Sch.-DM relationship constant. Fiscal policy is to a certain extent immobilised by heavy interest payments on the growing public debt. After some consolidation in 1984, the deficit of the Federal Government has tended to increase again. In these circumstances, "fine tuning" of economic policy with respect to given socio-economic goals seems to be out of the question. The traditional and highly institutionalised process of fine-tuning (forecasting, evaluation of forecasts, designing measures to improve the expected economic performance) has degenerated.

Austro-Keynesianism, in the narrow sense in which the term was used here, has faded out. This was acknowledged by the Austrian government. In the *Economic Report 1985*, Chancellor Sinowatz stated[4] "The former design of Austro-Keynesianism was the remedy of the 1970s. The success of that 'deficit spending' was based on the precondition that only short-term economic fluctuations had to be smoothed out. The phrase "diving through the crisis" symbolised this objective pretty well. For a long-lasting stagnation, however, such as that at the beginning of the 1980s, this system was not designed" (Author's translation). That does not necessarily mean that the basic Keynesian ideas about macro-economic policy were abandoned. But Austria is too small, and too much integrated into the world economy, to carry through expansionary strategies by itself. The Austrian government supported various attempts on the part of the OECD secretariat, in the first half of the 1980s, to induce leading industrial countries to follow a less restrictive policy stance. And I am sure that the government looks sympathetically to the recent US proposals for a coordinated international policy for economic growth.

Given the limited scope for demand management, how could *unemployment* be kept at a relatively low level? The answer is: employment strategies were shifted from demand management in the goods markets to supply-side measures in the labour market. A *shortening of the working week* appears to have narrowed somewhat the gap between productivity growth (measured as output per person employed) and output growth. The last step towards a 40-hour workweek happened to fall in the depression

4) **Wirtschaftsbericht 1985 (Bericht der Bundesregierung zur Lage der Österreichischen Wirtschaft)**

year 1975. A further reduction of hours is under way now. But, of course, spreading out the volume of working hours to a larger number of workers is not a panacea, especially if employees want higher real wages rather than a shorter working week.

Furthermore, open unemployment was reduced by *adjusting the labour supply* to the actual demand for labour. The Austrian authorities, since OPEC I, have considerably reduced the admission of foreign workers. In addition, various measures (e.g. early retirement schemes) kept the supply of domestic labour constant during the long recession in the early 1980s, although the population of working age increased considerably. One might object that the Austrian policy-makers just converted open unemployment into hidden unemployment. But this is only partly true, because early retirement was quite attractive for many elderly workers.

5.5 Structural adjustment

Austria's above-average economic performance in the early 1980s, and the somewhat unusual macro-economic policy-mix, attracted international attention. The London *Economist* wrote an article about Austria under the headline "A Small House in Order".[5] I had the opportunity to explain Austria's incomes policy to the Joint Economic Committee of the US Congress. The American Enterprise Institute held a symposium about the Austrian economy. In the OECD country reports, Austria's performance met with approval. Criticisms emerging in the US, when the high exposure of Austria to Eastern European countries became public, receded into the background as soon as the Latin American debt crisis unfolded.

More recently, however, international praise of the Austrian economy has become less frequent. The last OECD *Economic Survey of Austria* (July 1986) still acknowledges the above-average economic performance but points to structural weaknesses and criticises the excessive budget deficit of the Federal Government. Only for political scientists interested in "neo-corporatism" is Austria still a favourite model.

The gradual change of opinion has both ideological and practical reasons. The ideological reasons can easily be identified. The prevailing neo-classical view of how the economy works, and of what economic policy can achieve, makes it difficult to understand and evaluate objectively the Austrian system: a mixed economy with nationalised industries, numerous subsidies called investment promotion, and an incomes policy under which entrepreneurs in oligopolistic markets are asked to submit their intended price increases to a commission of the social partners for approval.

---

5) Sarah Hogg, "A small house in order", (survey of Austria), London, The Economist, 1980

But there are also, of course, practical reasons for concern. Economic policy in Austria, after the fading of Austro-Keynesianism in the narrow sense, failed to develop a consistent programme of *structural change* based on the virtues of the Austrian system of consensus strategies. Public opinion and policy in the last few years have been preoccupied with environmental issues assuming that the economic problems of the country were either solved or could be left to routine decisions. It is true that the product and industry structure of Austria's manufacturing industry has changed very little in the past. Iron and steel, and other basic products, still hold a large share. Many firms operate in markets where producers of less developed countries compete or are about to compete. The concentration on basic products, and the obvious failure to take up profitable lines of high quality finished products, together with the reluctance to dismiss workers and close plants with chronic losses, explain the crisis of the nationalised industries which rely heavily on government subsidies.

On the other hand, *productivity* in Austrian manufacturing industry is still growing faster than in the OECD area as a whole (or than in Western Europe). Both facts - the slow change of the production pattern and the above-average productivity increase - may reflect characteristic properties of the Austrian socio-economic system which cannot be changed rapidly and at low cost. The consensus climate at the enterprise and plant level, as well as the skill of the employees, facilitate productivity gains within the given spectrum of products. But it impedes a radical change in the production pattern which might be more easily achieved in a system in which hire-and-fire is socially accepted and which facilitates the decline of old firms and the growth of new ones.

The discussion of whether and where the Austrian economy needs a more dynamic impetus, and of how this can be achieved without giving up the virtues of the Austrian system, continues. One might argue that to exploit the productivity gains of an existing structure is an acceptable strategy so long as the terms of trade losses resulting from an sub-optimal structure are small when compared with the productivity gains. But whatever the nature and dimensions of the structural problems may be, it is difficult to believe that the Austrian economy would now be in a better shape if more unemployment had been accepted at an earlier date.

PART III - POLICIES FOR INTERNATIONAL ECONOMIC RELATIONS

Chapter 6

DECISION-MAKING AND INSTRUMENTS FOR SOCIALIST FOREIGN TRADE

József Bognár[1]

The structure of decisions on questions of external economy derives from numerous factors in the socialist economic system.

6.1 Evolution of socialist foreign trade policies

The first period of social-economic evolution in the socialist countries was dominated by the *transformation and import-saving* model, which was accompanied by an "inclination to turn inwards". We speak of a "transformation model", because the consolidation of the new social-economic system had priority, while the postulates of economic rationality were secondary. We speak of an "import-saving model", because at that time the socialist system gained power in economically less developed countries - countries which aimed at catching up the economically most developed countries within a historically short period. In that period, the mutual uncertainty caused by differences of system, and the atmosphere of political suspicion and hostility - which also found expression in blockades, embargoes and discrimination - restricted trade to acts involving a *simple exchange of goods.*

In this model the decisions

a) were made by governments,

b) involved only exchanges of goods, and

c) aimed at a balanced exchange.

Once the system had been consolidated, the weaknesses of the transformation/import-saving/centralised model became very obvious; a shortage economy resulted, technical progress and restructuring proved slow by international standards, economic activity did not produce sufficient income, and central control was unable to select between good and bad enterprises.

---

1) Director, Hungarian Scientific Council for World Economy, Hungarian Academy of Sciences, Budapest

Gradually the governments recognised that they had to build economic development on new foundations: since the previous model was reproducing the shortages, difficulties and lags, not as coincidences but as consequences of the nature of the model.

The change-over of economic development on to new foundations assumes a *reform*, of which reappraisal of the role of the external economy forms an organic part leading to recognition that external economic activity is a factor in growth and development. From another approach, the progress and success of the reforms largely depends on changes in the external economic factor. Favourable changes in the external economic factor demand not only an internal reform but also a system of regular and mutually recognised international economic relations. Consequently, in the socialist economies the "opening up", like the economic reform, is not a coincidence or an initiative of some individuals or trends that "can be retracted tomorrow", but a new stage in the history and evolution of the socialist economic system.

In the 1980s economic reforms have been introduced in every European socialist country and also in China, although these reforms exhibit not only similarities but also numerous different features and approaches. In some economies (Hungary, China, and earlier in Yugoslavia), as a result of the reform processes, the amount of change reached the critical border beyond which we can speak of a new model replacing the old one.

In other East European economies, the change began, for the time being, with rationalisation of the old model (fewer plan indices, enhancement of the role of profit, improvement of financial responsibility and of incentives, better adjustment to the different character of the various economic sectors, emphasis on the role of prices, greater sectoral flexibility in the satisfaction of demand, permission to establish joint ventures, etc.). But progress evolves, with some cyclical fluctuations, towards more up-to-date solutions.

We do not want to discuss here the historic, social, political and economic reasons for these differences. That would demand a separate study.

The external economic opening plays a very important role in both models; but it emerges in peculiar circumstances, since in the period of barter trade no export sector or genuine export orientation had been developed. Consequently, the economies introducing reforms, and opening up their external economic relations, usually amass debts, and can achieve a lasting external economic equilibrium only by building up a new export structure. This circumstance, of course, endangers the reform, since the conservatives often argue that before the transformation from the import-saving/centralised model the external equilibrium of the economy had been relatively stable.

6.2 Reconciling interests in the new model

We now examine the interconnections and problems of external economic decisions in the light of the new model.

In substance, the external economic decision is extremely complex from the aspect of interconnections, timing (export-led investments) and their consequences, since many differing interests and institutional attitudes must be reconciled and translated into action - especially where the state and cooperative ownership are preponderant.

The system and mechanisms for the reconciliation of interests played a vigorous part in the new model. It is beyond doubt that even in export- or trade-oriented endeavours the various interests can be clearly distinguished. It is obviously useful to pay attention to these, since their influence on the different attitudes and actions is all the more forceful the less the attention given to them.

In setting export goals or promoting development for export purposes, sectoral and branch interests clearly surface, aiming at the improvement of the operational conditions of the sector or industrial branch in question. Exports are an instrument rather than a goal of this improvement, since an autonomous organism is involved. This appears not only in questions such as incentives, premiums, preferential wages, retention of foreign exchange, etc. but also in problems such as technical alternatives, credits, interest rates and rates of return, as well as in the economic processes embraced by the investment.

The interests of the exporter or potential exporter companies appear even more definite and characteristic. Technically, the biggest exporter companies are assembly plants, since foreign or domestic suppliers often provide 60-70 per cent of the selling price of the end-product. The companies developing high technology are linked to external markets in all their essential activities, of which imports and exports make up a large proportion; and both also involve software. The cycle of products developed and manufactured by them differs completely from the cycle which characterised the technology of the past; i.e. their financing, research and production systems differ from those to which they had been accustomed.

In general, the demand for high quality and high use-value products surpasses the supply. This circumstance offers a favourable position to the producers, and it often even leads to the avoidance of risks. In the European socialist countries, the companies produce for three markets: the domestic, the socialist, and the convertible currency market. They aim at dividing their products among the three markets by confronting the *achievable benefits* (not only profit, but also foreign trade authorisation, better material supply, foreign exchange retention, import connections, etc.) with the requirements of quality, technology and marketing. Of course, these requirements cannot be isolated from the innovative and technological abilities and discipline of the manufacturers concerned.

The arguments and differences between the manufacturing companies producing for export and the conventional foreign trade companies have recently become very active, culminating especially in the determination of export prices. The differences cannot always be smoothed out through the mechanisms of interest reconciliation, but independent export authorisations are increasingly demanded by producers and are increasingly accorded. New organisational forms are also developed, such as "trading houses", and sometimes the conventional foreign trade companies also establish institutions which correspond to the new requirements.

The foreign partners of the Hungarian companies are also the focus for arguments and changes in the system of marketing and distribution. In general, the earlier methods are not considered satisfactory; consequently joint companies are established in many countries for the distribution of Hungarian goods; and there are also endeavours to establish firm ties with large foreign companies, and at joint distribution in third markets, linked with industrial cooperation.

Of course, the large foreign companies have their own interests and organisation (independent of the Hungarian connection), which must also be taken into consideration in the course of reconciling interests.

It is obvious from what has been said that company interests have become much stronger in recent years; this enables the companies, on the one hand, to engage in autonomous activity in a broad area, and on the other, compels the government (in its macro-economic policy) to give maximum attention to company interests in elaborating economic conditions, and to establish - in the course of reconciling conflicting interests - a positive link between company interests and other concerns of economic policy.

To avoid any misunderstanding, we should stress that some kind of company interests - even if truncated and distorted - also exerted an influence in the economic system of the early period; but in formulating macro-level economic decisions the makers of economic policy tried to subordinate company interests to the macro-economic aims. This endeavour was unsuccessful, since in the socialist economy too the weight of differing economic interests continued to play a role in determing economic actions.

The interest systems which dispose of relative autonomy or special features include the operational machinery responsible for the *balance of payments and foreign exchange equilibrium* and for the maintenance and development of international monetary relations - embodied in the *bank of issue* and the *domestic banking system.* The different interests provide new opportunities and also make new forms of initiative possible. So care must always be taken, in the process of reconciling interests and moderating conflicts, that the new opportunities and initiatives should be expanded rather than restricted. Experience has shown, also, that new opportunities always arise in the course of a well-arranged reconciliation of interests. Of course, new opportunities may also lead to new conflicts of interests.

6.3 Tasks for the financial system

Among the interests represented by the banking system - especially the bank of issue (in Hungary the National Bank of Hungary) - I should like to stress a number of points.

a) The dollar-rouble problem (which has already been touched upon in the description of company interests) is one. Trade among the socialist countries is transacted in roubles, which are non-convertible; i.e. situations may arise when we have a surplus of roubles but a shortage of dollars. In such a situation, obviously, attention must also be paid to the question of how many dollars we use for our rouble exports, since the problem of the balance of payments in convertible currencies is complicated and difficult in all circumstances. In such cases company interests and "banking interests" clash vigorously. (We hope for the establishment of an international monetary system which creates at least a link between the two monetary systems, but that is a different matter.)

b) Clashes about desirable export markets are also possible, since companies wish to sell according to the market situation, while the bank must consider the ability to pay of the different potential customers. I believe it is superfluous to emphasise the magnitude of the problem and how much ground it creates for clashes at a time when the number of heavily indebted national economies is over one hundred. (It is another point that in such cases various kinds of barter agreements are possible, or may even be indispensable.)

c) It is the task of the bank of issue to construct the system of operations connected with the international credit policy of the economy, the repayment of credits and the servicing of debts. The credits raised are usually linked to the development of export capacities, which creates a strong connection, of action and reaction, between the policy of the bank and that of the companies. On the other hand, the companies, too, raise suppliers' credits in establishing cooperation arrangements and other links involving production. Such credits are "self-extinguishing", but their terms cannot be independent of conditions in the international monetary and credit markets. It is also the task of the bank of issue to maintain the country's credit standing, which is inseparable from the economy's exporting ability - of which the development is consequently decisive.

d) Business relations between banks may, of course, also promote cooperation in production and marketing, and may even facilitate the establishment of *joint ventures*.

e) Finally, through the contacts of the bank of issue with the IMF and the World Bank, domestic producers and exporters obtain numerous new opportunities extending from restructuring loans to participation in World Bank tenders. I believe it is superfluous to point out that clashes of interests and opinions occur in this sphere too; these are finally settled either in mutual negotiations or, in more difficult cases, by government decisions.

6.4 Domestic and external objectives are interlinked

Among the interest systems influencing the external economic processes and decisions, domestic consumption must be mentioned, including the imports which cover it in part or, for some goods, totally. Imports must also be interpreted as an internal economic process, though stemming from the outside world; when imported raw materials are processed, domestic technology is developed by imported capital goods; consumer goods are used up. Some of the imported products could also be produced by the domestic economy, if with lower profitability or, indirectly, at the expense of potential exports. On the other hand, imports may assist in promoting the qualitative improvement of export products, may save on investments, and may relieve manpower shortages.

The most important energy and raw material imports establish a permanent community of interests and a stable relationship with the economy of the exporting country. However, there is another side to this relationship: continuously growing exports are necessary to pay for the imports concerned, which can still further strengthen and stabilise the relations between the two economies.

It is well-known that vigorous arguments are usual among technical experts about large-scale technical imports, since such an import is not likely to be a once-for-all transaction but will, rather, stimulate relations between the interested parties. A relevant example is the supply of cars in countries with no automobile industry of their own. Today, the tendency in a small market with an adequate industrial background is gradually to establish assembly plants in which 50 to 60 per cent of components and sub-assemblies are supplied by domestic industries. It is obvious that production for export also benefits these producers of components and sub-assemblies. In this way, imports for the satisfaction of domestic demand become the focus of economic activity and exports.

The mechanism for reconciling interests involved in "import-led" economic development and exports is especially complicated; it has many facets, since it affects supply, industrial development, investment, economic efficiency and foreign marketing problems. This is true even if a single company "transfers" part of its products and creates out of the additional resources thus released profitable exports to other countries. This is, however, the simplest case, since alternatives are also possible when the counter-payment production has still to be developed and made suitable for exports. In such cases the decision made, after the reconciliation of interests, affects industrial policy (what should be developed in order to update technology), the distribution of investments and credits, contributing to the international transfer of technologies and the profitability, structure and country breakdown of exports. This also determines the methods, opportunities and constraints connected with supplies to consumers and industry.

The agreements and decisions made in the course of reconciling interests are obviously implemented by *economic instruments* - either built into the five-year plan, or applied continuously. Actions linked to international economic decisions clearly cannot be kept in abeyance until the next plan cycle. This statement is especially important at present: on the one hand, the life cycle of products has become shorter; on the other, interdependence between the national economies has grown, and consequently an increasing proportion of decisions linked to external economic questions are "responsive actions".

On governmental activity in decision-making on external economic questions, I wish to make two preliminary observations.

The first point to note is that the external economy covers substantially more than foreign trade, since it includes all problems of production, development and selection which are interconnected in the "domestic economy" with exports, imports and international economic cooperation. In the contemporary situation, at a time of economic interdependence, when we see the beginning of a universal economic boom, the possible responses and endeavours of the national economies take a new form connected with the discipline of the world economy. It is obvious that it is not possible, and indeed would not serve any useful purpose, to separate rigidly the domestic from the international issues, since the "responsive actions" of the national economies exert a decisive influence on the future evolution of world economic processes.

The second point to be made is that every national government has maintained, in essence, its traditional structural form of sectoral and branch ministries, although the problems which governments have to tackle - the economic and social processes - have become more complex and can no longer always be approached through the conventional structure. Of course, individuals working in an old structure can also make decisions with a new substance; but there are experiments afoot in many countries to bring about new forms and methods within the governmental system. It should, however, be pointed out that these experiments are conducted along *professional* rather than *political* lines, but a change in this respect is primarily a question of political power.

6.5 The tasks for government policy

What then are the questions about which the governmental organs must make decisions in the socialist economy, in the circumstances of the new mechanism?

We clearly cannot strive for a complete answer to this question, but would like to stress - in a sketchy way - some decisive interconnections.

In the first place, the task of the government is to elaborate the external economic concept and to create a projection of economic policy and of the plan. External economic policy is part of economic policy as a whole, but a component which substantially influences all important interconnections. In this context, we consider as components of external economic policy the monetary and international financial policy, as well as all elements of national economic activity connected with the external economy, such as production for export, imports, factors stimulating exports, technical progress, prices, etc. All these factors must find expression in the concept of external economic policy.

In every economic policy there are objectives derived from scientific analysis of different situations, and determinations which arise from the policy instruments, the functioning of the organisational systems - and human nature. The system of interest reconciliation - if efficiently used - is very suitable for establishing harmony between the abstract objectives and the realistic conditions and possibilities.

In more detail, the governments' task therefore involves:

a) formulation of an "instrumentarium" for furthering the external economic policy to be developed and promoting its acceptance within the framework of general economic policy;

b) management of export development credits and other financial means in concert with the bank of issue;

c) commissioning, analysis and utilisation of world economic forecasts for forward-looking economic, social and scientific planning;

d) building up an information system for use by the governmental organs engaged in the external economy, through which they can learn in good time of every international economic event, phenomenon and trend;

e) international initiatives to broaden the world economic potential of the Hungarian economy, including negotiations with the Common Market, bilateral agreements, etc.;

f) initiatives and decisions about cooperation with foreign equity capital, the establishment of joint companies, and the settlement of questions concerning the activity of joint companies;

g) development of a *continuous* system of external economic decision-making, and also fixing its relationship to the original plans.

As is obvious from this enumeration, the decisions made, and actions undertaken, by the governmental organs engaged in the external economy take into account the interests and ambitions of the different actors. They are partly of a "coordinating-reconciling" nature, and are partly connected with the internal and external operational conditions of the micro-sphere. It is obvious that in both respects the decisions are made not on a hierarchic-administrative basis, but have in mind and support the interests of the companies. The aim of the government is not the restriction and cutting back of the micro-sphere, but creation of a dynamic balance between micro- and macro-actions. This attitude is also in harmony with the requirements of economic rationality, since the real economic results are produced by the micro-sphere; the task of the macro-sphere is rather to create the economic conditions promoting success.

In a difficult situation, of course, restrictions may also be needed, or companies may have to be liquidated. But in the course of economic evolution there have always been, and always will be, difficulties; and new activities have always been developed making some earlier activities unreasonable or irrational.

Incidentally, this economic policy and system of decision-making *automatically* also promote international economic relations, which represent an indispensable driving force for the progress of the national economies.

Chapter 7

GROWTH AND THE FOREIGN BALANCE: EXPERIENCE AND PROBLEMS OF THE GERMAN DEMOCRATIC REPUBLIC

Wolfgang Heinrichs[1)]

In the past decade the national economy of the GDR, like other socialist economies, was faced with the challenge to convert the primarily extensive economic growth onto an intensive path. The aim was that this conversion should involve no losses in growth. The GDR economy - an open system and also a net importer of energy and of major mineral materials while a net exporter of machinery and equipment - had considerable difficulties in maintaining and restoring the conditions of balanced foreign trade. Moreover, political pressures were exerted and former embargo practices, reminiscent of cold war times, were revived. New restrictions on the transfer of technology, on the import of grains, and on credits were imposed by those circles uninterested, or no longer interested, in mutually advantageous East-West trade relations. As a result, the economic and trade relations of the GDR with the non-socialist economic region were considerably strained and, more seriously, the foundations of confidence, laboriously created in the process of détente, were severely shaken. Notwithstanding this general trend, the relations between the GDR and several western industrial countries continued to develope over this period.[2)] This move was politically and economically motivated and originated in reasonable and realistic efforts made by groups intent on restoring momentum to détente and thus taking advantage also of the economic relations between East and West.

Certainly, the economic strategy adopted at the XIth Party Conference of the SED (1986) is chiefly prompted by domestic requirements for accelerated scientific, technical, economic and social development. This is also a basic interest common to the CMEA national economies, i.e. to elevate the socialist international division of labour to a qualitatively new level. However, the lessons of the 1970s and 1980s concerning the possible repercussions of relations with the non-socialist countries on the internal development of socialist economies should not be forgotten. The lessons to be learnt should be worth remembering by all socialist countries embarking

---

1) Director, Zentralinstitut für Wirtschaftswissenschaften, Akademie der Wissenschaften der DDR, Berlin, GDR

2) Including Belgium, FRG, France, UK, Japan, Canada, Austria, Sweden

upon mapping their economic strategies for the long-term development of foreign trade.

Ultimately, a realistic rather than a petty distrustful approach to the period ahead must take as the point of departure for economic relations between the national economies, or between economic groupings of different social systems, the close interdependence between the political and economic goals and interests. It is also to be expected that East-West economic relations will react sensitively to whether détente or confrontation dominates in relations between the two social systems.

7.1 A new phase of intensive growth

Economic calculations[3] have shown that the optimal growth rate for a structured economy, such as that of the GDR, given the material and cultural living standards reached so far, lies around 4.5 to 5 per cent annual growth of national income produced. In such conditions of growth, increasing investments (through increasing amortisation and net investments) in the manufacturing and non-manufacturing branches are possible simultaneously with a stepwise rise in the living standards of the people. The directive on the development of the GDR national economy covering the period 1986 to 1990[4] provides, among other things, that from year to year a growing share of the national income produced is to be used domestically as an increment to accumulation and consumption. And it is intended to reduced progressively that part of the national income which at present has to be spent on interest and credit repayments, and on the adjustment of those foreign-trade transactions where domestic expenditures exceed considerably the proceeds obtained in foreign currency.

The major road to carry out these ambitious tasks is to secure a stable growth in productivity and efficiency which is irreversible, repeatable over the long-term, and increasingly carried by the economic utilisation of high technologies. This makes inevitable an accelerated renewal of the production base. The proportion of renewed industrial production in the GDR in 1980 amounted to about 20 per cent; it rose to 27.5 per cent already in 1985. By 1990 the aim will be 30 per cent, an average which will be open to deviations upward or downward according to industry

3) Such research is carried out at the Central Institute of Economic Sciences of the Academy of Sciences of the GDR, using different model calculations.

4) See the Directive of the XIth Party Congress of the SED (Socialist Unity Party) on the 5-Year Plan on the Development of the National Economy of the GDR in the years 1986-1990, Berlin 1986, p. 15 ff.

and group of products. It is crucial that the rate of renewal of goods and technologies should be substantially increased, and that the proportion should be raised of those that exceed world standards in terms of technology and economy. The mechanism of foreign markets, especially the dynamics of cost-benefit relations, has, no doubt, to be more effectively utilised. As is well-known, the economic contribution of the modern development of productive forces is to upgrade the cost-benefit relations by minimising expenditures for manufacture and by raising the user value of commodities *in a synchronised manner*. In this sense, the increase in quality of products plays the key role. Even a partial abandonment of the economic utilisation of this potential effectiveness would, from the very outset, mean resting content with a lower than attainable economic utilisation of this high technology. Ability to produce products of international standards of quality, by the use of modern techniques, will in the final analysis decide "... whether the domestic and external demand for high-quality products can be satisfied rationally and in the quantities needed."[5]

The material stimulation of the industrial combines to accelerate the scientific-technical rate of renewal will be further intensified, as will be shown below, by the continued perfection of management, planning and economic accountancy (economic mechanism) since the beginning of 1986 and is now being made more effective by new pricing measures. Differentiated regulations will also provide specific support for export-promoting effects. Basically and primarily the functioning of the economic mechanism can only be verified by a properly working economy rather than by theoretic models - however intellectually attractive they might be as repeatedly claimed in academic circles.

The accelerated renewal of the production base is accompanied by a higher rate of finish of imported and also, to an increasing extent, of indigenous energy sources and raw materials. Finishing processes penetrate all stages of production, from basic materials through intermediates to final products. Higher finish, as well as re-use of secondary raw materials, both achieved by the scientific and technical processes of renewal, become the crucial elements in a resource-saving and thus non-polluting growth. In the past few years, the GDR has been able to gain much practical experience in this field. (See *Table 7.1*). Compared with 1985, national income produced in 1990 is to increase by 24-26 per cent. Centrally-run industry will see an increase in labour productivity (on the basis of net production) of 49-51 per cent, with a reduction in the specific consumption

---

5) Report of the Central Committee of the SED to the XIth Party Congress, Berlin 1986, p. 51

Table 7.1

Indexes of development of the national income and of productive consumption[a]
(1975 = 100)

Year	National income produced	Productive consumption	Productive consumption per unit of national income produced
1980	123	122	101
1985	152	135	88

A reduction in productive consumption by 1 % corresponds to an increase in the national income:

in 1970 of 3.0 billion marks
in 1980 of 4.8 billion marks
in 1985 of 5.3 billion marks

[a] Material inputs

Source: from "Erfolgreicher Weg der Gestaltung der entwickelten sozialistischen Gesellschaft in der DDR", *Zahlen und Fakten*, Berlin 1986, p. 40.

of economically important raw materials by about 4 per cent a year, of economically important energy carriers by 3.3 per cent a year, with a increase in the utilisation of productive equipment (by increasing the shift coefficient) by about 20 per cent and, ultimately, with an increase in the output-capital ratio (capital efficiency) in industry by 12 per cent. This increase in effectiveness, as set out in the new 5-Year Plan, must result in the acceleration of the scientific-technical renewal of the production base and of the technical and social infrastructure. The major share of investment is specifically planned to serve this particular aim. The share of rationalisation investments in manufacturing industry is to increase to about 80 per cent by 1990, with a simultaneous reduction in the expenditure on construction and a further shortening of the construction periods for the start-up of new investments. By comparison with 1975/1980, when the share of rationalisation investment in total investment was 53 per cent, and in the next five years rose to 64 per cent, the increase to 80 per cent by 1990 will be the fastest so far. By 1990, the GDR economy will reach a level of rationalisation and scientific-technical modernisation equal to that of the developed industrial countries. These plan figures also contradict the misunderstanding that sometimes arose about the actual role of high technologies in the growth of the GDR economy. The scientific, technical and economic potentials of the high technologies are to promote growth and efficiency primarily, and to a large extent, by the rationalisation of the existing production base. The kind of rationalisation which in earlier stages of development was overshadowed by extensive investments is now subject to a fundamental change of function. Its scientific, technological and economic level has now been substantially raised by modern technologies. It should become effective over the entire national economy, by contrast with the capacity-expanding investments of the past decades which represent a so-called "island solution" of progress. Together with growing consumption power up to 1990, the margins for manoeuvre in trade policy, both for capital and consumer goods, will be widened in an attempt to participate still more intensively in the international division of labour, and to make use of its benefit more effectively for achieving the domestic aims of development.

In 1985/1990 the GDR's commodity trade with the USSR and the other socialist countries is expected to account for two thirds of the GDR's total international trade. However, against the background of an increasing quantity, an important change in quality has emerged and is bound to be brought about in line with the progressive implementation of the complex programme of scientific-technical progress to be achieved by the member countries of CMEA up to the year 2000. Also, in future, scientific-technical cooperation with the USSR based on the long-term development of modern productive forces, will be of overriding importance for the steady development of the GDR national economy in accordance with the "Long-term programme of development of cooperation between the GDR and the USSR in the fields of science, technology and production covering the period up to the year 2000". The intense involvement of the GDR national economy in the international socialist division of labour is illustrated by selected data in *Table 7.2*.

Table 7.2

Trade between GDR and USSR

Foreign trade turnover GDR/USSR (in bn. foreign-currency marks)		Share of specialised products in the export of the GDR to the USSR (in %)	
1971/75	99	1970	1
1976/80	177	1980	38
1981/85	303	1985	49
1986/90	more than 380		

Source: As Table 7.1, pp. 96-97

On the foundation of stable political and economic relations with the USSR and other CMEA countries, the GDR's economic and trade relations with the non-socialist world will also be further developed as the growth-oriented economic and social policies come into effect. This course is supported by the stabilisation of the foreign trade balance achieved in the first half of the 1980s in relations with the non-socialist countries. From 1981 until now a positive trade balance has been reached in trade with the non-socialist world in every year. The foreign trade turnover of the GDR with the socialist economic region over the period from 1971 to 1975 amounted to some 88 billion marks. In the period 1981 to 1985 it rose to about 270 billion marks. From 1981 to 1985, overall foreign trade secured an export surplus of 26 billion marks. The apprehensions voiced by some western experts on the GDR, who saw in this development a significant weakening of the consumption and investment capacity of the GDR, and, also predicted an inevitable stagnation of growth because of a temporary redistribution of national income to stabilise the foreign trade balance, have proved unfounded - or at least could not be confirmed in the way they expected. By contrast, over this period economic growth even accelerated compared with 1975/1980. Undoubtedly, there are several long- and short-term factors that require deeper analysis. But there is already no doubt that the GDR authorities, by taking their strategic decisions in good time, were a major factor in this development. In making these strategic decisions, it was possible to give due consideration to the clear international dynamics of modern productive forces. They find their explicit expression in the further development of the economic strategy, and their progressive implementation will help to widen the room for manoeuvre in East-West cooperation in science, technology and production and to putting this cooperation on a longer-term basis. Incidentally, this analysis indicates that developments in the CMEA countries in the second half of the 1970s and in the very early 1980s were very different, so that generally accepted evaluations of the past and the future course appear to be very complicated.

7.2 Agriculture in the trade balance

Compared with the developments in import and export structures and terms or trade in the later 1970s and early 1980s, the years ahead will, in all probability, bring about some deep-going changes to be taken into account. This refers, for the GDR economy, primarily to the use (commitment) of foreign-currency proceeds, obtained from the export of the products for the metal-working and other processing industries, the import of important energy carriers, agricultural (grain) and industrial raw materials on the basis of the traditional models of exchange. Especially since the early 1980s a fundamental change has begun in the GDR national economy, with its effects becoming fully perceptible only in the years up to 1990 and thereafter.

This change proceeds along two lines: one is a more intensive use of indigenous energy and raw material resources with a higher degree of processing; the other is the continuous reduction in the specific consumption of energy and raw materials, with an increase of the share of value added in total production and a decrease in the energy and material intensity of national income. Given the GDR's economic structure and its foreign-trade intensity, it is obvious that these two lines will entail direct and-through the input-output relationships - also indirect effects on the product composition of the future import-export structure. One of the main effects will be that the amount of manufactured goods needed to pay for the import of agricultural and industrial raw materials, for each unit of national income produced, is likely to decrease. There will be a "release" of export funds, consisting of consumer and capital goods, available either for the technological renewal of our own production base and the supply of the internal market, or for an extended transfer of technology and an expanded international exchange of consumer goods. This will be illustrated in greater detail by relevant economic calculations to be considered in the stepwise replacement of grain imports.

In the GDR, as in most of the European member countries of CMEA, animal production, from the 1960s till the second half of the 1970s, grew faster than crop production. The growing imports of feed grain, chiefly from the non-socialist countries, made it possible, by circulation through the animal, to raise the production and the consumption of meat and meat products for domestic consumption and, in addition, for exports. Thanks to a relatively stable price level for grain and other crops on the world market, this policy was justifiable for a certain period and under definite political conditions. When strict economic criteria are applied, the policy was even profitable because of world market conditions: at least it was more profitable than other possible alternatives which would have produced the same result, i.e. ensuring a stable supply of the population with meat, meat products, animal fat and milk products in growing quantities and in constantly improved quality (see *Table 7.3)*. Moreover, our own experience, reinforced by the experience of other socialist countries during the 1970s, implies that a stable supply of foodstuffs, rising progressively, is one of the major factors influencing both political stability and the conditions for balanced domestic and foreign trade. All other considerations, including enterprise and economic interests, must be subordinated to it.

However favourable was the realisation of this approach for the

Table 7.3

Basic foodstuffs: State deliveries and consumption 1970-1985

Year	State deliveries				Per-capita consumption of basic foodstuffs			
	Slaughtered animals	Milk	Eggs	Wool	Meat, meat products sausages	Butter	Eggs and egg prod.	Drinking milk
	000 tons	000 tons	million	tons	kg	kg	number	litres
1970	1631	5681	3505	3306	66.1	14.9	239	98.5
1980	1953	6829	4712	5735	89.5	15.2	289	98.7
1985	2590	7528	4835	7315	96.2	12.7	305	105.6

Source: As Table 7.1, pp. 51 and 86.

socio-political goals, it proved indispensable to strengthen the pressure for the intensification of agricultural production and the marketing of farm produce, and, if possible, to elevate them to the level of industrial production. A development well balanced between industry and agriculture, according to *uniform* standards of effectiveness, is needed and should be achievable. The drastic price changes for grains on the world market, and the misuse of the international grain trade as a political instrument for exerting pressure, were not the original causes for accelerated intensification of our own agricultural production, yet served as catalysts. The data in *Table 7.4* indicate the recent and expected future results of our efforts. The progressive intensification of agricultural production will at the same time permit the replacement of the hitherto necessary imports of feed grain. In the long-term, it will produce a favourable effect by widening the room for manoeuvre in the transfer of technology in East-West relations. For, on average, grain imports (some 3.6 million tons a year) were using up 20 to 50 per cent of the proceeds of exports to the non-socialist countries. But in 1981 to 1985, it was possible to reduce this amount to 2.5 million tons, in 1985 even to 1.5 million tons. In the period to 1990 the net import of grain will be completely eliminated. The only way of replacing the grain imports is to increase the hectare yields in crop production, accompanied by a more effective utilisation of other production factors. In 1981/1985 it was possible to achieve growth in agricultural production with a 15 per cent cutback in costs of mineral fertilisers per unit of crop production, a 3 per cent reduction in feed costs per unit of animal production and a 14 per cent reduction in energy- fuel- and gas costs per unit of agricultural production. A saving of 20 per

Table 7.4

Crop yields per hectare
(grain equivalent in quintals per hectare)

Year	Total	grain	potatoes	sugar beet
1976-1980	40.3	35.8	175	269
1981-1985	45.4	41.3	206	294
1990 (planned)	50 to 52	47 to 49	250 to 270	370 to 390

Source: As Table 7.1, p. 85

Note: A record grain harvest, and record yields, were achieved in 1985 (11.6 mn. tons and 46.2 quintals per ha.). Helped by improved incentives, agricultural production from *individal holdings* increased; from 1980 to 1985, sales from these holdings rose by 44 % for slaughterings, 50 % for wool, 70 % for fruit, and 51 % for vegetables. Individual holdings accounted in 1985 for 30 % of State deliveries of slaughterings, 31 % of wool, 36 % of eggs, 30 % of fruit and 11 % of vegetables.

cent of grain imports in 1981/1985 was made possible by an average saving of 1.5 per cent a year in feeds. Over the same period, exports of meat were increased by 26 %, of butter by 19 %, and of eggs by 92 %, to the socialist as well as non-socialist markets. The following calculations illustrate the economic benefits to be derived from the progressive replacement of grain imports. A ton of imported grain costs about 1000 marks (wholesale price in domestic currency) and this corresponds to about 400-500 foreign currency marks. By contrast, the cost of home-produced grain is about 400-500 domestic marks per ton. Thus an expenditure in domestic currency of 400-500 million marks would make it possible to produce about 1 million tons of grain in the GDR, whereas the import of the same amount requires about 400-500 foreign currency marks. Compared with root crops, grain in the GDR is among the agricultural products having the highest productivity. The entire technological process, from soil cultivation, sowing, fertilising, harvesting and storage up to processing as food or feed is fully mechanised and provided with automatic controls at appropriate stages. For this reason, the losses during harvesting, transport and storage are comparatively low, together with any losses during processing. This period was also characterised by a fundamental reform of both agricultural prices, and of economic and organisational arrangements in the interest of better management. The aim was to ensure more effective consideration of natural factors and scientific knowledge in agricultural production, as well as making use of cooperative ownership for a better division between plant and animal production according to the requirements of natural rotation.

Thus the structural shift in foreign trade as a condition for economic growth becomes apparent, (e.g. the suspension of grain imports), as do its consequences for interdependency in international economic relations and, accordingly, for the GDR's import and export structure. This shift consists much more in the attainment of higher efficiency of existing resources within the economy than in any quantitative expansion of the use of resources. The shift will affect the basic internal conditions for balance, such as the balance between industrial and agricultural production, together with the dynamics and structure of foreign trade profit-and-loss accounting. Certainly, more profound empirical and theoretical analyses would be required to elucidate the reciprocal relations between the intensive type of growth, the national economic structure and the shift in foreign trade conditions - not least to ascertain more exactly their effects on the economic relations between East and West.

7.3 New incentives for new exports

In recent years the GDR combines have evolved into economic units in which the continued process of intensification of the national economy originates and is being pushed ahead. Within them, science and production are closely interrelated. Starting from Research and Development, through their own introduction of methods of rationalisation and production, up to the sales on domestic and foreign markets - all is controlled on the basis of the combine's own responsibility and strictly evaluated by economic guidelines, net production and economic return. The very fact that in addition to these indicators there have still to be added the parameters "Products and performance for the population" and "Export" is not solely attributable to international requirements, but is also the result of the high measure of foreign trade intensity of the GDR economy. Among the 127 currently operating, centrally-run combines in industry, there is hardly one to be found which does not have an export share of at least 30 per cent. The combined results from the totality of these indicators for evaluating the performance of the combines are aimed at promoting export-oriented management - although not disregarding the needs of the domestic market. The need for intensification of all these effects, with the object of accelerating the renewal of an adequate supply of products conforming with international standards, has now become part and parcel of the central problems faced in the further improvement of the economic mechanism.

At present, the following regulations are at the stage of first practical testing, or are on the threshold of immediate introduction into economic practice:

a) Determination of ceilings for costs and prices for new export products;

b) Introduction of price premiums in accordance with improvements in quality and effectiveness for newly marketed products;
c) Introduction of price deductions for outdated products.

On a)
The fixing of cost and price ceilings for new export products is based on the assumption that modernisation of the product implies a steady increase in efficiency. This increase has to be confirmed in terms of a cost reduction per unit (allowing for quality and other user characteristics) of the new product. The cost and price ceilings are, so to speak, the economic framework within which research and development has to operate in order to transform scientific and technical innovations into an actual gain in efficiency; the ceilings also make it possible to prevent price increases at variance with the actual price-benefit relationship. In determining the upper limits of prices for export commodities, the provisional proceeds in foreign currency play a prominent role. The price ceilings can be realistically determined only by scientific-technical and marketability comparisons with the world standard. In determining the price ceilings it is implicitly assumed that the upper limits of costs are fixed, thus making it possible to provide sufficient information for an attempt to open up further possibilities of cost reductions even during the R&D stage. Since in defining the price ceiling the foreign currency proceeds likely to be obtainable when the new product comes on the market is the basis for calculation, a certain pressure is exerted to shorten the time required for development and transfer into production. In the advanced combines, these regulations have already produced favourable effects. Nevertheless there are still many combines which still have to adjust to market-oriented work, necessarily beginning already at the R&D stage. In most cases, these are the combines which today face difficulties in accelerating the rate of renewal, irrespective of the fact that with the introduction of new products an above-average foreign currency revenue will have to be earned.

On b)
Price premiums, within the system of evaluating the performance of the combines, are to be considered mainly as an *extra profit* resulting from an increase in efficiency, once again composed of increases in user-value or quality *and* cutback in costs. The mechanism for allowing these extra profits has triple effects on the combines. First, they apply to particularly new products which are able to reach the planned increase in production and efficiency. Compared with the older products, whose prices included only the standard rate of profit, the new products provide a perceptible advantage in raising net production and profit. Second, already in the

R&D stage, it is necessary to make use of all possibilities of cost reductions. It is obvious that the earlier the costs of new products approach their minimum, the more beneficial are the gains in extra profit; and *vice versa* the longer a number of combines adhere to the practice of attempting to keep back reserves for a later reduction in costs, the less are the opportunities to extract extra profits. Third, the benefit to the combine is the greater, the more the cost-conformable production volume of new products can be achieved during the first two years, because such price premiums are always limited to two years. The industrial prices covering the first two years will be fixed in such a way that they ensure the same export profitability as the comparable product depending also on the actual foreign-currency proceeds.

On c)
There is no doubt that the process of product renewal cannot be stimulated only by price premiums and by the mechanism of extra profits. It also requires price deductions for those products which have exceeded the standard life-cycle. Such deductions make it substantially more difficult to obtain the net production and profit required under the system of performance evaluation. These regulations came into effect on 1 January 1987, so that the system of incentives for the combines to export foreign currency-profitable products is further enlarged. There is no doubt that, as a result of these regulations, additional changes in the economic mechanism will have to be made for the promotion of exports of high-quality products conformable to world market standards. Against this background of export promotion, it is intended to widen further the room for manoeuvre for exports with the aim of making still more effective use of the benefits of the international division of labour in order to fulfil our national economic, technical and social tasks. This will certainly benefit also the further development of the GDR's economic and trade relations with the non-socialist countries.

Chapter 8

INTENSIVE DEVELOPMENT AS AN INSTRUMENT FOR EXPORT-LED GROWTH IN THE GERMAN DEMOCRATIC REPUBLIC

Peter Sydow[1)]

In every national economy - and the German Democratic Republic is no exception - growth strategy is both subject to external constraints and involves internal structural changes. No national economy can decisively determine global political or economic developments but will rather have to adjust to them. But a government can influence the process of adjustment through its political, social and economic aims - which requires internal structural adjustment, both social and economic.

8.1 Social growth strategies for the 1990s

On the threshold of the 1990s, the growth strategies of socialist countries have to address three major concerns and offer practicable courses of action conforming with their national circumstances:

a) To avert a nuclear holocaust and to establish world peace on stable and enduring foundations, an active policy governed by reason and realism is vital. Readiness to engage in political dialogue to preserve peace must be linked with effective economic growth to create further social progress and to guarantee social security, the right to full employment and education, and a peaceful future.

The consequent demands on the GDR's growth strategy are indeed very exacting. They are reflected in the central policy of combining economic achievement with social prosperity.

b) The new challenges to the organisation of the national economy concern all aspects of the growth process, and in particular the development and application of the new technologies - sources of growth which appeared unattainable in the 1970s when the traditional sources of growth were approaching exhaustion. This calls for management of a new stage of economic strategy in the GDR, organising all phases of the cycle of intensively extended reproduction for maximum efficiency[2)]. Only in this way can

---

1) Professor, Central Institute of Economics, Academy of Sciences of the GDR, Berlin

2) Directives issued by the 11th Congress of the Socialist Unity Party for the Five-Year Plan for the GDR's national economic development 1986-1990, (English translation), Verlag Zeit im Bild, Dresden, p. 10.

the GDR hold its place among the leading industrial nations and protect not only its political, but also its economic, scientific and technological security.

c) The further evolution of international economic and technological cooperation is essential in view of the continuing internationalisation of production and labour rooted in the maturity of socialist production relations and in the dynamics of modern production forces. Standing on the watershed between two systems, as a member of CMEA and a major partner of the USSR, and because of the importance of its foreign trade, the GDR has a permanent interest in undisturbed international economic relations.[3] The GDR must play its part in raising economic integration with the USSR and other CMEA countries to a qualitatively new level.

The central feature of the CMEA's "Comprehensive programme for scientific and technological progress to the year 2000" is the elaboration of division of labour arrangements in many areas for the production of products and processes that will determine the state of the art on the international level.

By contrast with the aim of a mutually advantageous development of the international division of labour, the "hawks" in the West have engaged since the early 1980s in a strategy of economic encirclement cutting off the socialist community from international progress. They seek to gain both economic and military superiority by monopoly of new scientific and technical development. The result is major disturbance of global economic relationships; embargoes and boycotts have almost frozen exchanges, especially in key advanced technologies. Discrimination and protectionism, together with other negative impacts of the capitalist economic and monetary systems, represent additional constraints. Thus the economic relations of the GDR, and of other socialist states, with the rest of the world have been severely strained.

Yet the synthesis of the largely common interests of European and overseas countries with different economic systems offers, in our opinion, a sensitive but viable base for making greater use of the economic and scientific potential of East-West (European) economic interaction.

---

3) The GDR is a net importer of energy and of a wide range of minerals, and a net exporter of machinery, equipment and instruments. The share of exports in its national income is, more than 40 per cent.

8.2 Implications of intensive development

Intensification of social production has been the main path of economic growth in the GDR for about ten years.[4] The dynamic development and use of science and technology has resulted in fast growth of productivity and efficiency, saved labour, reduced specific consumption of materials and energy (i.e. inputs per unit of output), and greatly improved the cost-benefit ratio in the economy. The centrally-managed combines in industry and other sectors have proved their viability as the backbone of the socialist planned economy. Central planning by the state, the system of balances, the improvement of commodity-money relations and the grant of greater responsibilities to enterprises have combined to constitute a modern operational mechanism for a socialist economy which can respond to the challenges of the scientific and technological revolution and to international demand while creating conditions for the gradual improvement of domestic living standards.

A review of the recent growth path should not be confined to the observation that a favourable break in trend did occur. While I cannot analyse here all the experiences in the light of reproduction theory[5], I can at least make the following points:

a) Intensive growth in the socialist reproduction cycle is a process of social, economic and techno-scientific change, passing through various stages of maturity as the advanced socialist society continues to take shape. What marked the process in the early 1980s is that we managed to proceed to comprehensive intensification and to initiate a thorough-going renewal of production[6].

b) Comprehensive intensification presupposes, and produces, changes in all phases of economic progress, geared to improved economic performance chiefly by the development and effective use of key technologies. The aim is to keep abreast with the accelerating pace of the international scientific and technological revolution, and to take the lead in selected branches. That will guarantee a sustained and irreversible long-term increase in productivity and efficiency.

c) The *social aim* of our economic strategy is to use economic achievement

---

4) Programme of the Socialist Unity Party of Germany, (English translation), Dresden, Verlag Zeit im Bild, p. 23

5) W. Heinrichs (ed.): Grundfragen der sozialistischen Reproduktionstheorie, Berlin, Dietz Verlag, vol. 1/1982, vol. 2/1987

6) Report of the Central Committee to the 11th Congress of the Socialist Unity Party, (English translation), Dresden, Verlag Zeit im Bild, p. 31

to increase living standards, so that social security will be guaranteed, the housing problem resolved by 1990, and working conditions improved. Higher incomes and a better supply of consumer goods and services will make it possible to translate economic advances into fresh social vigour.

d) This new type of socialist development does not only modify material processes. It is first and foremost dependent on a *steady* evolution of socialist production relations in which the human person is an active factor, and whose all-round development is the focus of all efforts.

The national income per employee in the productive sector has risen from 28,000 marks in 1980 to over 34,000 marks in 1984. Growth in industry has been almost entirely due to the application of scientific and technological knowledge, resulting in 445 million man-hours saved annually from 1976 to 1985. In the following five years these economies are expected to rise to 500-600 million man-hours, which would mean another increase in labour productivity by over 23 per cent. This upward trend - the most important source of economic growth - when combined with decreases in productive consumption, will allow a rise in the national income produced by 24-26 per cent in 1985-1990.

Savings per unit of output in current labour costs, in capital utilisation and in input of energy and materials accounted for 40 per cent of the growth of national income in 1980-1985; in that period national income produced rose faster than productive consumption for the first time. This break in earlier trends is expected to continue[7].

Sustained growth of national income by 4-5 per cent a year corresponds with the level of economic, scientific and technological capabilities of the GDR. This rate of growth is necessary to finance the development and application of key technologies and an adequate rationalisation of productive capacities while gradually raising living standards. National income growth of this order (with a progressively increasing volume of competitive manufactures for the world market) will ensure that the strategic aims can be achieved with an effective export surplus allowing the GDR to react flexibly to the international market and to service its international debt.

The new pattern of growth is assured chiefly through the concentration and expansion of the scientific and technological potential (supported by allocations of 4 per cent from the national income produced) in the following major areas:

---

7) See also W. Heinrichs, Chapter 7 of this volume, especially Table 7.1

- accelerated development and application of microelectronics;
- increased application of modern computers;
- design of fully-automated production lines for flexible manufacture;
- processes, technologies and equipment to reduce energy consumption and to upgrade brown coal;
- new solutions for a fuller use of all raw materials;
- greater reliance on biotechnology;
- manufacture of high-value consumer goods;
- new solutions for higher yields in agriculture;
- design of modern construction methods and processes;
- new scientific and technological solutions for public transport and telecommunications;
- development of low-waste and non-waste technologies and methods, and
- preservation, promotion and restoration of health.

The knowledge to implement these priorities is expected to come from scientific and technological activities in industrial combines working in close collaboration with institutes of the Academy of Sciences and the universities.

Systematic links between science and production by contractual cooperation between these establishments will ensure that *basic research* will be geared to the prospective requirements of the economy while the remaining research potential is coordinated to resolve short-term and medium-term *production-related* tasks.[8)] In both kinds of R and D, the international state of the art will be the criterion.

8.3 Renewal and modernisation of production

New technologies, processes and products developed in these ways are prerequisites for the *renewal* of production in all branches. Such a renewal will become effective only if it has a favourable impact on the cost-benefit ratio in two senses: first, that costs will be reduced to internationally determined levels and, second, that the quality, technical standards and operational reliability of products will simultaneously be raised to meet the requirements of the international market.

The average rate of product renewal in industry in 1985 was 27.5 per cent. That will not be sufficient for the coming years, because the correspon-

8) According to the principles for economic relations between industrial combines and institutes of the Academy of Sciences and institutes of higher learning and the Ordinance on Research Activities (see Gesetzblatt der DDR, Teil I, No. 2, 16/1/1986), the parties conclude economic contracts of different types.

ding rate among trading partners and competitors also tends to go up. So the present aim is to renew over 30 per cent of the products in all industrial branches each year through 1990. For consumer goods, rates of renewal of between 30 and 40 per cent appear to be required in order to cope with the growing domestic demand and also to open up export opportunities. By 1990 it is planned to have a total of 15,000-16,000 new designs in production. For at least 60 per cent of these, the designs must meet international top standards. These rates are dictated not only by the market situation, but also by the need to translate new technical findings into products quickly enough to pay off the initial outlays for R and D and to meet domestic and foreign demand at lower costs for the economy.

Renewal of production must comprise all stages of production (from the primary material to finished product); i.e. renewal must be managed as a planned process of extended reproduction. The economic strategy complies with this necessity by providing that materials undergo refinement or upgrading. In rolled steel, for instance, the portion of high-grade products was 80 per cent in 1985 and is to reach 90 per cent by 1990. Brown coal, remaining the GDR's main source of energy, will increasingly be used as a feedstock for the chemical industry (7 million tonnes in 1985, 11 million tonnes in 1990, in oil equivalents). Deeper cracking of oil makes it possible to provide a bigger proportion of carburants and basic chemicals without having to increase the quantity of imported oil until 1990. By 1990 the yield of white products from oil should reach 75 per cent. These developments indicate that more productive use of imported inputs should be combined with more rational use, and conservation, of indigenous materials. Together with recycling of waste products, this approach will make it possible to cover rising needs for materials without increasing imports and at the same time to ensure a resource-saving mode of growth (with reduced environmental pollution). Critical analysis of what has so far been achieved reveals a substantial potential for further economies.

There are many opportunities, too, for increasing labour productivity. Improved preparation of production and scientific organisation of work should affect 1.2-1.3 million workplaces by 1990 and set free manpower for other productive occupations. Some 450,000 workers will see their strenuous working conditions alleviated or eliminated.

Better use of existing productive capacities plus an efficiency-oriented investment policy are the keys to unlock these reserves. In 1985, about 60 per cent of industrial machinery and equipment in the GDR was less than ten years old, one-third less than five years old. The degree of automation of industrial equipment rose from 48 per cent in 1980 to

53 per cent in 1985. Against this background capacity utilisation per calendar day can very well be increased by about 20 hours; this will require, of course, corresponding arrangements for social facilities and services.

Thus an important concern in the next few years will be further strengthening of the techno-material base of the economy, mainly through socialist rationalisation. An investment volume of nearly 350 billion marks might be available in 1986-1990 (against 319 billion in 1981-1985). These funds will chiefly be employed

- to increase labour productivity by application of key technologies;
- to promote the production and effective use of domestic raw materials and fuels (above all, by higher degrees of refinement);
- to continue the housing construction programme;
- to accelerate the output of consumer goods, and
- to enhance the economy's export power.

To raise the output-capital ratio by 12 per cent between 1985 and 1990 calls for a higher proportion of rationalisation investments (1981-1985: 63 per cent; 1986-1990: 80 per cent), so as to reinforce present fixed assets with ultra-modern technological processes and to cut down further the gestation periods of investments.

These aims imply consequences for the production profile of the metal-working industries. Moreover, the industrial combines are challenged to expand their own production of equipment for rationalisation by over ten per cent a year. In this way, 25 per cent of the investment could be secured, modern production facilities be utilised and imports be dispensed with by 1990.

The rationalisation of production is thus the main road to employing new technologies and processes for comprehensive intensification.

8.4 A flexible trade strategy

Export orientation of economic growth takes on a new content from comprehensive intensification. This much-debated question has often been looked upon onesidedly and over-simplified by regarding export sales merely as the principal means of financing imports. But the essence of the question seems to transcend the commercial solvency of the economy. In terms of political economy, the answer seems to be that a kind of techno-scientific and economic capability needs to be achieved by which *both exports and imports*, closely linked with an active international division of labour, become a method of economising social (past) labour and in their physical form enable production cycles to continue with increased efficiency. This requires the planning of production for export by internationally defined techno-scientific and economic criteria and the use of "imports for production" similarly and as rationally as possible.

In many sectors the GDR's economy has pursued this strategy with success. This is shown by the big export share in the output of many industrial combines and their resulting revenues. Without these achievements, and, above all, without the active participation in specialisation and cooperation arrangements with the Soviet Union, the many disturbances in world markets would hardly have allowed the GDR to honour all international obligations on time, or to reach the present level of production and consumption while maintaining the pattern of external economic links. Of particular importance has been the conceptual evolution of industrial combines, notably the incorporation of foreign trade organisations while the state monopoly of foreign trade is maintained, and the decision to make their exports a major criterion for evaluation and to let the combines fulfil their functions in the government's system of economic balances.

The flexibility of the socialist planned economy was also proved when fuel oil imports had to be reduced and replaced by indigenous energy resources, and by energy conservation measures, without cuts in production growth. A comparable process was set on foot to replace grain imports[9]. The manufacture by industrial combines of their own equipment for rationalisation - when imports would cost more - is another move in the same direction. A powerful impulse for structural change on the macro-economic level has come from the recent fall of energy prices.

These examples go to show that the objective is not simply to replace imports, or to increase exports, perhaps at the expense of domestic production or consumption. Export-led growth has become a structural requirement for the national economy. Its effective implementation presupposes comprehensive intensification so as to develop export capability in balance with the needs for imports. The present stage is basically an effort to produce a growing volume of saleable goods to meet the increasing demands of our own economy and those of our commercial partners.

An effective increase in national export power means renewing and concentrating the range of scientifically and technologically attractive products with lower inputs. That includes stepping up imports where they are of maximum benefit for the rationalisation and concentration of production or research. It also includes finding substitutes for imports where efficient domestic capacities meeting the demand exist or can be developed.

---

9) See W. Heinrichs, Chapter 7.2 of this volume for relevant estimates

The bilateral long-term programmes of cooperation with the Soviet Union, Czechoslovakia, Poland, Hungary, Romania and Bulgaria, and the CMEA's Comprehensive Programme for Scientific and Technological Progress provide the impulse to press on with socialist international specialisation and cooperation in science and production in keeping with the criteria of comprehensive intensification. At the same time, they offer increasing opportunities for adapting the pattern of East-West economic relations, bilaterally and multilaterally, to the requirements of the 1990s.

Chapter 9

THE EUROPEAN MONETARY SYSTEM (EMS): FIRST LESSONS AND NEW CHALLENGES

Henri Bourguinat[1)]

There is a kind of paradox about the favour accorded by economists to the EMS. At the inception of the European monetary experiment, a deep scepticism was the rule. Seven years later, the success of the EMS is generally acclaimed, not only in Europe but all around the world. Occasionally, someone even proposes to generalise the system to the whole world economy and to develop a "World EMS System" with a "target zone" mechanism derived in fact from that in Europe.

A long time ago some major flaws were foreseen:

a) the grid of pegged parities would rapidly cause difficulties to the weakest currencies, as happened with the "snake" during previous attempts in 1972-1978;

b) the Exchange Rate Mechanism could not resist major fluctuations of the American dollar without internal damage;

c) it was sometimes argued that interventions by the central banks of participating countries in defence of agreed parities would necessarily prejudice monetary targets;

d) it was also suggested that the enlarged credit facilities would create a "Moral Hazard", postponing the necessary adjustment measures by members and facilitating inflation.

In reality, the seven years of EMS functioning have shown that it behaved better than was first intended. Not only did the system not collapse, nor have the currencies of any members been withdrawn (as sterling or the French franc withdrew from the "snake"). The EMS has even developed the ECU (European Currency Unit) which is now (BIS, 1986)a major currency in the international financial markets with the Deutsche mark and the US dollar. It has also resisted, very much better than was expected, the last two large swings of the dollar, even the dollar's marked decline since mid-1985.

Can we go so far as to say that the EMS is a real success and that its future is guaranteed? Before adopting such a proposition, we must answer three different questions.

---

1) University of Bordeaux, France

First (section 9.1), we have to show that in terms of exchange rates and prices, the EMS has performed well, better than originally expected. Particularly since 1983, convergence is clearly improving and the EMS appears effectively now as a "stability island" in the general system of floating rates. But we must also demonstrate that this convergence is limited in terms of trade performance among European partners. This conclusion leads (9.2) to the problem of the permanence of this convergence. Is this tendency, observed in changed parities and convergence of inflation rates, reinforced by progress in the field which is the final and principal aim of the EMS: the reinforcing of the integration process? We suggest that the answer is rather negative. Finally, we try to establish (9.3) in what conditions the ECU could become the pivot of a really common European currency.

9.1 The progress of convergence

There has been incontestable progress towards a greater convergence of the participating economies. Nevertheless, these improvements are often debated and we must distinguish between several levels manifesting significant differences.

Nominal and real exchange rates

One of the most generally mentioned positive results of the functioning of EMS, in spite of the nine official realignments during 1979-86, is that EMS has strongly contributed to the exchange rate stability of the participating currencies. This conclusion, established for several years, is more and more robust. Using as a general indicator of variability the standard deviation coefficient, it is obvious that the EMS currencies behaved in a way substantially different from the behaviour of the same currencies in previous years.

Different studies afford several interesting results. Ungerer (1983), for instance, showed that the short-run volatility of the EMS currencies with respect to each other has diminished significantly since 1979, while the volatility (daily and monthly) of the dollar, the yen or sterling has considerably increased. More recent studies bring out three other interesting results:

a) in terms of *nominal* effective exchange rates, it is clear (Padoa Schioppa, 1985, de Grauwe and Verfaille, 1986) that the standard deviations calculated on monthly percentages show that the short term variability has strongly decreased if we compare 1979-1985 with 1973-1979. If we calculate these standard deviations from *real* effective exchange rates, the same decreasing instability is clearly revealed (*Table 9.1*);

b) if we compare the short term variability of the EMS member currencies with that of non-members, we must emphasise that a difference emerges between *intra-* and *extra-*EMS currencies;

c) *Table 9.1* also demonstrates that the variability of *overall* real exchange rates is weaker for all EMS currencies than for the three major extra-EMS currencies (dollar, yen, sterling). For this reason, we recognise that the EMS is becoming the "stability island" often claimed by its supporters. We remark too, that the more stable real effective exchange rates confound the forecast, often made, that the intra-EMS pegs would increase real exchange movements. If the period under review is extended from 1979 (March) to 1986 (April), *Table 9.2* shows also that the dollar and sterling have had the biggest short-term variability with respect to the ECU after the EMS was established. But, at the same time, sterling's variability against the dollar was not significantly less than that of the other EMS countries (Musso, 1986).

It is interesting to add that the *medium-term misalignments* of the EMS currencies, defined (Williamson, 1985) as deviations of the real effective exchange rate from the "Fundamental Equilibrium Exchange Rate", were less for the EMS currencies than for sterling, the US dollar or the yen. That suggests that the EMS major currencies registered more limited deviations from purchasing power parities than the outside currencies.

Real interest rates and inflation rates converge

It has sometimes been argued that this improved stability of exchange rates has been achieved at the cost of a great volatility of the participants' interest rates. In fact, this conclusion does not seem fully correct. It is true that the period 1979-1986 is characterised by a jump of real interest rates for the EMS participants, as for the whole world, in accord with the general decline of inflation; on the other hand, *Tables 9.3* and *9.4* show that while the variability of short-term interest rates has been as low in the UK as in France or West Germany since 1983, nevertheless UK long-term rates have been more variable, being exceeded only in Italy, Belgium and Ireland (countries where progress in reducing budgetary deficits has been the slowest). One author (Russo, 1986) has correctly inferred from these differences that interest rates in the UK probably incorporate a higher risk premium than interest rates in the other EMS participants. Be that as it may, the intra-EMS convergence of real interest rates is certainly attributable both to the increasingly well established leadership of German monetary policy as well as to the centripetal function of the EMS. The European monetary experience has acted as a force permanently bringing together the participant economies and preventing important divagations. This force also appears to have succeeded in the field of inflation rates. Here we have to recall that one of the most radical criticisms heard in 1978 and 1979 concerned the alleged incapacity of the EMS to enforce substantial convergence in costs and prices. Seven years later, everybody must admit that there has been important progress in bringing down consumer price inflation in all EMS countries, especially in France, Ireland and Italy.

Table 9.5 shows that adherence to the EMS has coincided with falling inflation rates; in this respect the EMS has certainly played a very useful role. Indeed this movement has been general over the whole world; although French and Italian inflation rates in 1985 were still maintained well above the 2-3 per cent levels of West Germany and the Netherlands, it is obvious that the differences are decreasing. During 1985, in spite of the new slow-down in West German and Dutch inflation rates, the variance of inflation has been further reduced as compared with previous years; in autumn 1986, differences between the four main countries in the narrow band of the exchange rate mechanism were little more than 1-2 points. As a consequence of this growing convergence of consumer prices, and simultaneously of the last two realignments (Italian lira and French franc), we can be sure that real exchange rates are also converging (specially since the end of 1985).

Against this undeniable evidence of convergence, particularly of the inflation rates of the member countries, it is often said that this is the consequence of worldwide disinflation rather than of the integrationist properties of the EMS. If, in reality, as *Table 9.5* shows, the reduction of inflation is general, it is nevertheless certain that the EMS has had a decisive role in this evolution - not so much in fact from a *positive* but rather from a *negative* point of view. It has prevented member countries like France or Italy, which began with double-digit inflation, from remaining out of step with other countries by obliging them to adopt a more severe wage discipline and a stricter budgetary policy: this is especially true of France. The introduction of the *"politique d'austérité"* since 1983 has exactly corresponded with the necessity of maintaining the French franc in the exchange rate mechanism.

Finally, in spite of the more and more homogeneous evolution of consumer prices and of real exchange rates, it is evident that this convergence is still incomplete, especially in respect of the trade balances of the member countries.

Intra-European trade imbalances

One of the most striking negative results of European cooperation is the increasing divergence of trade balances. Seven years after the beginning of the EMS, West Germany and the Netherlands have much stronger merchandise balances which, frankly, contrast with most other partners (*Table 9.6*).

Since 1981, these two countries have trebled their commercial surpluses. By contrast, the positions of most other European countries have not improved, although they have also benefited from the drop in the dollar until 1985. These divergences are likely to widen further unless - which is very doubtful - West Germany agrees to boost its domestic demand, or unless, after the usual lag ("J curve"), the last realignments prove effective.

It is indeed possible to explain this counter-performance of intra-European trade. Elements such as oil shocks and dollar rate swings could be mentioned; from this last point of view, it is certain that the overvaluation of the dollar during the second period induced stronger growth of the EMS members' exports towards the outside world than within the EEC area. On the other hand, it seems (Bourguinat, Cazals and Ithurbide, 1985) that the EMS has not succeeded in substantially modifying the exchange practices of European traders; for example, they did not reduce their currency hedging in trade with European countries any more than in trade with outside partners. In general, EMS markets do not appear to be treated differentially. Similarly, the direct investment inquiry in France (1981-83) shows no substantial preference for investing in EMS countries.

The fairly good results of examining a variety of fields lead us to the heart of the question of the permanence of this improving convergence.

9.2 Convergence but for what?

It would be stimulating to bring together the aims pursued in the European Monetary attempt. The EMS was first promoted to bring order into intra-European parities and to stabilise exchange rates; its final aims have been different. Since the early 1970s, two other important aims have been pursued: first, to sustain economic and commercial integration by monetary cooperation; second, to take the first step towards a European common currency. How far have these two intentions been fulfilled after seven years functioning of the EMS? Two main observations will be presented.

Poor intra-European trade performance

Theoretically, the EMS is the monetary element of the more general unified trade structure whose name is the European Economic Communities. One would expect that the evidence of convergence, just mentioned, would normally bring about a net increase of intra-European trade. In fact, one of the main features of EC performance is that the greater stability of the mutual exchange rates has not contributed to the growth of trade within the system. If, following de Grauwe (1986), we compare the two periods 1973-78 and 1979-84 (*Chart 9.1*), we reach two conclusions: (a) the annual growth of intra-EMS trade declined from an annual average 4.9 per cent in 1973-78 to 2.2 per cent in 1979-84. The decline of the growth of trade between EMS and non-EMS countries is much more modest;

(b) during both the pre-EMS and post-EMS periods, it appears that the growth of intra-EMS trade was substantially less than the average growth of trade of the EMS countries with non-EMS industrialised countries; after 1979, intra-EMS trade continued to grow at less than half the rate of extra-EMS trade, despite the increasing stability of exchange rates inside the European system.

We thought immediately of the changing influence of the dollar between the two periods, especially on EMS exports. But de Grauwe and Verfaille show that even if we exclude trade with the US, EMS trade with other non-EMS countries increased at a slightly faster rate than the EMS trade with the whole group of non-EMS countries. Thus, dollar appreciation cannot explain the difference.

As a consequence, the internal trade-creating effect of the EMS seems to be decreasing. Once again, the improvement of exchange stability and stabilisation of inflation rates is significant but did not stimulate the growth of trade of the member countries. The reasons for this failure are diverse and we cannot review them all here.

Nevertheless, we cannot fail to observe the indisputable gap between the monetary effects of the EMS and its "real" effects. From this point of view, it seems that there is a kind of life cycle in the integration process, which contrasts with traditional customs union theory. It appears that after an initial period during which the *static effects* (due to the increase of competition) of liberalisation of trade were effectively captured the expected second wave of gains derived from *dynamic effects* (imputable to new structures reinforcing interdependence) did not really emerge.

It is possible that this disappointing result may have been due to incomplete achievement of the European Common Market, and, further to the fundamental fact that the EC is no longer large enough for the contemporary scale of the international division of labour: in several industries, from now on, the efficient area is the whole world, and not only a regional market, however large.

Chart 9.1

Average annual growth of trade (exports + imports) of EMS countries in constant prices
(in per cent)

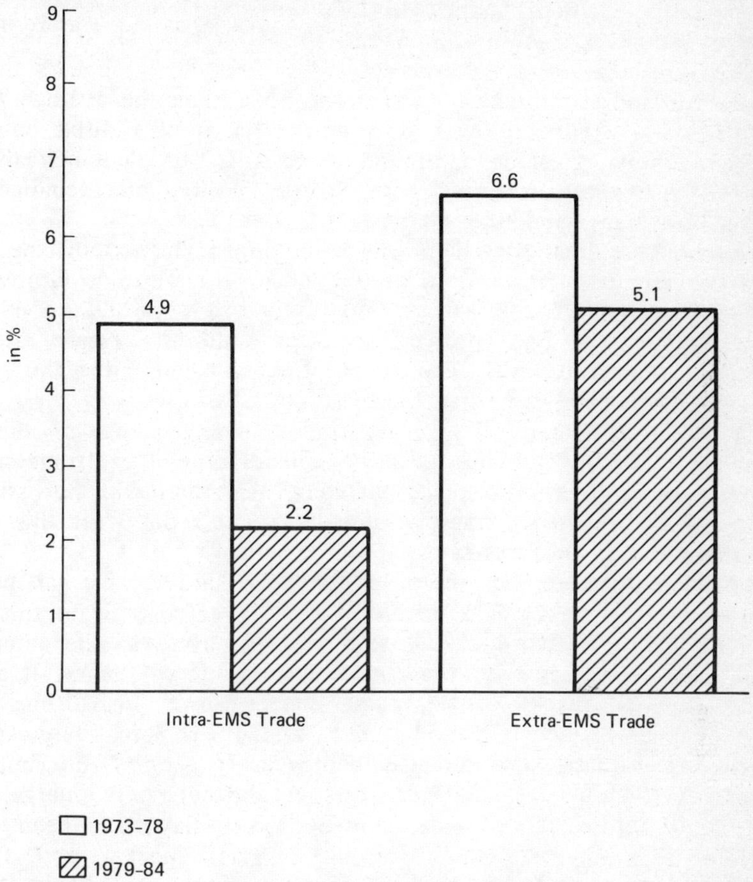

Notes: (1) The extra-EMS trade relates to the trade (exports + imports) of the EMS countries with non-EMS industrialised countries (Austria, Canada, Japan, Norway, Sweden, Switzerland, US, UK).
(2) The export figures of each country were deflated by the index of export unit values of the same country; to obtain import figures in constant prices, export unit weighted by the share of each exporting country in the total imports.

Source: de Grauwe and Verfaille (1986)

An EMS deflationist area?

One other disappointment of the EMS which must also be mentioned is seen in the growth rates of member countries. Thus if we compare growth rates of industrial production in the EMS countries with those in non-EMS countries, it is obvious that the European countries appear as a group of *low* growth economies; this differential deflation was particularly manifest by comparison with Japan and the United States during 1979-84 (*Table 9.7*).

Here we find one crucial issue for the EMS experiment. It is obvious that the price of reducing average inflation in West Europe has been a severe restraint of demand in the more inflationist countries. This is particularly evident in France since 1983. To realign their inflation rates with Germany and the Netherlands, the "less virtuous" countries have had to reduce drastically their growth of domestic demand. Investment particularly had to suffer. As a consequence, the EMS group appears as a *differentially deflationist* area. This failure is certainly not entirely to be imputed to the EMS project. Nor, it would be legitimate to link "eurosclerosis" and the EMS. The roots of the lag in European growth are certainly deeper and more structural (lack of flexibility, wage indexation, technological factors etc. ...).

Nevertheless, it would be unfair to consider only the progress made in bringing down consumer price inflation and in stabilising exchange rates and to forget the commercial imbalances and the weakness of the growth rates. Finally, it seems that the most inflationist members have found an evident interest in accepting the price and monetary discipline of "virtous" West Germany. This medicine has prevented them from making a "band apart", and has certainly allowed them to move away from double-digit inflation. Contrarywise, they have had to accept, at least in the short run, the drawbacks of this same choice (lower growth rates and the higher unemployment). But it is true to say that this rough therapy was much better than a lax domestic behaviour in these countries, which sooner or later would have led them to undertake more drastic adjustments with, at the beginning, more frequent intra-EMS parity realignments.

9.3 The ECU and the future of the EMS

It was originally foreseen that the first phase of EMS would be followed by a second, involving the permanent creation and development of ECUs to complete the monetary union. But, if phase two has been delayed, the expansion of the ECU is already a reality, at least on private financial markets; on the other hand, the use of the official ECU remain limited. So we have to ask whether the reinforcement of the links between the two ECU circuits is the condition for the improvement of monetary integration or whether other fundamental determinants would have to intervene.

Private versus official ECU

One of the more significant developments of the EMS is the recent progress of the European Currency Unit (ECU). Surprisingly, what was originally a simple unit of account is now used as an international instrument for more than 5 per cent of all the new international bond issues (*Table 9.8*). The ECU also appears, according to the BIS, as the fifth international money instrument for the assets and liabilities of the reporting banks (after the dollar, the DM, Swiss franc and Yen), with a total around $ 50 billion (*Table 9.9*). The private ECU markets had already shown strong vitality. The merits of the ECU, formerly appreciated principally by the Italian and French borrowers, are now accepted by other operators, even some outside the EEC. The initial advantages of the ECU, briefly mentioned, are now enlarged: ECU paper is not only appreciated by the borrowers in countries of high inflation. Its composite nature provides a useful diversification, which limits exchange risks and permits also the promotion of sophisticated investment strategies. We can note that the ECU also begins to be used as an invoicing currency by a few Italian and French industrial groups, but this movement is still limited and happens because of the exchange rate controls. Is this evidence enough to consider the ECU as the possible basis for the Common Currency Union which is projected for Europe? The problem is more important than it has ever been. At a time when the dollar is called into question as an exclusive international currency, it could seem attractive to reinforce the ECU by making it one of the elements of a "tripolar" International Monetary System (dollar, yen, ECU). But, in reality, at this stage, two difficult and crucial problems remain unsolved.

(a) First, there is the question of the link between the *private* and the *official* ECU. If the first is prospering, the second is still underdeveloped and suffers greatly from the lack of a real European Central Bank. For the moment, it is created only in the form of three-month swaps by the EMS central banks of 20 per cent of their gold and dollar reserves. The ECU mechanism (Allen, 1986, Meyer, 1986) has not yet provided a well-defined lender of last resort; consequently, one important concern is: what would happen in a severe liquidity crisis of the European banks?

The steps taken in 1985 and 1986 to develope the official ECU are certainly not negligible (Miscossi, 1985). They lead to a loosening of the prevailing restrictions on the use of the ECU for transactions between central banks and, for some purposes, with some non-members ("third holders"). For the first time, but still within limits, the member countries may mobilise their official ECU holdings to obtain currencies for an intervention within EMS margins rather than at the limits of the band. A second reform includes a modest liberalisation of the 50 per cent rule on members' obligations to accept ECUs offered in settlement of intervention balances. Last, it was decided in July 1986 that the settlement of net claims positions in ECUs would be closely related to that of the money-market in so far as holdings of official ECUs would be encouraged (Morgan Guaranty Trust Co, 1986). These technical measures, important as they could be, do not hide the fact that the gap between official and private ECUs is still very large. The main difficulty is to find the specific conditions for improving use of the ECU.

(b) A second concern about the ECU is certainly the steady hostility of the West German monetary authorities to the extension of private uses of ECUs by their nationals. The Bundesbank is firmly resisting opportunities for its nationals to borrow in ECUs. This would be considered as indexation, which is precisely forbidden by the German fundamental monetary law (art. 3). As long as Germany maintains its position, the future of the ECU will be compromised and the prospect of a Common European Currency, circulating in parallel with national units, appears to be out of the question.

This point seems to be decisive since the Deutsche mark represents one third of the basket and West Germany is the dominant economy in Western Europe; this country is the key to the solution. Beyond academic discussion about the currency/non-currency nature of the ECU, the future of ECU as the pillar of the European Monetary Union depends upon the decision of Germany.

The ECU as the third pillar of an oligopolist currency system?

If we consider that the future of the world monetary system must depend on a "tripolar" basis, with, for example, three vehicle currencies, the question is whether the ECU would be the third international unit, beside the dollar and the yen. Obviously, as long as the two questions raised above remained unsolved, the evolution of the international payments organisation toward an *"oligopolist currency system"* would continue to be blocked. This would be particularly regrettable, especially at a time of dollar weakness. At this moment, in fact, the ECU could offer a substitution currency vis-à-vis the dollar and could constitute an advantageous instrument of diversification. It could usefully absorb the pressures on the "hard" currencies, particularly the DM, and so constitute an interesting instrument of diversification. Nevertheless, in spite of this possibility, one question would remain: could the ECU at this moment be regarded as a true common currency or is it rather a disguise, or simply the nth money of the EMS whose axis obviously would then be the DM?

The answer depends on at least two profoundly different elements.

Should the UK joint the EMS?

The case for entry of the UK into the exchange rate mechanism is crucial not only for the UK itself but also for the whole EMS. By entry, the UK could gain a first advantage by substituting an exchange rate target for the monetary target after the disarray of the latter (Brittan, 1986). Another specific advantage, particularly if there were a change in the political majority, would be that full adhesion to the parities grid would provide a formal institutional arrangement constituting an external constraint for moderating the continuing rise of British labour costs. The objection that sterling is a petro-currency now seems exaggerated in view of the recent fall in the oil price. Nevertheless, a difficulty about full EMS membership would remain if, as Goodhart (1986) has shown, the price to pay for full entry of UK into the exchange rate mechanism would be volatility of interest rates: in his view, if intra-European exchange rates were pegged for a long time, it would be necessary (since countries still have widely different flexibility factors) to accept frequent and wide gyrations of interest rates. Forcing the exchange rate to be absolutely fixed for a long time, would also, according to Walters (1986), mean a single nominal interest rate for two countries having very different rates of inflation. This common nominal interest rate would drive real interest rates up in the already low-inflation country and down in the high-inflation country. As a result, this mechanism would cause inappropriate signals in both countries.

All the above arguments are, in fact, debateable. To the latter, the answer could be that the margin on either side of the official peg would allow for a time, immediately after the last realignment, the more inflationary country to maintain higher nominal interest rates. More generally, the result of joining for the UK would be determined (Goodhart, 1986) by the choice between a more or less "hard" or "soft" option. Particularly with a "wide band", or with more frequent realignments in the EMS, the inconvenience of full membership would be lighter. On the other hand, the softer the options were, the weaker would be the incentive for greater convergence and for stronger internal discipline.

For the European system itself, also, the entry of the UK would be important. first, from a technical point of view, Britain's full participation would provide a second reserve currency in the ECU. Some observers foresee a possible instability between rival currencies. But, on the contrary, sterling's entry would provide a wider basis of diversification, particularly if the speculative capital funds moved out of dollars. The position of the City of London as a world financial market in a more integrated European financial area would also be strengthened. All these internal considerations in favour of the UK's full membership are transcended by another more general argument: Britain's full participation in the EMS would reduce the risk of West German hegemony, a risk which still exists and which would be much more significant in future if capital movements were completely free among the EMS countries.

Liberalisation of capital movements: the new challenge for EMS

The EC Commission has recently adopted "directives" which stipulate the next stage towards total liberalisation of financial transactions in Europe. Italy, France and Belgium are chiefly concerned by this movement towards financial deregulation which, in addition, coincides with the French suppression of exchange controls. In reality, this new step could be decisive in inducing progress towards European Monetary Union and also in influencing progress towards convergence between the European member countries. At this level, it is important to emphasise that capital controls have been the central element of the eight preceding years of the EMS. In view of the two-tier exchange market in Belgium, refusal to allow foreign residents to borrow locally in France, Denmark and Italy, and miscellaneous regulations which limit investment abroad, free capital movements have been severely limited. One can really ask whether these prohibitions have not been the master work of the EMS since 1979. Following Rogoff (1985) or Giavezzi and Giovannini (1986), we have to conclude that restrictions intended to discourage arbitrage between the domestic and the offshore market have constituted the main obstacle to European portfolio diversification. They have been equivalent to a tax on holdings of foreign securities by domestic residents and have strongly increased the transaction costs for assets denominated in such currencies. Before each devaluation of the French franc, the Euro-franc rates, especially, have climbed to tremendous levels. Finally, it is obvious that the risk premium generated by restrictions on European capital movements has played a decisive role in limiting intra-European financial integration: it has prevented the equalisation of nominal interest rates and has allowed the member countries to safeguard a minimum degree of freedom in their monetary policies. This arrangement has proved to be very practical among partners which have had divergent inflation rates and also vis-à-vis the "n^{th} currency".

With full relinquishment of capital controls, the EMS would enter a new epoch: it is obvious that the constraints imposed by the EMS on member countries would become very much stronger than before. It was already demonstrated during the preceding years (Galy, 1986), in terms of Sargent and Haugh-Pierce tests, that nominal and real French interest rates (short and long) have been more and more determined since 1979 by West German rates[2]. This proves that the EMS, even before the liberalisation of capital movements, has led towards a partial hegemony of German monetary policy. Nevertheless, during this period, France and other member countries were able temporarily to resist some pressure from the "n^{th} currency" and to maintain some differences in nominal interest rates. In the near future, with free capital movements, the evolution might be quite different. If the risk premium and transaction costs on weak currencies were to disappear, the integrative capacity of the EMS would be greatly strengthened. Interest rates would then not only be strictly correlated, but in such circumstances, would tend to equate. Also, a delicate problem of assignment could intervene. If the members were to be affected by recurrent differences in flexibility or by wide discrepancies in competitiveness, one cannot clearly foresee how accommodating mechanisms could be developed without movements of factors, unless the exchange rate realignments themselves become more frequent.

9.4 Conclusion

Finally, we may take a look at the elements which together create what might be called "the dilemma of the EMS". If the EMS were to take the next step by freeing capital movements, it would accelerate progress toward monetary and economic integration. But, at this moment, to do so would risk increasing the hegemony of the DM and of the West German economy. The counterpart could then be an increase of internal tensions between the leader currency and its followers. The full entry of the UK would appear at this moment as a means of reequilibrating the EMS and of preventing it from becoming a DM monetary area. But, on the other hand, it appears that British entry might require a mechanism with a wide band or with internal crawling pegs. In such a case, it is no longer sure that the EMS would be able to play the same major role as it played during 1979-1986, when it ensured a real convergence of the member countries' inflation rates and, above all, promoted an internal discipline of costs and wages in even the most lax countries.

At this point, the importance of the challenge appears great: the EMS should enlarge and deepen its mechanisms but it is absolutely necessary to avoid two risks: at one extreme there is the danger of weakening

---

2) During 1973-1979, by contrast, interest rates were dependent on the American rates

the EMS by a too "soft" exchange rate agreement; on the other hand, the system must not become too rigid. At present, when the EMS is just on the verge of freeing capital movements, the choice of the right speed at which to complete this step is more crucial than ever.

References

P.A. Allen (1986), "The ECU: Birth of a New Currency", Group of Thirty

BIS (1986), Bank for International Settlements, 56th Annual Report

H. Bourguinat, M. Cazals and Ph. Ithurbide (1985), "L'entreprise française face aux variations de change: Dollar contre S.M.E.?" Economica 1985

S. Brittan (1986), "Fallacies on EMS Entry", Financial Times, 1 April

Commission of the European Communities (1984), "Five years of Monetary Cooperation in Europe; March 1979-March 1984", II 74/84-E

M. Galy (1986), "Contribution des facteurs externes à la détermination des taux d'intérêt" Cahiers économiques et monétaires de la Banque de France, no. 25

F. Giavezzi and A. Giovannini (1986), "The E.M.S. and the dollar", Economic Policy, April

Ch. Goodhart (1986), "Should the U.K. join the EMS?" Paris, Table Ronde du GRECO (Groupement de Recherches Coordonnées du CNRS), June

P. de Grauwe and G. Verfaille (1986), "The European Monetary System" - Table Ronde du GRECO (op.cit)

S. Micossi (1985), "The Intervention and Financial Mechanism of the EMS and the role of the ECU". Banca del Lavoro, December, no. 155

Morgan Guaranty Trust Company (1986), World Financial Markets, August

T. Padoa Schioppa (1985), "Policy Cooperation and the EMS Experience", in W.H. Buiter and R.C. Marston (eds) International Economic Policy Coordination, Cambridge, England, Cambridge University Press

K. Rogoff (1985), "Can Exchange Rate Predictability be achieved without monetary convergence? Evidence from the E.M.S.", European Economic Review, no. 28

M. Russo (1986), "Why the time is ripe". Lecture to the Bow Group, House of Commons, London, May 1986, mimeo

M. Scarcinelli (1986), "The EMS and the International Monetary System; toward greater stability", Banca del Lavoro No. 156, March

H.O. Ungerer, E. Evans and P. Nyberg (1983), "The European Monetary System: the experience of 1979-82" IMF, Occasional Papers, no. 19, May

Sir A. Walters (1986), Britain's economic renaissance: Margaret Thatcher's reforms 1979-1984, Oxford University Press, 1986

Table 9.1

Standard deviation of monthly changes of the effective real exchange rates (%s)

	Intra-EMS variability			Total variability		
	1973 March 1979 March	1979 April 1983 March	1983 April 1985 July	1973 March 1979 March	1979 April 1983 March	1983 April 1985 July
Belgium	1.0	0.8	0.5	1.0	0.9	0.5
Denmark	1.8	1.2	1.0	1.8	1.4	1.1
France	1.5	1.2	0.6	1.5	1.3	0.8
FR Germany	1.2	0.6	0.3	1.4	0.9	0.6
Ireland	2.3	0.9	0.5	1.3	1.5	1.1
Italy	2.1	0.9	0.8	1.8	0.9	0.7
Netherlands	0.9	0.8	0.4	0.9	0.9	0.7
UK	–	–	–	1.9	2.3	2
Japan	–	–	–	2.2	2.9	2.0
US	–	–	–	1.3	2.0	1.7

Source: World Financial Markets

Table 9.2

Short run variability of exchange rates[a]
(monthly data; March 1979-April 1986)

Currency with respect to:	ECU	US $
US $	2.82	–
DM	0.52	3.01
FF	0.78	3.10
HFL	0.49	3.00
LIT	0.71	2.72
UK £	1.98	2.86
BF	0.80	3.07
DKR	0.70	2.92
ECU	–	2.82

[a] Standard deviation calculated on monthly percentage changes

Source: EC Commission

Table 9.3

Short term real interest rates[a]
(monthly data in per cent)

		1972-1979	1979-1985	1983-1986[b]
UK	average	–2.78	3.09	5.4
	variance	185	91	20.9
France	average	–0.91	1.92	3.52
	variance	201.6	111.19	21
FRG	average	1.24	3.58	3.16
	variance	167.8	35	22
Netherlands	average	–1.12	3.65	3.50
	variance	312.2	40.6	25
Italy	average	–2.44	2.08	5.16
	variance	104.6	172.5	29
Belgium	average	–0.4	5.44	4.24
	variance	700	36,5	32.7
Ireland	average	–2.5	1.94	5.10
	variance	155	193	47.5
Denmark	average	–0.61	4.34	3.89
	variance	595	63	41.6

[a] Real interest rates are calculated by dividing the nominal interest rate by the rate of increase of the consumer price index in the preceding 12 months. Variance: standard deviation as per cent of mean.

[b] January 1983-March 1986.

Source: EC Commission and M. Russo (1986)

Table 9.4

Long term real interest rates[a]
(monthly data in per cent)

		1972-1979	1979-1985	1983-1986[b]
UK	average	−0.71	2.64	5.12
	variance	566	129.79	18.2
France	average	0.39	3.32	5.27
	variance	402	68.5	15.4
FRG	average	2.73	4.01	4.88
	variance	25.6	24.6	12.0
Netherlands	average	0.73	4.99	5.67
	variance	262	17.3	10.6
Italy	average	−2.5	1.76	3.50
	variance	141.6	170.4	24.6
Belgium	average	0.23	5.0	4.04
	variance	1233	16.8	17.8
Ireland	average	−0.83	1.83	5.40
	variance	394	201.6	32.65
Denmark	average	3.96	7.0	6.96
	variance	66.5	21.3	10.35

[a] Real interest rates are calculated by dividing the nominal interest rate by the rate of increase of the consumer price index in the preceding 12 months. Variance: standard deviation as per cent of mean.

[b] January 1983-March 1986.

Source: EC Commission and M. Russo (1986)

Table 9.5

Consumer prices: % change on preceding period

	1981	1982	1983	1984	1985	1985 IV	1986 I	1986 II	1986 III	Latest % change on year[a]
Belgium	7.6	8.7	7.7	6.3	4.9	0.3	0.2	0.1	0.2	0.9
Denmark	11.7	10.1	6.9	6.3	4.7	0.8	0.1	3.3	0.1	4.6
FR Germany	6.3	5.3	3.3	2.4	2.2	0.3	0	–0.3	–0.5	–0.9
France	13.4	11.8	9.6	7.3	5.9	0.6	0.1	0.7	0.6	2.1
Greece	24.5	21.0	20.5	18.3	19.4	9.7	6.0	4.3	2.0	21.9
Ireland	20.4	17.2	10.4	8.6	5.4	0.2	1.6	1.2	0.2	3.1
Italy	17.8	16.5	14.7	10.8	9.2	2.2	1.6	1.0	0.5	4.7
Luxembourg	8.1	9.4	8.7	5.6	4.2	0.9	–0.4	–0.6	–0.3	–1.0
Netherlands	6.7	5.7	2.7	3.2	2.3	0.6	–0.4	0.4	–0.9	–0.1
UK	11.9	8.6	4.6	5.0	6.1	0.5	0.7	1.3	0.1	3.0
EUR (12)	12.1	10.7	8.6	7.4	6.1	1.1	1.0	0.8	0.4	3.1
USA	10.3	6.2	3.2	4.3	3.6	0.9	0.2	–0.2	0.7	1.5
Japan	4.9	2.7	1.9	2.2	2.1	0.4	0	0.3	–0.5	–0.4

[a] Latest month shown against corresponding month of 1985

Source: EC Commission, *Tendances Conjuncturelles* Suppl. A, No. 12, December 1986

Table 9.6

Merchandise trade balances (cif/fob)
billion ECU (seasonally adjusted)

	1981	1982	1983	1984	1985	1985 IV	1986 I	1986 II	1986 III	Change 1986-III from 1985-III[a]
Belgium/ Luxembourg	–5.4	–3.1	–2.4	–4.9	–3.5	–0.8	–0.3	–0.3	0.1	+0.8
Denmark	–1.5	–1.9	–0.7	–1.1	–1.5	–0.5	–0.4	–0.6	–0.6	–0.3
FR Germany	11.2	21.6	18.5	24.1	33.0	9.4	10.8	13.3	14.7	+6.0
France	–17.3	–24.5	–15.6	–13.1	–13.4	–3.0	–2.3	–3.6	–2.6	+1.0
Greece	–4.0	–5.8	–5.8	–6.0	–7.3	–1.6	–1.9	–1.5	–1.6	0
Ireland	–2.5	–1.6	–0.6	0.1	0.4	0	0.3	0.1	0.2	+0.1
Italy	–13.6	–12.5	–8.5	–13.4	–16.1	–4.1	–2.8	–0.1	–0.5	+2.1
Netherlands	1.3	3.5	4.5	4.7	3.9	1.1	1.2	1.5	1.6	+0.6
UK	–0.4	–3.3	–9.7	–14.0	–11.5	–2.5	–3.4	–3.9	–5.8	–3.3
EUR (10)	–32.0	–27.5	–20.4	–24.1	–16.1	–2.1	1.0	5.0	6.5	+7.0
USA	–35.5	–43.4	–77.9	–155.0	–194.9	–47.8	–47.1	–42.2	–43.5	+41.4
Japan	7.8	7.0	23.1	42.6	60.5	17.3	16.8	20.3	21.9[b]	+6.7

[a] In billion ECU; + = improvement, – = worsening.

[b] June-August

Source: As Table 9.5

Table 9.7

Industrial production: % change from preceding period (seasonally adjusted)

	1981	1982	1983	1984	1985	1985 IV	1986 I	1986 II	1986 III	Latest % change on year[a]
Belgium	2.7	0	2.0	2.5	2.4	1.8	0.9	–0.3	1.3[b]	6.7
Denmark	0	2.7	3.2	9.7	4.2	1.8	–1.9	4.6	–3.7	0
FR Germany	–1.9	–2.9	0.6	3.0	5.7	0.8	–0.3	0.8	0	2.9
France	–2.3	–1.5	0.8	2.3	0.8	0	–1.2	1.5	2.2	4.5
Greece	–0.6	–4.2	–0.7	3.5	2.6	–1.1	–2.9	4.0	..	1.0
Ireland	5.4	–0.9	6.6	12.4	2.3	3.3	1.1	–0.4	1.7[b]	8.1
Italy	–1.6	–3.0	–3.2	3.4	1.2	0.2	3.7	0.6	–3.5	5.4
Luxembourg	–5.7	0.9	5.4	13.3	6.9	4.3	1.5	–0.8	..	0.8
Netherlands	–2.0	–4.1	3.2	4.1	4.0	2.6	1.9	–2.8	1.6	5.2
UK	–3.4	1.9	3.6	1.3	4.8	0	–0.8	–0.4	1.6	1.3
EUR (12)	–2.1	–1.4	1.1	2.6	3.4	0.8	–0.3	2.0	–0.4	2.1
USA	2.1	–7.4	7.8	11.9	2.5	0.5	0.8	0	0.8	2.2
Japan	1.0	0.3	3.6	11.1	4.6	–0.9	0.2	0.2	–0.9[b]	–3.1

[a] Latest month shown against corresponding month of 1985

[b] June-August

Source: As Table 9.5

Table 9.8

Bond issues in ECUs
($ million)

	ECU issues	Total issues	ECU %
1983	2,191.4	50,098.2	4.37
1984	2,937.5	81,717.2	3.59
1985	7,036.3	135,445.6	5.19

Source: OECD

Table 9.9

Bank assets and liabilities in ECU
($ million)

	Assets		Liabilities	
	Total	Non-banks	Total	Non-banks
December 1983	11.9	3.9	10	1.1
June 1984	20.9	6.3	16.5	1.7
December 1984	28.1	7.9	22.3	1.9
June 1985	38.8	9.9	33.4	4.3
December 1985	54.2	12.3	48.2	6.4

Source: Bank for International Settlements, 56th Annual Report

Chapter 10

THE NEW PROTECTIONISM WITH NONTARIFF INSTRUMENTS

Dominick Salvatore[1]

During the 1950s and 1960s the volume of international trade and the economies of most nations in the world, particularly the industrial countries, grew at an unprecedented rate. The merchandise trade of industrial countries grew at an average rate of about 8 per cent a year and this fuelled a growth in real GDP of over 4 per cent a year. This period can truly be regarded as a golden age of growth and stability.

The growth of international trade was made possible by successive rounds of trade liberalisation achieved under the Dillon Round (1960-1), the Kennedy Round (1964-7), and by the Tokyo Round (1974-7). Tariffs were cut until today they are less than 5 per cent on most industrial products. Effective tariffs (i.e., tariffs on value added) are somewhat higher than nominal tariffs but they are still very low both in absolute terms and by historical standards. Generally resisting liberalisation has been trade in agricultural commodities.

The general trend toward trade liberalisation was reversed, however, from 1975, when the world faced the deepest world-wide recession since the Great Depression of the 1930s[2]. This gave rise to what has come to be known as the "new protectionism", characterised by the imposition of many new nontariff barriers (NTBs) in the form of "voluntary" export restraints, orderly marketing arrangements, antidumping measures, countervailing duties, and so on, as industrial nations sought to protect industry after industry from the adjustments required by international trade in a climate of slow domestic growth and rising unemployment.

Thus, while tariffs were being reduced on most industrial goods as part of the Tokyo Round of trade negotiations, the number and importance of NTBs have grown so rapidly that they have now become more important than tariffs as obstructions to international trade. This fact did not go unnoticed during the Tokyo negotiations, and indeed codes were negotiated to restrict and regulate the use of NTBs. These codes, however, failed to stem the tide of new NTBs, to the point where today these represent

---

1) Chairman and Professor, Department of Economics, Fordham University, New York

2) The Annual Report on Exchange Rates of the IMF for the year 1975 was the first to find a larger number of increases than declines in restrictions on international trade.

the most serious threat to the postwar trading system and world welfare (Salvatore, 1986a, chapters 9 and 20).

From 1975 to 1979, world trade grew at about 5 per cent a year (as opposed to an average of 8 per cent during the previous two and a half decades), and fell to a yearly average growth of about 3 per cent from 1980 to 1985. Until now, the slowing down of the great trade engine of growth can be attributed mostly to the reduced growth of the world economy rather than to the rise in protectionism (though *causality generally runs both ways*). The great danger, however, is that the continued proliferation of NTBs will lead to sharp retaliation and result in an actual decline in world trade, as nations revert more and more to bilateral trade deals. This will result in a misallocation of resources internationally, a slowdown in structural adjustments in mature economies and in growth in developing economies, and in an increasing threat of a trade war in which all nations would stand to lose (Salvatore, 1986b).

There is also the danger that trade restrictions (inappropriately) applied to protect domestic employment during recessionary periods will not be eliminated once the recession ends. There will then be a recession-protection ratchet effect: a recession leads to protection but the end of the recession will not lead to the removal of the protection. Until now, demands for protection have often been successfully resisted by governments with the well-known arguments for the benefits of free trade and for fear of foreign retaliation. Exceptions are made for several mature industrial sectors such as textiles, steel, and automobiles. The danger is that the list may greatly expand in the future. Even the Reagan administration, in spite of its alleged adherence to the free market and thus to free trade, has imposed significant new trade restrictions in the form of NTBs.

In section 10.1 we briefly examine the major forms of nontariff trade barriers in the United States and in other industrial countries. In section 10.2 we explore the causes of the new protectionism and examine some of its effects. In section 10.3 we present econometric results on the causes and effects of one of the few readily quantifiable forms of NTBs - the escape clause petition for trade protection in the United States. Section 10.4 explores the relationship between the new protectionism and industrial policies in the major industrial countries. Section 10.5 examines how the new protectionism is likely to shape the future international trade regime. The general conclusions from the paper follow.

10.1 Nontariff trade barriers and the present international trade regime

The original conception of the postwar trade regime was to set up an International Trade Organisation (ITO) to oversee and regulate all trade distortions. The General Agreement on Tariffs and Trade (GATT) was instead created with a more limited scope. GATT sanctioned "grandfather" clauses, such as the US escape clause provisions and the Antidumping Act of 1921, and allowed other deviations from the liberal design, such as the EEC Common Agricultural Policy (CAP). In fact, GATT lacks even the mandate to compile a comprehensive list of all nontariff trade barriers in existence in member countries.

Current trade restrictions can be classified as tariff barriers, explicit nontariff barriers, and implicit nontariff barriers. As noted above, *tariff barriers* are now very low as a result of successful rounds of multilateral trade negotiations. Nontariff barriers (both explicit and implicit) have increased very rapidly, however, during the past decade while tariffs were being reduced. *Explicit nontariff trade barriers* generally refer to quotas, "voluntary" export restraints (VERs), and safeguards (such as antidumping measures, countervailing duties, and orderly marketing arrangements). These are either directly subject to GATT rules (e.g. quotas) or are recognised as being subject to the rules of the present international trade regime. Here, some degree of consensus exists as to what constitutes a fair or an unfair practice. Safeguard arrangements are covered by Article XIX of GATT, but the regulations are often disregarded. For example, according to GATT rules, a nation adversely affected by foreign safeguards is allowed to retaliate or demand a compensating reduction in other foreign tariffs. In fact, no such compensation usually takes place through prior bilateral agreement. This tends to undermine GATT and to sacrifice the interests of third parties.

While explicit nontariff trade barriers present considerable difficulties for GATT and for the functioning of the international trade regime, it is implicit nontariff trade barriers that lead to the greatest problems and controversies. *Implicit nontariff trade barriers* cover all those administrative regulations that are imposed to achieve some domestic objective, such as assistance to a domestic industry (e.g. steel) facing structural difficulties and large declines in employment, and without the declared intention of limiting imports, but which, nevertheless, discriminate against foreign suppliers and end up by limiting imports. Examples of these are government subsidies, discriminatory procurement regulations, discriminatory application of health and safety standards, and all those regulations of the domestic banking and distribution systems that favour domestic over foreign firms. Not only do the trade effects of these regulations often defy quantification, but sometimes it is impossible even to identify them without detailed analysis of all the policies followed by each government. Even then a great deal of disagreement remains on whether a particular trade-distorting domestic measure does or does not represent an implicit NTB. Claiming interference with their internal affairs, nations often refuse to provide information on what they regard as purely internal regulations and sometimes refuse to acknowledge even the existence of these regulations. Needless to say, there is strong disagreement on whether or not to include these regulations in international trade negotiations and on what standards of fairness to apply.

During the Tokyo Round negotiations, the United States pressed to make these implicit trade restrictions more transparent and to turn them into explicit barriers by devising rules of behaviour to fall under the jurisdiction of GATT. Among the results of the negotiations was a new code on government procurement. One of the first and most important applications of the new code concerned the purchase of telecommunications equipment between United States and Japan. Here and in other cases the new code provided only limited success and failed to overcome long-standing disagreements. As a result, the field of implicit nontariff trade barriers remains one of the most controversial and potentially dangerous aspects of the present international trade system.

Very serious problems also exist in agricultural trade due to widespread domestic subsidy programmes. As it is well known, most nations have very elaborate domestic agricultural support programmes and jealously shield their agriculture from outside competition by a powerful array of subsidies, tariffs, quotas, health regulations, and so on. Particularly troublesome, and the source of much conflict, are the EC's Common Agricultural Policy (CAP) and the US farm subsidy programme, especially the former. CAP covers 90 per cent of EC agricultural production and guarantees uniform prices, generally above world prices, throughout the Community. Imports of agricultural commodities are severely limited by a system of quotas and variable tariffs that make agricultural commodities from non-members as expensive as Community products. Subsidies are then utilised to encourage the Community's export of surplus agricultural commodities (OECD 1982).

While in the 1960s the United States was willing to accept the burden that CAP imposed on itself in order to favour European unification, it grew increasingly critical in the 1970s and 1980s of a system that sharply restricted US export of agricultural commodities to the EC and to the rest of the world. To be sure, the problems over agricultural trade and US exports are also the result of the US's own price support programme, which sets a floor beneath prices of many agricultural commodities, and of the large overvaluation of the dollar during the first half of the 1980s. But the entrance of Spain and Portugal into the EC and the potential loss of another 1 billion dollars of agricultural exports by the US brought renewed trade tensions, with the US threatening retaliation against an equal amount of EC exports to the United States. This heightened trade tension came at a very delicate time and threatened the planned opening in September 1986 of an ambitious new round of multilateral trade negotiations. For its part, the EC has expressed its willingness to start new global trade-freeing negotiations covering agriculture, but demanded that the US also be ready to cut its own subsidies and protectionist measures that benefit its farmers.

Much more data are available on explicit nontariff trade barriers than on implicit NTBs, and we will now concentrate on the former. (We return to the analysis of implicit nontariff trade barriers in sections 10.4 and 10.5.)

Despite the availability of more data on explicit NTBs, it is impossible to estimate the tariff equivalent of all explicit NTBs because of their nontransparency and also because their effect varies over the course of the business cycle. Most studies attempting to measure explicit NTBs have focussed on identifying the share of world trade in manufactured exports that is subject to explicit NTBs. *Table 10.1* presents two such estimates.

Table 10.1

Consumption of restricted manufactured goods as a percentage of total consumption of manufactured goods

	US	EC	Japan
1980	20.3	23.7	15.7
1981	32.7	26.0	15.7
1982	34.8	26.3	15.7
1983	35.0	28.0	15.7

Source: Balassa and Balassa (1984).

US	Italy	France	UK	W. Germany	Canada	Japan
34.1	33.7	27.2	22.1	19.5	9.6	7.4

Source: Cline (1984). Estimates for 1983.

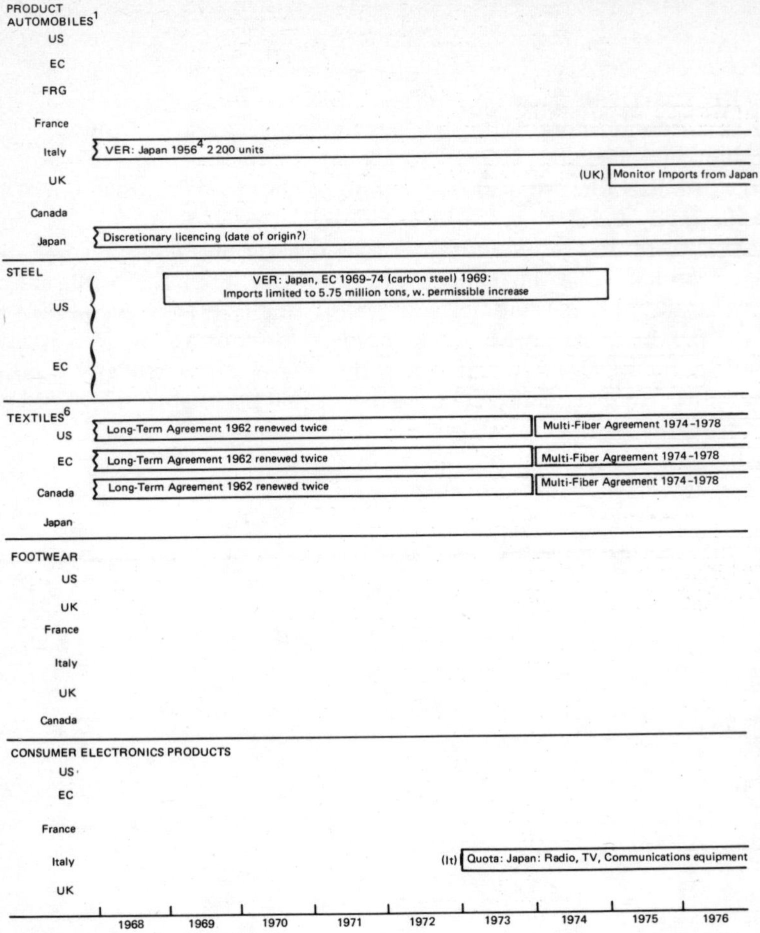

1. See chapter 7 of source for interpretation.
2. Extented for period 4/1/84-31/3/85.
3. Does not supersede ongoinig bilateral agreements implementedby individual member countries.
4. May precade 1956. The restraint agreements were grandfathered in GATT when Italy joined.
5. Private sector agreement carried out by two trade associations, supported by the Government.
6. See chapter 6 of source for details on bilateral agreements.

BPS - Basic Price System
EC - European Community
LDC - Less Developed Country
OMA - Orderly Marketing Agreement
QR - Quantitative Restriction
T+Q - Tariffs and Quotas
UR - Unilateral Restraint
VTR - Video Tape Recorder
VER - Voluntary Export Restraint
VRA - Voluntary Restraint Agmt.

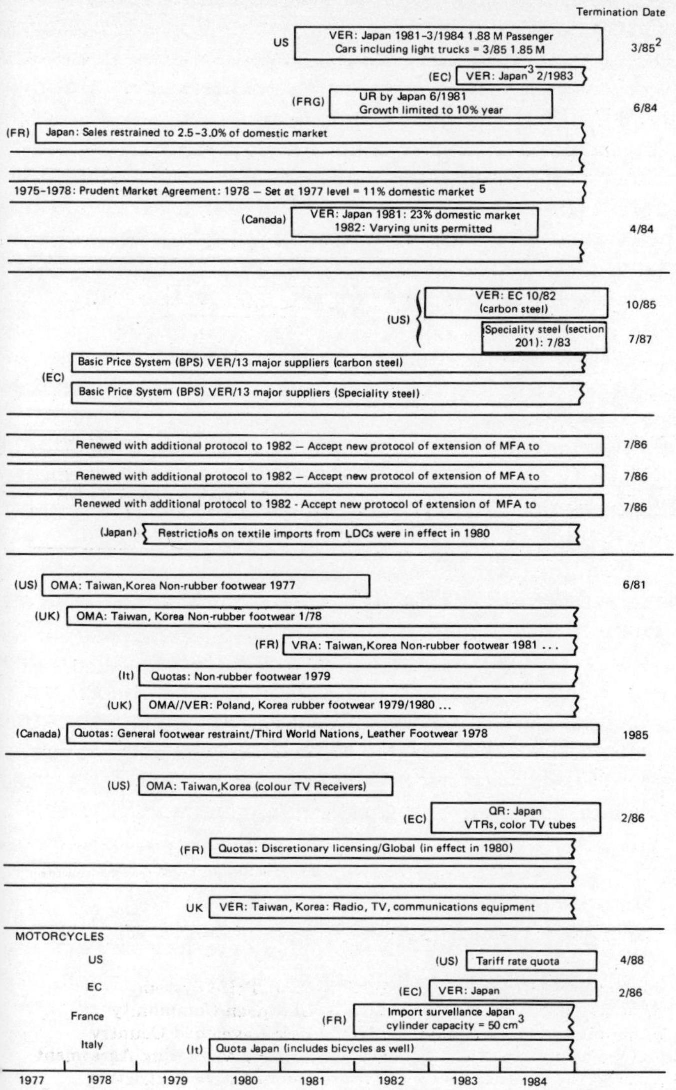

Source: OECD, Costs and Benefits of Protection (1985), pp. 32-33

The top part of the Table shows that the share of total consumption of manufactured goods subject to NTBs is higher in the US than in the EC, and much higher than in Japan, and it has increased sharply since 1980. The bottom part of the table shows somewhat different estimates for 1983 (from another study) for the seven largest industrial market economies. The differences between the two sets of estimates are due to the differences in definitions and methodologies in the two studies[3]. The much lower figure generally reported in most studies for Japan is said to reflect the fact that Japan relies much more heavily than the United States on implicit rather than explicit NTBs. Indeed, according to some, it could be argued that all Japanese trade is managed (Page, 1981, p. 29). In general, NTBs are more overt in the US than in other countries. Thus, the figures in *Table 10.1* reflect only acknowledged or explicit NTBs.

Table 10.2 summarises the products affected and the pattern of NTBs. It shows that the patterns of NTB protection are broadly similar in the major industrial countries. The products involved are textiles, apparel, steel, and more recently, automobiles, machine tools and electronic consumer products. According to OECD (1985), explicit NTBs (mostly in the form of VERs) have quadrupled from 1968 to 1983. For the most part, they have been directed at Japan and the Asian NICs (S. Korea, Taiwan, Hong Kong, Singapore). OPEC also reported that the percentages of these nations' exports affected by VERs and orderly market arrangements more than doubled (from 15 to over 30 per cent) between 1980 and 1983. As experience of successive Multi Fibre Arrangements (MFA) shows, the scope of these explicit NTBs has constantly expanded until today more than 43 supplier nations are affected by bilateral agreements and the number of product categories specified is more than 50. At the same time, the yearly increase in imports allowed under successive MFAs has been sharply reduced and restrictions against dominant suppliers have tightened considerably.

10.2 Causes and effects of NTBs

From the above discussion, it is clear that nontariff barriers are much less transparent and quantifiable than tariff barriers. It is in this basic difference between tariff barriers and NTBs that we must seek

---

3) The estimates of restricted imports as a percentage of total manufactured imports differ widely between the two studies. Balassa and Balassa put their estimate for the United States at about 13 per cent, while Cline puts it at about 45 per cent. Other studies (see, for example, the 1981 one by Page) report still different results. Most studies, however, do find that the size and scope of NTBs have increased significantly since the mid-1970s.

the cause of their opposing trends, in number and significance, over the past decade. Specifically, since the mid-1970s, recession, slow growth, and increased competition from Japan and the NICs have led to large employment losses in such large and mature industries as textiles, steel, and automobiles in industrial nations, and this has led to irresistible demands for protection[4]. Industrial nations have responded with sharp increases in NTBs (at the same time as tariff barriers were reduced) in order to minimise the apparent departure from the principle of an open, multilateral trading system. Thus, while cyclical conditions, and large and growing pockets of unemployment in industrial nations, were the cause of the increased demand for protection, their response with more NTBs as instruments of protection can be related to their desire to preserve at least the appearance of continued movement toward trade liberalisation. Nontariff trade restrictions also seem to have been utilised, at least in part, to compensate for negotiated tariff reductions, while at the same time by-passing Article XIX of GATT which permits safeguard measures only on a non-discriminatory basis.

One of the most common and increasingly used forms of NTBs is the "voluntary" export restraint (VER). This is used to limit exports of textiles, apparel, steel, automobiles, consumer electronics, and other products. Though these restrains are called "voluntary", they are essentially quotas imposed on the exports of a specific product, from a particular nation, for a given period of time, and under the administration of the exporting country. The exporting nation accepts these restrictions out of fear or threat of even more stringent and direct restrictions on its exports. The most clearcut example (and the one on which most information is available) is the VER imposed by the US on automobile imports from Japan. This is briefly described below[5].

In April 1981, the US negotiated with Japan a VER that limited Japanese automobile exports to the US to 1.68 million units a year for three years. In April 1984, the restraint was renewed for another year, 1.85 million automobile exports being allowed. These restraints were deemed essential at a time when the US automobile industry was incurring huge losses and almost 250 000 of its workers were idled by Japanese imports. In 1985, the US decided not to press Japan to continue its quota on auto exports. Japan, however, in an effort to ease trade frictions with the US, decided unilaterally to limit automobile exports to the US to

---

4) As pointed out in section 10.4, rising protectionism since the mid-1970s can also be traced to widely fluctuating and disequilibrium exchange rates.

5) An in-depth analysis of Japanese automobile trade with the US is presented by Feenstra (1986).

2.3 million units per year, or 24 per cent of the US market. This self-imposed limitation was still in effect in July 1986. As shown in *Table 10.2*, Japanese automobile exports have been even more severely restricted with VERs by Italy, France, UK, and West Germany. Today, practically the entire international trade in automobiles (which is about 8 per cent of total trade in manufactures) is "managed".

More generally, the causes and effects of VERs can be examined by the use of *Chart 10.1* (adapted and extended from Hamilton, 1985a). Dh is the demand curve for a homogeneous importable commodity (say, a particular grade of steel) in the home country, Sh is the home supply curve of the commodity, while Shu is the home supply curve of the commodity *plus* the export supply curve of the commodity to the home country from countries whose exports are unrestrained. Finally, St is the total supply curve of the commodity to the home country. It includes the home supply curve of the commodity plus the supply curve of exports of the commodity to the home country from *all* of the rest of the world, including the dominant-supplier country whose exports to the home country are restrained with a VER. Note that since St is positively sloped, it is assumed that the home country is sufficiently large to affect the supply price of exports from other countries, including the dominant-exporting country.

From the Chart, we see that in the absence of the VER (i.e., before the VER is negotiated) or of other trade restrictions on imports of the commodity, the price of the importable commodity in the home country is OA and consumption is AE, of which the home country produces AB, imports BC from countries other than the dominant-supply country, and CE from the dominant-supply country. Suppose that now the home country wants to increase the domestic production of the importable commodity

Chart 10.1

The effects of a VER

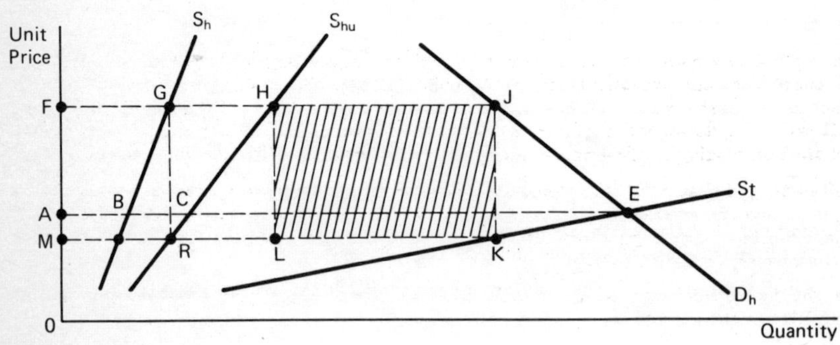

from AB to FG by negotiating a VER with the dominant-supply country only[6]. To expand domestic production from AB to FG, the home country must negotiate a VER that restricts the exports of the dominant-supply country from CE to HJ. The price in the home country then rises from OA to OF and consumption falls to FJ, of which FG is produced domestically, GH is imported without restriction from other than the dominant-supply countries, and HJ from the dominant-supply country. Thus, the exports of countries other than the dominant-supply country expand, while those of the dominant-supply country contracts when compared to the free-trade case. This is often observed in the real world and often leads to the subsequent extension of the VER to other supplying countries. For example, when steel exports from Japan to the US were restricted, exports from other nations, especially S. Korea and other NICs, increased, and this led to VERs against S. Korea and other nations as well[7].

Because of the large-country assumption for the home country, the dominant-supply country would be willing to supply the lower negotiated quantity of exports (HJ as compared with CE) at the price of OM (as compared with OA under free trade). However, since the VER is administered by the exporting country, the dominant-supply country will export the commodity at the price of OF, so that the recipients of export licences in the dominant-supply country earn the rent of FM=JK per unit and JKLH in total (the area of the shaded rectangle in the figure). Had the home country tried to increase domestic output from AB to FG by imposing the more traditional *import* quota of HJ on the export of the dominant-supply country, it would itself have collected the JKLH in revenue. If the home country had imposed instead a *global* quota of GJ on import from *all* countries, it would have collected the JKRG in revenue. In any event, the *ad valorem* tariff equivalent of the import quota on the dominant-supply country, of the global import quota, or of the VER on the dominant-supply country is FM/MO[8].

The above analysis can help us to understand better the reasons for this rising popularity of VERs during the past decade. Even though

6) The home country may want to do this in order to reduce unemployment in the industry, or to counteract the tendency of productivity increases to result in unemployment in the fact of sluggish growth in the demand for the output of the industry. Negotiating a VER with the dominant-supplier country means that other countries can continue to export the commodity to the home country without restrictions. This is often the case.

7) It is often alleged that since NICs have little bargaining power vis-à-vis industrial countries, there is a greater predisposition on the part of the latter to impose additional NTBs on the exports of the former rather than on each other's exports. This seems to have been the case especially in textiles.

8) While the figure has been drawn so that the tariff equivalent of the import quotas and of the VER are the same, this need not be the case.

the home country fails to collect any rent, since the VER is supposedly voluntary, it allows the home country to bypass the GATT regulation that forbids quantitative and discriminatory import restrictions[9)]. The country against which the VER is imposed also seems to find VERs preferable to facing the risk of possible stronger and more permanent trade restrictions. In addition, the rent collected by exporters creates a constituency in the exporting country that lobbies the government for the retention of the VERs[10)]. Finally, we can see from the chart that the non-restrained countries also benefit from a larger volume of exports to the home country and from higher export prices. The losers are, of course, consumers in the country that imposes VERs because of the restricted range of imports and higher prices[11)]. However, as is well known, consumers are very numerous and cannot usually organise themselves as effectively in resisting VERs as producers of the domestic import-competing product can in lobbying for trade restraints. In addition, since producers are much fewer in number, they stand to gain much more individually than single consumers stand to lose from a trade restraint. As a result, the incentive for producers to organise, and the resources that they have at their disposal, are also likely to be much greater than for consumers.

It is possible that some governments which are opposed to more permanent trade restrictions agree to negotiate VERs in order to appease their more vocal constituency while minimising actual restrictions on international trade. Specifically, a government may originally negotiate a VER with the dominant-supplier country only. Over the years, however, the supply of exports shifts to unrestrained nations, and by the time VERs are negotiated with these other nations as well, several years may have passed, thus giving the domestic import-competing industry time

---

9) It must be pointed out, however, that while VERs are not against the letter of GATT they are certainly against its intent.

10) So strong is this interest group that when the US declined to ask Japan to extend the VER on automobiles past the deadline of April 1985, Japan decided to continue it (at an increased rate). It is true that Japan did this in order to avoid greater trade conflicts with the US, but the suspicion remains that, on balance, Japan found this arrangement beneficial. However, since export licences are usually distributed to firms according to their past volumes of exports, with only periodic and incomplete adjustments to reflect relative changes in efficiency among exporters, domestic resources in the exporting country are not likely to be utilised most efficiently with a VER. There is, in addition, the welfare loss from society's point of view due the lobbying itself and the bribery and corruption to which VERs and other NTBs usually give rise.

11) For example, since a VER is imposed on the volume rather than on the value of exports, Japanese automobile firms began to export more expensive automobiles to the United States (i.e., they moved up-market or upgraded their exports). To the extent that this increased quality and higher price were "forced" on US consumers, there was a reduction in consumer welfare.

for restructuring and for its displaced workers to be absorbed into other industries. Whether or not we can impute these lofty motives to the actions of some governments, the substitution that we in fact observe from constrained to non-constrained sources of supply, when a discriminatory VER or other NTB is imposed, does indeed provide a safety valve or escape mechanism that may prevent even more stringent and permanent increases in traditional tariffs and import quotas. This strategic benefit from the use of VERs results, however, only if they are temporary and very selective in nature. If they become more or less permanent and more widespread, even this questionable second-best benefit of VERs and other NTBs over more traditional forms of protection vanishes. It must also be pointed out that a given VER becomes less and less restrictive (as contrasted to a given tariff rate) in declining industries (the predominant type of industry where VERs have been applied).

Other arguments for, and justifications of, VERs or other NTBs readily fall to the ground when juxtaposed with accepted theoretical arguments in favour of free or freer trade. For example, when the positive response of most industrial nations to demand for protectionism with more NTBs is related to legitimate concern for domestic equity and income distribution, trade theory clearly prescribes that where divergences between private and social costs and benefits are domestic in nature, taxation and subsidisation at the point of divergence rather than trade intervention is the first-best policy[12)]. Similarly, the difficulties faced by large and mature industries in industrial countries today can more effectively be overcome by subsidies to stimulate structural adjustment than by NTBs. While NTBs are less quantifiable and sometimes (as in the case of implicit NTBs) less identifiable, their effects on prices, production, employment, balance of trade and payments, and comparative advantage are generally the same as for more traditional trade restraints. These are well known and are not repeated here. We are primarily interested here in the differential causes and effects of NTBs as compared with traditional tariffs and import quotas, *because of NTBs' inherently less identifiable and measurable characteristics.*

As pointed out by OECD (1985), the new protectionism has had only limited success in protecting domestic employment when compared with the employment effect of changes in macroeconomic circumstances. For example, it was estimated that the US-Japan VER on automobiles resulted in an increase of 22,000 jobs in the US at a time when recession was

---

12) See, Bhagwati (1971). Not everyone subscribes to this, however. The Cambridge Economic Policy Group (CEPG), in particular, believes that in cases of real wage rigidity, protection represents the only effective way for an industrial nation, such as the UK, to escape balance of payments and domestic unemployment problems.

reducing employment by more than ten times that amount. Protection also accelerated the substitution of capital for labour in production, further reducing employment. For example, OECD pointed out that the capital-labour ratio in the textile industry (perhaps the most highly protected industry in industrial countries today) has gone from being well below the manufacturing average in the 1950s to about 20 per cent above it in the 1980s. This capital deepening, together with a slowly rising demand for textiles, accounts for over two-thirds of the decline in employment in this industry. Thus changes in import penetration have had only a minor effect on employment. Furthermore, while one of the alleged most important objectives of the new protectionism is to allow mature industries to reorganise along more rational lines, it actually provided the incentive to attract more firms into these industries. For example, more than one-third of the textile firms in existence in the US in 1982 have been established since 1976, and in France more than one-fifth of new manufacturing firms are in textiles. The new protectionism has also a way of becoming ever more inclusive, as firms shift their operations to other nonprotected nations and products. Thus, the Orderly Marketing Arrangement for colour television which the US originally aimed at Japan was subsequently extended to S. Korea and Taiwan and it also seems to have deterred other nations, such as Mexico and Singapore, from entering the market.

The rapid rise and spread of the new protectionism, or neo-mercantilism, that we have seen during the past decade is also inextricably intertwined with the most important and crucial policy controversies that the US and other industrial countries are now facing and are likely to continue to face in the foreseeable future. These include proposals for a domestic industrial policy; the calls for stabilising exchange rates in general, and the international value of the dollar in particular; the need to deal with the threat to the mature industrial countries, particularly the US, emanating from the NICs; disagreements on how to solve the world debt problem; and the calls for reform of the international economic system. These relationships have already been analysed in detail in Salvatore (1986b) by some of the world's most distinguished international economists[13)]; we will summarise and extend that discussion in sections 10.4 and 10.5.

Before moving on to those topics, however, it may be useful to analyse the causes and effects of one particular type of NTB - the escape clause trade complaints and actions under the escape clause in the US. The reason for concentrating on this is that it is one of the few quantifiable

---

13) Among these are: M. Bailey, B. Balassa, R. Baldwin, J. Bhagwati, J. Bilson, W. Branson, M. Corden, R. Cooper, A. Deardorff, O. Emminger, G. Helleiner, L. Klein, M. Kreinin, P. Krugman, R. McKinnon, M. Michaely, M. Mussa, R. Stern.

forms of nontariff protection, with data going back to 1948. The hope is that studying this form of NTB will shed some additional light on the causes and effects of other more recent but less quantifiable forms of nontariff protection.

10.3 Escape clause petitions and US import trade

In the US, tariff protection is most common in low-skill-intensive industries in which the US has a comparative disadvantage. These industries are generally concentrated in only one or a few regions of the nation and, because of this, they have limited political influence. On the other hand, NTBs are concentrated in large and mature industries producing fairly homogeneous products with capital-intensive production techniques, with labour of medium skill level, and located in many regions (hence their greater political influence). One important type of NTB is the VER (examined in the previous section). Another is the escape clause procedures set up under US trade legislation.

Section 201 of the Trade Act of 1974 establishes an escape clause procedure, whereby an industry may petition the US Tariff Commission (USTC) to conduct an investigation to determine if the domestic industry is being, or is likely to be, injured by increased imports[14]. If the USTC finds injury or the threat of injury, it recommends to the President the import restriction (a tariff, an import quota, or an orderly marketing arrangement) and/or the adjustment assistance that it deems necessary to remedy or prevent the injury to the domestic industry. The President may accept the recommendation of the USTC, may impose a different remedy, or choose not to protect the industry.

The US may also protect a domestic industry from unfair competition from abroad resulting from dumping or subsidised exports by imposing countervailing duties. These are called "less than fair value" (LFV) cases because the trade practices that they are intended to control involve, in legal terms, the sale of products to the US at less than "fair value". LFV clauses go back to the Antidumping Act of 1921 and the Tariff Act of 1930 which were "grandfathered" into GATT. In these cases countervailing duties are automatically imposed upon the determination of the USTC that dumping or subsidised exports are injuring or likely to injure a domestic industry. LFV cases are much more numerous than escape clause cases, but the latter are much larger, on average, and affect twice as much

---

14) Such an escape clause was established by executive order from 1948 to 1951, by section 7 of the Trade Agreements Act of 1951, and by section 301(b) of the Trade Expansion Act of 1962.

trade as the former. Between 1948 and 1985, there have been 209 escape clause petitions and investigations, of which 69 were affirmative and 32 led to some trade action being taken to relieve domestic industry.

In order to analyse the causes and effects of escape clause petitions and actions, we estimated the two-equation model presented in *Table 10.3.*Before examining the table, however, we should note the changes in the trade laws introduced by the Trade Expansion Act of 1962 and the Trade Act of 1974. The Trade Expansion Act of 1962 (in operation from 1963 to 1974) required that the escape clause petitioner *demonstrate that injury was due to increased imports that resulted primarily from the trade concessions negotiated under the Act.* This clause was removed from the Trade Act of 1974 (in operation from 1975 to 1979), thus easing the criteria for filing escape clause petitions and for receiving a favourable ruling.

Table 10.3

Model of escape clause actions in US import trade: 1948-1985

(1) $N_t = 13.363 - \underset{(0.066)}{0.329Y_t} + \underset{(2.606)}{3.110S_{t-1}} - \underset{(0.995)}{3.898D62} + \underset{(1.369)}{4.159D74}$

$R^2 = 0.68$ SEE = 2.47 DW = 2.24

(2) $M_t = 0.00412 - \underset{(0.00020)}{0.00046N_t} - \underset{(0.00493)}{0.00076S_t} + \underset{(0.00167)}{0.00163R_{t-1}} + \underset{(0.04026)}{0.98757M_{t-1}}$

$R^2 = 0.96$ SEE = 0.0048 Durbin h = 0.25

Legend:

M = Import penetration measured by the ratio of the value of imports to GNP
N = Number of escape clause protection petitions
S = Ratio of successful escape clause petitions to number of petitions
R = Dummy variable assuming value of 1 for years of dollar overvaluation
Y = Level of real GNP in the US
D62 = Dummy variable assuming value of 1 for years 1963 to 1974 (for the Trade Expansion Act of 1962)
D74 = Dummy variable assuming value of 1 for years 1975 to 1979 (for the Trade Act of 1974)

Numbers in parenthesis are standard errors

Equation (1) shows that the number of escape clause petitions filed in a given year is inversely related to the level of real economic activity in the US in the same year and to the change in the trade laws instituted by the Trade Expansion Act of 1962; but it is directly related to the number of successful escape clause petitions in the previous year and changes in the trade laws under the Trade Act of 1974. This is exactly as predicted on theoretical grounds. That is, in years of strong economic activity and employment expansion, it is reasonable to expect fewer escape clause petitions to be filed. On the other hand, the larger is the ratio of successful petitions in a given year, the larger is likely to be the number of petitions filed during the following year; that is, successes encourage more petitions because the greater is the perceived return and incentive for filing.

As predicted, the coefficient of the dummy variable for the years during which the Trade Expansion Act of 1962 was in operation is negative, reflecting the more stringent provision of the Act for filing escape clause petitions and for receiving a favourable ruling. The opposite is the case for the coefficient of the dummy variable for the years during which the Trade Act of 1974 was in operation. Thus, all of the estimated coefficients of equation (1) have the correct sign, and all, except the coefficient of the ratio of success variable, are statistically significant at better than the 1 per cent level. The Durbin-Watson statistic indicates the absence of serial correlation in the error terms, and the regression "explains" 68 per cent of the variation in the number of petitions filed during the period of the study.

Equation (2) shows that the level of import penetration in a given year is inversely related to the number of escape clause petitions filed and to the ratio of successful petitions in the same year, but it is directly related to the dummy variable for the years during which the dollar was overvalued (R) lagged one year and to the level of import penetration in the previous year. The number of escape clause petitions filed gives a measure of protectionist *pressure* (the "harassment" thesis), while the ratio of successful petitions can be taken as a measure of the *degree* of actual protectionism. Thus, equation (2) postulates that import penetration will be smaller, the greater the levels of protectionist pressure and of actual protection. Variable R is lagged one year because it is well-established that it usually takes from 12 to 18 months for the trade balance (and, therefore, for the level of import penetration) to be significantly affected by exchange rate changes[15]. Equation (2) also postulates that import penetration in a given year is directly related to the import penetration in the previous year. The introduction of the lagged dependent as an explanatory variable in equation (2) results from taking all right-hand variables (RHVs) in equation (2) as expected values, with expectations generally formed on the basis of a distributed lag of current and past values of the RHVs.

From *Table 10.3*, we see that while all the estimated coefficients of equation (2) have the correct sign, only the coefficient of the number of petitions filed and the level of import penetration in the previous year are statistically significant at better than the 5 per cent level. The ratio of successful petitions was nearly significant only at the 10 per cent level. The lack of significance of this variable was not due to multicollinearity with the number of petitions filed, since removing the latter did not increase the statistical significance of the former. The lagged dummy for years of dollar overvaluation has the correct sign but is not statistically significant. Substitution of each year's value for this variable results in a negative sign (confirming the postulated inverse J-curve effect), but is also statistically insignificant. This does not mean, of course, that overvaluation of the dollar has no effect on import penetration, but rather that the pattern of response is too complex to be captured by the use of a simple dummy. Since the Durbin h is statistically insignificant, no serial correlation correction was necessary in estimation because of the presence of the lagged dependent among the explanatory variables (Johnston, 1984, 360-262). The coefficient of multiple correlation is 96 per cent, but equation (2) suffers from the presence of a dominant variable (the lagged dependent).

Two important conclusions follow from the estimation of the above model. The first is that the demand for escape clause protection is cyclical

---

15) During the first year of overvaluation, lower-priced imports and higher-priced exports could temporarily narrow the nation's trade deficit (the inverse J-curve effect). It would have been much more useful to use the actual exchange rate of the dollar to measure its effect on the US trade balance and import penetration. A dummy variable had to be used, however, because the model is to be empirically tested for the period from 1948 to 1985 and the exchange rate of the dollar was fixed until 1971. The US dollar was generally overvalued during the years 1958-60, 1969-1972, 1975-77, and 1982-85 (see, Cline, 1980, chapter 3). For the 1958-60 subperiod, the overvaluation of the dollar was inferred from the sharp worsening of the trade balance during those years. It is well known that the floating exchange rates that prevailed among industrial countries from 1971 did not result, in general, in equilibrium exchange rates.

in nature, rising or falling with the level of domestic economic activity. The second is the confirmation of the harassment thesis. That is, the possibility of filing an escape clause complaint is in itself effective in reducing import penetration, independently of the rate of success in actually obtaining a favourable ruling. This is consistent with results of other empirical studies utilising cross-section industry data for LFV cases in the US (Finger, 1981, and Herander and Schwarz, 1984). Both conclusions were anticipated on theoretical grounds and both have important implications for the functioning of the present and future international trade regime.

10.4 The new protectionism and industrial policies

There is a close link between the new protectionism, especially that of the implicit NTB type, and the call for industrial policies in industrial countries. As is well known, an important aspect of an industrial policy involves the granting of government subsidies both to "sunrise industries", such as high-tech industries, in order to stimulate their growth and development, as well as to "sunset industries", such as the steel and textile industries, in order to encourage their reorganisation along more rational lines. These government subsidies certainly affect the international competitiveness of these industries. Indeed, an important objective of the call for an industrial policy for high-tech industries is to counteract foreign subsidies. Similarly, demands for subsidies to mature industries, such as the steel and textile industries, often arise from mistakenly attributing the declining employment opportunities facing these industries primarily to foreign competition, rather than to slowly increasing demand.

Exchange rate volatility, or frequent and large fluctuations of exchange rates about equilibrium levels, by increasing uncertainty in international trade and payments, can also lead to demands for protectionist measures (IMF, 1984). Even more important in giving rise to protectionist pressures are exchange rates which remain overvalued (such as the US dollar) or undervalued (such as the Japanese yen) for relatively long periods of time (such as the first half of this decade - Salvatore, 1986a and 1986b). In cases such as these, however, the appropriate policy is reform of the international monetary system so as to restrain wild fluctuations in exchange rates and prevent large and persistent disequilibria, rather than to use industrial policy.

Opponents of an industrial policy in the US and elsewhere believe that such a policy would only delay required structural adjustments and reduce the overall growth of the nation over time. Whatever unfair trade practices are used by other nations should be corrected through trade-liberalising negotiations, and not through import restrictions which only invite retaliation. The only function for trade restrictions would be to make structural adjustments less disruptive and smoother. But then trade restrictions would have to be temporary and should not be used to prevent adjustment. Yet, even here, trade theory (Bhagwati, 1971) tells us that this is better accomplished by subsidies (which are more efficient and transparent) rather than by trade restrictions (which are less efficient, run the greater risk of becoming more or less permanent, and lead to retaliation).

Krugman (1986) points out that one of the allegedly most successful cases of industrial targeting by Japan, the steel industry, is no success at all because the Japanese steel industry has had consistently lower rates of return on investment than the national average. If anything, Krugman argues, the targeting of the steel industry from the 1950s to the early 1970s has reduced Japanese national growth. Krugman also states that it is unclear whether semiconductors (the other alleged most successful case of industrial targeting in Japan) can in fact be considered a success[16]. On the other hand, he points to some clear examples of targeting failures, such as Synfuel in the US and the Concorde in the UK and France. To this, supporters of an industrial policy in the US and elsewhere reply that comparative advantage can be crated by targeting, as for example, in synthetic rubber, jetliners, and lunar landers and in the new advanced technology that sprung from them. They also point out that Lockheed, Chrysler, and Continental Illinois in the US, and many other large companies (indeed, entire industries) in other nations, have sometimes been saved by large and direct government support.

Without necessarily advocating an industrial policy, it must be pointed out, however, that Krugman may not have fully considered all of the external economies that Japan anticipated (and has in fact obtained) from its steel industry since the 1950s. A large and very efficient domestic steel industry (by international standards rather than by Japanese domestic standards) may have been wanted by Japan in order subsequently to target such large steel-using industries as shipbuilding and automobiles, which have been most successful and profitable for Japan. Indeed, Japan is known to operate in just this way (i.e., taking a very long-run view of an industry and sacrificing short-term profits in that industry, *or even long-term profits* in a complementary industry, in order to maximise the long-run *joint* profits of the two industries). It likely that, through MITI (the powerful Ministry of International Trade and Industry), Japan was able

---

16) These are the two industries in which some of the greatest trade frictions exist between the US and Japan. This reinforces our contention that the new protectionism is closely related to industrial policies.

to provide all sorts of indirect subsidies to its steel industry while the industry was being built in the 1950s, and subsequently during the period of lower than average national returns. Similarly, it is not true that the jury is still out on semiconductors. Japan seems to have accomplished yet another feat by driving out of business all but a handful of the most powerful US companies (such as IBM and AT&T) that manufacture semiconductors.

Apart from most professional economists, there was widespread support for an industrial policy in the US in the early 1980s. What was proposed was the establishment of a development bank to provide subsidised loans to targeted industries. These were to be the older and mature industries, such as textiles and steel, and new high-technology industries, such as the information industry. Rapid domestic growth in the US during 1983 and 1984, however, reduced considerably the calls for a national industrial policy and the 1984 Presidential campaign all but killed the idea. It is more likely, however, that the demand for an industrial policy has been overshadowed in recent years by the widespread call for protectionism. Indeed, the US may have had in fact an implicit industrial policy all along, one that forced a large reallocation of labour from "sunset" heavy industries to more technologically advanced "sunrise" industries, such as the information and the telecommunication industries. This was to be reinforced by the Reagan tax reform plan, which would greatly discourage investments in heavy industries. In the meantime, high-tech industries were to be (and to some extent are being) greatly stimulated by the large defence spending. One thing is certain - industrial policies are closely related to the new protectionism and are likely to shape the future of the international trading system.

10.5 Nontariff trade barriers and the future of the international trade regime

During the past decade, the world has slipped more and more toward bilateralism and managed trade. Unless arrested, this process can undermine the entire world trading system and have very serious consequences for world welfare. Particularly dangerous is the rapid spread of implicit NTBs, which are less transparent than other forms of protectionism and, therefore, much more insidious. Reversing the present drift toward protectionism will not be easy and would necessarily involve (i) the rapid expansion of the world economy, (ii) eliminating excessive fluctuations and large and persistent disequilibria in exchange rates, and (iii) a return to established GATT principles.

One of the best antiprotectionist measures is the rapid expansion of the world economy. This will not only slow down the decline of mature industries (such as textiles and steel) in developed nations but will also lead to the creation of many additional job opportunities in the rest of the economy to absorb new entrants into the labour force and to provide employment opportunities for displaced workers in declining industries. Together with increased assistance (in the form of financial assistance, job retraining, and relocation allowances to displaced workers), this would greatly reduce demands for trade protection and arrest or reverse the drift toward increased protectionism. Another important step is the reform of the present international monetary system so as to avoid future excessive fluctuations and large and persistent disequilibria in exchange rates. While, in the past, this seemed impossible because the major nations were unwilling to give up some of their autonomy for the sake of international cooperation and reform, it seems somewhat more feasible after the Plaza Accord of September 1985.

Perhaps a more promising way to reverse the trend toward greater protectionism lay in the agreement to begin a new round of multilateral trade negotiations in September 1986. These negotiations should promote: (i) a return to GATT's most-favoured-nation principle, (ii) the resolution of trade disputes through GATT rather than bilaterally, (iii) the replacement, whenever possible, of "voluntary" export restraints by more open and transparent devices such as tariffs, and (iv) agreement on the question of how far it is legitimate for nations to promote their high-technology industries by restricting market access, by subsidies to exports and to R and D, and by government procurement provisions favouring domestic suppliers. It seems that most industrial and developing nations (e.g. Brazil) are today claiming a greater share of high-tech industries than is consistent with the world growth of these industries. This not only leads to current trade problems but also sows the seeds for even greater trade problems in the future.

While generally agreeing with this liberal prescription, some (e.g. Goldstein and Krasner, 1984) sharply disagree with this way of achieving it. They prescribe a specific course of action to attack explicit NTBs and a different one for implicit NTBs. For explicit NTBs, Goldstein and Krasner advocate a "tit for tat" strategy, first expounded by Axelrod (1981). According to this, a large nation, such as the US, should unhesitatingly adopt a policy of unilateral trade retaliation as defined by GATT to force other nations to remove unfair NTBs of the explicit type. This is like the case of the "prisoner's dilemma": it would pay a nation to impose explicit NTBs in the absence of retaliation, but with retaliation both nations would be better off by dismantling their explicit NTBs. For this strategy to work, however, both nations must agree as to what is an unfair explicit NTB. Goldstein and Krasner believe that such a condition is generally met, and they give several examples where retaliation drove the other country to the bargaining table and to a resolution of the trade dispute. They believe that the unwillingness of the US to make general use of this strategy arises from the mistaken fear of starting a trade war. The result is a perpetuation and proliferation of explicit NTBs in other nations (as well as in the US).

By their very nature, implicit NTBs are those on which no agreement can be reached as to what constitutes a fair or an unfair practice. Many nations regard these as purely domestic policies and part of their state's sovereign rights. Here Goldstein and Krasner point out that it is futile for the US to try to force other nations to eliminate their implicit NTBs through international negotiations. Rather than waste its efforts in a futile attempt to change the basic and socio-economic-political institutional characteristics of other nations (such as industrial targeting in Japan or the EC's CAP), the US should itself adopt similar policies in order to counteract the effect of such policies abroad and to further its own industrial objectives. The trade conflict between the US and Japan in telecommunications and semiconductors may be cases in point. This means that while negotiations can be very useful in eliminating or reducing tariffs and explicit NTBs, some disagreement and trade controversy on implicit NTBs are inherent in the present international trade regime and cannot be negotiated away.

The logical conclusion, therefore, is that industrial policies, which are rejected on first-best theoretical grounds, re-enter through the back door as a second-best and inevitable aspect of the future world trading system. While the US and most other nations do not have a full-fledged explicit industrial policy, most do provide much help to many of their industries. In the EC and in the US, agriculture is highly protected by domestic subsidies, and mature industries are protected by trade restrictions. Similarly, high-technology is aided through all sorts of direct and indirect subsidies in the EC and Japan, and through military expenditures, the space programme, and aids to education in the US. To the extent that nations are unwilling to give up these policies, implicit NTBs will be part of any future international trading system and, inevitably, so will some trade friction. What is important is to negotiate for a reduction of traditional trade barriers and explicit NTBs, and accept as inevitable the existence of some implicit NTBs. Nations could counteract with appropriate domestic policies the most disturbing effects of foreign implicit NTBs in a manner that minimises the resulting trade controversies.

The future international trading system must also consider the legitimate interests of less developed countries (LDCs). Because the exports of many LDCs are in competition with commodities produced with low-skill labour in industrial nations, industrial nations seem somewhat more protective against the exports of LDCs than against each other's exports. This is unfortunate because it comes at time when many LDCs are finally switching from a less efficient import-substitution direction to a more efficient export-oriented strategy, and at a time when many LDCs are unable to service their huge foreign debts. It would be unenlightened, and against the long-term interests of both developed and less developed countries, if, as a result of the limited bargaining power that LDCs have vis-à-vis industrial nations, the trade and development interests of LDCs were to be neglected in the new round of multilateral trade negotiations.

10.6 Summary and conclusions

During the past decade, the number and importance of nontariff trade barriers have grown so rapidly that they have now become more important than tariffs as obstructions to international trade. Unless arrested, this process can undermine the entire world trading system and have very serious consequences for world welfare. Particularly dangerous is the rapid spread of implicit NTBs, which are less transparent than other forms of protectionism and, therefore, that much more insidious.

Industrial nations have responded to increased demands for protectionism with nontariff barriers (while tariff barriers were being reduced) in order to minimise the apparent departures from the principle of an open, multilateral trading system. One of the most common and increasingly used forms of NTBs is the "voluntary" export restraint (VER). This is used to limit exports of textiles, apparel, steel, automobiles, consumer electronics, and other products. Since a VER is supposedly voluntary, it allows the home country to bypass the GATT regulation that forbids quantitative and discriminatory import restrictions. The country against which the VER is imposed also seems to find a VER preferable to facing the risk of possibly stronger and more permanent trade restrictions and the rent collected by exporters creates a constituency that lobbies the government for the retention of the VER. Finally, the non-restrained countries also benefit from higher export volume and prices. The losers are consumers in the country that imposes VERs because of the restricted range of imports and higher prices. VERs and other NTBs have had only limited success, however, in protecting domestic employment.

Two important conclusions follow from estimation of a model of the causes and effects of escape clause trade complaints and actions in the US. The first is that the demand for escape clause protection is cyclical in nature, rising or falling with the level of domestic economic activity. The second is confirmation of the harassment thesis: the possibility of filing an escape clause complaint, is, in itself, effective in reducing import penetration, independently of the rate of success in actually obtaining a favourable ruling. The reason for concentrating on this form of NTBs is that it is one of the few quantifiable forms of nontariff protection, with data going back nearly four decades.

The industrial policy of granting government subsidies both to "sunrise industries", such as high-tech industries, in order to stimulate their growth and development, as well as to "sunset industries", such as steel and textiles, in order to encourage their reorganisation along more rational lines, certainly affects the international competitiveness of these industries, and has been an important driving force behind the growth of the new protectionism in the past decade, particularly in its implicit NTB form. It is also likely to shape the future of the international trading system.

Reversing the present drift toward protectionism will involve (i) the rapid expansion of the world economy, (ii) eliminating excessive fluctuations and large and persistent disequilibria in exchange rates, and (iii) a return to established GATT principles. For explicit NTBs, Goldstein and Krasner, however, advocate a "tit for tat" strategy, according to which a large nation, such as the US, should unhesitatingly adopt a policy of unilateral trade retaliation as defined by GATT to force other nations to remove unfair NTBs of the explicit type. For implicit NTBs, where it is impossible for nations to agree on questions of fairness, these authors propose that the US should adopt industrial policies similar to those adopted by other nations. Acceptance of their analysis means that implicit NTBs will be part of any future international trading system and, inevitably, so will some trade friction. In future trade negotiations, nations should then concentrate on reducing traditional trade barriers and explicit NTBs, while counteracting with appropriate domestic policies the most disturbing effects of foreign implicit NTBs, but in a manner that minimises resulting trade controversies.

References

M.C. Aho and J.D. Aroson (1985), Trade Talks, New York: Council of Foreign Relations.

S.J. Anjaria, U. Iqbal, N. Kirmani and L.L. Perez (1982), Developments in International Trade Policy, Washington, D.C., International Monetary Fund.

R. Axelrod (1981), "The Emergence of Cooperation Among Egoists", American Political Science Review, June.

B. Balassa (1978), "The New Protectionism and the International Economy", Journal of World Trade Law 12:409-436.

B. Balassa and C. Balassa (1984), "Industrial Protection in Developed Countries", The World Economy, June.

R.E. Baldwin and A.O. Kruger (eds.) (1984), The Structure and Evolution of Recent US Trade Policy, Chicago, University of Chicago Press.

J.N. Bhagwati (1971), "The Generalized Theory of Distortions and Welfare", in J.N. Bhagwati et al., (eds), International Trade: Selected Readings, Amsterdam, North-Holland.

J.N. Bhagwati (1982), Import Competition and Response, Chicago, University of Chicago Press.

J.N. Bhagwati and T.N. Srinivasan (1976), "Optimal Trade Policy and Compensation Under Uncertainty: The Phenomenon of Market Disruption", Journal of International Economics, June.

A.M. Costa (1986), "The Need for New Multilateral Trade Negotiations: Why it is Urgent to complete the New Round of GATT", in D. Salvatore (ed.), The New Protectionist Threat to World Welfare, North-Holland.

W. Cline (1983), Trade Policies in the 1980s, Washington, D.C., Institute for International Economics.

W. Cline (1984), Exports of Manufactures from Developing Countries, Washington, D.C., The Brookings Institution.

S. Cohen (1985), Uneasy Partnership: Competition and Conflict in US-Japanese Trade Relations, Cambridge, Mass.: Ballinger.

R.C. Feenstra (1986), "Automobile Prices and Protection: The US-Japan Trade Restraint", in D. Salvatore (ed.), The New Protectionist Threat to World Welfare, North-Holland.

Federal Reserve Bank of Kansas City (1985), The US Dollar - Recent Developments, Outlook, and Policy Options, Kansas City.

J.M. Finger (1981), "The Industry-Country Incidence of "Less than Fair Value" Cases in US Import Trade", Quarterly Review of Economics and Business, Summer.

J.M. Finger et al. (1982), "The Political Economy of Administered Protection", The American Economic Review, June.

J.L. Goldstein and S.D. Krasner (1984), "Unfair Trade Practices: The Case for a Differentiated Response", The American Economic Review, May.

C. Hamilton (1985a), "Economic Aspects of Economic Export Restraints", in D. Greenway (ed.), Current Issues in International Trade, London: Macmillan.

C. Hamilton (1985b), "Voluntary Export Restraints and Trade Diversion", Journal of Common Market Studies, June.

C. Hamilton and J. Whalley (1983), "Optimal Tariff Calculations in Alternative Trade Models and some Possible Implications for Current World Trading Arrangements", Journal of International Economics, June.

M.G. Herander and J.B. Schwartz (1984), "An Empirical Test of the Impact of the Threat of US Trade Policy: The Case of Antidumping Duties", Southern Economic Journal, July.

IMF (1975), Annual Report on Exchange Rates, Washington, DC.

IMF (1984), "Exchange Rate Volatility and World Trade", Occasional Paper 28. Washington, DC.

IMF (1986), World Economic Outlook, Washington, DC.

P.R. Krugman (1986), "Targeted Industrial Policies: Theory and Evidence", in D. Salvatore (ed.), The New Protectionist Threat to World Welfare, North-Holland.

R.I. McKinnon (1984), An International Standard for Monetary Stabilization. Washington, DC, Institute for International Economics.

M. Michaely (1984), Trade, Income Levels, and Dependence, New York, North-Holland.

OECD (1979), The Impact of Newly Industrializing Countries on Production and Trade in Manufactures, Paris.

OECD (1982), Problems of Agricultural Trade, Paris.

OECD (1985), Costs and Benefits of Protection, Paris.

S.A.B. Page (1981), "The Revival of Protectionism and its Consequences for Europe", Journal of Common Market Studies, September.

D. Salvatore (1986a), International Economics, Second Edition, New York, Macmillan.

D. Salvatore (1986b) (ed.), The New Protectionist Threat to World Welfare. New York, North-Holland.

B. Scott and C.L. Lodge (1985), US Competitiveness in the World Economy, Boston, Harvard Business School Press.

L. Turner and N. McMullen (1982), The Newly Industrializing Countries: Trade and Adjustment, London, George Allen & Unwin.

United Nations (1986), World Economic Survey, New York.

World Bank (1986), World Bank Development Report, Washington, DC.

Chapter 11

COMPARING THE FOREIGN ECONOMIC STRATEGIES OF MARKET AND CENTRALLY PLANNED ECONOMIES

Paul Marer[1)2)]

Comparative economics should go beyond the simplistic classification of countries as capitalist vs. socialist, or as market economies vs. centrally planned economies (CPEs), because those terms veil important similarities between countries belonging to different groups as well as significant differences within them.

This chapter compares the foreign economic strategies of selected countries in Asia, Latin America, Western Europe and Eastern Europe. Two related aspects of these economies are examined: the degree to which the authorities pursue *economic policies* to keep the economy "open" vis-à-vis the rest of the world, and the role of government in the economy - a key feature of a country's *economic system* which can be decisive in determining a country's foreign economic strategy.

Section 11.1 discusses foreign economic strategy options and instruments; 11.2 summarises the foreign economic strategies of selected Asian, Latin American, and West European market economies; 11.3 those of the CPEs. Owing to the author's imperfect understanding of the facts and to space limitations, oversimplifications in depicting economic strategies or systems are inevitable. 11.4 identifies the main forces that appear to shape the foreign economic strategies of nations. 11.5 concludes the chapter with a discussion of the links between foreign economic strategies and economic performance.

11.1 Foreign economic strategy options and instruments

By contrast with what some textbooks suggest, a country's real international economic policy choice is not between free trade, absence of restrictions on foreign direct investment (FDI), and unimpeded capital flows on the one hand and complete economic isolation on the other; in the real world there are many ways and combinations of handling

---

1) Professor of International Business, School of Business, Indiana University, Bloomington, Indiana, USA

2) The author would like to thank Joseph Battat, Jozef van Brabant, Elton McGoun, and Aleksander Lukaszewicz for valuable comments on the first draft.

external economic relations.

The discussion of foreign economic strategy is approached here from two perspectives. One is the degree of openness toward trade in goods and services and cross-border flows of capital, technology and entrepreneurship. The other perspective focuses on the role of government in the economy, more specifically on two aspects of its role: the extent to which the government owns the means of production and the extent to which it intervenes in the operation of the economy by planning and regulating the operations of particular industries and of individual firms. Speaking broadly, the role of government may range from laissez faire, to guidance, to pervasive control.

A key aspect of a country's economic system is the role of the government - or, more broadly, that of the authorities, a term that may encompass not only the central administration but also the ruling party if it performs certain key governmental functions, as, for example, in countries ruled by Communist parties. It will be argued here that under certain kinds of economic system the authorities have greater flexibility to choose between alternative foreign economic strategies than under some other kinds of economic system where the system itself predetermines certain aspects of foreign economic strategies. For example, the closer the role of the government approaches that of a laissez faire situation, the more "open" will be - for better or for worse - the foreign economic strategy. At the other end of the spectrum, the closer a country's economic system is to that of a traditional, Soviet-type CPE, the less feasible it will be for that country to pursue foreign economic strategies that - for better or for worse - are "open". Below I define the term "openness" and discuss foreign economic policy's main instruments.

The subject matter of this chapter is a comparative analysis of the foreign economic strategies of nations. The appropriate focus, therefore, is on governmental objectives and policies, together with the rules and regulations designed to implement them. The focus, thus, is not on how "open" or "dependent" or "vulnerable" an economy may be to external economic influences, but on the intentions of the authorities regarding those matters. The distinction is important because economic objectives and observed outcomes may not be fully consistent. Why and how such a paradox may arise is discussed and documented in the chapter.

Foreign economic strategy is comprised of three elements: trade strategy, attitude toward FDI, and willingness to integrate with the international financial system. Trade strategy focusses on policies regarding the export of goods and services. FDI strategy concerns policies toward cross-border flows of capital joined with entrepreneurship (often technology also, in embodied or disembodied form). External financial strategy focusses on policies toward cross-border flows of capital without entrepreneurship. Foreign economic strategy is thus defined as the sum total of policies in each of the three areas, trade policy being the most important.

Foreign trade strategies

Much of the literature defines openness on the basis of the relative importance of foreign trade in the economy, measured by the foreign trade participation ratio (FTPR): the sum of exports plus imports as a share of GNP. I prefer not to use this definition, for several reasons. First, FTPRs make it difficult to compare the foreign economic strategies of countries of different economic size or levels of development, because the ratios tend to be correlated negatively with size of country and positively with development level. Second, a country's FTPR may rise as the unintended and paradoxical consequence of policies designed to reduce dependence on foreign trade. This may happen if the imports needed to build, maintain, and operate new production capacity exceeds the value of the imports that the new production capacity was suppose to displace. Third, the ratios are computed in domestic not world prices and the former may well be distorted. For example, a high level of protection will inflate the domestic prices of tradeable goods even as it discourages exports. For all these reasons, it seems preferable to classify foreign trade strategies on the basis of the objectives and actions of the authorities rather than on the basis of observed outcomes.

Two of the basic and contending foreign trade strategies are *export promotion* (EP) and *import substitution* (IS). To be sure, such policies can rarely be found in pure form. Rather, they describe only broad tendencies.

The common features of EP - outward-oriented - policies are that there is at least as much incentive to earn as to save foreign exchange, that exports are not concentrated excessively in unprocessed primary products but involve also manufactures (of the kind appropriate for the level of development of the country), and that imports needed by producers are not excessively regulated. Incentives to export tend to be fairly uniform, not discriminatory across commodity groups. Exporters may receive production or export subsidies, tax concessions, or preferential access to credit. Alternatively, EP policies could be no more than the absence of policies that discriminate in favour of sales in the domestic or protected regional market; for example, the exchange rate is not overvalued. And since exporters, if they are to be competitive, must be given ready access to raw materials, intermediate goods, and manufacturing technology at world prices, a genuine EP policy requires a fairly liberal import régime.

The hallmarks of an IS régime are high levels of long-term protection of many industries, fairly detailed and bureaucratic regulation of imports, and disincentives to export. IS régimes have a mix of policy instruments under which imports are allocated by category of commodity, type of domestic user, source of foreign exchange, and the specific priorities of the authorities. IS régimes often have overvalued exchange rates that encourage imports and discriminate against exports [Krueger 1983, p. 6], but that is not an indispensable feature.

Foreign direct investment

FDI is defined as cross-border flows of capital linked with entrepreneurship (often also with technological know-how). Much of FDI is by multinational corporations (MNCs) that are perceived by host countries as agents that generate benefits as well as costs in the local economy and as a quasi-political institution that may interfere with national sovereignty.Although empirical verification of the numerous direct and indirect benefits and costs of FDI is difficult, there is consensus that FDI tends to make a positive net contribution to the economies of host countries by bringing in capital, technology, entrepreneurship, as well as management and marketing know-how. Nevertheless, in many countries FDI is not welcome, for political reasons. The issue is that of national sovereignty. Foreign-owned firms can exercise decision-making power from foreign headquarters and remain subject to the authority of a foreign government. Therefore, it is often alleged, FDI may thwart the capacity of the host government to achieve its economic or social goals.

FDI may be regulated so as to maximise the host country's economic benefits or to minimise perceived limitations on its sovereignty. Regulation typically serves both purposes. All countries discriminate against foreign ownership of local firms in industries regarded essential to national security, defence, public utilities, airlines, shipping lines, communications; in some countries foreigners may also be excluded from banking, insurance, real estate, agriculture, forestry, extractive (mining and petroleum) and basic industries (iron and steel, petrochemicals, etc.). Many countries prohibit the acquisition (takeover) of locally-owned firms by foreign investors and/or require local participation or majority ownership. Many countries impose performance requirements, involving the use of local labour, local content, import limitations, and export performance. Performance requirements are forms of protection because they distort flows of trade and investment in ways that favour the host country to the detriment of others. At the same time, the vast majority of countries also offer investment incentives, such as tax concessions, subsidies, and tariff preferences. Their effectiveness to attract FDI is questionable because the incentives of one country are largely neutralised by the incentives of others, and because incentives cannot create profitable operations if markets are small, infrastructure poor, and host-government policies disruptive [Root, Chapter 24].

In some countries where foreign ownership and control of production affiliates is prohibited, minority joint ventures or contractual service arrangements may be permitted. These may include service contracts, coproduction schemes, licensing, and various types of industrial cooperation agreements (ICAs).

The range of accommodation between host governments and MNCs lies between a laissez-faire policy at the one end and the exclusion of all foreign ownership or control at the other. In practice, all governments impose at least mild restrictions. But the greater the restrictions on foreign ownership and control, and the more pervasive the performance requirements, the less "open" is the economy.

Foreign financial integration

Willingness to borrow relatively large sums from foreign sources - be they international financial institutions, governments, or private lenders - is a sign of openness. Taking on large debts not only finances imports but also commits the borrower to the future expansion of exports to meet debt service obligations. This fails to apply only if a country repudiates its foreign debt outright - the most overt sign of a country turning sharply inward, since it would have great difficulty financing and thus maintaining imports. Willingness to lend large sums to foreigners is also a sign of openness because it implicitly commits the lender to the future expansion of imports, since the rest of the world will have to earn the lender's currency to service the debt.

Openness is best indicated by willingness to borrow (or to lend) when appropriate, up to prudent limits, but not by the actual size of foreign debt (or assets): this is because countries in strong balance of payments positions may not need foreign credits and because indebtedness beyond certain limits suggests imprudent borrowing, not greater openness. Willingness to borrow (lend) may be signalled by the government's own involvement in international credit transactions and by whether the authorities allow national enterprises to enter foreign capital markets and foreign private financial institutions to do business on the domestic market. In brief, one indicator of a country's openness is the nature and strength of the links between domestic and foreign financial institutions, including membership in international financial institutions such as the International Monetary Fund (IMF) and World Bank.

11.2 Strategies of selected market economies

"Market economy" is a term used here loosely to designate economies where a significant part of the means of production is privately owned. In such economies the prices of factors of production as well as of intermediate products and final goods and services are responsive to market forces, although market imperfections and government intervention may move many individual prices away from those that would prevail in their absence.

This section gives examples of market economy countries located at various places in the "open to closed" spectrum of policies for trade, FDI, and financial integration, as well as the extent of government participation in, or control of, the economy. There is no attempt here to undertake a systematic or a representative survey of all market economies or to suggest how one could identify more precisely the kinds of foreign economic policies that countries follow; the purpose is to illustrate the wide spectrum of policies as well as outcomes among market economies.

If we focus on trade and FDI policies, two notably successful countries that have pursued an EP strategy are Hong Kong and Singapore. Hong Kong's strategy involved little government intervention beyond creating and maintaining an excellent physical and social infrastructure, while Singapore's strategy encompassed extensive government intervention to engineer social and industrial policy objectives. Because the economy of Hong Kong is dominated by small- and medium-sized family firms, its industrial exports do not involve extensive FDI: MNCs account for only about 10 per cent of manufactured exports, even though Hong Kong is quite open to FDI. In Singapore, by contrast, the participation of foreign firms is high: MNCs account for more than 80 per cent of manufactured exports [Sheahan, p. 17]. The role of FDI in these two small states is an example of why outcomes may not be accurate measures of policies - in this case attitudes to FDI.

Both countries responded to recent external economic shocks - the energy and raw material price explosions of 1973-74 and 1979-80 - *not* by borrowing significant amounts but by belt-tightening and by adjusting quickly to new conditions on the world market, while continuing liberal import policies. To be sure, after the first oil shock, Singapore did have large trade deficits for several years but it eschewed debt-financing in favour of equity financing through FDI. Nevertheless, both states serve as centres of international finance, so in this respect, too, their economies are quite open.

Three notably successful countries that have pursued EP, combined with considerable import protection and control over FDI are Japan, the Republic of Korea and Taiwan. Between 1964 and 1978, Brazil also placed a strong emphasis on EP and was more open to FDI than either of the three Asian countries.

The import protection policies of Japan, Korea and Taiwan differ from the more extreme variants of IS policies pursued by scores of countries in that

(a) initial periods of broad-based import substitution policies, pursued during the 1950s, were supplanted by general policies of export promotion;

(b) the main purpose of selective import protection was not to coddle declining industries but to shelter, temporarily (!) infant industries with prospective advantage.

All three countries have pursued rather restrictive policies on FDI. Japan, in spite of its recent liberalisation, still restricts FDI in scores of industries. In those that are open to FDI, it permits the entry of foreign companies only as minority partners and generally limits foreign ownership in *existing* Japanese companies to less than 25 per cent. A great deal of foreign technology has been acquired, however, through licensing.

While S. Korea shares many of the attributes of Japan, its government relies less on building a consensus and more on direct controls over industries and individual firms to push them in the desired direction. To illustrate; the government requires manufacturers of textile goods to negotiate each year export prices higher than a national average benchmark price which it sets, penalising firms that fail to comply. The case of Hanil Co. is not atypical. In 1984 Hanil made about three million sweaters for K-Mart, a US department store chain. In 1985 the government ordered it to cut production by 120,000 sweaters because the average export prices that Hanil negotiated the previous year were too low (*The Wall Street Journal*, March 19, 1985). Korea has permitted FDI more readily than Japan but less so than Singapore, or even than Brazil and Mexico. In the mid-1970s, more than half of foreign firms were required to achieve export targets, with the activities of many limited entirely to export. Nonetheless, majority-owned foreign firms accounted for less than one-fourth of Korea's manufactured exports in 1980 [Sheahan, p. 21].

Taiwan's early postwar policy (1953-61) was IS, although in relatively mild form. During the early 1960s it changed into an EP strategy by introducing a unified and realistic exchange rate, relaxing exchange controls, and reducing the effective rate of protection. FDI was not excluded but limited and controlled in many ways. In 1953-72, public and private foreign capital contributed less than 6 per cent of cumulative investment [Fei, pp. 26-29 and 311]. Even today, only selected foreign investors are favoured and performance requirements are imposed [*Investment*, Vol. III, pp. 263-68].

The three countries differ considerably in their attitude toward international financial integration. Japan, owing to its high domestic savings rate and trade surplus, has had little need to borrow abroad during the last decade (during earlier periods it obtained substantial foreign loans). Although in recent years Japan has become a leading lender to the rest of the world through equity and portfolio investments and has been liberalising its financial markets, for a long time during the postwar period it had more restrictions on the international financial involvement of its banks and firms than did most industrialised countries.

S. Korea built up a large foreign debt during the 1970s and early 1980s. However, its rapidly growing exports have kept its debt-to-export and debt-service ratios reasonable, thereby avoiding a payments crisis. By contrast, Taiwan followed a very conservative course. After both the first and second energy price explosions, which initially hurt Taiwan's economy, it quickly converted large trade deficits into surpluses and decided to guard its autonomy by foregoing both foreign debt and equity finance despite its low level of development and the negative real rate of interest in the 1970s. "The decisions of Taiwan and Singapore to forego debt financing seemed at the time to conflict with market signals and to represent a kind of artificial closure to world-capital markets" [Tyson, p. 254].

Although Brazil's performance has not been on a par with those of Japan, Korea, or Taiwan, its economy also performed well between 1964, after it modified its highly protectionist strategy, and 1980, the first year in which the adverse effects of a prolonged and severe balance of payments crisis have been felt. After 1964 Brazil developed a complex system of direct promotion and control of industry and exports - a system similar in many respects to that of S. Korea, though with somewhat less aggressive EP and greater reliance on foreign investment [Sheahan, p. 23]. But during the 1970s and early 1980s it accumulated foreign debt at a much more rapid rate than it was able to expand exports, triggering a prolonged payments crisis. Unlike the countries in East Asia, one of Brazil's responses was to turn inward so that, once again, it is emphasising IS. It has also become much more restrictive toward the entry and operation of MNCs, excluding foreign firms entirely from certain fields, such as small computers and health-care equipment. Its government also owns or participates directly in the productive activities of many enterprises.

The third pattern of EP has been followed by members of the European Economic Community (EC) since 1958. They have established free trade for industrial products for EC members while maintain moderate protection of manufactures *vis-à-vis* non-members and erecting a strong wall of protection around agriculture.

The effect of EEC integration in manufactures was a rapid increase in *intra-industry* specialisation, based on slightly differentiated products, more so than *inter-industry* specialisation based on differing factor endowments. That is, much of trade expansion has taken place among products within the same industries: differentiated consumer goods to provide variety, and differentiated components, parts, subassemblies as well as machinery and equipment to fill special niches. The essence of integration was market extension, making possible economies of scale that could not be achieved by supplying only one national market. It intensified competition, forcing producers to cut costs, sell more aggressively, and search out new products. Profitable firms could generate sufficient revenues or credits to finance the introduction of modern, cost-effective technology as well as the R&D required for continuous product improvement. Integration also stimulated the inflow of FDI. These were some of the important dynamic benefits of integration for economic growth, reinforced by a gradual liberalisation of factor movements.

The EC countries have pursued a relatively open policy toward FDI as well as towards international financial integration. To be sure, France has periodically frustrated the attempts of foreign firms to take over French firms and has imposed strict though temporary controls over capital outflows for balance of payments reasons, as did Italy for the same reasons. Even the Federal Republic of Germany, whose economy is the most "open" in respect of trade and FDI, still retains certain capital controls (for example, German firms cannot borrow in foreign currency).

From the mid-1950s till the early 1970s, it was chiefly US-based MNCs that took advantage of the opportunities represented by preferential access to the whole EC market for firms located within the EC. They found the most advantageous locations to set up facilities to serve the entire EC market. US multinationals thus played a significant role in the economic integration of Western Europe.

Among countries that have pursued inward-oriented strategies for long periods, we also find significant policy differences. A large group of countries, encompassing much of Latin America and also India, have attempted to promote industrialisation through broad-based IS, without strong export orientation. Attitudes toward FDI have varied but significant barriers to entry and onerous performance requirements have been common characteristics. For example, for many years Mexico has pursued a policy of progressive "Mexicanisation" of foreign-owned companies, requiring that they be converted into joint ventures with local partners. Another example is India. In 1977 its authorities demanded that Coca Cola and IBM transfer both their know-how and the majority ownership of their Indian subsidiaries to Indian nationals. Both firms refused and ceased operations in the country. More generally, the economy of India operates with a very large public sector and with myriad economic controls, with the government regulating everything from how many plants can produce a product to how much a factory can produce, to what its product-mix must be, and to specifying the location of where new plans can be built by the private sector. Some countries in this category accumulated very large foreign debts and today face severe debt-servicing difficulties (e.g. Mexico), while others were able to keep foreign debt at more manageable levels (e.g. India).

Lastly comes a group of the most inward-oriented countries whose economies, for all practical purposes, are closed to outside economic influences. Some have pursued the most extreme versions of IS (e.g. Sri Lanka until 1976) or have placed a low priority on development in order to preserve the existing social structure, or sovereignty, or both (e.g. Burma since 1962). None has allowed FDI in any form or has taken out large foreign loans.

Table 11.1 summarises the patterns of openness and government intervention found for the market economies whose policies were discussed on previous pages.

11.3 Strategies of centrally planned economies

CPEs are characterised by predominant state ownership of the means of production, and hierarchical-bureaucratic control over most economic decisions. The degree of differentiation between the state and the economy is low: the activities of producers, consumers, and workers by and large depend on the decisions of the authorities. For the most part, only specialised foreign trade enterprises can conduct import and export transactions, although in some countries selected producers are being increasingly allowed to deal directly with foreign customers and suppliers. Most producing enterprises, however, are insulated from the foreign buyers of exports or foreign suppliers of imports. Not being independent of the state, producers bear little of the costs or risks of their activities. Because the state routinely reimburses producers for costs incurred, and because output does not have to be "marketed" (since the authorities arrange the distribution of whatever the enterprises were told to produce), the budget constraint on enterprises is "soft".

"Expansion drive" characterises behaviour at all levels: a desire to produce as much as possible without worrying about the costs, the quality, and saleability of the output. At the macro level, the expansion drive stems from the commitment of the authorities to rapid growth and industrialisation; at the micro level, it stems from the "soft budget constraint" and the pressure and incentives that stress the growth of output [Kornai].

Table 11.1

Degree of openness of the foreign economic strategies of selected market economies

Country	Foreign trade	Financial integration	Foreign direct investment	Government intervention
Hong Kong	high	high	high	low
Singapore	high	high	high	guidance
Japan	high	moderate-high	moderate-high	guidance
S. Korea	high	high	moderate-high	guidance
Taiwan	high	moderate	high-moderate	guidance
EEC	high-moderate	high	high	guidance
Brazil				
1964-80	moderate-high	high	high	guidance
1980-86	moderate	high	moderate	guidance-control
Mexico	low-moderate	high	moderate	guidance
India	low	low	low-moderate	guidance-control
Sri Lanka	low	low	low	guidance-control
Burma	low	low	low	guidance-control

Source: see text

While in market economies output levels are constrained by demand, in CPEs the constraint is resource availability. "The drive to realize ambitious output plans generates constant pressure on resources and a widespread perception of shortages of resources as a barrier to plan fulfillment" [Tyson, p. 245]. The result is a perpetual sellers' market, with an insatiable demand for inputs, including imports.

The foreign economic strategies of the CPEs, as well as the outcomes, differ not only as between countries, but for each country in its relations with market economies versus those with other CPEs. Much of the latter takes place within the so-called Council for Mutual Economic Assistance (CMEA or COMECON),[3] the integration group between the USSR and

---

3) Council for Mutual Economic Assistance (CMEA), whose full active members are the USSR, Bulgaria, Czechoslovakia, the German Democratic Republic, Hungary, Poland, Romania, Mongolia, Cuba, and Vietnam.

countries of Eastern Europe that shares certain features with, but also has many differences from, the EEC.

Strategy and instruments in trade with market economies

If we focus not on what the authorities say but on what they do, the most common and distinctive feature of the foreign trade strategies vis-à-vis market economics of CPEs is protection. The evidence is twofold. First, the authorities import little if demand can be satisfied from domestic or CMEA sources. Consequently, no domestic producer faces import competition or is forced out of business because imports are cheaper or better. Second, the authorities are continually attempting to replace convertible-currency (CC) imports with domestic production or purchases from the CMEA, a policy analogous to extreme versions of attempted IS pursued by many market economies. In CPEs, the instruments of protection are not tariffs or quantitative restrictions but the central control over all foreign trade and foreign currency operations, although the administration of control may be delegated to varying degrees.

The fact that the CC imports of many CPEs had increased rapidly during the 1970s does not contradict the statement that CPEs are extremely protectionist. The main purpose of CC imports is not to alter production patterns on the basis of the country's comparative advantage but to alleviate the many domestic shortages that constrain the ability of the planners to achieve their objectives, determined to a greater or lesser degree by political-ideological considerations. For the authorities the "gains" from trade consist in reducing shortages, not in altering production patterns on the basis of the country's comparative advantage [Comisso, p. 200].

During the 1970s many CPEs increased imports from the West rapidly, a significant part on credit. While in a certain sense a rapid increase in imports can be taken as "opening" the economy to the West, assessing whether that really was the intention of the authorities is important in judging the trade policies of individual CPEs. Imports from the West may increase rapidly:

(a) to replace less efficient domestic production and thus employ resources more efficiently;
(b) to build capacity to increase CC exports;
(c) to substitute domestic production for CC imports;
(d) to obtain technology and inputs to help produce exports intended for the CMEA markets;
(e) to alleviate shortages and bottlenecks in the domestic economy created by overambitious expansion drives, planning mistakes, and inefficiencies;
(f) to borrow and import to maintain domestic absorption (consumption plus investment) in the face of deteriorating terms of trade.

Only motives (a) and (b) represent genuine "opening". If motives (c) through (f) dominate, imports from the West may increase rapidly but without a corresponding increase in export capability.

A detailed study of the Hungarian experience suggests that (d), (e) and (f) were the predominant reasons for CC import expansion during the 1970s [Marer 1986a]. The situation was probably not too different in Poland [Poznanski 1986a] or the GDR. For Romania, objectives (c) and (e) were probably the most important. The point, again, is that one must be cautious about inferring policy positions on trade on the basis of observed outcomes.

Be that as it may, since growing imports must be paid for and foreign debts must be serviced, policies of *selective* export promotion may be pursued periodically also. Irrespective of what the authorities may say about giving high priority to export promotion *generally*, since producers have many reasons to prefer to sell on the domestic or on the CMEA market, and since access to imports is strictly controlled, the economic system and policies of CPEs discriminate against CC exports. The initial response of the authorities to the pressure to expand CC exports is to enlarge the production of energy, raw materials, simple semimanufactures, and (in some countries) agricultural commodities because the production of these standardised goods need not be oriented toward foreign markets; exporting is largely a matter of so allocating a portion of the output. But once the relatively easy possibilities have been exhausted and inventories run down, the authorities may initiate economy-wide EP campaigns. The timing and intensity of the campaigns vary, depending on country-specific circumstances and policies. In Eastern Europe, EP campaigns are typical responses to balance of payments crises. Since 1977, China has pursued such a campaign without such a crisis; in the USSR no such campaign has taken place in recent decades.

The main instruments of EP are not market-type incentives determined jointly by production costs, foreign prices, and exchange rates but (the often somewhat arbitrarily set) export targets of the authorities. Firms that agree to increase their exports are then rewarded by preferential access to investment credits, domestic and imported CC inputs, tax concessions, and bonuses and perquisites (such as foreign travel) to enterprise managers and other key persons. But EP campaigns typically do not yield sustained improvements in export capability because their focus is short-run and because they tend to divert to the CC market intermediate goods of good quality at the expense of supplying domestic manufacturers.

Strategies and instruments in trade between CPEs

Trade between the European CPEs takes place under the auspices of the CMEA, an arrangement that resembles that of the EEC in that the basic purpose of both is to integrate the economies of member countries by promoting preferential trade between them. But the mechanisms, the policies, and the outcomes differ greatly.

As regards the *mechanism* of integration, the fundamental difference is that in the EC much of international commerce is conducted by private enterprises seeking profit opportunities wherever they can find them, so that a reduction of the barriers to the movement of goods, factors of production, and financial capital across national boundaries goes a long way toward integration. In the CMEA, by contrast, all movement of goods, factors and capital requires explicit action by governments. Integration, therefore, demands more overt management and an elaborate bureaucratic structure.

Because the currencies of CPEs - and the transferable rouble serving as the CMEA's unit of account - are inconvertible, trade decisions and settlements are bilateral. Because intra-CMEA prices do not reflect relative scarcities within the bloc, a substitute mechanism has emerged. Goods in short supply ("hard" goods) are balanced against commodities in surplus ("soft" goods), where "hardness" and "softness" reflect domestic priorities, not prices [Marrese].

Trade policies within the CMEA are also driven by a desire to reduce shortages by importing "hard" goods. As long as trade partners could make such goods available for export, trade expansion and integration were promoted. For some years after World War II, the more advanced East European countries were able to supply machinery, equipment, and other manufactures (not too different in quality from those in the West, where they could not trade owing to the reciprocal trade denial policies during the Cold War) in exchange for energy, raw materials, and agricultural products from the less developed countries of Eastern Europe and the USSR (supplying also turnkey plants and heavy-industrial machinery). But gradually, the incremental supply of hard goods available for exports to CMEA partners declined, for the following reasons:

- as the quality and modernity of manufactures fell more and more behind world market levels, trade partners became less and less eager to purchase them;
- the expansion drives in these economies - coupled with the wasteful use of inputs as each country built up parallel industries- increased the shortage of energy, raw materials and (except in Hungary and Bulgaria) agricultural and food products. But the shortage has not affected the intra-CMEA prices of these goods, which re-enforced the shortages;

- the expansion of trade with the West (where hard goods are available in unlimited quantities) pre-empted a growing share of hard goods available within the CMEA.

Nonetheless, the volume of trade within the CMEA continued to increase through the 1960s and 1970s largely because of the willingness of the USSR - until the early 1980s - to supply "hard" energy and "relatively hard" raw materials and semimanufactures[4)] in exchange for increasingly "soft" East European manufactures. To be sure, the production of those manufactures requires growing purchases from the West of technology and inputs. The more difficulties the East European countries have obtaining CC inputs, the "softer" become each country's manufactures for export to CMEA partners also.

Today, the constraints on Soviet energy and raw material supplies, the scarcity of hard goods of all kinds throughout the bloc, and the severe shortage of CC in every CMEA country are limiting the further expansion of intra-CMEA trade. When states have only additional soft goods to trade, their interest in trade expansion declines - which was, by and large, the case in intra-East European trade since the early 1970s. When a country wants to increase the exports of soft goods only, and demands in exchange increased quantities of hard goods - the Soviet position in recent years - its partners become reluctant to expand trade, irrespective of the fact that currently the USSR exports to Eastern Europe more hard goods than it imports.

A key difference between intra-EEC and intra-CMEA trade is the kinds of manufactures traded. Whereas much of the increase in intra-EEC trade has stemmed from *intra-industry* specialisation, ranging from components to finished products, intra-CMEA trade has involved mainly *inter-industry* specialisation in finished products, such as the exchange of Hungarian buses or Polish construction machinery for Soviet trucks. Specialisation in components, or by stage of processing beyond raw materials or standard intermediates, is the exception [Pecsi]. Thus the production of finished manufactures tends to be vertically integrated within each country (paralleling the high degree of vertical integration within enterprises), so that the small and medium-sized East European countries are unable to gain the static and dynamic benefits of economies of scale and specialisation.

This pattern of trade in manufactures is fostered by the planners'

---

4) "Relatively hard" because imports from the USSR were less attractive than imports from the world market in terms of quality and timeliness of deliveries. E.g. the best grades of cotton, needed as input into textile exports intended for the West, are not available; or the USSR is willing to export only ores with a higher waste content than it is economical to process.

preference for economic independence and by the mechanisms of intra-CMEA trade. Each country fears that dependence on inputs imported from CMEA partners may jeopardise the fulfillment of the plans in case of supply breakdowns, which are frequent in terms of quality and timeliness of deliveries. Aspects of the CMEA mechanism that hinder specialisation include:

- lack of strong interest by producers in exports, especially pronounced in the USSR where enterprises are often not willing to modify products to meet the requirements of "marginal" buyers from Eastern Europe.[5] By contrast, exports to the USSR are often very important for East European producers, whose output is often tailored to the requirements of the Soviet market;
- trade negotiations are conducted by ministries, not by enterprises. For central authorities it is less cumbersome to agree to trade tractors for buses than tractor parts for bus components;
- much of trade takes place on the basis of quotas included in the five-year trade agreements. It is thus necessary to forecast demand for machinery and equipment as far ahead as eight years because plan coordination begins three years before the current plan period ends. This does not facilitate the matching of product specifications between trade partners;
- prices in the CMEA reflect neither costs of production nor relative scarcities. To illustrate the problem this creates: in the late 1960s Poland and Czechoslovakia agreed to produce tractor parts and components for each other's markets; to resolve the debate about what each part or component was worth, they agreed to barter 10 kg of exports for 10 kg of "similar type" imports. Subsequently, the uncertainty about whether this yielded gains or losses was a factor in the decision to terminate the agreement.

Foreign direct investment

Throughout much of the postwar period, the economies of CPEs have been closed to FDI by Western firms. However, since the early 1970s, several economies began, gradually, to modify their attitudes toward MNCs. The USSR, Poland, Hungary, Romania, and Bulgaria began to promote industrial cooperation arrangements, mostly with MNCs, to license technology, to build turnkey factories, or to subcontract or co-produce a product. Subsequently, four East European countries began to promote - half-heartedly, to be sure - joint ventures in which Western partners could have minority interest [Marer and Miller]. In 1979 China, and in 1986 the Soviet Union,

---

5) For examples, see Bauer, et al.

also announced that joint production ventures on their territory are permitted. In recent years, China and Hungary have also created "special economic zones" where foreign firms can own and control fully export-oriented production ventures. Both countries view joint ventures as a way to obtain modern plant and equipment and know-how. In spite of a host of difficulties, by the end of 1986 China succeeded in attracting $ 7 billion (actually invested) [People's *Daily*]. Hungary agreed to some 70 joint ventures, about half in manufacturing, with a modest total of $ 80 million of foreign capital committed [Varga].

These reforms represent significant changes in the attitudes of some CPEs; others - Czechoslovakia, Albania, North Korea - have continued their uncompromising stance vis-à-vis the MNCs. Those that have liberalised their FDI laws have proceeded at varying paces and with notably different results. Even so, it is possible to make the general statement that the actual contribution of ICAs and joint ventures to the *general* upgrading of the technology, the productivity, and the export-competitiveness of the host countries has ranged from modest to insignificant.[6] So far China has been no exception to this generalisation [Battat]. Up until now, relatively few Western companies have entered into large-scale ICAs or joint ventures in CPEs, not only because of the political risks and constraints, but also because the economic mechanisms and policies of the CPEs have kept the expected gains much below potential.

A Western firm will invest capital, technology, and management resources in a foreign venture if it has a good chance of obtaining profitable access to natural resources or new markets, or if it can source products or components more competitively than from alternative locations. Not many investments in CPEs promise those gains because:

- time-consuming negotiations, complicated requirements, and regulations (that may not be spelled out clearly and may change) increase the costs and risks for Western investors;
- access to natural resources is typically not allowed, China, with its offshore oil leases and large joint venture in coal, being an exception. In any event, given the declining trend in world energy and raw material prices, there is not likely to be much investor interest in natural resource ventures in the immediate future;
- poor infrastructure (especially the communication and transport systems), and the absence of networks of independent suppliers and subcontractors of basic inputs, parts, components, and services, may make local

6) See Marer, 1986a; other country studies published in the same OECD series on technology transfers; and Monkiewicz and von Czege.

operations difficult. Even if suppliers can be found, Western firms may not have routine commercial access to them;

- on most ICAs and practically all joint ventures, CPEs typically impose stringent export-performance requirements, or simply close access to the domestic market, even though there is no guarantee that the venture in the host country can become a cost-competitive producer on the world market. In the light of labour and other costs and productivity levels, it is doubtful that the CMEA countries have a comparative advantage *vis-à-vis* most NICs in labour-intensive manufacturing. They could, however, become competitive with products and technologies embodying relatively large amounts of high-skilled labour. China, on the other hand, has already succeeded in attracting investment in labour-intensive manufacturing and has great potential in this area. In any event, since factor and product prices and exchange rates are administratively established and changed, computations of cost, revenue, and profit in CPEs are notably uncertain;
- nonconvertibility of CPE currencies increases the uncertainty and risk of profit repatriation;
- in view of the relatively small size of the markets of the individual East European countries, inability to penetrate from an East European base the entire CMEA market (that of the USSR often being the prime target) limits severely the interest of MNCs in investing in Eastern Europe. The difficulties of selling on the other CMEA markets stem from the inconvertibility of the currencies, the shortcomings of CMEA trade mechanisms and the apparent unwillingness of the prospective East European host countries actively to promote such deals. Their reluctance stems from their urgent need to earn more CC and the apparent unwillingness of the USSR and other CMEA partners to make firm advance commitments to import the output of the joint venture, much less to pledge to pay in CC or at least in hard goods. Given the potential size of their markets, this is not a problem for the USSR or for China, provided that domestic market penetration through a joint venture is a feasible option.

Admittedly, not all of the constraints enumerated may be relevant to each and every prospective venture. It is also true that ingenious ways have been found to sidestep the obstacles. But in today's world in which more than 100 countries compete to attract MNCs through ICAs, joint ventures, and wholly-owned subsidiaries, a realistic assessment of the competitive positions of the CPEs is needed. Notwithstanding numerous cases of successful foreign ventures in CPEs, their environment is not, on balance, very attractive for FDI, China being a partial exception.

Until now, FDI between the CMEA countries themselves has not taken place on any significant scale, although sizeable investment contributions have been made (mostly by the East European countries to the USSR) for natural resource development and transport projects, in return for assured quantities of future deliveries of products. There has been no significant FDI in manufacturing, for the same reasons that hinder trade specialisation.

International financial integration

One indicator of the extent of a country's financial integration with the rest of the world is the amount it is willing to borrow (lend) abroad; another is its willingness to join international financial organisations such as the IMF and the World Bank. Although standardised measures of indebtedness, such as debt-service and debt-export ratios, are far from perfect, they suggest differences in willingness to depend on external finance[7].

Table 11.2 compares these ratios (CC debt only) for eight CPEs and four heavily indebted NICs for 1981. Countries are divided into four categories, from the most heavily indebted to slightly indebted. Although focusing on one or the other ratio might place a country into a higher or lower category, important differences between the countries emerge clearly. Under either measure, Poland became one of the most heavily indebted countries of the world by the early 1980s, even more than Mexico or Brazil. Among the heavily indebted we find Hungary, the GDR, and Romania (although more recently Romania has cut its debt by pushing exports even at the expense of exacerbating severe shortages in the domestic economy). Among the moderately indebted countries are Czechoslovakia and Bulgaria[8]. China and the USSR were among the least indebted countries of the world. Especially surprising is the policy of China: at the end of 1981 the country's net foreign deposits exceeded its borrowing by about $ 6 billion (Wharton, report of August 31, 1982); when so many countries began to face severe debt-servicing difficulties, China - one of the world's poorest countries - was a net foreign lender through 1984. Very modest also was the indebtedness of the USSR - simultaneously a creditor of Eastern Europe and (like Eastern Europe) of selected developing countries also.

Four of the eight CPEs have become members of the IMF and the World Bank: Romania (1972), China (1980), Hungary (1982) and Poland (1986).

---

7) One problem with these indicators is that if a country borrows beyond prudent limits, it will have to reschedule or default, steps that are usually accompanied by major cuts in imports.

8) Bulgaria took out very large debts through 1978 but then reduced its debt burden.

Table 11.2

Debt-service and debt-export ratios of selected countries in 1981

	Debt-service ratio %	Debt-Export ratio %
Most heavy indebted		
Poland	102	399
Brazil	57	331
Mexico	see below	293
Yugoslavia	see below	215
Heavily indebted		
S. Korea	see below	120
Hungary	45	90
GDR	44	95
Mexico	45	see above
Romania	35	see below
Yugoslavia	33	see above
Moderately indebted		
Romania	see above	49
Czechoslovakia	26	46
Bulgaria	23	22
S. Korea	21	see above
Slightly indebted		
China (1982 data)	11	-19
USSR	7	29

Sources: [Tyson], Table 1, except USSR: [Wharton], April 27, 1982, and China: [Wharton Outlook], October 1985, p. 163.

To summarise the foreign trade *policies* (but not the trade *outcomes*): all CPEs are found to be highly protectionist because no import competition is allowed, a significant share of trade is not on the basis of comparative advantage, and exports are discriminated against. Nevertheless, the Soviet Union, the countries of East Europe, and also China had increased CC imports rapidly during the 1970s to help alleviate shortages caused by their development strategy, by the wasteful use of inputs, and by the increased difficulties of obtaining hard goods from CMEA partners. All these countries except the USSR had also tried, at various times and with varying intensity, to promote manufactured exports. But only China has been conspicuously successful. Between 1977 and 1984 the rate of growth of the value of China's exports has approximately matched the rapid expansion of its imports [Sheahan, p. 55]. After several decades of rapid growth of intra-CMEA trade, numerous constraints now hinder its further expansion.

Many CPEs are attempting gradually to establish links with MNCs; today, many CPEs are promoting industrial cooperation and are willing to serve as host countries for joint ventures. In this area, the direction of *policies* is toward opening, although the *outcomes* do not indicate this, owing to systemic impediments to attracting Western corporations. There are notably large differences between CPEs in willingness to assume foreign debt, ranging from Poland, one of the world's most heavily indebted countries, to China, a net creditor to the rest of the world during the early 1980s.

Table 11.3 summarises the pattern of foreign economic strategies and the role of the authorities in CPEs.

Table 11.3

Degree of openness of the foreign economic strategies of centrally planned economies

Country	Foreign trade	Financial integration	Foreign direct investment	Government intervention
USSR	low-moderate	low-moderate	low	control
Poland	low-moderate	high	low-moderate	control
Hungary	low-moderate	high	low-moderate	control-guidance
Romania	low-moderate	high-moderate	low-moderate	control
Bulgaria	low-moderate	moderate	low-moderate	control
Czechoslovakia	low-moderate	moderate	low	control
GDR	low-moderate	moderate-high	low	control
China (1979-)	moderate	moderate	moderate	control-guidance

11.4 Determinants of foreign economic strategy choices

What factors explain differences in the foreign economic strategies of nations, not only between market economies and CPEs but the significant variations within each group, and the policy changes of individual nations? Some subset of the following variables appears to be significant.

Resource endowment: Countries poorly endowed with natural resources and not self-sufficient in agriculture realise the importance of exporting manufactures: Japan, Taiwan, Korea, Singapore, and Hong Kong are examples. This view is expressed powerfully in the Hong Kong doctrine of "sweet peaches", meaning that it must continually offer goods desirable to the rest of the world [Johnson, p. 563]. By contrast, most countries of Latin

America and Eastern Europe are much better endowed with natural resources and opportunities for agriculture, so that they had less apparent need to open up their economies to essential imports.

Size of country: Size is relevant not only in terms of diversified resources but also in opportunities to be self-sufficient without a huge sacrifice in economic efficiency. Size may be a partial explanation of why the USSR, China (until 1977), India, and Brazil (up to 1964) have pursued inward-looking policies.

Level of development: Very poor countries, with no industrial base beyond traditional clothing and housing activities, few skilled workers and entrepreneurs, and poor infrastructure are unlikely to achieve much capacity for growth by opening the economy. At best, they could export a few primary products but those sectors will have few linkages to the rest of the economy. For such countries, some combination of protection and state promotion of new activities is probably necessary [Sheahan, p. 15]. India after it won its independence, and the poorest countries of Africa and Latin America may be cases in point. More developed countries, on the other hand, tend to prefer "open" policies; so may poor countries where the colonial administration has developed infrastructure and human resources (Taiwan, Hong Kong), where there has been an influx of disciplined labour and entrepreneurs (Taiwan, Hong Kong), and where the state has provided broad-based educational opportunities (Taiwan, Hong Kong, Singapore, S. Korea, Japan).

Historical experience and tradition: Countries invaded or blatantly exploited by outside powers, and countries with long traditions of antagonism toward each other, are likely to place a high priority on maintaining their sovereignty and achieving economic independence. Therefore they are apt to pursue policies believed to achieve those objectives. China certainly, much of Africa, to a certain extent India, and in some degree the countries of Latin America, the USSR, and Eastern Europe are cases in point. For example, when the Austro-Hungarian Monarchy - a large and economically integrated entity in East Central Europe - disintegrated after World War I, the successor states (Austria, Hungary, Czechoslovakia, Poland, Romania, Serbia) were left with one-sided production capacities, so that relatively free trade between them became essential. But political relations between the newly independent countries were so antagonistic that all of them imposed high trade barriers and opted for IS industrialisation.

> Thus, protection invoked in the name of self-sufficiency inevitably pushed the countries of East Central Europe much further away from one another than the countries of the area as a whole from those of Western Europe. Notwithstanding the circumstances of proximity, natural opportunities and historical traditions,

> the volume of trade among the countries of the region shrank considerably ... [which] had a strong and negative influence on [their] economic growth during the period following World War I [Berend and Ranki, pp. 90-91].

After World War II, this historical tradition strengthened policies of attempted autarky and has continued to hinder regional integration in Eastern Europe. Historical traditions that may influence policies also concern such matters as the role of the state in economic development: very strong, for example, in Russia and China and significant in Japan and Korea.

Economic or political doctrine: During the 1950s, many economists in Latin America, and experts associated with the UN Economic Commission for Latin America, accepted the economic doctrine and policy recommendations of Argentine economist Raul Prebisch. He held that there is a persistent, long-run tendency for the terms of trade of developing countries specialising in exporting primary products to deteriorate; the policy prescription was IS industrialisation behind import barriers. In Latin America this policy was a continuation of what most countries in the region had already practised since the depression of the 1930s. After winning political independence, many developing countries in Asia and Africa followed the Latin American lead [Root, Chapter 18]. IS became a way of life because policy-makers underestimated its costs and overestimated the obstacles to EP. Much of East Europe also inherited from the interwar period a tradition of protectionism and attempted IS industrialisation [Berend and Ranki, pp. 82-91]. Superimposing on that a Marxist-Leninist political orientation, which proclaimed the "law of imperialist exploitation" of poor by rich countries, has reinforced this tradition. Decision-makers in the CPEs, and many economist in the Third World especially in Latin America, were influenced by Marxism-Leninism, notably during the 1950s and 1960s.

External political relations: The more antagonistic are political relations between prospective trade partners, the more inward-looking will be the trade polices pursued. During the Cold War, the West practised policies of trade denial toward China, the USSR, and Eastern Europe, while the CPEs pursued policies of autarky from the West and integration among themselves. Even today, trends in East-West economic relations to some degree mirror trends in East-West political relations.

Economic system: This is clearly a very important determinant of the foreign economic policies of nations. The key aspect is the degree of differentiation between the state and the economy: the extent to which the state identifies its interest with those of *individual* producers and whether the price system makes it possible to assess the economic performance of producers. Differentiation is uniformly low in all CPEs; it ranges widely in other economies. Low differentiation is highly correlated with inward-oriented policies, more generally with lack of competition. Numerous features of a Soviet-type CPE reinforce the inward orientation of its policy-makers, as was noted above.

Domestic political strength of the authorities: A policy of export promotion involves trading off costs in the short-run for longer-term gains. Governments viewed as legitimate, and with strong political support, are more likely to be in a position to take a long-term view. Weak governments, by contrast, are always looking for short-run solutions. It is also easier for weak governments to lose macro-economic control if the money supply and/or wages increase too rapidly. Loss of macro-economic balance leads or contributes to balance of payments pressures, which in turn reinforce the short-term "crisis-management" policies, under which import controls become more pervasive.

Learning from experience: Many countries have altered policies or changed course as they learned from their own experiences and those of others. Many developing countries began the post-World War II period with a strong orientation toward inward-looking policies, and then changed to outward-oriented policies, though there have been examples of movement in the other direction also [Sheahan, p. 6].

To conclude, the foreign economic strategies of the nations may be classified into three broad categories, though with significant differentiation within each group. Much more work needs to be done to define more precisely and to classify nations. As a first approximation, using as examples the group of economies discussed above, the main categories, and the most plausible reasons why nations belong to them, are:

(a) The "open" economies of the industrialised countries and the East Asian NICs. The key determinants of policy choices seem to be: for the industrialised countries, their proven international competitiveness (which in part can be traced to the relatively open policies which they pursued for long periods during earlier development stages); for the Asian NICs, their sense of dependence on world markets for imported food and raw materials which have to be financed by the export of manufactures. However, only the trade and financial policies of most countries in this group can be termed generally "open". With respect to FDI, the practices range from being fully open (most of the industrialised countries except Canada and France, plus Singapore and Hong Kong) to being only moderately open. In the latter groups some countries are "moderately open" (they could also be designated "moderately closed") because government regulations represent a significant barrier to entry (Japan), and/or because detailed performance requirements are imposed on foreign investors (S. Korea, Taiwan). Even with respect to international financial integration, the practices of some relatively open countries vary. For example, Hong Kong is the world's third largest financial centre, with more than one hundred private foreign banks maintaining 1,000 offices, many with branches or correspondent relationships all over the world [*Investment*, Vol. III, p. 62]. In Taiwan, by contrast, most domestic banks are publicly owned, the few foreign banks allowed are restricted primarily to lending in foreign currencies, and earnings from investment without prior approval cannot be repatriated [*Investment*, Vol. III, pp. 263-4]. Relative openness of foreign economic strategies may be associated either with low or with considerable government intervention, the latter taking the form of significant government ownership of the means of production and some type of "guidance" of the private business sector.

(b) The "inward-oriented" economies of most countries in Latin America, of many in Africa, and of several in Asia (e.g. India, Pakistan). Their common policy feature is strong import substitution and extensive government ownership and operation of public services, mining, and heavy industrial firms. Interestingly, the extent of government involvement in the economy appears to be as great in most of the East Asian NICs as in Latin American countries. For example, both S. Korea and Taiwan allocate as large a share of fixed capital through state enterprises; but the share of GDP originating in state enterprises is apparently greater in S. Korea and Taiwan than in much of Latin America [Sachs]. The difference between the East Asians and Latin Americans lies more in the way state-owned enterprises are managed and in the longer time horizon, and greater market-conformity of government intervention to guide the private business sector. In part, the IS policies in this group are explained by the larger size of many Latin American economies, and of India and Pakistan, and their superior resource endowments; the costs of IS are perceived to be less and the costs of inevitable dependence on world markets as weaker, than in East Asia [Tyson, p. 248]. The low levels of development of some countries, and the prevailing economic philosophy or Marxist-Leninist political orientation of some leaders, probably also helped to determine their strategies. Attitudes toward foreign direct investment have varied, though on balance have been more restrictive than in the countries of group (a). Many nations have become "open" only in their willingness to borrow large sums, although their high levels of indebtedness may be more the unintended consequence of domestic economic policies, and the unforeseen results of external developments, than conscious policy choices.

(c) The "extremely inward-oriented economies", primarily the CPEs plus a few others (such as Burma). Although the CPEs and the inward-oriented economies in group (b) have pursued similar development strategies, a key difference between them is that the CPEs have a Soviet-type economic and political system, which causes trade policies to be highly protectionist and their economy to be inflexible in responding to external economic signals. Historical experience and traditions, as well as adversary relations with the West, have reinforced these systemic and policy features. A key similarity between the CPEs and other inward-oriented economies is that the high levels of indebtedness of both may in large measure be attributed to the domestic economic policies pursued. As CPEs undertake comprehensive, market-oriented reforms, the room for significant differentiation in foreign economic policies is, gradually, being created.

11.5 Consequences of alternative strategies

I draw four main conclusions from the foregoing discussion of alternative foreign economic strategies, first stated briefly, and then elaborated.

First, that outward-oriented strategies are associated with significantly better overall economic performance than are inward-oriented strategies pursued over a long period.

Second, that the key aspects of a successful foreign economic strategy are an export-oriented trade policy in manufactures and good macroeconomic control over the domestic economy; policies toward foreign direct investment and external financial integration are less important.

Third, that the economic mechanism of countries with a Soviet-type CPE system imposes a severe constraint on their policy-makers' ability to implement successfully a change from an inward- to an outward-oriented economic strategy without fundamental reforms in the economic mechanism.

Fourth, that pursuing for a long time policies intended to replace imports with domestic production regardless of comparative advantage, or policies intended to achieve economic independence regardless of costs, typically leads to outcomes the opposite of those intended.

Let me elaborate briefly on these conclusions.

The *first conclusion* is that open economic strategies are associated with significantly better overall economic performance has been amply documented (Krueger-1983 and 1985; Sheahan). As regards the economic performance of CPEs, evaluations based on their official statistics tend to overstate performance because:

- the officially reported growth rates of CPEs tend to be significantly upward-biased (Marer, 1985);
- in any event, growth rates do not reveal how much of what CPEs produce would be purchased by enterprises, consumers and CMEA importers if convertible currency imports were to be allowed at realistic exchange rates; and

- CPE economic systems and policies "hide" both unemployment (within the factory gates and farms) and inflationary pressures (revealed primarily through shortages and forced substitutions rather than price increases).

The two preferred measures of economic performance, in my view, are trends in export competitiveness in manufactures on the world market and improvements over time in the standard of living. If the export competitiveness of CPEs is measured by changes in the market share of their manufactures, say, from the mid-1960s till the mid-1980s, then all CPEs have performed poorly [Poznanski, 1986b], even though during this period Western discrimination, substantial as it may have been, did not increase and probably decreased. Concerning the standard of living, most experts would probably agree that although in most CPEs the improvements until the early 1980s were substantial, the rate of improvement (taking the quality of goods and services available also into account) has been substantially less in the USSR and Eastern Europe than in Western Europe.

The *second conclusion*, that good economic performance is tied closely to a country's timely move toward outward-oriented trade policies, combined with good macroeconomic control, is based on both logic and fact. This is not to deny that economic performance is influenced also by the values, the character, and the cohesion of the nation; by its inherited environment; and by economic and political developments outside its borders; or that ability to shift policies is influenced by the domestic political situation and by the economic strength of the country. Even so, the point is that inward-oriented, extreme versions of import substitution policies, pursued for extended periods, hinder economic development, for the following reasons:

- the small size of domestic markets in all but a few countries constrains economic growth under import substitution policies because industry can expand only up to the size of the domestic market (which itself remains below potential because output is typically priced higher than on the world market). In many cases plants must be of a minimum size to operate efficiently and at low cost. An export-oriented régime, however, makes it possible to establish plants of economically efficient size;
- efficient manufacturing entails the use of a wide variety of inputs. In countries pursuing import substitution policies, producers are often forced to obtain inputs from protected domestic suppliers, whose costs, quality control, design, engineering, product innovation and timeliness of delivery may leave much to be desired. Forced reliance on their products thus raises the costs and lowers the quality of output throughout the economy;
- the demands for particular inputs are often fairly specialised so that under an import substitution régime there is often only one or a

small number of domestic suppliers. Consequently, delivery problems encountered by one firm or in one sector disrupt the operations of other firms and industries quickly. Under an export promotion régime, exporters have access to the world market to obtain inputs;

- that only one or a very few firms produce a given product under an import substitution régime means that domestic competition is difficult to promote. Many firms with monopolistic or oligopolistic power cannot be broken up because they would then lose economies of scale or supply lines would be disrupted. Under an export promotion régime, domestic firms are less likely to have monopoly power;
- under an import substitution régime, where the authorities directly control imports, even the most capable bureaucracy will make mistakes, because it is not possible to foresee the full consequences of limiting this or that import. The bureaucracy may also be corrupt or show favouritism based on "connections". In any event, firms needing imports will have a built-in incentive to misrepresent their needs to improve access to imports. The authorities counter with more regulation and pervasive import control becomes a way of life. The resulting bargaining games misdirect the energies and initiatives of government officials and managers;
- the high degree of across-the-board protection restricts competition and the entry of new firms. One reason is the bureaucratic allocation of imports, either on the basis of quotas granted during a base period or in proportion to output shares. If the resale of inputs is costly or prohibited, market shares - and thus production structures - will remain rigid, and the growth rates of most firms and industries fairly uniform;
- since import substitution régimes often increase imports faster than exports, they will tend to face recurrent balance of payments problems, constraining economic growth.

Export promotion policies promote good economic performance partly because they improve the efficiency of resource allocation - its static benefits - but mainly because they improve the ability of the economy to capture various dynamic gains: those associated with increased competition, greater specialisation, economies of scale, and government intervention in the form of positive incentive rather than negative restrictions.

Another key variable affecting performance is macroeconomic control, which may be weak for diverse reasons. Macroeconomic control refers to the ability of the state to keep (open or hidden) inflation in check and (in market economies) the exchange rate realistic. Poor macroeconomic control leads to loss of export competitiveness in manufactures, which in turn strengthens import substitution policies; permanent and rather extreme forms of such policies in turn reinforce weak macroeconomic control owing to the excessive protection provided to (often monopolistic or oligopolistic) domestic producers. To be sure, a high degree of openness makes a country, especially a small economy, highly vulnerable to external shocks, which the authorities may try to counteract with expansionary fiscal and monetary policies, which in turn can cause macroeconomic imbalance if not loss of control. Such imbalances appeared after the first oil shock in Australia, Austria, Belgium, Denmark, Finland, Iceland, Ireland, Luxembourg, the Netherlands, New Zealand, Norway, Spain, and Sweden. In all these countries, increased government spending and decreased taxes led to the loss of macroeconomic balance, with accelerating inflation contributing to a deterioration in the balance of payments [Blondall].

In scores of developing countries, the loss of macroeconomic control has more fundamental causes. Many developing countries seek to remedy insufficient voluntary savings in their economy (the so-called "savings gap") through budgetary deficits, which breed inflation and external payment problems. Reluctant to correct the deficits by cutting domestic spending (and thereby falling short of development targets), or by exchange rate devaluation (in the belief it would not work, would cause more inflation, or for political reasons), the authorities respond with import and exchange restrictions. Inflation, overvalued exchange rates, and import controls all too frequently limit export expansion [Root, Chapter 18].

The "expansion drives" of CPEs often have parallel results. For example, a detailed study of Hungary's foreign economic policy, published in Hungary, concludes:

> Attempted import substitution by the centre was reinforced by the expansion drives of enterprises. At the same time, this attracted huge imports, in part because manufacturing decisions were made without due attention to our comparative advantage and on the other because the manufacture of uneconomic products was not discontinued. [In addition,] imports increased also because poor investment specialisation reinforced Hungary's technological backwardness. Thus, despite the excessive preferences given to import substitution - and in spite of the expectation that this will lower imports - the Western raw material import content of a unit of production increased continuously. While in 1959 1,000 forint of industrial production required 32 forint of materials imported from capitalist sources, by 1975 the same increased to 44 forints [Facsady, p. 34].

For developing and for planned economies alike, the consequences of such policies are predictable:

> ...rapid growth in import demands; a diversion of resources to production for the home market; and an intensification of inflationary pressures which show up either openly in rapidly

rising prices or covertly in shortages, black markets, and the like. [Tyson, p. 151].

Mexico and Poland, countries with different economic systems, are good examples of especially lax macroeconomic controls contributing to poor economic performance.

Mexico reacted to the second explosion of oil prices during 1979-80 by accelerating, in response to domestic political pressures, its growth-cum-debt strategy. Savouring an unrealistic vision of mushrooming future oil revenues, an excessively ambitious expansion of investment and public-sector spending was pursued. Foreign lenders were willing to provide finance, even though Mexico's exchange rate became increasingly overvalued, which hurt non-oil exports and led to massive capital flight in expectation of the inevitable devaluation [Tyson, p. 261].

In Poland, the Gierek leadership also pursued a strategy of accelerated growth, making export projections that were continuously much too optimistic, while foreign lenders provided finance. During the 1970s the authorities gradually lost control of the growth in investment and wages, the national plan becoming little more than an aggregation of the demands of powerful industry heads and regional political leaders [Poznanski 1986a]. There, too, the ultimate reason was political: party leaders pursued only their individual interests. Political leaders divided up power and authority among themselves so that each became free to act. Even when a collective decision was made, it was often not implemented because opponents of the decision controlled the organisation that had to implement it [Comisso, pp. 232-3].

> Procedures and rules no longer applied, and targets became irrelevant to real economic capacities. Make-shift solutions became the mode, while economic and administrative actors could literally purchase permission to act as they wish or use the threat of spontaneous group protest to claim the resources they wanted... On lower levels the attenuation of rules was reflected in wage drift; on higher levels it materialised as bribery and corruption... The upshot was that those who were in principle politically responsible for state actions in practice found themselves unable to control them [Comisso, pp. 234-5].

In recent years many countries have recognised the costs associated with extreme inward-looking policies (as well as those associated with insufficient macroeconomic control) and have begun to change them.

Our *third conclusion* is that such a transformation is much easier for economies that are predominantly market-based than for CPEs, whose protectionist trade policies are determined more by their economic *system* than by feasible policy choices. Whatever the ownership arrangements, in the absence of a real market mechanism (as distinct from central planners using market-type instruments to implement the central plan), including substantial domestic and import competition, no real transformation is likely even if imports from the West increase rapidly, if attitudes and laws toward FDI are liberalised, and if large and foreign loans are taken. This conclusion suggests that to maximise the benefits and to minimise the costs of opening up the economy, comprehensive economic reforms are needed.

> The administrative instruments of central planning have proven themselves to be powerful tools for the compression of demand, but they have also proven themselves to be poorly designed for the promotion of supply except via the rapid mobilisation of capital and labour resources, a choice constrained [today in many countries] by current and future scarcities [Tyson, p. 282].

Comprehensive economic reforms, in my view, must include:

- Giving up detailed, administrative directives to producers;
- Replacing directives with profit maximisation (subject to constraints) by enterprises, with realistic and enforced timetables of implementing hard-budget constraints on producers;
- The above, in turn, requires a reform in the price system under which individual prices are less and less determined administratively and more and more by supply and demand forces;
- The above, in turn, requires that the monopolistic concentration of producers be eliminated whenever the economies of scale allow it and that gradually introduced import competition be relied upon to exert competitive pressures on monopolistic domestic producers;
- A key element of the reform must be also the elimination of the foreign trade monopoly (less essential for primary products than for manufactures) and the introduction of unified and realistic exchange rates.

It is self-evident that the introduction of such comprehensive reforms is an exceedingly complex and politically difficult task; even under favourable circumstances, it can be implemented only gradually. In this regard, significant progress among the CPEs has occurred only in Hungary since 1968 and in China since 1979. (Yugoslavia has introduced a set of reforms that in many ways are different from those sketched above, and are uniquely applicable only to that country). Although the distance between the traditional CPE and the economic systems prevailing in Hungary and China (the two sharing similarities as well as differences) is substantial, both countries have a long way to go before they have in place a system that can accomplish the economic objectives of their systems' directors.

Is integration within the CMEA an alternative to the comprehensive economic reforms and opening to the West? I do not believe so, owing to the many well-documented shortcomings of the CMEA mechanism, fundamentally rooted in the domestic CPE systems of its members. Suffice it to point out that regional integration for the East European countries has meant for years attempting to secure the largest possible quantities of energy, raw materials, and intermediate goods from the USSR and from each other because that source of supply was considered to be the most secure, because prices were (temporarily) lower than on the world market, and because imports could be paid "advantageously" in part with "soft" manufactures. But whatever short-term gains this policy may have provided to some members, it proved to be unwise, for several reasons. The USSR is not satisfied with the arrangements. One reason is that this form of integration required the USSR to invest in energy and raw material development beyond the point considered economic. Furthermore, supplying growing quantities of these goods has preempted the CC revenues that it badly needs. In addition, the USSR is becoming less and less satisfied with the quality and modernity of goods received in payment. In the long run, the East European countries have also not benefited because this relatively easy access to energy and certain raw materials has allowed them to perpetuate their economies' excessively energy- and material-intensive structure of production, an important reason why their products have continued to lose competitiveness in the world as well as in the CMEA markets.

The *fourth and basic conclusion* of this chapter is that the pursuit of economic security through excessive protectionism - whether it appears openly, as in some industrialised countries, or in disguised forms, as in the CPEs and a certain group of developing countries - typically leads to outcomes the opposite of those intended by the policy-makers.

References

[Bauer] - Tamás Bauer, et al., Járműprogram és gazdaságirányítás [Public Vehicle Program and Economic Mechanism], Budapest: Közgadaságtudományi Intézet, 1980.

[Battat] - Joseph Y. Battat, "China's Special Economic Zones: Strategic Consideration", paper presented at conference on "The Role of Foreign Investment in National Development, with Special Reference to China", Hang-Zhou Zhejiang Province, November 1985.

[Berend and Ránki] - Iván T. Berend and György Ránki, East Central Europe in the 19th and 20th Centuries, Budapest, Akademiai Kiadó, 1977.

[Blondall] - Gisli Blondall, Fiscal Policy in the Smaller Industrial Countries, 1972-82, Washington, DC, IMF, 1986.

[Comisso] - Ellen Comisso, "Introduction: State Structures, Political Processes, and Collective Choice in CMEA States", International Organization, Vol. 40, No. 2 (Spring 1986).

[Facsady] - Júlia Facsady, "A befelé fordulás (importhelyettesítő stratégia) magyarországi multjáról és gyökereiről" [The History and Roots of Hungary's Turning Inward (Import Substitution) Strategy], Külgazdaság Vol. XXX (July 1986).

[Fei] - John C.H. Fei, Gustav Ranis and Shirley W.Y. Kuo, Growth With Equity: The Taiwan Case, New York and Oxford, Oxford University Press, 1979.

[Gacs] - János Gacs, "A fokozatos importliberalizálás megvalósításának feltételei, lehetősége és várható következményei a magyar gazdaságban" [Conditions, Possibilities, and Expected Consequences of Gradual Import Liberalisation in Hungarian Economy], Külgazdaság (Budapest), XXX, No. 4 (April 1986).

[Investment] - Investment Climate in Foreign Countries (Volume I: OECD and Other European Countries; Volume III: Asia, excluding Japan; Volume IV: Western Hemisphere, excluding Canada) Washington DC, US Dept of Commerce, 1983.

[Johnson] - Johnson, Chalmers, "The Nonsocialist NICs: East Asia" International Organization, Vol. 40, No. 2 (Spring 1986).

[Kornai] - János Kornai, "The Hungarian Reform Process: Visions, Hopes, and Reality", Journal of Economic Literature, Vol. XXIV, No. 4 (December 1986).

[Köves] - András Köves, The CMEA Countries in the World Economy: Turning Inwards or Turning Outwards, Budapest, Akadémiai, 1985.

[Krueger, 1983] - Anne O. Krueger, "The Effects of Trade Strategies on Growth", Finance and Development, June 1983.

[Krueger, 1985] - Anne O. Krueger, "Import Substitution versus Export Promotion", Finance and Development, June 1985.

[Marer, 1985] - Paul Marer, Dollar GNPs of the USSR and Eastern Europe, Baltimore, Johns Hopkins University Press for the World Bank, 1985.

[Marer, 1986a] - Paul Marer, East-West Technology Transfer: Study of Hungary, 1968-1984, Paris, OECD, 1986.

[Marer, 1986b] - Paul Marer, "Economic Reform in Hungary: From Central Planning to Regulated Market", in Joint Economic Committee, US Congress, East European Economies: Slow Growth in the 1980s, Vol. 3: Country Studies on Eastern Europe and Yugoslavia, Washington DC, US Government Printing Office, 1986.

[Marer and Miller] - Paul Marer and Joseph C. Miller, "US Participation in East-West Industrial Cooperation Agreements", Journal of International Business Studies, Fall-Winter 1977.

[Marrese] - Michael Marrese, "CMEA: Effective but Cumbersome Political Economy", International Organization, Vol. 40, No. 2 (Spring 1986).

[Monkiewicz and von Czege] - Jan Monkiewicz and Andreas Wass von Czege, "Western Direct Investment in CMEA and Technology Transfer: Some Preliminary Observations", Occasional Paper No. 44 of the Institut für Außenhandel und Überseewirtschaft der Universität Hamburg, July 1986.

[Nehrt] - Lee Nehrt, The Politico-Economic Analysis of Countries, New York, Gabriel Haugue Chair Monograph Series No. 1 of the Manhattan College, School of Business Research Institute, 1981.

[Pécsi] - Kálmán Pécsi, The Future of Socialist Economic Integration, Armonk, New York, M.E. Sharpe, 1981.

[Poznanski, 1986a] - Kazimierz Poznanski, "Economic Adjustment and Political Forces: Poland Since 1970", International Organization, Vol. 40, No. 2 (Spring 1986).

[Poznanski, 1986b] - Kazimierz Poznanski, "Competition Between Eastern Europe and Developing Countries in the Western Market for Manufactured Goods", in Joint Economic Committee, op. cit., Vol. 2: Foreign Trade and International Finance.

[Root] - Franklin R. Root, International Trade and Investment, Cincinnati, South-Western Publishing, 1984, fifth ed.

[Sachs] - Jeffrey D. Sachs, "External Debt and Macroeconomic Performance in Latin America and East Asia", Washington DC, Brookings Papers on Economic Activity, 1985:2.

[Sheahan] - John B. Sheahan, "Alternative International Economic Strategies and Their Relevance for China", World Bank Staff Working Paper No. 759, 1986.

[Tyson] - Laura D'Andrea Tyson, "The Debt Crisis and Adjustment Responses in Eastern Europe: A Comparative Perspective", International Organization, Vol. 40, No. 2 (Spring 1986).

[Varga] - Gy. Varga, "Joint Ventures in Hungary", paper presented at the Tenth US-Hungarian Economic Round-table, Budapest, December 1986.

[Wharton] - Wharton Econometric Forecasting Associates, Centrally Planned Economies: Current Analysis (serial publication), and Centrally Planned Economies Outlook (semiannual).

COMMENTS ON PARTS II AND III - DOMESTIC AND EXTERNAL MACRO-POLICIES

Márton Tardos[1)]

My comments refer to three papers about the macro-economic policies of three German-speaking countries - two market economies: *Kloten* (Ch. 4) on the Federal Republic of Germany, *Seidel* (Ch. 5) on Austria; and one socialist economy, *Sydow* (Ch. 8) on the German Democratic Republic. One feature is common to all three economies - successful economic development. It is difficult to define the reason for this undoubted fact; I am inclined to think of factors analysed by social anthropologists rather than by economists. The German-speaking peoples are more industrious and more disciplined, by virtue of their cultural heritage, than most European nations. I cannot elaborate any further on this idea, but mention it because it represents a challenge to our relatively limited knowledge and demonstrates the need for more effort to understand the non-economic factors influencing national performance.

For the success of the FRG, I would stress the *Soziale Marktwirtschaft* as a specific feature. *Kloten* points out that in the early 1950s there was no attempt in the FRG at central coordination, because that would not have been in accord with the generally accepted neo-liberal concepts; even the Socialist Party (with its *Freie Wirtschaftsordnung*) put the emphasis on the *Wirtschaftsordnung*.

The pressures resulting from the inflows of foreign exchange, as well as from the cessation of the inflows of East German labour, certainly enhanced the importance of business cycle policy. The Act of June 1967 might be called a synthesis of the Keynesian message with the Freiburg school's liberal approach.

The subsequent development seems to show that the simultaneous fulfilment of the following four objectives - monetary stability, external balance, full employment and rapid growth - was not feasible. According to *Kloten's* arguments, the main lesson from this experience is the need for monetary stability, which can be considered as a prerequisite for economic stability. The government could achieve this aim if it were not involved in rescuing insolvent firms, if monetary and fiscal policy were to give clear guidelines to the parties in the labour market, if foreign trade were to be balanced and, last but not least, if the demand for public services were to be constrained.

The real lesson for those who would like to learn from the experience

---

1) Institute of Economics, Hungarian Academy of Sciences, Budapest

of the FRG is, however, the not very far-reaching recommendation in the paper that there is a need for some, but limited, central coordination and for a continuous and predictable monetary policy. I think that there are strong and convincing reasons for the statements emphasising the need for some central actions, but also the restricted possibilities for such actions. The success of the central authorities in practice is based more on the art of using power than on science. But we must also admit that this is a clear sign of the weakness of our knowledge.

Seidel's paper on Austria deals mainly with the same question: how the central regulation influences the successes and failures of the economy. The peculiarity of Austria is the *"Sozialpartnerschaft"*, which means that the representatives of the main social groups - workers, capital owners etc. - try to solve their conflicts by compromise reached by negotiations behind closed doors.

Seidel turns our attention to the question of what theory underlies Austrian practice. He quotes former Chancellor Kreisky's saying: "Austro-Keynesianism has as much to do with Keynes as Austro-Marxism with Marx - namely nothing".

On the actual practice of the central authorities *Seidel's* view is again very ambiguous. He writes about incomes policy, which in his view does not work; about an expansionary monetary and fiscal policy, which worsens the balance of payments; about aggregate demand management, which may fail in the short-run but, even if it succeeds, conceals structural defects and delays adjustment. Now we are in trouble again: we are looking at an Austrian success story, but with some weaknesses (slow-down in growth, increasing unemployment etc.) and our knowledge about the underlying reasons is very vague.

Turning to the GDR, *Sydow* emphasises the need for a shift from extensive (thriftless) growth to an intensive pattern. The specific feature of the GDR policy is the maintenance of the centralised hierarchy of the centrally planned system. Some other countries, in view of the rigid nature of mandatory planning, have turned in the direction of market forces (Yugoslavia, Poland, China, Hungary). The GDR is trying to solve the problem with a change called *"Vervollkommnung der Planung, Lenkung und Wirtschaftsrechnung"* (perfection of planning and control) and does not accept the call for "radical reforms".

The undoubted advantage of the GDR approach is its harmony with the existing political system. Some of the decision rights of government and the enterprises are reallocated to the combines without challenging the hierarchical system of mandatory planning. The change might bring positive results - not only because hitting mandatory targets is acceptable to people brought up in a Prussian environment - but also because management by the combines can easily overcome difficulties when enterprises in the combine have contradictory interests; the combine can find a compromise between the aims of the central agencies and those of the enterprises without losing the information gathered by the latter. The shortcomings of the concept are connected with the unavoidable fact that, even in the best organised system, combines will have contact with outside economic agents (producers of raw materials and of semifinished goods not produced in the combine, and buyers of their products). The problem of harmonising demand and supply in such cases remains unsolved.

Domenico Mario Nuti[1]

The GDR: can success continue?

Sydow (Ch. 8) reports the success story of comprehensive intensification of growth in the GDR and attributes the success to intra-CMEA division of labour, as envisaged by the CMEA Comprehensive Programme for scientific and technological progress up to the year 2000. The benefits of planned integration are contrasted with the discrimination and protectionism practised by non-socialist economies in their "strained" relationships with the GDR. It might be said, however, that the GDR enjoys a special relationship with the EC and other Western trade partners through its own special relationship with the Federal Republic. Without going as far as saying, as some have suggested, that the GDR has the same benefits that would accrue from membership of EC, there is no doubt that the close trade and credit ties with the FRG have solved precisely those structural problems - due to the mismatching of supply and demand structure - that have hindered and slowed down economic growth in other socialist countries, especially at times of economic crisis.

Also important in explaining GDR growth performance is the flexibility accorded by a combination of central planning and sectoral integration (through vertically integrated central combines which considerably reduce the size of planning tasks and therefore the drawbacks of centralisation); one can only agree with *Sydow*, while stressing at the same time the specific features that make that form of organisation particularly effective in the GDR, namely its economic diversification, the large size of its industrial sectors affected by economies of scale (also thanks to industrial exports), and its heavy reliance on imports for materials and energy.

---

1) European University Institute, Florence

There is no doubt that the policy course suggested is wise: high technology and export-led growth are a good course for any economy seeking high productivity for a stationary and fully employed labour force. The questions, however, remain open of whether a highly centralised economic system, though tempered by sectoral decentralisation, is best at implementing this policy course; and of whether CMEA can really take full advantage, especially in the short run, of the opportunities for economic integration which might give the GDR new advantages in the international division of labour. Might not economic reforms both in the domestic economy and CMEA institutions and rules be required for the policy outlined by *Sydow* to bear fruit? His optimism is not unreasonable but remains to be demonstrated.

FRG: success or failure?

Kloten (Ch. 4) stresses the importance, and at the same time the limits, of qualitative instruments of macroeconomic policy, referring to the FRG experience with the Stability and Growth Act and subsequent developments. The Act set as targets monetary stability, external balance, high employment and an appropriate real rate of growth. New public economic bodies were entrusted with policy responsibilities: the Economic Policy Council and the public sector's Council for Financial Planning. Indeed, concern about growth had been added after some controversy, and tempered by reassuring references to "the framework of a market economy", i.e. on the understanding that no predetermined growth rates would be part of macroeconomic policy; only anti-cyclical policies would have to be adopted. With monetary policy aimed simply at stabilisation, an exchange rate policy aimed at overall equilibrium in the balance of payments (i.e. compatible with persistent surpluses in the current account), and little room for incomes policy, the only active policy instrument remained fiscal policy, with specific stances - both at central and local levels - in different phases of the cycle.

In these circumstances, it is not surprising that *Kloten* should find that "In retrospect it becomes obvious that the target of stabilising overall economic development on a high level, in a stable monetary environment, was not reached". In spite of increases in the government share of GNP, unemployment grew while growth fell substantially below potential. *Kloten* attributes this policy failure to the poor quality of economic forecasts; Bundesbank intervention in interest and exchange rates at odds with the Act and its targets; procyclical behaviour of local authorities; an erratic tax policy; electoral considerations distorting financial policy; trade unions' disillusionment and ensuing frustration and militancy, intensifying the distributive struggle.

Kloten observes that the "Stability and Growth Act degenerated more and more into an empty shell" and concludes that "Even the best law will not live up to the expectations put on it, if social forces fail, especially if political opportunism hinders an exact execution of the law". He also stresses - if I understand him correctly - that targets were over-ambitious (this is how I read his reference to "too high conditions for success"). He draws from the FRG experience the lesson that a successful macroeconomic policy must be oriented towards the medium-run and (a) have little need for forecasts; (b) not put too high demands on the public sector; (c) make monetary policy continous and predictable; (d) provide "guidance" (in the sense of clear signals about government wishes, backed by monetary and financial policy) to wage negotiations; (e) ensure foreign balance without recourse to protectionism. I would draw different conclusions from the FRG experience: namely, that ambitious targets cannot be attained by supply side economics alone (i.e. by purely qualitative policy instruments); that stated policy targets were pursued by FRG governments (and Bundesbank governors) with different intensity, actual achievements reflecting precisely real priorities and intended trade-offs, so that one should talk not of policy failure, but of success; that a successful policy *à la Kloten* would amount to an effective demobilisation of public policy and would aim only at modest policy targets, i.e. close to the spontaneous course of economic events. One can hit a target by drawing a circle around the spot where the arrow has struck; but why bother? What kind of "policy" is this?

Austria: the end of a special case

Seidel reports, as one would have expected, that in 1973-85 the Austrian economy proved to be somewhat more shock-resistant than the average of industrialised countries. What is the secret of Austrian success? Not Austro-Keynesianism, because there is no such thing - argues Seidel - but a macroeconomic policy mix of comprehensive and institutionalised incomes policy (guaranteed by the central bank, which would only adopt restrictive policies if the economy was clearly overheated) and fairly expansionary fiscal and monetary policy. This has proved a better mix than fighting inflation by a restrictive monetary policy and attributing unemployment to wage rigidity.

Of course the Austrian thirty-years' experience with neo-corporatist institutions must have played an important role and cannot be repeated overnight, but the strategy of asking unions for wage moderation from an expansionary instead of a deflationary stance must also have been important. Usually social contracts do not work, because wage moderation is asked of unions for their own good in return for future uncertain employment gains, while the government meanwhile deflates, often brutally. The Austrians have synchronised the sacrifices and the gains associated with wage moderation, and this seems an important lesson.

An expansionary policy in the face of world recession was feasible, in Austria, because of its insignificant external debt; thus external deficits could be maintained for a while, in spite of the AS link with the DM and the temporary real revaluation of the AS. Only in 1977 was the balance of payments deficit a primary concern, but it was only stabilised instead of being reduced. Subsequent payments problems arose from capital movements, not trade. Anti-cyclical policy however was much more moderate after the second oil shock. This is regarded by *Seidel* - and by official policy pronouncements - effectively as the end of the specifically Austrian policy mix which had proved so successful in the past; not because of a change of mind on the part of policy makers but because the world has changed. Once the room for manoeuvre afforded by neo-corporatism and international credit-worthiness has been exhausted, Austria is now in the same boat as everybody else, dependent on "a coordinated international policy for economic growth".

One remaining instrument is indicated by *Seidel* as mitigating unemployment, i.e. the reduction of the working week. This however is not very convincing: such a reduction for the same weekly wage per worker raises unit costs just as a money wage rise would, and has the same adverse effects; while if money wages are reduced to match the shorter working week the ensuing reduction in real wage per worker is not as beneficial to employment promotion as it would be if it was accepted without shortening the working week. It remains to be demonstrated that the net benefits of a shorter week (if any, in view of greater organisational and other costs) can be significant.

Would the Austrian economy have been in a better shape if more unemployment had been accepted at an earlier date? *Seidel's* answer is "no". Others might think of possible advantages of earlier unemployment, such as lower external debt, earlier restructuring, lower inflation; the elusive and uncertain nature of these possible benefits, and the high human and real cost of such an alternative for the countries that have followed it, strongly support *Seidel's* conjecture.

Fritz Breuss[1)]

In the reviews of the prospects for the world economy (in Part I), not enough was said about the constraints on world trade, and hence on East-West relations, stemming from the "new protectionism". Thus *Klein* and *Bond* (Ch. 2) presented a rather rosy picture of medium-term growth of GDP in OECD countries at annual rates of 2-2½ per cent, and of a gradual depreciation of the US dollar, according to their simulations, increasing world GDP. I regret that, in the light of *Salvatore's* excellent paper (Ch. 10) on the emergence of the new protectionism with non-tariff instruments, I must doubt whether the game of unlimited depreciation of the dollar, without retaliations, can be played for ever.

Salvatore raises a most important, indeed a burning issue for the near future of international trade and the world economy. Starting in 1975 the general trend toward trade liberalisation (after the seven GATT rounds) was reversed. The deepest world-wide recession since the Great Depression of the 1930s, together with the increased competition from Japan and the Newly Industrialised Countries can be identified as "causes" for the rise of protectionism. Arguments for new forms of protectionism (the old form of tariff protection being contrary to GATT rules) are increasing unemployment and payments imbalances after OPEC I and OPEC II.

Salvatore distinguishes two kinds of Nontariff barriers (NTBs): (a) *Explicit* NTBs such as quotas (directly subject to GATT rules); "voluntary" export restraints (VERs) allowing countries to bypass GATT; safeguards such as anti-dumping measures; countervailing duties; orderly marketing arrangements. The data (available only for these NTBs) indicate that NTBs are highest in the USA and lowest in Japan. Why is this? The answer is that Japan uses more *implicit* NTBs. (b) *Implicit* NTBs: all administrative regulations protecting a domestic industry (such as steel) facing structural difficulties and a large decline in employment. Such NTBs are nearly impossible to identify statistically, but they exist! In addition, there is a huge area of protectionism in agricultural trade in the form of widespread domestic subsidy programmes (e.g. the EC's Common Agricultural Policy and the US farm subsidy programme), which leads from time to time to the US-EC "trade wars" in agricultural trade.

Salvatore takes the example of the VER, negotiated between the US and Japan, to limit Japanese automobile exports to the US (first to 1,68 million units per year, starting in April 1981; renewed in 1984). Who is the winner and who the loser? Clearly the exporters (Japan's car industry)

---

1) Austrian Institute for Economic Research (WIFO), Vienna

won a monopoly (or export) rent via increased car prices in the US market; consumers' welfare is reduced. But it helped also to make the US car industry profitable again after a long period of troubles. However the OECD study on "Costs and Benefits of Protection" (1985) showed impressively that the "new protectionism" had only limited success in protecting domestic employment.

Salvatore's regression model demonstrates that the demand for "escape clause" protection in the US is cyclical (rising when the level of domestic activity is low); it also confirms the "harassment" thesis. What is meant under "escape clause" protectionism? Under the Trade Act of 1974 a US industry may petition the US Tariff Commission to conduct an investigation to determine whether the domestic industry is, or is likely to be, injured by increased imports. Then a recommendation to the President to restrict imports is possible (via tariffs, import quota, orderly marketing arrangements, etc.).

Furthermore, the author points to a close link between the "new protectionism" (especially the implicit NTB), and the call for "industrial policy" in industrial countries. An important and paradoxical aspect of such a policy involves the grant of government subsidies both to "sunrise industries" (high tech industries), and to "sunset industries" (such as steel and textiles). In both cases, international competitiveness is affected. It is an open and much debated question whether one of the most successful cases of industrial targeting by Japan, namely the steel industry, was good or bad (as *Krugman* suggests[2)]) for economic growth. If one takes into account the external economies for its steel industry since the 1950s (for targeting large steel-using industries such as shipbuilding and the automobile industry) the Japanese steel policy was highly successful in *Salvatore's* view.

Exchange rate volatility (large fluctuations of exchange rates), by increasing uncertainty in international trade and payments, can also lead to demands for protectionist measures. It is nearly futile to mention that the increase in protectionism is reducing the potential world trade growth and is therefore an additional constraint on the so-called "export-led" strategies of some Eastern European countries. This aspect was not taken into account explicitly by *Bognar* (Ch. 6) or *Heinrichs* (Ch. 7). By contrast, *Marer* (Ch. 11) sees "direct protectionism" as a central feature of CMEA trade policy, on the import side.

The GATT aims at tackling some of the new aspects of protectionism. Let me therefore say a word on the bargaining power in GATT negotiations

---

2) See References to Ch. 10

(not mentioned by *Salvatore*). Since the Kennedy round the big trading countries and blocs (US, EC, Japan) have generally dominated the negotiations. Not only are the legitimate interests of the less developed countries often neglected, but also the interests of smaller industrial countries are not properly represented. Why is that? Modern international trade is increasingly based on intra-industry specialisation: broadly speaking, large countries - because of the comparative advantages of large-scale and research-intensive production - can gain more from intra-industry trade than small countries. Because of this asymmetry of trade gains, and because of the weak bargaining power of small (industrial) countries, in my opinion[3] GATT should allow the smaller industrial countries to compensate for their diminishing gains from trade.

---

3) See also: Fritz Breuss: Österreichs Außenwirtschaft 1945-1982, Vienna 1983, p. 244

Ante Čičin-Šain[1]

Outward-oriented growth in socialist countries

I would like to comment first on the problems of the outward-oriented growth patterns now envisaged by several socialist countries. I refer to the papers by *Bogomolov* (Ch. 1), *Bognár* (Ch. 6), *Heinrichs* (Ch. 7) and *Sydow* (Ch. 8). This is among the most important issues faced at present by socialist countries. I would like to say two things:

- First, socialist countries now face the need to change their overall development patterns towards "export-led growth", both on external and internal grounds. While it should be obvious that balance of payments problems can best be tackled by measures aiming at increased exports, it must also be pointed out that profound changes of development patterns have to be pursued for "internal" reasons as well. The economic reforms

---

1) Professor, Economic Institute and Faculty of Economics, Zagreb

envisaged now by most socialist countries cannot be successfully carried out if they are not accompanied, or preceded, by substantial changes in foreign trade mechanisms.

- Second, I would like to show that to effect the changes in foreign trade mechanisms needed for export-led growth requires much greater systemic changes than seems to be generally appreciated. I will summarise the necessary systemic changes within a formal scheme, which might perhaps be regarded also as a pattern by which such changes could be pursued:

(a) Actual and formal dismantling of the government foreign trade monopoly. It must be said that this monopoly has, in fact, largely been overtaken by actual developments in several socialist countries. It seems, therefore, that this first step can be based on the developments which have already occurred, or which are in progress.

(b) Consistent introduction of decentralised foreign trade mechanisms which, evidently, have to be accompanied by appropriate macro-economic policies.

(c) Reform of the exchange rate system: present implicit and/or open multiple exchange rates should be replaced by a unified exchange rate. This is likely to be the most important, and the most difficult change, to carry through. To benefit from a decentralised foreign trade mechanism, all foreign trade participants must know what to trade and how to trade. For this purpose it is crucially important to have one common, generally-known and reliable yardstick. This common yardstick can, as far as I can see, be nothing else but the unified exchange rate. In the absence of such a common yardstick, decentralised foreign trade could, very easily, result in considerable losses instead of expected gains. The unified exchange rate system, however, cannot reasonably be expected to succeed unless it is accompanied by appropriate changes in other parts of the national economic system. I will mention only the most important of these.

(d) A thorough reform of the internal price system. Internal prices, including prices of production factors, must be determined so as to reflect accurately the relevant scarcity ratios. The implementation of this principle will be greatly facilitated through increasing liberalisation of imports. Since the price reform can hardly be achieved without considerable increases of the general price level it must be accompanied by -

(e) Adoption of active exchange rate policies, which - to be successful - must be accompanied by corresponding interest rate policies. A shift towards positive real interest rates becomes indispensable. This implies further -

(f) Substantial changes in the role and structure of the banking and financial systems in general.

All this could (and should) be elaborated in much more detail. My object is simply to draw attention to the intrinsic logic of the systemic and policy changes needed to effect the desired and necessary moves towards "open" or "export-led" development patterns.

The European Monetary System

In his very stimulating and thought-provoking paper, *Bourguinat* (Ch. 9) deals with three closely interrelated issues.

(a) He presents what might be called the EMS success story. His data clearly show the convergence of monetary and exchange rate policies achieved among EMS member states during 1979-1986. The success of EMS is convincingly displayed by the data reflecting the convergence processes among nominal and real exchange rates, on the one hand, and real interest rates and inflation rates, on the other. This indicates, also, that the overall economic policies of EMS members have been successfully harmonised, probably to the benefit of all participants. This aspect of EMS experience should be very interesting for any group of countries considering a move towards this or some other form of monetary integration.

(b) *Bourguinat* then deals with certain problems of intra-European trade. This part of his analysis shows some somewhat paradoxical results: the convergence achieved in the financial sphere has not been adequately reflected in the development of intra-EMS merchandise trade. This trade has not increased in line with other parts of member countries' international trade; further, trade balances among EMS members have been moving in opposite directions. While these somewhat surprising results could be discussed and interpreted in different ways, I think they are not so important for our present concerns as to divert our attention from some other, much more important, aspects of the EMS story.

(c) Thirdly *Bourguinat* deals with the role of the ECU and the future of the EMS. This aspect is most important not only for EMS members, but also for the future development of the whole international monetary system. Our recent unsatisfactory experience with the US dollar as the key international reserve currency provokes serious consideration of the ECU's potential for taking up the role of a third - why not a first or second? - pillar in an (oligopolist) international currency system.

In this connection I note that *Bourguinat* also raises the question of the "...steady hostility of the German monetary authorities to the extension of private uses of ECUs by (German) national residents." The other, perhaps equally important, question is the possible entry of the UK into the EMS.

Aleksander Lukaszewicz[1)]

Marer (Ch. 11) attempts a broad and generalising analysis of the most typical foreign economic strategies used by the market economies and centrally planned economies. He examines three aspects: trade strategy, attitudes toward foreign direct investment and willingness to integrate with the international financial system.

Reviewing the last two decades, *Marer* finds that the main difference in foreign economic strategies between the market and centrally planned economies lies in the outward-orientation of the first group and the inward-orientation of the second. This is ascribed to the salient features of the economic mechanisms inherent in each type of economy. Marginal mentions can be found of the role of political factors and the development level; they are disregarded as determining any situation or process analysed.

According to *Marer*, the consequences of alternative strategies are the following:

- In the long-run the outward-oriented strategies are associated with significantly better overall performance;
- These strategies have been accompanied by good macro-economic control over the domestic economy, yet rather weakly correlated with foreign direct investment or external financial ingration;
- The real shift from inward to outward-oriented economic strategy in the centrally planned economies requires fundamental reforms in the economic mechanism;
- In the long-run, import-substitution policies aimed at greater economic independence typically lead to outcomes the opposite of those intended.

My comments concentrate on only a few arguments which seem to be most relevant.

(a) The question arises whether the assessment of economic results in the long-run can be separated from the assessment of social results - broadly conceived - in the same period. These two sides of the social process can by no means be separated. The choices made by the socialist countries in the past have always given priority to the social aspects. This does not mean, of course, that the policies in this respect were always successful in terms of both resource allocation and all distributional effects.

(b) The next question is whether the level of socio-economic development, or rather its rate of progress, may be put aside in judging the strategy choice and political options. The same question arises in comparing

1) Professor, Department of Economics, University of Warsaw

different economies, particularly those with different socio-political systems. (c) Both in the past and today the political factor in international economic relations has always been present; not seldom is it the dominating factor distorting the economic interflows which could be considered as natural and mutually beneficial. The presence of the political factor cannot be taken as justifying every decision made; yet more often than not its impact leads to a situation in which the *economic security* of a country becomes a main determinant of the strategy choice.

These three points appear in *Marer's* analysis, but only far back in the shadows. I cannot share this attitude.

Marer's critical assessment of the operation of the centrally planned economy relates mainly to a past period - the time of what was called the command economy. In general, I agree with his strictures (apart from my comments above), including his remarks on the strategy for foreign economic relations derived from that planning system. But what strikes me as unbalanced is his failure to appreciate the process of reform which has been gaining in strength and spreading for some years now throughout most socialist countries. Hungary and China are not, as he suggests, the only examples - as is demonstrated by several chapters in this volume on the socialist economies. Moreover *Marer* pays little attention to the new ventures in foreign trade strategies undertaken by virtually all CMEA countries, giving high priority to the outward-orientation of future development.

Obviously, the success of any shift of direction depends on the exporting abilities, import capacities and competitiveness of exported goods and services. But the heavy, deliberate politicising of international economic relations is a serious impediment, insurmountable for some countries. It is simply inconsistent to stipulate the need for fundamental reforms while forgetting the real obstacles against which these reforms collide.

PART IV - THE MANAGEMENT OF ENTERPRISE STRATEGIES

Chapter 12

PROBLEMS OF CONTROLLING MARKETS AND RESOURCE ALLOCATION IN CONDITIONS OF EXCESS DEMAND: THE POLISH CASE

Jan Lipiński[1)]

The purpose of this paper is to discuss some questions arising in a socialist economy about interactions between central decisionmakers and state-owned enterprises, taking into account the behaviour of workers and consumers. The paper concentrates on a certain field of those interactions, namely the markets for industrial (non-food) products and the allocation of resources needed for industrial production.

My discussion is confined to the Polish economy which, I should remind the reader, is at present subject to a fundamental economic reform, which began in 1982. This reform has adopted the principle of granting the state-owned enterprises autonomy in decisions on all important activities, including investment. Central control of those activities should be exercised, in the first place, by applying so-called "economic" instruments. No restriction of that autonomy would be permissible, unless justified by specific circumstances.

The autonomy in decisions ought to be backed by the principle of self-financing, also adopted by the Polish economic reform. A state-owned enterprise should finance all its activities out of its own funds or by bank credit; any subsidy needs special justification. On the other hand, no enterprise can be deprived of any part of its funds, except by taxes or tax-like deductions.

The supporters of the reform expected at the start that it would open the way to a considerable increase in the role of the market mechanism in coordinating and guiding economic activities. They expected, too, that the scope of that mechanism would no longer be confined to agricultural products and consumer goods but would also be extended to producer goods.

Those expectations, however, have not yet been realised. In fact, owing to a coincidence of both "real" and social circumstances, the Polish

---

1) Professor, Central School of Planning and Statistics, Warsaw

economy is still characterised by excess demand for a wide range of commodities and resources, which we have not so far managed to overcome. Yet the implementation of the economic reform has not been suspended or delayed. To be sure, the scope for autonomous decision-making by an enterprise has been somewhat restricted by administrative measures concerning resource allocation and price formation. Yet, except in some particular situations, the state-owned enterprise has retained the right to decide what and how much to produce, how much to pay to workers and how to divide the profit.

We are thus faced in Poland with the coexistence of forces which might seem unreconcilable, or at least very difficult to reconcile with each other.

What is the impact of such circumstances on the operating of commodity markets and resource allocation? How can we assess the effectiveness of various instruments applied by the centre to cope with the difficulties that arise? What measures might be regarded as reasonable in such a situation?

Such are the questions I want to approach in this paper, as regards the industrial sector. I am unable, however, to make an exhaustive analysis here. I must select some questions that I consider the most important and to leave out others. And even these selected questions are discussed only briefly, in a highly simplified way.

The difficulties examined here seem to be affected by the prevailing structural forms of commodity markets and by the typical behaviour of the managements of state-owned enterprises.

12.1 Structural forms of markets

I begin by examining those structural forms of "partial markets" for industrial products which are likely to prevail in a small or medium-sized economy, not opened to foreign competition. By a *partial* market, I mean a market for a group of commodities which are close substitutes for each other. For my present purpose, I retain the traditional distinction between various structural forms of partial markets corresponding to different degrees of concentration of sellers or buyers (polypoly, oligopoly, monopoly etc.). The prevailing structrual market forms depend in the first place on the forms of industrial organisation adopted. If the organisers of the economic system in a small or medium-sized country wish to restrain the appearance of a monopoly - individual or collective - they ought to resist any attempt to form big industrial organisations on a horizontal basis, embracing the whole or the greater part of an industrial branch.

But even in the absence of such organisations, other factors may favour the formation of a monopoly or an oligopoly. This is likely to happen, first of all, in industries characterised by a high indivisibility of capital equipment coexisting with limited particular markets - features commonly found in a small or mediumsized national economy (unless open economies).

It might be objected to the foregoing that account is not taken of the possible accessibility of a partial market to outsiders. In fact, under the new economic system in Poland, the state-owned enterprise has the right to choose what to produce. But the actual freedom of choice is limited, in the short run, by the kind of capital equipment at the disposal of an enterprise. Thus an enterprise wishing to enter another partial market might have to convert its capital equipment or to build a new plant. A smaller enterprise, comprising one or a few plants, might be prevented from doing that by insufficient financial funds. A big multi-plant enterprise would probably be able to do it, but might not be interested in entering another partial market, because, in a small or medium sized economy, it would probably enjoy a monopolistic or a nearmonopolistic position. Thus a typial partial market in such an economy would probably be well protected against competition from outside and would therefore be likely to take an oligopolistic or monopolistic structural form.

The structural form of a partial market seems to be more important for the operating of a balanced or demand-restrained market than for the functioning of an excess-demand market. In fact, in an excess-demand market, even a seller having a small share in the total supply of the commodities concerned predominates over a buyer. But even in that situation the structural form of the market is far from negligible, because it seems to exert a considerable influence on the effectiveness of central control.

12.2 Motives for behaviour of enterprise managements and their market implications

By the *management* of an autonomous state-owned enterprise, I mean a team which, beside the manager, embraces anyone who can exert a significant influence on the most important decisions about the activities of the enterprise.

The typical behaviour of an enterprise-management in Poland is likely to be governed by the following chief motives:

(a) to keep the enterprise in motion, ensuring a tolerable level of output and sales;

(b) to take care of the current material interests of the workers employed in the enterprise.

On (a). A state-owned enterprise in Poland is no longer subject, as a rule, to obligatory output tasks of the central plan. There is, however, a level of output and sales which is regarded by the bodies supervising the enterprise as the lowest tolerable level. To avoid a negative appraisal of its work by those bodies, the management of the enterprise seeks to prevent output and sales from falling below that level. The latter may depend on various circumstances that will not be analysed in this paper. Anyway, it is likely to change with the capacity of the capital equipment, as well as with the available material and labour resources.

On (b). The typical management of a state-owned enterprise in Poland is likely to focus its attention on wages and bonuses for workers and on welfare expenditures for their benefit. It does so not only when faced with a strong and firm workers' council, but also if the workers' self-management is weak. The management is forced to behave in that way in a situation of excess demand for labour; otherwise the enterprise might be abandoned by workers and thus unable to ensure the tolerable level of output. But even apart from the labour market situation, the management would have to avoid any major discontent among workers which might provoke a disturbance in production.

It should be noted, however, that the typical management of a state-owned enterprise does not seek to maximise the earnings of workers but seems to be content with keeping pace with other enterprises in the same industry or operating on the same local labour market. Its intention is not to be left much behind the others, but also not to get much ahead of them for that might provoke a negative opinion of the public and an unfavourable appraisal by the supervising governmental or party organs.

Such an attitude induces the management to accept any demand for higher wages that does not exceed the prevailing rate of wage rise in the industrial branch or on the local labour market. To finance such a rise in wages, and to pay the taxes due on the wage payments, the management must ensure an appropriate increase in the gross income of the enterprise - the value added per worker employed. It does not seek, however, to maximise it but seems to be satisfied with attaining a certain level or a certain rate of growth. It seeks to achieve it, as well as ensuring a tolerable level of output and sales, with minimum effort and worry.

That typical attitude of the management of a state-owned enterprise is reflected in its behaviour on the market for the products it supplies. I have already pointed out that most partial markets for manufactured goods in the present-day Polish economy are still characterised by a dominance of sellers over buyers, due to excess demand or a monopolistic (or near-monopolistic) position of the producer. Yet the typical state-owned enterprise seems to be much less aggressive in dealing with its customers than a monopolistic enterprise in neo-classical models.

Let us take the formation of prices. It seems that even if price formation is free, with no administrative constraints, there would be no tendency on the part of most state-owned enterprises to impose prices aimed at maximising their profits or gross incomes. Those enterprises would nevertheless take advantage of their predominance over customers to set prices covering any level of production cost, whatever the waste of resources. Those prices would normally contain a profit margin sufficient to cover bonuses for workers and welfare expenditures at the level prevailing in the branch or the local labour market, and to enable the enterprise to pay the taxes on profits.

It should also be noted that the typical management would prefer to avoid, if possible, any considerable shift in the product-mix, even if that might bring about an increase in the profits or gross income of the enterprise. This is because such a shift would require in most cases an additional effort from the manager and the staff. The management would therefore prefer to retain as long as possible the current product-mix and would try to impose it on buyers, taking advantage of their privileged market position.

To sum up, the typical attitude of the management of a stateowned enterprise in the present-day Polish economy seems to be *conservative*. The manager and other members of the managerial team are likely to seek a quiet life for themselves and for the enterprise. They seem to be satisfied with those efforts that are necessary to keep the enterprise working and to retain their posts. At the same time, they want to avoid an unfavourable appraisal by the public and by any supervising body. Such an attitude makes them less "aggressive" in the market in situations of monopoly or excess demand than would be enterprises seeking to maximise their profits or gross incomes. At the same time, they seem to be reluctant to engage in innovations or adjustments, even if financially profitable, if these require a considerable additional effort. They are likely to refrain from such steps, unless they consider them necessary to attain tolerable results (i.e. to ensure a level of output tolerated by their supervisiors), while ensuring a level of wages acceptable to the workers. If, however, the enterprise enjoys a monopolistic position or encounters excess demand for its products, it can easily attain, in most cases, those tolerable results without any genuine innovations in the product or in the production process.

12.3 Demand - supply relations in the present Polish economy

This part of the paper contains a general outline of current relations between demand and supply in the present Polish economy in the area of industrial products and resources engaged in their production.

I begin with final industrial products - consumer goods and capital goods. Although some of the partial markets for these products are already balanced, or coming close to a balance, most of them are still characterised by an excess of demand over supply. The supply is constrained, according to the industrial branches or regions, either by the capacity to provide raw materials and intermediate products or by the available labour. The relative importance of those constraints, in the national economy as a whole and in individual industries, depends among other things on the balance of payments and foreign trade policy. The capital equipment engaged in producing final industrial goods is still in relative surplus in most cases but it badly needs replacement.

Because of such constraints, excess final demand engenders on the one hand excess demand for raw materials and intermediate products (accompanied by excess demand for convertible foreign exchange), on the other hand an excess demand for labour.

The excess demand for commodities is accompanied by a rise in their prices (the mechanism will be outlined below). But rising prices do not bring about a balance between demand and supply, for the following reasons:

a) For *consumer goods* bought by households to satisfy their substantial needs, the rise in retail prices is likely to encourage the workers employed to demand a compensating rise in money wages, in order to prevent a fall in real wages. Moreover, some professional groups of special economic importance often manage to obtain a rise in money wages more than proportional to the rise in prices. They act then as "wage leaders" because, if they are successful, they are normally followed by other groups of workers wanting to catch up.

Most of these claims for higher money wages are accepted by the managers of enterprises, for the reasons pointed out above. To be sure, efforts have been made to check such increases by imposing on enterprises a special tax on wage payments exceeding a given standard. So far, however, that tax has not proved effective, owing to its poor design and to tax reliefs too easily granted by fiscal authorities. The rise in the money wages of workers in the enterprises is followed, though with a delay, by decisions to raise wages and salaries in public services and to increase the old-age pensions. In these ways, the restraining effect of rising retail prices on household demand for consumer goods is considerably weakened or even neutralised.

b) The rise in prices of capital goods would no doubt reduce the demand for them, if the investment activities concerned were subject to hard financial constraints. This condition is fulfilled for a part of the investment expenditures of enterprises. It does not, however, apply to central investment decisions. Accordingly, the demand for capital goods generated by those central decisions seems to be price-inelastic.

In such circumstances, it is still considered necessary to resort to administrative methods of allocating some important raw materials and intermediate products. The task of allocating them has been entrusted to selected agencies, dealing with their purchase and sale. The government has also retained central allocation of the available sums of convertible foreign exchange. The main basis for the allocation of scarce material resources is the distinction between "protected" and "unprotected" social and economic needs and the corresponding division of economic activities into two zones - "protected" and "unprotected". I shall briefly discuss the main ways of resource allocation in each of these zones.

12.4 Resource allocation in the "protected" zone

The satisfaction of protected (priority) needs in a situation of resource shortage calls for detailed and firm central planning; its implementation demands the application of non-price instruments, addressed to individual enterprises. For this purpose, two institutional forms of central control are applied nowadays in the "protected" zone of the Polish economy:

- governmental orders,
- operational programmes.

Both forms presuppose a detailed list of goods and services to be supplied, specifying the exact quantities. Those data are contained in the annual central plan. To implement the plans, a governmental organ or agency (or an authorised economic organisation) enters into contracts with the appropriate enterprises for supplying the required goods in the quantities required. Both forms presuppose too, as a general rule, a voluntary commitment of the entreprise concerned which has the right to decline the proposed contract. This general rule, however, is subject to a qualification: it does not apply to a situation when an order of particular importance is declined by all its possible suppliers.

Of these two forms, governmental orders have become predominant; the application of operational programmes has been reduced to a narrow area. It is therefore only the first form that will be discussed here.

Governmental orders may be applied at present in the following fields:

a) supplying some industrial products (consumer goods, durable capital goods, raw materials, intermediate products, components of final products, replacement parts etc.),

b) implementing some investment projects,

c) performing some tasks related to the practical application of technical and scientific progress.

I concentrate on governmental orders applied in the first field.

To encourage autonomous enterprises to accept government orders, these orders must be made more attractive to them than the supply of commodities for other domestic purposes. It has been held that the best way of ensuring this,in a situation of acute resource shortage, would be to grant the performers of governmental orders and operational programmes a privileged share in the allocation of scarce resources. Accordingly, the enterprises engaged in implementing such orders or programmes are guaranteed a full supply of those raw materials and intermediate products which are subject to administrative allocation. They are not limited by any quotas. They are also granted a priority - next to producers of exported commodities - in the allotment of foreign exchange.

Therefore, although the governmental orders are intended to be applied as "economic" and not "administrative" instruments for implementing the central plan, their application is nevertheless closely connected with administrative methods of controlling the allocation of some important resources.

It was expected at first that guaranteed material supplies would prove so attractive to most enterprises that they would compete for government orders. It was therefore decided that such orders should be placed by tender. The competition should be open to all possible suppliers of the goods concerned - not only to state-owned and cooperative enterprises but also to private firms. The selection of tenders should be based on what have been called "efficiency criteria" (prices, quality, production costs, material outlays, foreign exchange outlays).

It is impossible, however, to ensure such competition in the following cases:

a) when the goods to be ordered are supplied by only one enterprise;

b) when only one of the possible producers is prepared to accept the order;

c) when the capacity of all possible and willing producers is insufficient (or hardly sufficient) to cover the order.

The more frequent are such cases, the less is the opportunity for placing government orders by tender. It is to be noted that in Poland orders placed in this way have covered only a minor part of the total value of goods supplied against government orders.

Thus the actual placing of government orders in the Polish economy has departed in many respects from the original idea. The system has nevertheless contributed, beyond doubt, to a sensible improvement of the demand-supply relationships for some important groups of industrial goods in the "protected" zone. This, however, has been made possible by a reallocation of scarce resources at the expense of the "unprotected" zone.

It should be observed that even the most reasonable control of economic activities in the protected zone cannot operate satisfactorily unless that zone absorbs only a minor part of the available resources of the national economy. In fact, the longer the list of priority needs and, consequently, the greater the proportion of available resources engaged in their satisfaction, the greater is the risk of not satisfying those needs because of the shortage of some resources.

12.5 Resource allocation in the "unprotected" zone

Enterprises in the "unprotected" zone must be content with the residual parts of the supplies of basic raw materials and foreign exchange left after satisfying the needs of the "protected" zone. It is therefore uncertain, even in the short run, whether it will be possible to achieve the plan figures for outputs of "unprotected" industrial goods, especially for those limited by material or foreign exchange constraints. Those figures cannot therefore express any firm decisions, but are only non- rigorous guidelines or expectations, permitting a wide margin of tolerance.

It would not be reasonable in these circumstances to allot to enterprises fixed quotas of permissible purchases of basic raw materials, for those quotas might not be covered by actual supplies. Instead, therefore, permits are granted for purchasing the actually available amounts of the materials concerned. That is the task of the allocating agencies mentioned above.

What is the criterion for granting the applications of enterprises for such permits? The main guideline for the agencies is to allocate the materials in question (after satisfying the demand of the "protected" zone) in accordance with the material balances contained in the annual central plan. Suppose now that the actual supply of a material is smaller than the respective plan figure (by an amount exceeding the planned reserve in the material balance). In that case, the appropriate allocating agency is instructed to make a proportional reduction in supplying that material to the producers of "unprotected" goods (while retaining the full satisfaction of all the priority needs). This is, of course, a primitive, oversimplified rule of allocation which does not take account of the complementarity in demand for various materials, nor of the interindustrial input-output relations.

Besides, the allocating agencies are not instructed how to divide the available supply of a material between different enterprises producing similar commodities. It might seem possible to organise a competition between those enterprises, based on the material-saving criterion. To my knowledge, however, no allocating agency has ever attempted to do that. Thus a wide area of allocation decisions is left to the discretion of the allocating agencies. The present administrative methods of allocating the available convertible foreign exchange, for "unprotected" needs, could be similarly described.

To sum up, the allocation of scarce transferable resources within the unprotected zone of the activities of state-owned enterprises is marked by a "gap" in regulation. On the one hand, it is subject neither to a self regulating market mechanism, nor to any effective control by means of "economic" instruments. On the other hand, the administrative allocation of some important resources (basic raw materials and foreign exchange) lacks definite and consistent criteria. That "gap" is normally filled by well known informal processes; there are various ways by which buyers of scarce commodities and resources compete to win their supplies.

12.6 Some ideas for improving demand-supply relations

We could, of course, come closer to balanced markets for industria consumer goods if we could ensure a faster growth of their supply tha of the demand for them. It is doubtful however, whether we could manag to attain balanced markets by the end of the present five-year perio mainly by an increase in supply, while allowing demand to continue t grow at present rates. Since the adopted draft of the five-year pla has ruled out any increase in the share of personal consumption in nationa income, the only way of attaining a sensible increase in the supply o consumer goods would be a rise in the efficiency of the economy.

It would be technically possible to make considerable progress i efficiency in most industries, without major investment, by reducing th waste of resources in enterprises. But a conservativeminded managemen of a state-owned enterprise would not be eager to take any remarkabl step in this direction unless submitted to hard economic pressure. Ho to exert such pressure without a balanced market? We are thus face with a sort of vicious circle.

In these circumstances, a rapid balancing of markets for industria consumer goods would call for a considerable reduction in households demand for them. That idea is supported by many outstanding Polis economists who want it to be applied not only to industrial products but to food products as well (except for some basic standard articles). It might be implemented in different ways, for example:

a) by permitting or even promoting a more rapid rise in retail prices than at present, while not allowing a faster rise in personal money incomes;

b) by retaining the rate of increase in retail prices while ensuring a slower rise in money incomes.

Here are my comments on that proposal:

(a) Irrespective of the method of implementation, it would imply a reduction in the average level of "real" personal incomes. According to supporters of this idea, it would not mean any genuine loss to the average household, because the supply of consumer goods and services would remain unaffected. I do not share that opinion. I think that a typical consumer prefers to stand in a queue, with the *chance* of buying a commodity at a moderate price, than to be unable to buy it at all because its price is too high or his income too low, while richer people can buy without a queue. This is why he is likely to oppose any significant reduction of money income, or any considerable uncompensated rise in prices, even if this were to mean a disappearance of queues.

(b) Supporters of the proposal suggest that most workers' claims for higher wages could be successfully offset by hard fiscal measures imposed on the enterprises. Accordingly, they demand a substantial change in the present construction of the tax on excessive (over-standard) wage payments, as well as the cancellation of discretionary reliefs from taxation. I share that demand, but I am afraid that even the best constructed tax would have only limited effectiveness. It might discourage managements from yielding to a demand for a rise in wages which would exceed the prevailing wage claims in the branch or the local labour market. It would, however, seem much less effective in inducing a management to resist claims in line with those prevailing, and especially for higher wages from a "wage leading" occupational group. To restrain such wage claims would call for a political pressure on the "wage leader".

It is even more doubtful whether any feasible fiscal solution could successfully curb a rise in wages to compensate for a rise in living costs. I am afraid that enterprise managers in most industries would have to yield to such wage claims, irrespective of the form of taxation. If an enterprise lacked the means, the competent fiscal authority might be unable, for political reasons, to refuse financial aid - by subsidy or tax relief. I am therefore inclined to regard price-compensating wage claims as a socio-political constraint on the economic policy of the Polish government - likely to be as severe as the resource constraints. This opinion, however, concerns the present, rather peculiar situation in Poland. I cannot say whether (or how far) it applies to any other socialist economy.

I doubt therefore whether the proposal to keep down real incomes is feasible, in the present Polish situation, as a general guideline for wage and price policies.

In formulating a reasonable price policy, we should take account of the fact that the extent of price-compensating wage claims seems to be different for different groups of consumer goods and services.

For some commodities, rising prices are likely to arouse a demand for higher money wages from a majority of workers. It would not seem reasonable to promote a higher rate of rise in their retail prices, because we could not expect to exercise in this way any major restraint on the demand for them, owing to the neutralising effect of rising money incomes. On the contrary, it seems that a reasonable policy for such commodities would be to keep down the rise in their prices. That would stimulate demand for them, because it should help to moderate claims for a rise in money wages. The slower the rise in the retail prices of that group of consumer goods, the smaller could be the pricecompensating rise in money wages.

In my opinion, if an excess demand for a group of commodities is considered inevitable, irrespective of price movements, it would be better, (at least not worse) to accompany it by a slower than a faster rise in prices.

For those commodities where rising prices would not be likely to provoke major successful wage claims from any large proportion of workers it would seem reasonable to promote even a considerable increase in their retail prices. It might indeed be possible in this way to reach a balance on the partial markets concerned, even without any substantial increase in supply.

The differences in the wage-claim effects of rising prices for various kinds of consumer goods depend of course on how households with different incomes and in different occupational groups estimate the importance of various kinds of needs, and the comparative advantage of different ways of satisfying these needs. I cannot, however, develope that subject in this paper.

12.7 Restraining demand for producer goods

How can we cope with similar problems of balancing the markets for *investment goods?* The demand for those goods is generated (a) by central investment decisions, financed out of the State budget or by bank credit; (b) by investment decisions of enterprises, which are financed out of their "development-funds" (fed by a proportion of depreciation quotas and by a fraction of profits) but may be topped up by bank credit.

Central investment decisions are not limited to public services and socio-economic infrastructure, but also comprise some big projects in the sphere of direct material production.

A well known phenomenon in some centrally planned economies is an excessive propensity to invest, displayed at the level of an economic organisation and at a sectoral or regional level. That attitude is accompanied in most cases by "soft" central planning of investments (easy acceptance of an investment proposal) and by "soft"[2] financing of investment expenditures (ease of obtaining supplementary funds to pay for an enlargement of the investment programme or to cover a rise in its cost).

Such circumstances, of course, engender a demand for investment goods which is both price-inelastic and in excess of supply (unless at the cost of consumer goods or by an increase in foreign debt).

The excessive propensity to invest, coexisting with "soft" central planning and "soft" finance, was characteristic of the Polish economy in the 1970s. This is no longer true for investment by enterprises. The typical, conservative-minded management of a state-owned enterprise in Poland is interested, no doubt, in replacing its old capital equipment but shows nowadays no interest in a substantial increase in its productive capacity. This cautious attitude of typical enterprise managements, however, seems to be outweighed by the large-scale investment proposals of various sectoral and regional bodies. Some of these big projects, begun on the basis of central decisions, have been granted a privileged status ensuring full and flexible financing (chiefly by bank credits), thus rendering the accompanying demand for investment goods price-inelastic. On the other hand, investment proposals initiated by enterprises themselves have been "underprivileged" and subject to special fiscal measures intended to reduce the enterprises' own financial resources; it is true that the enterprises concerned may apply for bank loans, but they are often unable to satisfy the criteria used by the banks or to accept the terms of repayment.

These fiscal and banking measures have not, however, been effective enough to reduce enterprises' demand for investment goods to the level of supply. Moreover the burden of fiscal measures may be alleviated for some enterprises by special reliefs. These factors all contribute to the persistence of excess demand for most investment goods.

To reduce the demand for *raw materials and intermediate products*, we would have to make it responsive to changes in prices. We could

---

2) The term "soft" has the meaning given to it by János Kornai in Economics of Shortage, Amsterdam, North Holland, 1980

not, however, ensure the price-elasticity of an unsubstitutable material without balanced, or demand-restrained, markets for the final products. In other words, we would have to bring about a situation in which a rise in the price of a material, when embodied in the price of the final product, would reduce the sales of the product. Since most materials are not easily substitutable in the short run, it seems impossible to set up self-balancing markets for raw materials and intermediate products so long as there exists excess demand for these commodities.

12.8 Mechanism of price formation

As already indicated, excess demand, still prevailing in the Polish economy, is accompanied by a general and continuing rise in prices. Why do prices rise? The answer requires an outline of the mechanism of price formation in Poland. I shall concentrate on the formation of prices for raw materials and manufactured industrial products.

Most *basic raw materials, and some standardised intermediate products*, are sold at "official" prices, fixed by a competent governmental organ. The original intention was to base most of these prices on the average prices applied in foreign trade for convertible currencies. Those prices were to be converted to zlotys at a rate of exchange set at a "submarginal" level, ensuring the profitability of 70-80 per cent of exports to the convertible currency zone. Official domestic prices of materials were to be automatically adjusted to any change in this basis or in the exchange rate (allowing a certain tolerance margin).

This general rule was to be modified for those raw materials in which Poland has a considerable share in the total supply on the international market (e.g. coal and sulphur). But since the amount of Polish exports of those materials might significantly affect prevailing international prices it would not be reasonable to adopt the international prices as the sole basis for the domestic prices.

Actual practice in setting official prices of materials deviates in many respects from these principles. The list of prices in fact set on the basis of foreign trade prices is shorter than was at first recommended. Moreover, owing to some inconsistent measures adopted at the start, some of those prices have lagged well behind the foreign-trade basis.

It was intended to fix the official prices of coal and energy on the basis of production cost. The price of coal, however, is actually fixed at much below the level of average costs. Its sales are therefore heavily subsidised.

Nevertheless, the official prices of most basic raw materials have been raised every year, to keep pace with the rise in the relevant basis. Prices intended to be cost-based have been raised in accordance with the rise in production costs - thus preventing, or at least mitigating an increase in subsidies. Prices intended to be set on the foreign-trade basis have been raised along with successive depreciations of the zloty (against the US dollar). Those depreciations have been regularly made in order to adjust the exchange rate to rising production costs of exported goods. Such changes in official prices have not been automatic. They have been subject to selective decisions by the government with a view to delaying the effects on prices of consumer goods.

A number of Polish economists, including the present author, have been recommending for a long time a return to the original intentions in setting prices for raw materials. If that were done consistently, the prices of most raw materials would have to be raised much above the present levels, and accordingly most subsidies on their sales could be cancelled. The cost effects of such an operation ought to be fully transferred into the prices of intermediate products and investment goods. The increases would, however, have to be neutralised, or at least alleviated, for the retail prices of some important groups of consumer goods, in order to avoid consequential major wage claims. This would call for subsidies to the sellers of those goods or for an appropriate reduction of some indirect taxes. Thus, instead of subsidising raw materials, we would have to extend the list of subsidised consumer goods.

The supporters of such a solution expect that it would have a considerable stimulating effect on material-saving efforts in enterprises. Those expectations, however, cannot come true as long as buyers of raw materials can fully compensate for a rise in their prices by raising the prices of their products without risking any major reduction of sales.

Most *manufactured products* have been sold at "contract" prices which, according to the price legislation, should be agreed between sellers and buyers. Some "protected" groups of those products were sold, at first, at "regulated" prices, set by producers on the basis of production costs in accordance with a compulsory rule for cost calculations ("justified" cost) and profit margins. But the area of "regulated" prices has now been reduced to a negligible part of the total supply of commodities. In this paper, therefore, I shall concentrate on "contract" prices.

The original idea was to permit free formation of all "contract" prices, without any administrative restrictions. It was expected that contract prices would then be set by demand-supply relations for particular commodities and would thus bring their markets into balance. Those expectations, however, have not been realised. Even in the period of free formation, contract prices were actually set by most state-owned enterprises on the basis of individual production costs plus a profit margin, fixed in most cases at a standard level which was tacitly agreed upon by enterprises in the same industrial branch. The state-owned producers did not normally seek to raise prices above such a level, even in a situation of excess demand. They nevertheless sought to cover any level of production cost, even if it included wasteful expenditures. That method of price formation, as already pointed out, can be attributed to the conservative attitude of typical managements.

It should be noted that prices set in this way by producers were usually accepted by buyers, without any genuine negotiations. They were therefore not true "contract" prices, in spite of their official designation.

After a short period of free formation, the contract prices have been subjected to administrative restrictions. Here are the most significant measures taken in 1983-85.

(i) The enterprises were not permitted to raise contract prices of their products, except to cover a rise in costs due to external factors or to an increase in the turnover tax. The most important among the external factors were central decisions to raise official prices of raw materials, fuel and energy or to increase transport tariffs, depreciation rates or taxes included in cost calculations. It was not permitted to raise contract prices in response to a rise in the wage cost.

(ii) In addition to the above restriction, a uniform percentage ceiling was fixed (in 1984 and 1985) for the permissible rise in retail prices of consumer goods.

Those measures were motivated by the following intentions of the centre:

- to slow down the rise in prices of final products (especially of consumer goods),
- to exert a downward pressure on the cost level in enterprises.

They proved, however, to be much less effective in these respects than had been expected. This can easily be explained. Application of measure (i) was difficult to check by an external inspector, who might be unable to estimate the exact contribution of external factors to a rise in the production cost of a commodity. And measure (ii), proved rather "soft" in practice. The uniform rate for permissible price increases, confronted with different rates of "justified" rises in the production costs for various commodities, compelled the price office to grant numerous individual permissions to overstep the price-rise ceiling.

Moreover, a manufacturer could easily evade either of those measures, by introducing at higher prices some sham new articles in place of some old ones. In spite of such shortcomings, measure (i) has been retained in 1986 for contract prices of producer goods. It reflects a popular but dubious idea of a "just" price, based on a "justified" cost level and ensuring a "reasonable" profit margin. That idea seems to underlie any form of administrative intervention in calculating production costs and fixing profit margins.

What instruments of price control might be effective in exercising presure on cost levels to reduce wasteful expenditures, even without pressures from the market?

I will present one solution, recommended by the Consultative Economic Council in Poland. The crux is abandonment of any direct administrative regulation of cost calculations in enterprises, and of any attempts to control prices of individual commodities - and to replace such measures by a control of average price movements in various *groups* of commodities. It is therefore proposed to fix every year, for a defined group of products, a maximum permissible average rate of price increase, or a permissible average price level (for a group embracing comparable goods). Such price ceilings should be set at a uniform level for all the enterprises producing commodities in the group concerned - irrespective of individual costs in particular enterprises. For those commodity groups of which a considerable part of output is exported, and for those where a significant part of supply is imported, the price ceilings should be based on expected average movements of foreign-trade prices, converted to zloty at the given exchange rate (taking account of any intended change in the coming year). For other commodity groups, an appropriate basis for setting price ceilings should take account of estimated external factors which might affect the expected average rate of rise in the production costs of the commodities concerned. It should be noted that such group price ceilings, irrespective of their basis, should relate to "producer prices", i.e. sale-prices minus turnover tax or plus subsidies.

A commodity group for which a uniform price ceiling ought to be set should embrace, if possible, only substitutable or comparable goods for which it might be possible to calculate an average price per physical unit or per unit of "utility" (if easily measurable). If a price ceiling were set for a larger group of commodities - in the form of a limit to the average rate of rise in their prices - it could not by applied to new articles, since it might then be easy for enterprises to evade it by introducing some sham innovations in their products.

Most supporters of such a solution recommend it not only in situations of excess demand, but also in balanced markets where there exists a monopoly (or a near-monopoly) of production. I am afraid, however, that a group price ceiling might prove much less effective where the total, or a greater part of, a group of substitutable products is controlled by a single enterprise. This is because it would be difficult in that case to make the price ceiling independent of the behaviour of that enterprise.

If, for example, that ceiling were to be based on the average level of export prices or on the average rate of their rise, a monopolistic producer might be encouraged to reduce the physical volume of his exports, by limiting it to those commodities which would be sold at the highest prices or would show the highest rate of rise in prices. That could constrain the area for effective application of group price ceilings.

I may observe that this solution has already been applied, beginning in 1986, for some groups of consumer goods, but not quite in accordance with the foregoing suggestions.

A consistent application of group price ceilings in situations of excess demand might perhaps contribute to a reduction of wasteful expenditures in enterprises. It is doubtful however, whether such a solution - or any other price-restraining measure addressed to enterprises - could greatly contribute to slowing down the rise in prices of manufactured goods. This is because - contrary to a widespread opinion - most state-owned producers of those goods are not mainly responsible for the rising trend in their prices. It is true that there is a lot of waste in their use of resources but we do not observe any remarkable increase in that waste. Nor do they seek the maximisation of their profits or of their workers' wages. To be sure, they often accept claims for a rise in wages more than proportional to the increase in labour productivity. Yet in this matter they are subjected in most cases to a pressure which they are unable to resist for socio-political reasons - a pressure generated, in the first place, by rising retail prices of consumer goods due to a rise in their production costs, or to an increase in the purchase-prices for agricultural products (enforced by the representatives of farmers in response to rising retail prices of commodities bought by farmers). Moreover, the main reason for the rising costs of manufactured products is the government policy of raising official prices of raw materials, due to their rising production costs or to devaluations of the zloty, in response to the increasing costs of producing exportable commodities.

It seems therefore that the continuing rise in the production costs of manufactured goods is chiefly due to external factors that enterprises are unable to control. The main role of enterprises consists in trying to transfer the cost effects of those factors to the prices of their products. I doubt if any administrative measure could prevent them from doing that.

We are thus faced in Poland with a feed-back, self-perpetuating mechanism of rising wages, costs and prices. This mechanism does not exert any major influence on resource allocation or on demand-supply relations in commodity markets. It has not greatly contributed to increasing or reducing the excess demand for commodities and resources - and it might continue to operate in a situation of balanced markets.

A particularly important part in this mechanism seems to lie with *central* decisions, namely decisions to raise official prices of raw materials and basic consumer goods, to increase purchase prices for agricultural products and to alter the exchange rate. It is true that those decisions are motivated by attempts to suppress or to reduce some major discrepancies in cost-price relations. Yet they contribute to the reappearance of similar disproportions at other stages of the economic process. The attempts to compensate for those consequences leads to the recurrence of the initial discrepancies, and so on.

It would therefore be possible for central decision-makers to break this inflationary spiral by dropping some of the measures described. The most reasonable action in present circumstances would be, in my opinion, to stop raising the official retail prices of basic consumer goods and services, notwithstanding the necessity of increasing subsidies on their sales. This would probably bring about a marked weakening in workers' claims for a compensating rise in wages, which would result, in turn, in slowing down the rise in the production costs of raw materials and manufactured goods, and would mitigate the rise in their prices, thus contributing to a further mitigation of wage claims and to easing the farmers' pressure for higher prices for agricultural products. We might then expect a progressive deceleration of the entire inflationary process without any marked deterioration of demand-supply relations.

12.9 Fiscal instruments for price control

Full implementation of the Polish economic reform will call for progressively curtailing the present scope of administrative regulation of prices and for replacing it - depending on circumstances - either by free, non-controlled price formation or by an "economic" control of prices by means of fiscal instruments. I will consider the possible application to that purpose of turnover-tax on the one hand, and of subsidies on the other.

Among Polish economists there are considerable differences of opinion about the applicability of turnover tax as an instrument of price control. Some are in favour of cancelling that tax altogether, or of neutralising its effects on price formation, by fixing a uniform and stable tax rate. Other economists take a contrary view, recommending the use of the tax as a major instrument for controlling retail prices of "unprotected" consumer goods, especially those where rising prices are not likely to engender important compensatory wage-claims. In their opinion, the tax rates fixed for those commodities ought to be differentiated for individual groups of goods, in accordance with demand-supply relations in various partial markets. A uniform tax rate ought, however, to be set for any group of substitutable commodities produced with the same capital equipment and by the same kind of labour.

That opinion takes account of the fact, pointed out above, that most state-owned enterprises are likely to fix prices for their products on a cost basis and are not inclined to raise them above that level even if they encounter excess demand. It is therefore for the central decision-maker to ensure the formation of retail prices in accordance with demand-supply relations. He can do that by applying differentiated and flexible rates of turnover tax.

Consider *subsidies*. Many representatives of so-called public opinion regard them as an evil phenomenon in the national economy, betraying inefficiency of the enterprises concerned and an excessive tolerance on the part of the fiscal authority. This is a naive, oversimplified view. The existence of subsidies, as well as their distribution and their level, depend, first of all, on the price policy; and in the present-day situation in Poland, no reasonable price policy would be conceivable without subsidising some goods. It is true that the present price policy in Poland deserves keen criticism - but not because it implies excessive subsidies. What ought to be criticised is not the level of subsidies but their distribution - namely, their concentration on coal and some other raw materials.

Moreover, the rates of subsidy are set in most cases on an unreasonable basis. The subsidy per unit of a "price-protected" commodity is usually determined, for each producer, as the difference between the official selling price and the enterprise's production cost plus a fixed profit margin. To be sure, the cost calculation ought to be "justified" and subject to inspection. But it is difficult for an external inspector to monitor a cost calculation when each enterprise holds a monopoly of information about its internal operations.

A reasonable basis for fixing the rates of subsidy ought to be independent of the individual production costs of each enterprise. Such a basis might be provided by group price ceilings (discussed in the previous section). The appropriate subsidy per unit of a "price-protected" good would then be the difference between the respective price ceiling and the price level at which the central authorities would wish it to be sold.

12.10 Expectations and proposals for the near future

To sum up, I will now present my general appreciation of what is likely to happen in the near future (2-3 years) and of what reasonable steps might be taken by the centre.

The domain of consumer goods is likely to remain divided into two areas:

(1) balanced partial markets,

(2) partial markets with excess demand.

Area 1 is likely to be extended. On the one hand, it will be possible to cover the demand for some additional "protected" commodities by a deliberate reallocation of scarce resources, initiated by the centre, On the other hand, some of the "unprotected" goods whose rising prices would not be likely to provoke any major wage claims may be subject to a larger extent than at present to a successful, demand-reducing policy for retail prices, implemented by the turnover tax.

There is, however, Area 2, where no market-balancing measures could be successfully applied. It comprises those consumer goods whose supply will have to remain "unprotected" (because any major extension of the "protected" zone would not seem reasonable) but for which a price rise could significantly stimulate wage-claims. The markets for those goods are therefore expected to remain subject to excess demand.

A similar division is likely to remain in the markets for investment goods; that depends on whether the centre, in planning investment, will be able to adjust the flow of financial funds to the available real resources, and to ensure "hard" financing of all investment expenditures, including central investment. Extension of the balanced area within this domain depends, in the first place, on the possibility of overcoming the investment ambitions of various lobbies. Since this is no easy task, the demand for some significant groups of investment goods will probably still exceed their supply.

The retention of a substantial unbalanced range of final products is likely to acompany an excess demand for some important raw materials and intermediate products, a corresponding excess demand for convertible foreign exchange, and, probably, a continuing excess demand for labour.

We must therefore reckon with the survival of a wide, though contracting, area of shortages, embracing significant groups of commodities and resources.

What could be done to alleviate some of the negative effects of such circumstances on the operation of the economy, especially in the realm of industrial products and materials? Would it be possible to improve the process of allocating raw materials or intermediate products for which demand exceeds possible supply? Those who control that allocation might seek to increase its efficiency by introducing or extending competition between buyers of a scarce material, based on materials saving or quality-improving criteria. But this could not be applied where the producer holds a monopoly, as in many segments of Polish industry.

Would it be possible to improve the operational efficiency of state-owned enterprises in spite of the absence of market pressures? The price and fiscal authorities might attempt the following measures:

(i) by a widespread and consistent application of group price ceilings, as described in Section 12.8;

(ii) by cancelling the right of fiscal authorities to grant enterprises any discretionary tax reliefs;

(iii) by fixing a uniform rate of subsidy for all state-owned producers of a commodity, independent of individual production costs.

If those measures were consistently applied, they would contribute, beyond doubt, to a "hardening" of the financial constraints imposed on an enterprise - and might thus exert an effective pressure on its management, compelling it to cut out waste.

I am afraid, however, that measures (i) and (ii) might not prove very effective for an enterprise holding a monopolistic or near-monopolistic position. Even apart from this qualification, the measures suggested above would not be sufficient to improve the product-mix of enterprises and the quality of their products. In fact, one cannot expect a radical improvement in these respects so long as the enterprises concerned encounter excess demand for their products.

Yet, even in such a situation, it might be possible to alleviate the present shortcomings in the product mix and quality, if it were not for the existing relationships between producing enterprises and trading enterprises. It should be noted that Polish industrial enterprises producing consumer goods have returned to their traditional practice of "coupled sales" to trading enterprises, refusing them some attractive commodities unless they buy in addition some other products which are difficult or even impossible to resell. Trading enterprises are normally prepared to accept that condition and to store unsaleable goods so long as there is room in the warehouses. It is only when the warehouses are full that trading enterprises are induced to reduce the prices of their accumulated commodities, which they do on their own account, without any loss for producers. They continue to behave in this way, because most of them have not yet encountered any major difficulties in financing their stocks. Just because of this kind of relationship between industrial and trading enterprises, the financial situation of a producer may long remain unaffected by consumers' demand. This, however, might be remedied by introducing sales on commission as an obligatory form of contract between industrial and trading enterprises.

* * *

I have indicated in this paper some measures to be taken by the centre, which might alleviate some of the negative effects of the prevailing demand-supply relations in the present Polish economy. Those measures, however, would be no more than palliatives - and even the best results that might be attained in this way in the near future would still be far from fulfilling the initial expectations of most supporters of the Polish economic reform.

Chapter 13

INVESTMENT DECISION-MAKING IN YUGOSLAVIA

Jadranko Bendeković[1)]
Ivan Teodorović[1)]

13.1 Introduction

Investment decision-making in Yugoslavia has undergone many changes, directly connected with the development of the planning system. These changes have followed a firm dedication to strengthening a socialist and self-managed society, as well as responding to the problems arising in the course of Yugoslavia's social and economic development. After 1945, Yugoslavia passed four new Constitutions (in 1946, 1953, 1963 and 1974). Each of them marked a new phase of social and economic development, the main idea being the further decentralisation of social management, the planning process and investment decision-making. Thus, the development of the planning system may be presented in four stages:

- Central planning (1947-1952).
- Global balances planning (1956-1961).
- Indicative planning (1961-1975).
- Self-management planning (1975 onwards).

Central planning represented a classical "top-down" approach. Hierarchically organised planning commissions at the federal, republican, communal and city levels were entrusted with comprehensive planning in their respective territories. The operational planning was carried out by the ministries and, down the line, by general and chief directors and planning sections in the enterprises. All vital decisions, at any level, were subject to direction by the central plan, leaving a very limited margin of freedom for the enterprises. Thus, the enterprise was not much more than a state institution, since its receipts and outlays were balanced through the state budget. Economic stimulation did not play a significant role and the decision-making process relied primarily on political actions.

Global balance planning was limited to the basic global aggregates, which offered planning agents the possibility of elaborating their plans independently although they were obliged to respect basic proportions specified by the higher level of the planning hierarchy. Instead of the former Planning Commission, which acted as a super-ministry controlling all planning activities, the Federal Planning Bureau was founded as an

---

1) Senior research fellows of the Ekonomski Institut, Zagreb

expert institution with no administrative power. Investment decision-making and financing were done through the Investment Fund, which allocated the capital through a mechanism of investment auctions and loan granting.

Indicative planning introduced an increased independence of the enterprises and the hierarchical subordination of the plans no longer existed. The Investment Fund was abolished and investment decision-making was passed to the banks. Planning decisions at the federal level were reduced to the key strategic issues and investment decisions at this level comprised only global proportions, except for investments in the social overhead sectors for which detailed projects were designed. The plans at the micro-level were formulated and implemented by the enterprises on the basis of information and their position in the market, subject to a set of economic policy measures designed to implement a plan. These profound changes to the planning system, poorly prepared and inconsistent, brought complex problems of vertical and horizontal coordination and of macro-economic efficiency at the lower level. The planning system left much room for relatively free actions by the federal units and enterprises, providing a considerable contribution to the reduction of the potential social conflicts in a pluralistic Yugoslav society. However, economic efficiency and performance were not satisfactory.

Self-management planning was introduced as a response to the problems mentioned above. It was aimed as a definite move towards the decentralisation of economic activities, which was considered as the way to improve the rationale of both social and economic development. This stage will be further discussed, especially with respect to investment decision-making.

13.2 Basic features of self-management planning

The most relevant features of the planning system are:[2)]

- planning comprises social, economic and spatial aspects of development;
- the process of planning is continuous and is carried out simultaneously by all planning agents through a top-down and bottom-up procedure;
- plans are classified as long-term plans covering a period of ten or more years, medium-term plans of five years, and annual plans;
- enterprises are entitled to set up "common programmes of development" through joint agreements which serve as a basis for the plans drawn up by those enterprises and socio-political plans;

---

2) The principles of the planning system are specified by the Constitution of 1974, the "Associated Labour Act" and the "Law on Premises of the Social Planning System and the Social Plan of Yugoslavia".

- plans are formulated on the basis of a compulsory, unified methodology and a set of economic indicators;
- economic activities are divided between those with a "special social interest", such as the economic infrastructure, and other, non-priority, sectors;
- all planning agents are supposed to harmonise their plans with other affected parties in order to reach a common agreement. These agreements are codified as "social compacts" and/or "self-management agreements" which are legally binding on those who have signed them;
- the chambers of commerce and trade unions also take part in planning, providing necessary professional help and initiatives especially in the process of harmonising of the plans;
- a socio-political unit has a constitutional right to undertake necessary measures where the process of planning is not progressing well and common agreement is not likely to be reached. In priority sectors, this means a right to determine a plan even without agreement on the part of the enterprises concerned.

Hence, the self-management system of planning was conceived as bringing about a further reduction of the state's role in planning by directly introducing the affected parties into the process of decision-making. However, in the last resort the state legislature can if necessary impose the plans. In addition, the role of the republics and communes was considerably strengthened, while the federal level has been assigned the role of coordination and harmonisation in reaching common decisions. Within this framework, investment decisions have been undertaken over the last ten years.

13.3 The investment system after 1974

As we have already indicated, a new system of planning has been adopted which provides an improved framework for coordination of decision-making. A number of institutional changes have also been made with the object of establishing a consistent, decentralised socio-economic system in a self-management framework. This has meant a higher degree of autonomy for the enterprises, local governments, republics and regions within the federation. The investment system assumed reliance on market mechanisms and on the system of planning.

Institutional changes that followed had to correct the inherited distortions of market mechanisms. At the same time, a system of social compacts and self-management agreements was introduced, primarily intended to define social priorities in sectors where market mechanisms cannot play a significant role, or for activities where evident market imperfections exist. However, over the course of time the role of this new system surpassed initial intentions and replaced market criteria by introducing some forms of nonmarket allocations.

The intention of changes in the system of planning was not to supersede the market, but rather to act as a mechanism for coordinating decisions made on the basis of market signals. Investment decisions were supposed to be a part of this procedure.

A major instrument for achieving the plan's objectives was the priority system for the allocation of investment. This system rested on the coordination of investment plans by enterprises, socio-political units and banks, through a series of self-management negotiations, self-management agreements, and social compacts. Such coordination was to guarantee the financing of agreed projects in priority development sectors, with the funding for nonpriority sectors to be determined residually.

The new system of investment had the task of identifying priority sectors whose share in total investment was to be guaranteed, and of using the self-management agreements and self-financing schemes among enterprises, instead of state and bank intervention, as a mechanism to achieve the desired distribution of the investment effort.

The basic institutional changes inaugurated a series of normative changes with respect to the elements of the economic system. The passing of new laws was slower than expected and under the pressure of economic policy, high investment pressure and conflicting development and economic interests, distortions in the market emerged, especially in the markets for capital, foreign exchange and labour. Thus indicators of market profitability were seriously influenced by such distortions.

The allocation mechanism had problems in defining and choosing the priorities. Assigning priority status to entire sectors (such as energy, raw materials) entailed certain risks, since it implied endorsement of a broad spectrum of projects, not all of which necessarily merited special treatment.

In addition, to the extent that enterprises and banks were able to circumvent the new priority allocation mechanism to direct their investment into profitable activities, this priority target was overshot. Finally, tensions between market indicators and sectoral priorities, coupled with autonomous pressures for investment in nonproductive sectors, played a role in the excessive growth of investment demand that spilled over into macro-economic imbalance during 1976-80. The mechanisms for directing investment resources toward priority sectors were not as effective as planned. As a consequence, the realisation of investment priorities resulted in financing an unsustainable total investment effort through excessive credit creation and foreign borrowing.

As a result of these, and of a number of other economic problems, the Long-Term Stabilisation Programme was designed and accepted at the beginning of the 1980s. This resulted in a number of new laws which directly affected and, therefore, modified the system of investment. The Long-Term Stabilisation Programme is in essence a programmatic document, finding ways and means for eliminating the earlier economic and political deviations. It demands full rehabilitation of economic laws and of the market under a more efficient planning system, and a consistent respect of real economic parameters (i.e. real income, real depreciation, real interest rate, balanced dinar exchange rate, anti-inflationary monetary policy, and modern fiscal policy) which will take into account the economic and social function of taxes in addition to the needs of the fisc.

The development policy of the Programme demands a change in the structure of the economy, and in particular an export-oriented economy mobilising the resources available through the use of comparative advantage under world market criteria.

In the system of investment, an improvement was accomplished in capital formation and capital allocation. The new Law on Expanded Reproduction (1982), brought new relationships into this system. In essence, the new law abolishes the treatment of accumulation as a residual factor; it changes the former sequence of priorities for income distribution in favour of accumulation, so that personal income per worker in the socialist sector depends on the amount of accumulation in relation to the operating fund and on gains in labour productivity.

Out of higher net income (gross income after taxes and contractual fees), and in relation to labour and capital engaged, proportionately higher capital formation is required. The formation of capital depends on capital intensity and the need for technological improvements. This also depends on the need for productivity improvements, as well as on the nature of the activity, thus curbing extra profits arising from market or other distortions. On the basis of this law, social compacts and self-management agreements are designed to set out objectives, criteria and mutual obligations for the agents involved.

With respect to capital allocation, this law confirms the interdependence of the planning process with investment decision-making in such a way that an investment project is an element of the planning process. The investment decision itself is autonomous at the level of the enterprise - more precisely for each basic organisation unit of associated labour

(BOAL). The decision has to be made by a majority of the persons employed on the basis of proposals elaborated by the management. The criteria for project formulation are defined, and this can be done by the enterprise or by external consultants. The project proposals have to prove market and social acceptability, which are elements in the decision process. Investment projects must be evaluated externally, by economic chambers, scientific or consultants' institutions or other self-management associations. The results of project evaluations are subject to the decision-making process. Since this law is not precise in defining terms such as project formulation, project evaluation and project implementation, projects had to be classified under the "Federal social compact on economic criteria for investment" (passed in 1985), elaborated further below.

Other laws introduced during this period deal mostly with the system of investment and some aspects of project evaluation. For example, the law on banking gives priority to financial aspects, and especially to the sources of finance. In other laws, the approach is partial and a difference is noted between aspects of physical and financial planning and evaluation. The solutions among republics and autonomous provinces differ as well. So it becomes evident that a minimum set of unified criteria and methodological approaches should be defined.

13.4 Investment decision-making

The essence of self-management is that workers employed in an organisation, either economic or non-economic, directly manage the means of production, independently organise the work and production, become incorporated in the work organisation and act as independent economic agents and legal entities in the country and abroad. Whatever they earn from their work, and from the use of the socially owned capital, belongs to them after fulfilling obligations to the society. In their decisions, therefore, they have to meet their individual organisational and social requirements. This is also true for investment decision-making.

In the investment decision process, three basic kinds of links are relevant: the planning mechanism, market mechanisms and socio-political mechanisms. These supply the necessary information and serve as check points for the decision-making process.

The initiative for investment decisions, leading to project preparation, can come from the enterprises, the integrated systems (PTT, the electric power generating industry, the railway system, etc.), the communes, the republics or autonomous provinces, and for some large projects from the Federal government in accordance with the new Law on Planning. The initiative, however, is concentrated at the enterprise level, since each enterprise is responsible for its own development.

Under the Yugoslav economic system, the business organisation behaves as an independent economic entity in a planned-market economy. The workers' incentives in planning, organising and implementing production and investment in the Yugoslav business organisation are derived from the basic objective function of the economic system as a whole. Since the workers decide the conditions and results of their work, they decide on all strategic economic aspects related to their business organisations. Consequently, they make different economic and managerial decisions regarding investment, production, marketing, distribution of income, price policy, financing, planning and organisation. In this decision-making process, the workers adhere to the principles of business success. Decisions which are of particular importance, and on which the workers decide directly, are the distribution of income, investment decisions, election of self-management bodies, adoption of self-management agreements and social compacts and the creation of development plans.

Self-management agreements are instruments intended to harmonise self-management relationships within the system of workers' management. Through such agreements, business organisations can independently, without the participation of government, define and harmonise their mutual relations and interests. All managerial decisions which have an executive character are usually taken through appointed delegates to the workers' council, or in the management board.

The organisational and managerial structure of Yugoslav business organisations is characterised by two representative self-management bodies. The first is the assembly of workers, which consists of all workers in the basic organisation of associated labour and acts as the supreme self-management organ. The second is the workers' council which is elected by the workers and acts as the main executive body. The Business Board, which is usually attached to the workers' council, is intended to provide relevant information and managerial expertise for self-management decisions and their execution. It has the function of a specialised professional service for the two self-management bodies. Every business organisation has a business organ, either an individual general manager (i.e. director) or a managing board which is appointed, or relieved of its function, by the workers' council. The general manager is appointed, through open competition, by a commission, which consists of representatives of the business organisation, trade unions and local authorities.

All investment decisions are brought to the assembly of workers on the basis of recommendations made by the workers' council. According to this procedure, workers are formally responsible for investment decisions. This means that any consequences are borne by the decision-makers, i.e. the workers themselves. In this respect, the role of professional consulting groups, which are not elements of the formal self-management structure, is very important.

13.5 Implications of the investment system for investment allocation

One of the most outstanding features of the Yugoslav economy is its extremely intensive investment activity, the rate of investment amounting to 31 per cent of GDP for the whole period from 1952 to 1982.

The investment rate demonstrates, in a certain way, the development strategy, as well as the outcome of economic policy measures. The average annual rate of gross fixed investment was relatively stable, fluctuating between 25.3 per cent (1983) amd 40 per cent (1978). We ought to note an escalation of the investment rate starting in 1974 and ending by 1981, with a peak in 1978. After 1979 the rate started to decline, corresponding with the beginning of the economic crisis (see *Table 13.1*).

Table 13.1

Yugoslavia: Share of gross fixed investment in GDP
(percentages)

1974	1975	1976	1977	1978	1979	1980	1981	1982	1983
28.8	32.4	34.9	36.5	39.6	38.4	35.1	31.0	29.2	25.3

Source: Statistical Yearbook of Yugoslavia, 1985, p. 85

In 1980-1984, the physical volume of fixed investment decreased, a consequence of very high repayments of foreign debts and slow economic growth after 1979.

The allocation of investment from 1974 until 1983 was such that on the average, 70 per cent of investment was absorbed by economic or productive activities and 30 per cent by non-productive activities;[3)] the long-run shares of productive and non-productive fixed investment in the GDP amounted to 21.3 per cent and 9.7 per cent respectively, thus bringing the rate of total fixed investment to 31.0 per cent. At the same time, the rate of accumulation (net fixed capital formation, plus investment in working capital) was 20.8 per cent.

The long run growth rate of GDP in 1974-83 was 6.4 per cent a year and the share of productive fixed investment 21.3 per cent, so that

3) In the Yugoslav economic system, productive sectors are: industry and mining, agriculture and fishing, forestry, water management, construction, transport and communications, trade, catering and tourism, and crafts.

the average annual marginal coefficient (known as ICOR - incremental capital output ratio) was 3.3. In the last few years, the ICOR was greater because the rate of productive fixed investment stayed relatively high while the rates of GDP growth were below the long-run average.

Industry and mining have had the highest share in the structure of total investments, reaching almost 40 per cent of the total by 1976 and then declining to 35 per cent by 1983 (*Table 13.2*). Because of this high investment, industry and mining have become the leading economic sector in the Yugoslav production structure, with 40 per cent of GDP. Agriculture has had a declining share during the peak of investment outlays after 1974, but increased its relative share by the early 1980s. The share of transport and communications is the second highest, reaching a peak of 15 per cent in 1979 and diminishing thereafter. Other sectors have minor shares in investment and the changes were relatively small.

Table 13.2

Yugoslavia: Sectoral structure of gross fixed investment
(percentages)

Year Sector	1974	1975	1976	1977	1978	1979	1980	1981	1982	1983
Industry and mining	34.1	39.1	39.9	38.8	37.2	35.7	37.5	36.6	36.1	35.1
Agriculture and fishing	7.7	6.9	6.5	5.8	6.1	6.1	6.0	6.8	9.0	9.8
Forestry	0.9	0.7	0.7	0.6	0.7	0.7	0.6	0.9	1.0	1.0
Water management	0.6	0.6	0.7	1.0	1.2	0.9	0.9	1.1	1.2	1.5
Construction industry	2.7	2.8	2.5	3.4	3.3	3.2	2.8	3.2	2.7	2.6
Transport and communications	12.1	11.4	12.9	13.2	14.7	15.0	13.9	12.7	11.5	13.1
Trade	4.2	3.6	2.8	3.3	3.7	4.1	3.7	3.5	2.8	2.4
Catering and tourism	2.3	2.2	2.7	2.5	2.2	2.4	2.3	2.7	3.0	2.8
Crafts	1.9	1.8	1.4	1.4	1.7	1.8	1.6	1.8	1.8	2.0
Non-productive activities	33.5	30.9	29.9	30.0	29.2	30.1	30.7	30.7	30.9	29.7
Total	*100*	*100*	*100*	*100*	*100*	*100*	*100*	*100*	*100*	*100*

Source: Statistical Yearbook of Yugoslavia, 1985, p. 86

After 1974, output growth rates were lower than in the previous ten years, while investment rates were considerably higher. The overall efficiency of investment decreased, an increase of investment by 1 per cent implying a rise of the GDP by only about 0.6 per cent.

Questions can arise about the allocation of investment between and within sectors.

Table 13.3

Yugoslavia: Structure of fixed investments by type
(percentages of total)

Year	New capacities	Reconstruction modernisation and expansion of existing capacities	Replacement and maintenance of existing capacities
1974	45.9	36.0	18.1
1975	51.1	33.2	15.7
1976	57.5	27.8	14.7
1977	56.9	28.0	15.1
1978	59.3	26.3	14.4
1979	60.0	25.3	14.7
1980	61.3	24.0	14.7
1981	62.3	22.8	14.9
1982	61.2	23.5	15.3
1983	60.4	22.9	16.7

Source: Statistical Yearbook of Yugoslavia, 1985, p. 192

Table 13.4

Yugoslavia: Source of financing of investment
(percentages of total)

Year	Enterprise funds	Loans from banks, other enterprises and governments	Government grants
1974	56.3	40.8	2.9
1975	52.7	44.2	3.1
1976	49.7	47.2	3.1
1977	50.5	47.1	2.4
1978	47.7	50.3	2.0
1979	49.0	49.0	2.0
1980	50.3	47.7	2.0
1981	52.6	45.4	2.0
1982	57.2	40.6	2.2
1983	61.1	36.5	2.4

Source: Statistical Yearbook of Yugoslavia, 1985, p.186

Most of the investment was allocated to new capacities, of which the share has increased to 60 per cent; The share going to reconstruction and replacements diminished (*Table 13.3*).

The new investment could have pulled up the economy but it is obvious that the priorities expressed by the plan were not the real economic priorities. In addition, the possibilities for a better allocation of investment given by the economic system, were outweighed by economic policy measures in such a way that suboptimal solutions were chosen.

The high investment ambitions are reflected in the analysis by sources of finance (*Table 13.4*).

From 1974 until 1983, enterprises self-financed over half of investment while bank and other loans accounted for most of the rest. At the end of this period, the proportion of enterprise self-financing increased (but the rate of investment was falling). The role of banks diminished, but this was due to lack of capital and its cost.

13.6 New developments in investment decision-making

The end of 1985 marked a sharp change in the institutional framework for investment decision-making, with the idea of imposing on the investors, the banks and government a more operational and professional approach to investment project planning.[4] Investors are now obliged to evaluate projects professionally and to have the results of the evaluation assessed by independent professional institutions or by experts from the banks. The findings must be submitted in documentary form to the banks when applying for loans. For this purpose, the common methodology, valid for the whole country, should be applied in order to allow comparative analysis of the competing projects.

The banks are not supposed to grant any loan without this professional evaluation. This expertise is part of the formal documentation needed for decisions on loan extensions. However, the crucial point is that the banks must now carry much of the risks of investment financing, being obliged to cover any losses on the projects from their own funds. The banks are also obliged to monitor the performance of the projects which they have financed.

The government, especially at the republican level, has been assigned a further and more operational elaboration of the legal framework regula-

---

4) The major changes were introduced by the "Social Compact on the Recommendation of the Social and Economic Feasibility of Intended Investments" and the "Law on Basic Principles of Banking and Credit System", both passed in December 1985.

ting the financing and implementation of the projects in order to set up a standard approach for the whole country.

Finally, it was decided to set up an integral information system for the benefit of all parties involved in investment decision-making, and to set on foot a specialised education system for project planners, but without specifying the necessary operational steps.

All the changes mentioned above represent, without doubt, an extremely important institutional step forward, opening the way for many improvements in the decision-making process. Three main lines of further action seem to be the most important and urgent: the operational methodology for investment project planning, the education of specialised experts and the establishment of centres for investment project planning.

The operational methodology for investment project planning (to be adopted by the end of 1986) covers the full cycle of an investment project, i.e. the preparation, the evaluation, the implementation and the follow-up stage of a project. At the micro level, the investor must prepare three main studies when planning a project: the pre-feasibility study, the feasibility study and the implementation study. These documents are to serve as an indispensable source of information for the enterprises, the banks, the government and all other parties involved in investment decision-making.

The crucial stage for planning purposes is the evaluation of a project, covering both its market efficiency and its socio-economic efficiency. To make the project planning consistent with the planning at the macro-level, a set of social parameters will be designed: the shadow prices, the cut-off rates and the social discount rate. The methodology proposed respects the usual international standards, but adapted to the conditions of Yugoslavia's economic system.

The specialised education system for investment project planning is definitely one of the most important prerequisites for the efficient implementation of the methodology. There is a genuine lack of experts in this field and a series of workshops is envisaged to upgrade the skills of the experts, primarily those in the enterprises and the banks. The participants in the workshops will be obliged to pass an exam to acquire the status of a "licensed investment project planner" and only those so qualified will be able to take part in the professional analysis of project planning.

The centres for investment project planning are envisaged as new professional institutions in the planning system with the function of bridging macro- and microplanning by offering consultancy services to potential investors. These centres may be established in the large enterprises and the banks, or as independent professional institutions; all have the a role of consultants with no administrative power.

It is hoped that these recent developments will introduce a higher standard of economic reasoning and rationality into investment decision-making and will reduce the political influence and political considerations to the necessary minimum. Yugoslavia's past experience shows no lack of new ideas and intentions, although it does show a lack of efficient and mutually consistent actions in upgrading its economic system and decision-making process. The years to come will show what real improvements will take place in these respects.

Selected Bibliography

J. Bendeković, Sistem investiranja u SFRJ, (Investment System in Yugoslavia), Ekonomiski institut Zagreb, 1971.

-, Analiza sistema investiranja SFRJ poslije godine 1965", (Analysis of the Yugoslav Investment System after 1965), Ekonomski pregled, No. 3- 4/1975.

- and I. Teodorović, Investment Project Evaluation in Yugoslavia, Ekonomski institut Zagreb, 1975.

-, "Self-Management Planning System: the Case of Yugoslavia", in Strategies of Planning and Development, Planning and Development Board, Punjab, Lahore, 1980.

D. Gorupic, The Enterprise and the Development of the Yugoslav Economic System, Ekonomski institut Zagreb, 1974.

M. Nusinović, and M. Teodorović, "Programirana raspodjela društvenog proizvoda" (Programmed Distribution of GDP) Ekonomski pregled, No. 9- 10/1979.

I. Teodorović, Industrijski razvoj i investicijske odluke u Jugoslaviji (Industrial Development and Investment Decisions in Yugoslavia), Ekonomski institut Zagreb, 1980.

- and M. Nusinović, "Investment Allocation in Yugoslavia" in Essays on the Yugoslav Economic Model, Center for Yugoslav-American Studies and Exchanges, Florida State University and Ekonomski institut Zagreb, Zagreb 1986, pp. 77-102.

D. Vojnić, "Investicije i društvena reprodukcija" (Investment and Social Reproduction), Informator, Zagreb 1977.

Dugoročni program ekonomske stabilizacije (Long-Term Programme of Economic Stabilisation), Centar za radničko samoupravljanje, Belgrade, 1982.

Koncepcija i model ocjene investicijskih programa (Concept and Model of Investment Projects Evaluation), Ekonomski institut Zagreb, 1983.

Doing Business with Yugoslavia, Yugoslav Chamber of Economy and Institute of Economics Zagreb, Belgrade-Zagreb, 1986.

Chapter 14

STRATEGIC PLANNING AND INNOVATION IN A YUGOSLAV SELF-MANAGEMENT ENTERPRISE - METALSERVIS

Aleksander Kraus[1)]

METALSERVIS, hereafter MS, was founded in 1947 as a trading enterprise supplying industry with production materials. In the 30 years of its business activity there were no large fluctuations. In the post-war economic development of Yugoslavia, MS gained the reputation of a reliable business partner. In 1975-1976 MS went through some kind of personnel crisis or crisis of management. The new, educated generation of experts had come in, but their arrival caused many disturbances. At that time, MS dealt with only one activity - wholesale trade on the domestic market. In 1976, the firm had about 800 employees. On January 1, 1977 the new management took over; changes began to be introduced and have remained in effect.

MS functions within the conditions of the Yugoslav economic and political systems, which today are going through a crisis. However, in 1977 we in Yugoslavia were all deeply involved in the consequences of the major legislation which, it was assumed, would help us to solve the many contradictions evident in the Yugoslav economy even at that time.

The struggle for a greater influence of the market model for running business, as against the dominant administrative regulation of the economy, has been pushed aside from the main scene. It has been replaced by a general reorganisation under the recent Associated Labour Act. The aim of this Act was to reconcile the contradictions and, by general consultations and agreements between the economic units, to remove the negative consequences of an uncontrolled operation of the market. Reorganisation of the existing economic entities took place in two directions: decentralisation within the existing enterprises to lower constituent parts with great independence, called BOALs (Basic organisations of associated labour), and forming larger economic units by merging the original enterprises into so-called COALs (Composite organisations of associated labour). This development of the Yugoslav economy many eminent economists nowadays call "consensus economy". It obviously coincides with the great difficulties which the Yugoslav economy is undergoing. The tempestuous ten-year development of MS has taken place in these circumstances and in the

---

1) President, Metalservis, Belgrade

actual conditions of the Yugoslav socialist model, i.e. with self-managing decision-making of the workers on all essential questions related to the activity of the firm.

14.1 Phase I - A new start

In 1977, MS was a sound traditional trading company where the employees did not live badly. There was a relatively small number of workers having university degrees and nothing new in the technology of running the business had happened for years.

Faced with such a situation, the first thing the new management insisted upon was the appointment of young and capable experts to the key positions in the firm. That process was very difficult, accompanied by much opposition and opportunism; but it had to be completed at any cost. Reorganisations then in progress were used, among other things, to appoint people with university degrees at the head of each organisational part of the firm. Getting familiar with the actual state of affairs and relationships in the firm and with the business system were accomplished during the first year. The level of applied technology in performing every-day functions of the system was assessed and a new internal structure of the system was analysed and outlined in compliance with the new legal provisions. A platform for the future development strategy, based on some relatively simple assessments, was already made at the time.

One of the important considerations was the fact that MS is located in Belgrade, the biggest market for metal goods in Yugoslavia. The highly concentrated industry in Belgrade and its immediate vicinity uses these goods for its own production (motors, autos, agricultural machinery, machine-building etc.). It was also obvious that a great part of the basic materials, semi-finished products and tools is manufactured out of Belgrade, while consumed in and around Belgrade. Our conclusion was that Belgrade industry is being supplied irrationally, i.e. that it keeps too large material stocks and thus makes its final products more expensive - which is untenable for a long period. Surveys showed that there are no big warehouses with modern equipment and that the warehouses of MS did not meet current criteria. It was also clear that competition in existing conditions cannot react quickly enough. It should not be necessary to underline that the Belgrade market is also the biggest for retail trade, which MS did not do at that time. In addition to the new personnel, a bright point for development was the land owned by MS 20 km from Belgrade, very suitable for quick construction of the modern warehouse.

Having in mind the inertness and relatively quiet life that existed in MS, it was very important to start the process of developmental changes with a project appearing relevant and logical to the majority of workers.

That project was the construction of an up-to-date storage complex. It was more difficult to explain to the workers that the warehouse, as well as the operation of the whole business, must be controlled by computer. However, that struggle was just about to take place. Thorough preparations were made for erecting the warehouse. For the first time, separate development departments were organised within the firm. Young experts were employed. Visits to get to know the contemporary achievements of storage technology in the developed European countries were arranged. A mixed group, including the new specialists and the older experienced and influential workers of MS, visited 16 modern warehouses in several West European countries. Intensive political activity was organised among the workers for explaining the necessity of undertaking large developmental activities. And the great battle to carry through the project began: finding investment funds, designing, construction licences, engineering and supervision of erection, ensuring punctual and best standards of work, repressing internal opposition etc.

A contemporary distributive centre, with 3 technological units was built within less than 20 months, on completely unsettled ground occupying 14 hectares:

- a 20.000 sq.m. hall for ferrous and non-ferrous metallurgy products,
- a 10.000 sq.m. hall with high-rack storage, and
- a 20.000 sq.m. outdoor warehouse.

Equipment from several well-known West European and American manufacturers was installed. The outdoor warehouse is equipped with two straddle carriers made by the American firm Mannesman Drot. In the hall for storing the technical goods are located high-rack fork-trucks of the British firm Lansing Ltd., as well as translators and high-rack storage made under the licence of the Italian firm Pianeli-Traversa. The warehouse is controlled by the computer unit of the domestic manufacturer Iskra-Delta, under licence of the American company PDP-Digital.

From the viewpoint of East-West economic cooperation, it is interesting to mention that during execution of this project there were other influences of the Western approach. The American consultant Bruce Payne was involved in MS for 6 months during 1978. His great experience contributed to the favourable environment created for going ahead with the project.

We also had the pleasure of visiting six famous European schools for business management training. Their approaches and ways of reasoning were precious for us in settling our current problems. We particularly stress valuable ideas gained from the Isvor-Fiat school in Marentino near Torino. This is of special importance, since MS deals with supplying parts and materials for the car manufacturing firm Zastava in Kragujevac where production is based on the Fiat licence. We were deeply impressed by other schools as well: Imede in Lausanne, the Henley school near London, the London Business School, IFL in Stockholm and the Oslo Institute of Business Administration. In all these ways we were exposed to the strong influence of fresh and modern approaches to the running of business, ideas which had to be adapted to the realities and conditions of the Yugoslav economic and political situation.

The warehouse project was successfully completed. When the Sava river flooded in April 1980, all the goods, the whole inventory and the warehouse workers were moved from 16 locations scattered all over the town to the new locations. The move was done by 470 truck tours within 10 days and nights with the help of the whole MS staff. The management took the lead participating with all the workers. The psychological foundations were laid for the future common work of the staff and the new management during that operation. When the warehouse was about to be finished there were a few attempts to dismiss the managing team of MS, but without the support of the majority of workers.

14.2 Phase II - Stabilisation

A great battle was won by construction of the warehouse. A significant strategic advantage was achieved over the competitors and the ground for future development prepared. After completion of the warehouse major efforts were devoted to raising the whole business system to a higher level of applied technology. Emphasis had certainly to be put on the quick introduction of data processing into all business activities of MS. The process of introducing the new working methods - one could say burning all bridges for return to the old methods - was very difficult, sometimes critical, but unavoidable and in the end very useful.

Another computer was purchased from the same manufacturer and formed the base of a computer network for the whole business system. The computer centre located in the management building in Belgrade took over the data processing of bookkeeping, finances etc. Great attention was paid to the preparatory phase of data processing; MS now has its own coding system for goods, customers, suppliers etc.

It is interesting that a certain natural relaxation, even some self-satisfaction with what had been achieved, was evident after the great efforts put into erection of the warehouse. As everything achieved so far was just a strategic base for the future, and since everyday life still went on by the inertia of old habits, so that the economic potential of the firm was insufficient, things were neither stable nor balanced. In such a situation it was necessary to decide quickly where and how to proceed. The first elements of a contemporary marketing concept of the firm had already been established.

We decided to follow two directions, both of them being developmental, but essentially different according to their fundamental characteristics. After construction of the warehouse and on the basis of the information system, the decision to develope further into retail trade on the one hand, and towards engineering on the other, had to act as a stabiliser of the approach to innovation and development problems. It took some time for the staff to understand that development is a permanent activity, that certain funds for continuous development have to be constantly set aside out of current income, and that development brings a stable future to everybody.

The psychological aspects of the stabilisation of novelties are not to be underestimated either. Some workers were dissatisfied by moving to the new location 20 km out of the town while the old storages of MS remained empty. Workers were retrained, new workers were brought in, and former unfunctional warehouses were adapted as department stores and retail shops. That process went on very easily and quickly and appeared completely logical to all the employees because retail trade is close to every citizen. Besides a standard range of MS goods, we were among the first in Belgrade to sell personal computers in retail shops.

We have rather easily succeeded in providing for the further financing of a team of experts in charge of capital construction. That group gradually became the core of an engineering department. It was made somewhat easier by the fact that during preparation of the Winter Olympic Games in Sarajevo, MS successfully accomplished important works within the environment protection project. These were basically engineering works, MS supplying pipes and equipment for new waterworks in Sarajevo. The engineering department's task was to cooperate closely with the wholesale trade department, particularly for capital projects and for supplying critical materials important for observing the terms of construction contracts. With respect to the engineering works we had in mind the future engagement of MS in foreign trade. We saw our biggest chance in capital projects abroad, particularly in developing countries where Yugoslav contractors are already active. We have also developed some technologies with our own know-how. This refers to the further development of warehouse technology, some branches of foundry technology and subsequently technologies within the area of chemical power sources.

Regarding development as requiring a systematic approach and a contemporary marketing concept, MS established its commercial and storage-manipulative network. For transport that means an integrated system connected with our regular flows of goods. The base of this strategy is the geographical and market location of Belgrade and the MS distributive centre. In 1978, MS opened its storage-manipulative branch in Bar, the southernmost port on the Adriatic Sea, connected by rail with Belgrade. In the distributive centre in Belgrade conditions exist for further development of the container terminal, with its good connections for cargo consignments: it is only 2 km from the airport and 2 km from a modern highway leading through Yugoslavia from the Austrian and Italian frontier down to the frontiers of Greece and Bulgaria. North-south routes through Yugoslavia are also of great importance, as are the advantages of the Belgrade-Bar railway; duty-free zones are about to be formed in Belgrade and Bar and in some other parts of the country. We also have in mind activities in connection with the Danube; MS is engaged in traffic on the Danube in Belgrade, Smederevo, Kladovo and intends to expand this sphere of activity.

Further activities of MS concern the development of foreign trade and representation of foreign firms. In view of the very strong technological base, and firm support in domestic industry, it was not too difficult, although there were doubts, to obtain from the Yugoslav authorities the right to engage in foreign trade activity. Very important penetrations in foreign trade arrangements for tools, bearings, fasteners etc. were made in 1983, though for only two years. The biggest deals were made with Poland, Italy and USSR; and there are business relations with more than thirty countries. MS participated in the first exhibition of the Yugoslav economy, held in Moscow in 1985 and in the second exhibition, "Days of Yugoslav science and technique", in 1986. By linking the goods flow both on domestic and foreign markets within one business system, MS has real chances of successful competition. Preparations for deeper engagement in the so-called small economy proceeded in parallel with foreign trade activities. The basic motive was and still is to promote involvement of the great number of Yugoslav workers temporarily employed in some West European countries. A number of favourable circumstances contribute. Our workers' experience of developed economic systems was of great use to MS, since they have considerable savings which they wish to invest. Some governments of countries where the Yugoslav workers are employed encourage their return by special funds. We started intense activity - certainly not without opposition - to establish relations with craftsmen, either in the socialist or the private sector, as quickly as possible.

Today we have about 500 collaborators in the field of small economy and have increasingly become a support for big industrial firms concerned in cooperation with craftsmen. MS provides programmes, production material, sales, advertising, development, data processing, financing etc., and craftsmen provide their work.

In view of the fast development of modern technologies and our technological lag, in 1984 we started another - at first sight hopeless

- project. The Belgrade Institute for Scientific Research, which dealt with development of chemical power sources, had, in our opinion, found itself in temporary difficulties. Again, MS committed itself, in spite of considerable opposition, and managed to take over this Institute. Thus MS has at last created a real potential within its own house for development of some important technological disciplines such as new materials and power sources (not only of chemical origin). This developmental step was certainly something completely new and unexpected from a traditional view of the trading function. For MS it represents a qualitative change which links the firm with everything happening in the world today in high technologies and the so-called third technological revolution.

It should be observed that Yugoslavia has more than 10 battery-charger factories. MS is now able, through its Institute, to engage intensively in developmental work in that field. Encouraged by that success, following our success, within only one year, of solving current, personnel and financial problems as well as other problems of Institute development, we became more occupied with high technologies. We were guided by the following strategic considerations. Belgrade has plenty of scientific, research, development and engineering centres, but only a few of them are directly involved in the economy. This fact compels us to take up these challenges; for at present MS is at the stage of gaining experience about mechanisms for securing the mutual interests of organisations concerned with the financing of actual innovation and of development projects and programmes. In our opinion, the weakest points of the present situation are the absence of adequate marketing of scientific research and developmental work, as well as deficiencies in managing these activities. We see our opportunities here, since MS is basically a marketing organisation, for which market activity and market analysis are conditions *sine qua non.*

A special aspect of our experience is the decision-making process. Taking into account the relatively complicated economic planning system, we have frequently faced problems that western businessmen do not meet. The main point for a western business executive is to know what has to be done; while for us, in MS, it has very often been equally important, sometimes even more important, to know how to carry a good idea through the numerous regulations and decisions required. In general, the position of the business executive in our economy is only now evolving. It might be said that during the whole of its ten-year development, MS has practised a method which could be conditionally called a "System-related approach in action". This method is in full conformity with the growing complexity of the problems to be solved, as well as with the turbulent background. In present circumstances, the planning system existing in Yugoslavia is not of great help to us. We must often take decisions by relying more and more on our own strategic observations and assessments.

In view of the increasing responsibility of business executives in the Yugoslav economy, and also of the still different understanding of the concept of risk in business management by comparison with some other countries, it can be said that precious new experience has been gained in the last ten years about the problems of management and organisation of economic activities in self-management conditions. I refer particularly to the position and role of trade in the market economy of self-management socialism. Many dilemmas have appeared with regard to ways of managing relations between the firm as a whole and its constituent parts. For this reason we have introduced some innovations. Every year, after the annual balance sheet, the employees, who elected the business executives, evaluate their work by a ballot. The experience is brand-new; however the first results are encouraging. The procedure is quite simple. The executives submit their written reports, including the operating results of each part separately and of the firm as a whole, for a public hearing. This is followed by a secret ballot in which the workers vote "yes" or "no" for each relevant executive. "Yes" means he continues in management, and "no" means he is replaced. Future experience will expose the good and bad features of this procedure; we believe that good features will predominate and that the work and self-management commitment of both executives and workers will be of better quality.

Fast inflation has afflicted the Yugoslav economy during recent years in addition to rather strained relations between the developed north and the underdeveloped areas in the south. One can also mention some differences in economic development between the east and the west of the country. These problems are increasingly affecting enterprises, so that business executives and decision-making bodies must take them into consideration.

The last phase of the strategic planning of innovations and MS development concerns the absorption of smaller factories and production plants. These have of course production autonomy, but for further successful market penetration, specially on international markets, they need stronger business systems. In the last two years MS has negotiated with about 40 minor production firms about merging and joint development on to a higher level of business organisation. This process is in full swing but so far does not run smoothly. However, some seeds have begun to sprout; thus in 1986 two or three such amalgamations will have been carried at the end of 1985, as MS expects a revival of civil engineering activity principally in the attractive tourist area of the south Adriatic coast - an area to which we anyway direct part of our strategic activities.

14.3 Phase III - Mastering the marketing concept

MS is at present passing through a disturbed period in order to establish a business system in which everything will function harmoniously. Obviously, this is a very complex work. It is necessary to make full use of the complementary advantages of MS and Belgrade mentioned above, while conducting relations within the firm so that stimulation of personnel, primarily by incentives, and involvement of workers can play a crucial driving role.

Today, MS has about 1700 workers, twice as many as 10 years ago - and that is just the beginning of a possible accelerated growth. In fact, all the activities which have been established can be quickly expanded, either into empty market spaces, or by amalgamation of the weaker or complementary units. At present, we are very seriously engaged in problems of joint ventures, technology transfers, international industrial cooperation, and protection of licences for industrial and intellectual property. We want MS to become a modern service for the optimal flow of new ideas, information, money, goods and people. We are interested in the Eureka project and are trying to be as active as possible in new technologies, new materials, introducing robots, new power sources and, certainly, computers. We have been working for two years in these directions and have just signed a joint venture contract with a partner from West Europe for construction of a plant for optical fibres manufacturing and processing.

In general, we consider that we have a good chance to become in the near future a creative business channel for the flow of high technology products between West and East as well as for traditional flows of products, reloading services, transport, activities in duty-free zones, joint ventures, tourism etc. Finally, MS now has over 250 employees with university degrees, more than 30 of them being Dr, MA or MSc. In 1977 there was not a single worker so qualified. Great attention is paid to the quality of the workers, because the purpose of everything being done for development is to live better today and tomorrow, without any ideological burdens.

Chapter 15

MARKETING AND INNOVATION STRATEGY IN A MAJOR HUNGARIAN ENTERPRISE - TAURUS

László Horváth[1)]

My aim is to outline the Hungarian practice of strategic thinking and plan preparation. A brief introduction reviews the more important general features of Hungarian practice, necessary because of the differences of approach from that in the West. This is followed by a description of the strategy evolved by *Taurus Rubber Works*, a major Hungarian producer of rubber goods, with some details of its marketing and innovation policies.

15.1 Strategic planning in Hungary

An indispensable precondition of strategic planning at enterprise level is *autonomy*, which applies to state enterprises in Hungary. Strategic thinking and planning began in the late 1960s after the reform of the country's economic mechanism. In its diffusion, large companies, among them Taurus, took a pioneering role. (Taurus is chosen as an example, because it stood out for its activity, and also because in that period the author was its General Manager). These enterprises followed the Western pattern and experience, which they adapted to Hungarian conditions. In about twenty years they developed principles and methods by which the Hungarian state-owned enterprises formulated concrete strategic aims, with due regard to the requirements of the socialist environment.

What *requirements* must a strategic plan meet?

Such a plan is a comprehensive, complex and consistent concept, covering a long period ahead, preparing the enterprise to cope with foreseeable future events. This means not only active but also passive preparation viz. the capacity to make maximum use of events and to minimise losses. By setting aside sufficient reserves, the concept should also enable the enterprise to adapt to unforeseeable events. It should set the enterprise's long-term goals, take stock of the measures upon which it can rely over the long run, find the way best suited for attaining the goals, provide satisfactory guidance to the decision-makers at every executive level, remain relevant and display a clear approach.

Although the complexity of the strategic plan means that it offers decisions about every important aspect of the tasks for the enterprise,

---

1) Chief Director, National Management Development Centre, Budapest

it would be wrong to conclude that a strategic plan is a voluminous document. The uncertainty and inaccuracy of long-term prognoses, and too many details, might lead to false decisions.

Table 15.1 is a synopsis of the process of strategic planning.

These remarks may have convinced the reader that there is no unbridgeable gap between western companies and socialist state-owned enterprises as regards the *content* of strategic planning; they differ only in their methods, of which some will be mentioned.

- To determine the *time horizon,* which is never uniform, the Hungarian enterprises apply a well-developed method founded on stable principles which take due account of the period of obsolescence of products, technologies and fixed assets, of the time spent by the permanent staff with the enterprise, etc. On this basis, the time horizon of a strategic plan in most enterprises is 8-12 years (rarely 15 years or more). The cycle of changes in the sphere of operation is longer: 20-25 years. The relatively detailed Hungarian long-term plan (up to 2000), available to the enterprises as basic information, facilitates strategic planning. From the national plan the enterprise planners may acquire information for elaborating prognoses and forecasts, directly or indirectly. (It is not compulsory to take the national plan as the basis for strategic plans).

- To analyse the *production structure,* a system of criteria has recently been elaborated in Hungary which, setting various conditions, helps in selecting the so-called strategic product groups. The process, often combined with the application of the portfolio matrix, helps in choosing the strategies worth following by dividing the product families into groups (competitive, potentially competitive and uncompetitive - the latter to be reduced) and has proved very useful.[2)]

- In the last decade several scientific works have dealt with the system of strategic goals.[3)] In the light of experience and discussions on the subject the following goals are regarded as strategic for the enterprise as a whole (the goals include partial goals, action goals, etc.):

(a) Market position

Plans regarding the market position of the enterprise extend to the way it intends to change its share on the main domestic and foreign

---

2) G. Varga et.al., A termelési szerkezet fejlesztésének müszaki-gazdasági kritériumai (The technical-economic criteria for the development of the product structure), Budapest, Kossuth Kiadó, 1978.

3) E.g. Horváth-Csath, Stratégiai tervezés: Elmélet és gyakorlat. (Strategic planning: theory and practice). Budapest, Közgazdasági és Jogi Kiadó, 1983, pp. 186-196, 319-345.

Table 15.1

The process of strategic planning

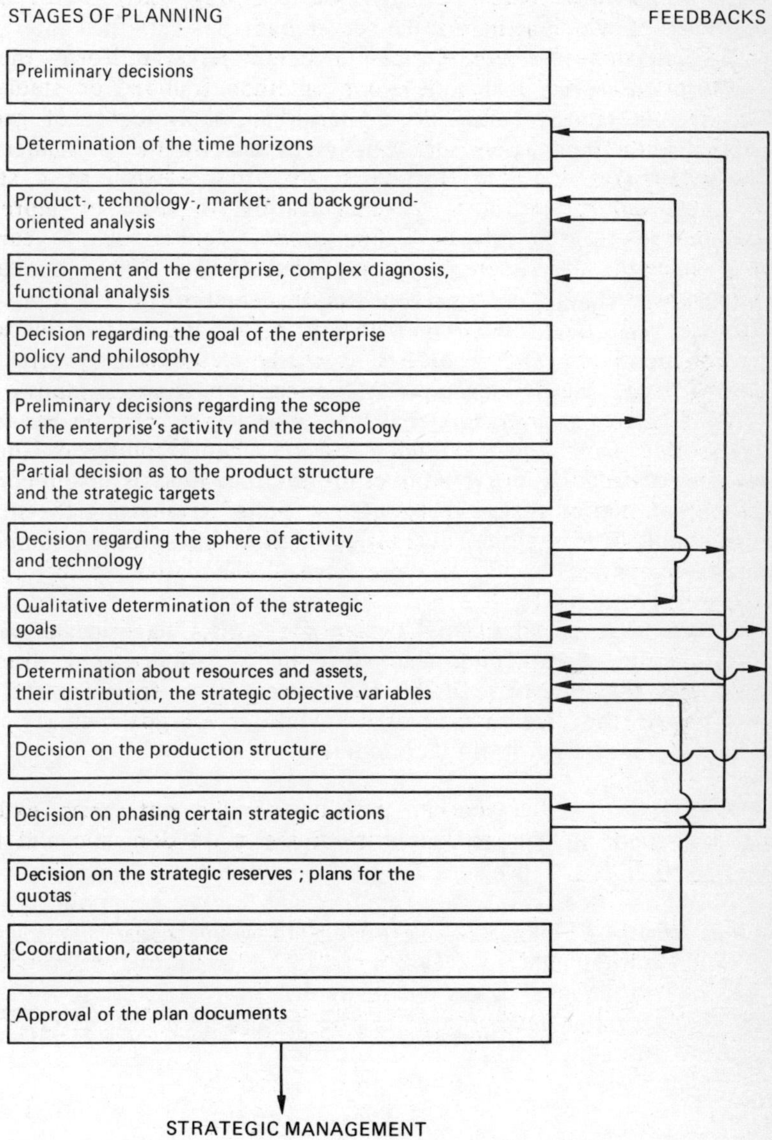

markets (with figures); the part it wishes to play on the market with its products and services by the end of the strategic time horizon; to what extent it wishes to expand its market organisation and the scope of its services; the markets it wishes to reach and the position it wishes to occupy there, etc.

(b) Technical position

What should be the main planned parameters of the enterprise's products - especially those of its most important strategic lines? to what degree does the enterprise wish to increase its capacities?

What should be the technical standard of the technologies applied? what should be the capacity and the quality of Research and Development at the enterprise? etc.

(c) Personnel position

What are the plans of the enterprise to improve the staff position in general? what should be the professional composition of the staff? what qualifications should those people have whom the enterprise wishes to put into executive posts? what policy is planned to support the work of the people engaging in development, management, organisation? what is the planned size and professional composition of the labour force? how can the enterprise ensure a reliable source of employees and workers? what facilities should be provided for the training and education of the personnel? what methods should be used in their training, and in what institutions should it take place? etc.

(d) Financial position

What should be the financial potential of the enterprise at the end of the plan period? what funds (including its own and external sources, loans, etc.) can the enterprise mobilise to attain its strategic goals? how will the enterprise be able to maintain the liquidity of its own resources? where will it be necessary to draw on external sources? etc.

(e) Enterprise size

An oversized enterprise causes problems as difficult as those of a too small one. If it is too big, it may become bureaucratic and inflexible, particularly if its excessive size is combined with a monopolistic status. If it is too small, it may become unable to concentrate and innovate. And since its market share is also likely to be small, its pricing policy will be exposed to its competitors' manoeuvres.

The goals for the development of the organisation are closely related to the size and strategic goals of the enterprise.

The strategic objectives related to human factors, determining the relationships between personnel and enterprise, are important elements of the system of strategic goals and are as follows:

Personal incomes. The goal related to personal incomes comprises the following: the personal incomes of the workers at the end of the plan period, compared with the earnings of their counterparts in enterprises operating nearby: the extra, non-monetary benefits, again compared with those granted by the competitors; the rate of increase in personal incomes over the strategic period.

Improvement of working conditions. This goal should be approached from various aspects, e.g. the changes foreseen in the environment, the reduction of heavy physical labour, measures to alleviate monotony, the provision of pleasant, aesthetic surroundings, etc.

Development of social, cultural and sports facilities. This too is a human-related goal which should include the development of institutions for children, for the aged, for pensioners, different forms of aid, etc.

Good atmosphere in the plant. Under this heading the plan should list all concrete measures that serve this aim, with stress on the provision of democratic management, a democratic institutional system, etc.

Assisting employees to start a career. The assistance given to members of the workforce to make a career; coordination with the enterprise's plans; with special attention paid to the careers of the expected relacements, etc.

15.2 Forming the strategy of the Taurus group

Plans for the development of the rubber industry, obviously with decreasing assurance and probability, were elaborated for the period up to the year 2000; in addition to the major enterprises, the plans applied to the development of some 60 small and mediumsize plants (the "Taurus Group")[4].

During the preparation of the plan several variants were examined differing:

- in the projection of Hungary's long-term demand for rubber goods;
- in the projection of the effects of foreign trade, primarily with the CMEA countries;

---

4) This part of the chapter has been based on the work of the TAURUS development team; its head is O. Dessewffy.

- in the projection of the rate of growth in production, in the evolution of enterprise organisation, in the production structure and in the direction of expansion.

For easier comparison the values were calculated at 1981 prices. The data published in US $ are for information, reflecting only proportions.

Analyses and conclusions

Rubber goods, being made of specially flexible material, play important roles in their respective applications. The rubber industry at present includes approximately 100 productive sectors. The technologies they apply are much the same but not convertible. About 100 000 lines are turned out, their common function being to ensure flexible means of power transmission or the storage of energy. They have many more technologically important secondary functions, not replaceable by other materials.

It is characteristic of the role of rubber production in economy and society that:

- most users - water conservancy, food production, mining, building materials and construction, vehicle building, engineering, chemicals, communication, transport and various services - belong to the most dynamically expanding sectors;
- the functions - power transmission, materials handling, transport, sealing, vibration damping, surface finish, insulation - assume growing significance for *technology;*
- the importance of rubber products in defence is also growing.

It follows that beyond a certain level of development which Hungary attained several decades ago, rubber manufacturing is a background industry which takes care of consumption, services, and investment. Within it, the relative weight of the branches producing consumer goods is declining, being replaced by plastics. While the 50 productive branches of the Hungarian rubber industry fall into a dozen or so categories, our conclusions refer only to two major product families: *rubber tyres* and *technical lines* (hoses, belting etc.). These account for 80 to 90 per cent of the goods produced by the rubber sector in Hungary, as well as worldwide.

The consumption of rubber goods in Hungary rose at an average rate of 9 per cent a year between 1960 and 1970 and at 8 per cent between 1970 and 1980. This means that the rise in demand surpassed the growth of GDP. The economy needs an extremely large variety of rubber products. From the present 40-50 000, the range may increase to 80 000, even to 100 000, over the long run. The magnitude of demand, the variety and character of the goods, make international and national division of labour and selective development indispensable.

World trade in rubber goods increases more rapidly than manufacturing. In the 1970s, foreign trade turnover rose 1.5-2.0 times faster than output.

Hungary's rubber exports followed the trend, rising faster than domestic sales. Over the last 10 years exports to socialist markers rose 2.7 times and to capitalist markets 13-fold. In 1980, Hungary exported 32.6 per cent of output, 12.6 per cent to socialist and 20.0 per cent to capitalist markets. Imports from the socialist countries rose slightly faster than exports to them; capitalist exports far surpassed capitalist imports. These facts support and justify the foreign market orientation of the development concept.

As regards *indices of efficiency*, labour productivity is around 50 per cent of that achieved in the countries with the highest international standards. Technical instrumentation and research facilities also lag behind modern standards (because of the different pricing systems comparison is rather difficult). While the specific consumption of material is near to the international level, the specific power consumption in Hungary is almost twice as great - in spite of improvements in the last 10 years. Analyses have shown that this lag can be compensated

- by a more up-to-date product structure;
- by the development of the infrastructure of production, and
- by a higher standard of management and organisation.

As regards the *human factors:* in the last 10 years the labour force in the rubber industry remained stable but the professional structure improved; the number of people interested in development and in the entrepreneurial spirit increased in the small, medium-size and major enterprises; the ratio of higher qualified workers is going up; the professional culture of the intellectuals (white collar workers) in the rubber industry is rising.

The development of the *organisational structure* of the Hungarian rubber industry is satisfactory. Its most important features are as follows:

- the trend in the relative weight of the large, small and medium-size enterprises has been most favourable and has made it possible for the small producers to develop more rapidly than the major companies; management at the large plants (e.g. by the introduction of the matrix system in the 1970s) has became more flexible; the establishment of an independent foreign trading organisation cum innovation centre within Taurus sees to the demand of the entire Hungarian rubber industry.

Development alternatives

The variant needed by the rubber industry must be based upon the powerful and selective development of the profitable productive branches and the gradual winding up of the non-profitable, or, as a minimum, the above average development of the dynamic sectors - bearing in mind that in the second half of the period sectors now little known will have to be rapidly developed. This is the only promising and lucrative strategy that can be applied with success given the principle of self-financing.

The risks inevitably involved will be compensated by maintaining the high standard of the technically and economically competitive branches to the limit of their possibilities. Making use of the favourable opportunities offered by some product families we shall wind up the outdated branches or, if for some reason this is not feasible, we shall maintain them as a necessary evil.

In preparing the framework for the firm's strategy decisions, two alternative projections were proposed for each of seven important variables. From the 128 possible combinations of these alternatives, four were chosen as a basis for strategic planning. These are displayed in *Table 15.2*.

Table 15.2

Selected combinations of variables

	Variants considered				
	I A	I B	II A	II B	Variants rejected
Projected growth rates	(% p.a. to 2000) for rubber goods				
1. Domestic demand[a]	3.5	3.5	3.5	3.5	5
2. Exports	8	8	10.5	10.5	–
3. Production	5	5	6.5	6.5	–
Projected shares					
4. % of exports to CMEA	40	40	40	40	30
5. % of tyres in production	50	40	50	40	–
6. % of home demand met by small & medium firms	18	18	24	24	–
7. Rate of technical progress[b]	even throughout				accelerating after 1990

[a] Based on alternative growth rates for the economy as a whole and for total consumption.

[b] No drastic technical changes were envisaged during the period; the tyre-casting technique is not expected to be introduced before 2000. Shares of other specific products were also examined.

The accepted economic strategy

On the basis of the variants, the main features of the accepted economic strategy are as follows (for more details see *Tables 15.3* and *15.4*).

- A common feature of every variant of the accepted economic strategy is that they count on a moderate rate of growth in domestic demand, a slow rise in socialist exports and an initially slow, then accelerating, growth. As regards the resources, the variants expect reductions in manpower.

Table 15.3

Product structure of TAURUS according to strategic variant IA
($ mn. at 1981 prices)

Main strategic units	1980	1985	1990	1995	2000
Steel radial truck tyres	30	45	75	110	180
Agricultural tyres	10	20	30	35	45
Diagonal truck tyres	40	30	10	–	–
Hydraulics and special hoses	20	25	30	40	50
Conveyor belting	15	15	25	30	35
Camping equipment	10	8	7	–	–

Table 15.4

Product structure of TAURUS according to strategic variant IIA
($ mn. at 1981 prices)

Main strategic units	1980	1985	1990	1995	2000
Steel radial truck tyres	30	45	85	130	220
Agricultural tyres	10	20	30	35	65
Diagonal truck tyres	40	30	15	5	–
Hydraulics and special hoses	20	25	40	70	95
Conveyor belting	15	15	25	30	35
Camping equipment	10	8	8	8	8

Variants I foresee a lesser rise in foreign trade than *Variants II* and therefore lower home consumption and a lesser rise in production. Dependence on the small and medium-size plants in meeting home demand will diminish.

Variants II are more export oriented. Accordingly they expect a considerably greater rise in production by the end of the period, and greater dependence on the small and medium-size plants in meeting home demand.

In *variants* I and II (growth in foreign trade and structural changes) A. and B. refer to the *production structure*, notably to the ratio of tyres to technical lines. However, development in both product families must be selective. For instance, in the tyre family, development will have to be concentrated on the manufacture of radial tyres for lorries, agricultural and earthworking machines. It would still be uneconomical to start the production of tyres for passenger cars in Hungary.

In view of the high flexibility of the development strategy, the need might arise for modification of the concepts if for reasons of foreign trade or foreign policy, strict autarchy must be practised; or if the spread of the casting technique results in radical changes in the status of this sector. (The introduction of the casting technology on a large scale may reduce the input of labour by 60-70 per cent and the capital investment by 50 per cent.)

The realisation of the development concepts depends on numerous human and material conditions:

- the long term development of the rubber industry must be effected with slightly decreasing *manpower*. This calls for 3-4 times higher labour productivity;
- an important criterion for the realisation of the concepts is the availability of the necessary *materials* and the reduction of the material content of the products;
- throughout the plan period the rubber industry will become a sector with *moderate power consumption*. Power conservation by modernisation of the supply systems and technology will continue to be a primary objective;
- the realisation of the development objectives will involve a *capital investment* of $ 70 million between 1981 and 1985, $ 150250 million between 1986 and 1990, $ 100-150 million between 1991 and 1995 and $ 150-250 million between 1996 and 2000. These high figures bring into question the realism of *variants* II, which envisage a higher rate of production and exports.

Since the value of production per unit of gross fixed assets will show little change, even with such high investment, the efficiency of the assets will remain essentially unchanged throughout the period. However, more ambitious plans would be unrealistic.

Another problem awaiting resolution is that of *organisation:* parallel with the modernisation of the production structure it would be desirable to develop also the small and medium-size enterprises and to give them a new relationship with the large company. To make maximum use of the potentialities offered for cooperation the producers should establish suitable and efficient forms of organisation (e.g. joint ventures, economic cooperatives, subsidiaries, associations).

15.3 Taurus's marketing and innovation strategy

Taurus's strategy is differentiated according to its principal markets (domestic, socialist, capitalist). In the limited space available, we shall deal only with certain elements of the strategy elaborated for trade with the capitalist countries only[5].

Trade policy concept

In the present keenly competitive international rubber market there are only two ways for some enterprises to survive: to merge with a large company; or to preserve their independence through ambitious innovative activity, development of an exceptional product structure, and on that basis to create a powerful marketing organisation. For Taurus, Hungary's largest rubber producer, only the latter way is open. It must adapt to the special features of the rubber industry and the rubber market: namely, that despite the existence of 4 000 producers the rubber industry is concentrated in a few countries and in a small number of enterprises.

In these circumstances, Taurus is faced by two conflicting problems: competition with the large multinational companies on the one hand, and, on the other, with thousands of small producers eager to remain in the field and develop in the shadow of the giants. In the long run, this complex situation will create steadily deteriorating conditions for marketing.

Competition on the foreign markets will become increasingly keen, a buyers' market must be counted upon in a large number of product groups and, simultaneously, there will be increasing competition by the rubber producers now recovering from the general recession and wishing to introduce new, more efficient techniques. Taurus will also have to grapple with more difficult conditions on the home market. Small enterprises were set up in Hungary which, in some productive branches, have managed to attain turnovers and rates of growth surpassing those of Taurus and are likely to compete on the foreign markets as well. An additional new competitive factor on the rubber market is the appearance of plastics, which will compete with rubber in the manufacture of technical goods and consumer articles. In market competition some non-price factors will also assume increasing roles, the most important being applications, accessory systems and services, quality, delivery terms, promotion, sales on credit, etc.

Analysis of the general market situation made Taurus realise that, with the conventional methods, it will not be able to hold its place in the competition. In this unusual situation, under the effect of a multitude of factors in many ways contradictory, Taurus had to find ways of marketing and innovation which would help attain its strategic goals.

---

5) **Based on the activity of a Taurus team; its head is E. Könczöl.**

The solution lies in the evolution and appropriate coordination of marketing and innovation adapted to the situation. *This calls for a differentiated and well-coordinated marketing and innovation strategy which takes maximum account of the competitive factors and is capable on the one hand of maintaining, even improving, the positions occupied by the enterprise, the concentration of its resources in the strategically most important sectors and, on the other, of making full use of market opportunities arising at any point in this complex competitive situation.*

Marketing and innovation

The combination of marketing and innovation shows different characteristics not only in the different productive sectors but even in some particular products; thus special marketing and innovative developments have been introduced at Taurus. Two examples follow.

(a) The importance of an entrepreneurial attitude

The manufacture of *special hoses for the oil industry* is one of Taurus's strategic lines. Thanks to successful production and rich experience, Taurus is in a position to implement technical development and to meet users' demands entirely from its own resources. The basis of non- stop innovation in this sector is the development of a type of deep drilling hose which in 1950 was granted an international patent. This technical achievement stimulated extensive technical development which scored great successes, e.g. in the production of deep drilling hoses for off-shore operation.

Relying on a secure background market (the Soviet Union), which more than covers the costs of development, a systematic extensive multi-stage marketing and innovation strategy was begun. In its first stage, the aim had been to intensify product specification and find new applications of the earlier technology. The result was more sophisticated air tube structures and the development of hoses suitable for new functions (e.g. concrete hose). Through the introduction of new technologies and the setting up of new capacities, the second stage of development was the manufacture of special-purpose hoses including a nearly complete family for the oil industry: jet-, dock-, steam-, choke- and kill-hoses, riser hose, and, the no.1 hit, the 200 m flow-line hose which Taurus was the first in the world to produce.

However, due to the specificity of the products, the utilisation of the very considerable Research and Development background depends on the efficiency of the marketing work. The goods are produced to the buyers' specifications and sold at competitive biddings. Development is generated by marketing; innovations must be derived from the requirements ascertained, often generated, by marketing. For the products concerned, the entrepreneurial attitude is of crucial importance. It determines the characteristics not only of marketing and innovation but also their coordination.

(b) The importance of the supply attitude

For the conventional rubber lines, primarily for tyres, the relation between market demand and innovation is less direct and less unconditional than for the special hoses. In tyres, in addition to the general technical standards, innovation manifests itself as an independent evolution which follows its own rules. For example, the latest low-profile tyres are based on Taurus's own development and on Semperit know-how. Semperit did a great deal to improve Taurus's supply situation. For these lines, innovation opens up new potentialities and imposes new tasks on marketing: *innovation in fact generates marketing*. Accordingly, the supply attitude is crucial and calls imperatively for the appropriate interpretation and coordination of marketing and innovation.

Marketing organisation

The elaboration of the marketing and innovation strategy was followed by continuous organisational activity. The aim is to develop an organisation able to cope with the increasingly stringent duties involved in sales, to take care of the highly differentiated work caused by the disproportion between the enterprise's extensive market strategy and its special competitive situation. Organisation takes place in two directions: to expand capitalist exports (for its dynamics see *Chart 15.1*), through the rapid reinforcement of the trade network (commercial organisations, agency network) and to effect a qualitative reorganisation of the sales system to implement the new marketing strategy.

One requirement was the faster integration of marketing, development and production. The system of product management has spread rapidly and now covers 75-80 per cent of the production value. The proportion of sales by the enterprise's own resources is likewise increasing.

To achieve these aims, Taurus had to introduce considerable changes. Since 1981, when the enterprise was granted independent foreign trading rights, the trading network has expanded powerfully. By virtue of its marketing strategy, Taurus is making efforts to increase its market share in a number of major countries (now 5) and to keep its positions also on the smaller markets (now 54) by concentrated marketing work. *Chart 15.2* shows Taurus's export structure, indicating also the points of gravity and the main directions of marketing activity.

Among the most important foreign trade organisations established by Taurus, the joint ventures founded in the West, and the sales network abroad, have developed at the fastest rate: they now handle 70 per cent

Chart 15.1

The trend of Taurus' sales
(1981 = 100)

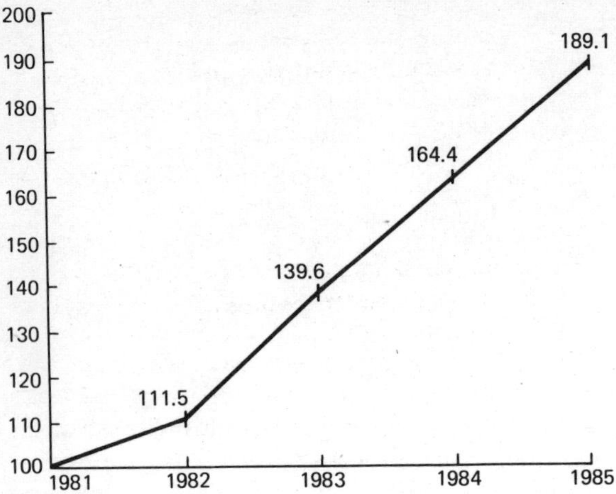

Chart 15.2

Market distribution of Taurus exports
(in per cent)

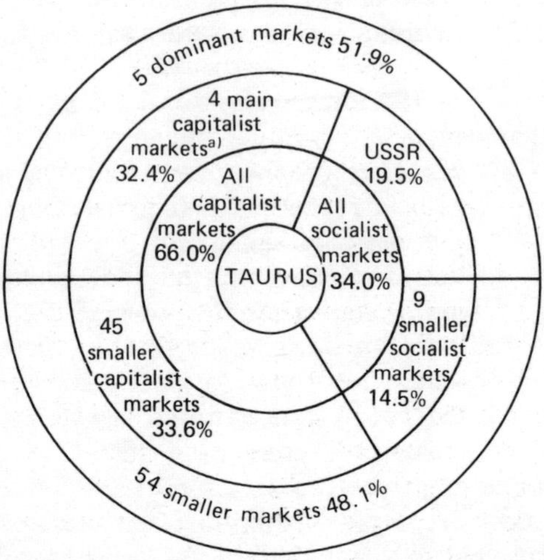

a) USA, FRG, UK, Austria

of the sales. The most important joint ventures operate in Taurus's principal markets: Taurus International Inc. (USA), Interchemol (FRG) London Chemical Co. (Great Britain) Chemol Wien (Austria). In spite of changes in the respective shares and of set-backs, the Taurus sales offices managed to increase their turnover (see *Chart 15.3*).

I hope that this survey has illustrated the problems that a major state-owned enterprise in a socialist country has to face when formulating its strategy. In judging the enterprise's activities, the reader should take into consideration that this kind of activity is relatively new in Hungary, and may still suffer from growing pains.

Chart 15.3

Taurus's own sales on the most important capitalist markets
(Total sales 1981 = 100)

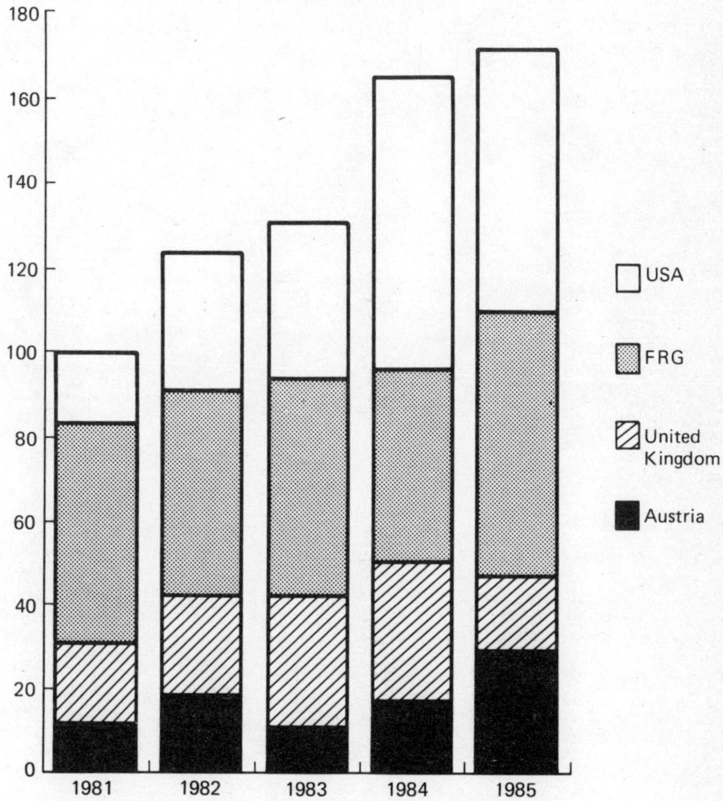

Chapter 16

RECENT DEVELOPMENTS IN PLANNING AND DECISION-TAKING IN LARGE CORPORATIONS

Peter Beck[1)]

"You can never plan the Future by the Past."

Edmund Burke

Few of us like uncertainty, but until this century mankind generally accepted the impossibility of determining one's destiny. The belief that only divine (or the devil's) intervention made prophecy possible was held by most cultures. Only during the last fifty years or so did the assumption spring up that application of the scientific method, of vastly expanded information flows and of hitherto unbelievable speed of processing information, can make prediction of the future possible.

Alas, experience over the last ten to fifteen years has rather dampened the enthusiasm for forecasting. During that time the world's economic climate because more uncertain than ever before and this made forecasting more difficult. This paper will attempt to argue that it is not uncertainty but complexity which has increased; life has always been uncertain and it is difficult to argue that to-day's uncertainties are greater than those of a thousand years ago. Secondly, the 'scientific method' of producing forecasts does not work and is not better than methods used in past times, such as astrology or reading of tea leaves. Indeed, Apollo's curse on the prophetess Cassandra, that she will have the power of predicting the future but that no-one will believe her, is still the curse on to-day's forecasters. Those who are believed tend to be proved wrong, whilst some who are ignored end up being right.

Acceptance of the impossibility of predicting the future and of the increasing complexity of modern economic life has had - and is having - considerable effects on the role of managers in business, on the ways successful businesses organise themselves and on the way they plan. It is the purpose of this paper to describe these.

---

1) Chairman, Strategic Planning Society, London

16.1 The first steps in planning

Up to the early 1950s there appeared to be little need for formalised planning activities within most businesses. Top managers saw themselves as the people who gave direction to their organisation and few would ever have thought of delegating this process to a planning department. Their decisions were based on their judgements about the future of their business and this judgement was formed by collecting relevant information and by debate and discussion with people they knew and trusted. Gathering information was expensive and slow, so that the decision makers got by with the minimum of information and a maximum of judgement. This they could do - and many throughout history did it very well - because they operated within systems which were small and simple enough to be comprehended. Furthermore, the time intervals between decision and effect were relatively short. Where this was not the case, e.g. where communications took a long time (as between Europe and South America before the advent of the telephone), delegation to the manager on the spot was seen as obvious. Choice of the right person for this job and provision of clear, but not necessarily detailed instructions were often the only decisions the top managers were able to take for such far flung areas.

By the mid-1950s the complexity of large businesses had increased to the point where it became more and more difficult for one person to comprehend and understand it all. Communication became faster and collection of information became easier. However, too much information does not help; it confuses. Before it can be used, it has to be sorted into the important and the trivial and the former has to be interpreted. These are judgemental processes. Once an organisation becomes too large or complex for such interpretation to be done by the decision maker (the manager) or by advisers he knows and trusts, there can be loss of direction and control because the expert making the choice may have quite different objectives to those of the decision maker.

For example, a motor car manufacturer in the early part of the century - Henry Ford in USA, or William Morris in England - would take his decisions, say about a new model, from information about the local market, the competitors in that market, many of which he would know personally, and the ability of his staff, most of who he would again know personally. The car could be on the the market within a year and, if not a success, the 'boss' would have learnt from his mistake and would try again.

How different is the life of his successors to-day! Their organisations employ tens of thousands of people, including thousands of managers. Decisions about new cars have to take into account the world scene, the strengths and weaknesses of the many competitors, technological and social developments and many other factors. Once the decision is taken, the new car may not be on the market for many years and the investment is such that the model may have to last a long time to recoup the enormous outlay in money and effort. No one person could study all the necessary information; thousands of people will have to be involved in providing advice and most will not be known by the top manager. How then can he be sure of their judgement and that their objectives when giving their advice are in line with his own? If the project is a failure, how can lessons be learnt, especially because in the time between decision and result many of the advisers and managers will have moved on?

Such developments made the manager - the decision maker - uncertain and less keen to take judgemental decisions; he was forced to seek help. But the very cause of this complexity - the information explosion - seemed to provide a helping hand. Means of data collection and processing improved at least as rapidly as the means of information transmission. Thus, by the early 1960s it became possible to construct complex mathematical models which could analyse and manipulate information and reduce a vast amount of data into simple and understandable conclusions. All the manager had to do was to accept the advice and to see that the decision, based on this advice, was carried out by his organisation. His views of the future became less relevant, and the manager soon found that he could use his time better in the day-to-day task of 'getting things done', rather than worrying about the long term.

Yet another development at that time assisted this process: the concept of the science of decision-taking, which assumed that a 'rational' decision-taker decides on an objective function to be optimised and then chooses the course which will achieve this. Future uncertainty was allowed for by probabilistic methods and with complex mathematical manipulation, made possible by the computer, 'optimal' decisions could be developed. Of course, the objective function varied from one organisation to another. Maximisation of profit to a company could be one, while maximisation of improvement in living standards of the population might be another. As long as the objective function could be expressed in numerical terms, the methodology seemed able to cope.

Initially, these techniques were largely used for the development and evaluation of capital projects. For major projects, like petrochemical plants or refineries, that meant assessing costs and income for a period at least ten years ahead. This required forecasts of demand, of product prices, of raw materials, tax rates, inflation, exchange rates and many more factors. Companies set up planning departments to provide the basis for such forecats and to ensure that sets of forecasts were consistent.

Early planning efforts therefore rested largely on forecasting - predicting the future. Later on, as the complexity of companies increased throughout the 1960s and 1970s, more than just project planning became necessary. It had been found that too many excellent projects, all in course of development, caused great strain on resources. Allocation of scarce resources, such as technical skills and finance, became necessary and this needed longer term forecasts of availability and demand for such resources. So the five (or ten) year forecasts were born in which the consequences of new projects could be integrated with the existing business. This needed even more forecasts and more computation.

Use of forecast-based planning had considerable effects on the organisation of large companies. It caused strong pressure for central planning and decision-making. Thus is was found necessary to have one central planning department to aggregate all plans and to ensure consistency of assumptions throughout the company. If, for example, all divisions of a company assumed different exchange or inflation rates, comparison between divisional forecasts would become impossible and the most important reason for the exercise - allocation of resources - would be negated. The central planning unit had therefore to send out their best estimates and everyone had to use them whether they agreed with them or not. Managers away from the centre therefore saw themselves more and more as administators of other peoples' plans. Efficient execution was their responsibility, success of the plans was not.

As rapid communication made it possible for the centre to obtain detailed and day-to-day information from all its peripheral sites, it appeared rational for the centre to have a major voice in the plans of operating units. The experts at the centre, after all, were believed to have far more knowledge about the future than the operators at the periphery.

The results of such central planning work looked impressive. The many tables and charts gave an assuring look of credibility to well-producted planning reports. All that had to be done was to carry out the plans and achieve the expected results. That, unfortunately, proved too difficult for most organisations, whether companies or government agencies. Many key assumptions proved to be wrong and reality played havoc with the best-laid plans. Initially, it was felt that with more experience and development of better and more sophisticated methods results would improve, but they did not. Eventually some companies started questioning the whole methodology.

16.2 Forecast-based planning examined

The basic assumptions behind this methodology, as it developed during the 1960s, are as follows:

(a) That it is possible to provide trustworthy predictions about the future;

(b) That all important aspects of a problem can be expressed in mathematical terms, either as numbers or as equations;

(c) That one can make a 'rational' choice of an objective function which has to be optimised and which, being rational, will readily be accepted by all decision-makers;

(d) That it is possible to arrive at one optimal solution for most business problems.

Let us now examine these assumptions.

(a) Predicting the future

Some fifteen years ago I was involved in a study of the quality of past predictions which had been used in the planning of projects. To everyone's surprise, it was found that most longer range forecasts had turned out to be wildly wrong and none was found to be right. It looked as if there was a bias towards wrong results in the forecasting methods used. The study identified at least three different types of forecasts[2]:

The *self-defeating* forecast, which, when believed, changes behaviour and thereby defeats the forecast. (See below for examples);

The *self-fulfilling* forecast, usually short term and therefore not very relevant for longer term planning; short term movements of exchange rates, following the publication of some influential forecasts,is an example;

Predetermined forecasts, where previous decision and actions have reduced uncertainty to a point where prediction becomes possible. Maximum availability of nuclear capacity by 1990 is an example. (Prediction of available capacity by then does not fall into that category, as there could be accidents or political moves leading to abandonment of some nuclear stations.)

Forecasts of natural phenomena, such as the path of Halley's Comet, the arrival of a spacecraft near Jupiter or the weight of a bridge from its design drawings, can be done with amazing accuracy. However, as soon as human endeavour and behaviour enters the equation - e.g. in

---

2) P. Beck, "Corporate Planning for an Uncertain Future", Long Range Planning, Vol. 4, p. 14, August 1982

costing the spacecraft, or in determining the time taken to construct the bridge - estimating becomes unreliable because the unpredictable effect of human behaviour enters the analysis.

We all believe that we act rationally according to our beliefs and values. The concept of the self-defeating forecast lies in the fact that these beliefs can change rapidly and with them can our actions. To give some examples:

During the 1960s there was general belief that fast economic growth could continue almost indefinitely and that it would be unconstrained by availability of raw materials. Only fringe-groups, such as the Club of Rome, took a different view and argued that raw materials, especially energy, will set limits to growth. At the time, most decision makers took little notice of the Club of Rome analysis and 'common wisdom' was defended by a series of counter-arguments. Then came the 1973 oil shock and with it a complete change in perceptions. Availability of energy, especially oil, was seen as finite and there followed a rapid reversal of behaviour. Conservation and displacement of oil by other energies became accepted wisdom - with the result that to-day we have a glut of oil. The Club of Rome prediction proved to be wrong, at least for the medium term, because at a certain stage the prediction *was* believed and people took action accordingly.

Similarly, the Club of Rome's predictions of substantial food shortages, if not world famine, were defeated, largely because the danger was believed and action was taken on food wastage, better husbandry, improved seeds and more pressure to reduce the growth of population. As a result, notwithstanding local tragic shortages, there is to-day a surplus of food. With hindsight, the Club of Rome proved highly influential in changing behaviour and attitudes; it failed to predict the future.

A different example arose when a famous US economist (and Nobel Prize winner) pointed out that the then economic problems of the US economy were predicted by his model, but nobody in government took any notice. That to him proved that his model was right. He did not go further and argue that the model only managed to be right because the government ignored it; had action been taken in the belief that the model was right, these economic problems might not have arisen.

One other example is worth quoting. In the 1960s, high growth and profitability for many years ahead was predicted for the petrochemcial industry. It first managed to achieve high growth and appealing profitability, to be followed by low growth and near bankruptcy.

The initial prediction brought in many new actors, each wishing to gain a share of the market. That increased competition and lowered prices, increasing demand but reducing profitability. The increased demand brought in still further capacity, but when prices reached rock bottom, growth slowed down; overcapacity and profitability reached disastrous levels, largely because the individual members of the industry all acted in the belief that the original predictions would be fulfilled.

Because mankind possesses imagination, the ability to learn from experience and a robust sense of self-preservation, our actions do not follow unchanging laws. Indeed, it might well be argued that discovery and announcement of some behavioural law (and presumably most economic laws fall into that category) which has held for centuries is changed by the mere fact that it is now known.

The story of Apollo and Cassandra and Edmund Burke's quotation at the head of this paper shows that past generations may well have had a more correct appreciation of human ability for prediction than many present experts. The Arab saying "Those who foretell the future lie, even if they tell the truth" should be the motto of every forecasting and planning department.

(b) Use of mathematical models

One of the benefits orginally claimed for forecasting methods based on mathematical models was that they removed the need for personal judgement about the ever-more complex future from the decision maker. Experts could provide him with information based on detailed study of the past, present and future, all encompassed by mathematical equations. That was the hope. In practice, however, personal judgement has not been eliminated; instead of the manager either using his own judgement or depending on that of some chosen adviser, he now, by using the results of the model, makes use of the judgement of the builder(s) of the model - whom he often does not know and with whom he rarely has the chance to debate.

As an example, many experts will have very different views about the relationship between energy price, economic growth and energy demand in a country. Model-builders will have to decide which of the many views to incorporate into an energy model, or whether to include a compromise, with which none of the experts might be happy. The ultimate answers from the model will include the effect of such a judgement, but the user of the answer is unlikely to be aware either of the assumptions included or of their effect on the result.

While, previously, judgement was overt and could be challenged, it is often difficult to disentangle cause from effect when using complex models. Model builders may well appreciate the doubtful nature of some of their assumptions, but if the results of their work are seen as interesting and topical, even they can start to believe that their handiwork is not just a model, but a portrayal of reality.[3)]

A fascinating example of such a problem comes from recent critiques of the modelling effort which lay at the foundation of the global energy study produced by the International Institute for Applied Systems Analysis (IIASA).[4)] The IIASA energy study utilised a series of interlinked models to develop two alternative views (scenarios) of the world energy picture up to the year 2030. Their purpose was to present comprehensive and internally consistent analyses from which 'robust conclusions' about the world's energy future could be provided to policymakers and energy planners. The study took some seven years and involved well over 100 scientists of many different disciplines and from many countries. After completion of the study, the models were analysed to see which of the many variables had major effects on the results, and which could be left out, because of their small effect. It was found that virtually ALL the variables were in the latter category. The results were largely dependent on the basic assumptions used to formulate the models and were independent of the variables. The examination concluded that "...despite the appearance of analytical rigour, the study's conclusions are evidently based on opinions rather than ojective robust analysis"[5)]

None of this implies that the IIASA energy study was 'wrong' or deliberately biased. It remains as 'good' or 'bad' as the opinions of the senior research staff who guided the study. (I have met some of them and have considerable respect for their judgement.) The worry is that the modelling process, far from illuminating the situation, appears to have been instrumental in transforming opinions into 'robust conclusions'. The IIASA example may be the largest example of this phenomenon, but it occurs everywhere. In the debate on energy there are Soft-energy tribes, who believe in conservation and renewable energy sources, and Hard-energy tribes, who argue for the status quo to continue. Both possess

---

3) Taylor, "The Baal Syndrome: When 'Spectacles' become 'Blinkers'," Training News, Shell International Petroleum Co., Shell Centre, London, No. 14, 1978

4) 'The IIASA Energy Study', Science Policy, Special Issue, Vol. 17, November 1984, including three articles on the subject by Keepin, Wynne and Thompson

5) Wynne, ibid, p. 199

complex models as weapons which prove to their own perfect satisfaction that their views are correct and can be scientifically proven by the models they use. Each accuses the other of using biased assumptions, believing his own to be the 'correct' one. By finding out to which tribe an author belongs, one can readily predict the result of his analysis. Equally, of course, there are tribes at war in the field of macro-economics (Keynesians and Monetarists are just two of them) whose models prove the righteousness of their cause.

All good fun, but it can mislead the decision maker, especially if the modellers provide him with the type of answer they believe he might like, so strengthening his prejudices and making him even less ready to listen to alternative views. Over 20 years ago, Frederic Schumacher wrote, in a review of European long term energy forecasts:

> "It is fashionable to-day to assume that any figures about the future are better than none. To produce figures about the unkown, the current method is to make a guess about something or other - called an 'assumption' - and to derive an estimate from it by subtle calculation. The estimate is then presented as the result of scientific reasoning, something far superior to mere guesswork. This is a pernicious practice which can only lead to the most colossal planning errors, because it offers a bogus answer where, in fact, an entrepeneurial judgement is required."[6)]

Amen to that; in the intervening period this 'pernicious practice' was indeed the cause of a vast number of 'colossal planning errors' in many industries and countries. Yet, with 20 years of bad experience behind us, the practice is still flourishing! Models can be very important tools for looking at the future, but only when used for research and not for prediction.

(c) Choice of the Objective Function

This turns out to be as judgemental and as subject to disagreement as any analysis of the future. An economist might talk about the maximisation of future profits, but how does one compare to-morrow's profits with those in ten years time? Argument about the choice of the 'right' discount rate can reach the heights of medieval disputations, although it often ends up with an arbitrary decision by the Finance Director, based on his understanding of last week's cost of money. Such discount rates affect the pattern of a company's development and R&D policy for many years

---

6) E.F. Schumacher, Review of Report on long-term energy propects for the EEC, The Economic Journal, Vol. LXXIV, March 1964

to come. Therefore, once again, judgement, perhaps made for the very best reasons years ago, becomes, by use in calculations, dogma.

Of course, decision-makers often have quite different non-economic objectives - a quiet life, fame, power - and their choice of experts to provide them with the many numerical analyses will, often quite unconsciously, reflect these.

(d) One optimal solution?

With the future uncertain and full of surprises, with models of the future depending on judgement rather than on neutral analysis and with the choice of objective also being judgemental, the concept of an optimal solution for a business problem, arrived at by scientific analysis and not dependent on personal views, falls to the ground. Most business problems have a number of possible solutions and it needs judgement by the decision-taker to decide which may be best: this is what happened in the past.

In the conditions of pseudo-scientific analysis described here, the judgements involved are those of the many experts employed in developing models and in collecting the many data needed before the models could run. It is they who have gained the power of MAKING the decision. The manager still has the power of TAKING the decision, but if only one solution is put to him, he has no flexibility except to say yes or no. If no, what happens next? Will the same experts come back with the same solution, or has he to engage a new set and will they perform better? The pressure for him to accept the proffered solution is therefore great.

16.3 The changing business environment

Although it has been known for some time that the basis on which forecast-based planning rests is weak or even false, the method has been in use for over 20 years and is still in use in many large and small organisations. One reason could be that, whatever the conceptual shortcomings of the method, it may have given good results in practice. The evidence is the opposite. Already by the late 1960s it was clear that the practical results were bad, especially when it came to project evaluation. The comment of one manager at the time was: "We are making 5 per cent on all those 35 per cent projects".[7] Yet, although many individual projects may have performed far worse than estimated, many companies were flourishing. This was, however, due more to the fact that the world's business environment at the time was very benign than to the planning techniques used. Fast

---

7) Bower, Managing the Resource Allocation Process: A Study of Corporate Planning and Investment, Harvard University Press, 1970, p. 18

growth, relatively steady commodity prices and exchange rates meant that mistakes had to be substantial before they could really damage a company. Thus much of the corporate environment of a large firm was at that time either relatively stable or under its own control.

From the early 1970s onwards the corporate climate started to change. Economic growth slowed down drastically and unexpectedly. Business became far more international, so that developments or inventions in one country could rapidly affect business practices around the world. Perhaps largely because to the 'microchip', technological change speeded up considerably, while on the economic front instability (e.g. in exchange or inflation rates) became the norm. All this meant that the corporate environment became uncertain and quite outside a company's (or even an individual country's) control. Furthermore, under conditions of low growth, planning mistakes, which could be shrugged off during periods of fast growth, could be (and often were) fatal.

As we moved into the 1980s the process of change speeded up still further; at the same time other fundamental changes in the world economy appear to be taking place - changes which are as yet hardly understood, but could have major influences on the business environment of the next decade. Two such factors are the gigantic increase in international capital movements and credit flows, at present some 35 times larger than the international flow of goods and services, while another is the declining demand for raw materials and labour per unit of manufacture.[8] Models based on relationships which may have held in the past, cannot cope with such a changing world.

By now, many companies in the forefront of technical change have recognised this and have changed their attitude to planning and decision making. Already by 1975 it was reported:

> "... the very nature of corporate planning is undergoing a dramatic change and the companies that fare best in coming years may well be the ones that adapt most quickly to new styles of planning. Today's changes are most visible in ... flexibility ... (and) ... speed (of response)."[9]

Experience since then has borne out that statement, but companies found that even more fundamental changes were necessary before they could ensure rapid and effective response to the everchanging environment.

---

8) P. Drucker, "The Changed World Economy", Foreign Affairs, Vol. 64, Spring 1986, p. 768

9) "Piercing Future Fog in the Executive Suite", Special Report on Corporate Planning, *Business Week*, April 28, 1975

Those who have made these changes appear to be flourishing, whilst organisations which continued as in the 1960s are finding to-day's world a hard and unrewarding place.

16.4 Living with uncertainty

Acceptance of uncertainty as one of the few certainties of the future proved difficult to many firms. Organisations and systems were based on the premise that Head Office would provide information about the future, take most major decisions on their reading of the future and leave managers to get on with the day-to-day business of running the enterprise. Although some managers may have resented their narrow role, even they accepted that the centre had far better access to expert opinion and that they were therefore in no position to outguess the central units.

Once the centre accepts that it has no firm answers, the system becomes virtually unworkable. How can one run a complex project evaluation programme, if the experts maintain that some of the data needed are impossible to forecast? Perhaps the first reaction was (and in some organisations still is) to ignore the problem and take the view that data MUST be provided and that wrong information is better than no information. I can give an example from my own experience. Some years ago my department was asked to provide estimates of exchange rates between the £ and the Can$ for the period 1987 to 2002. The information was needed for the evaluation of a complex international project. When told that the request was impossible and that no worthwhile estimates could be produced, there were bitter cries of 'sabotage'; complaints were made that,for lack of these data, work on a major and important project could not proceed. In the past, such pressure would have ended with the department providing the requested data; they would have been used in the evaluation and - for all we knew - they could have been instrumental in deciding on the scheme. Only the economist providing the data would have known that there must be a 99 per cent chance that the would prove wrong. At the time, we decided not to provide the data and the unit requesting them was forced to - and did - find other more realistic ways of developing and assessing their project.

A number of companies reacted in quite a different way. Managers became too scared of the future to take decisions which had long-term effects. "If the future is so uncertain, let us stop trying to plan ahead and take only those decisions which have short time horizons". Such firms could dispense with planning departments, reduce their R&D and their product development units and concentrate on short-term decisions. If their competitors did not take such a negative view and continued to invest in the long-term, the more timid companies could not survive. New products, new cheaper processes would come along and make such firms uncompetitive. As the commercial and economic climate deteriorated in the late 1970s and early 1980s such companies indeed found it more and more difficult to survive, unless they had moved into areas, such as some services, where the time horizon really is short.

There were other organisations - many of to-day's successful companies - which learned quite different lessons and adjusted their mode of working accordingly. They accepted that decisions required judgement about the future, that experts' opinons could prove to be faulty and that decisions should portray the manager's views, not the planner's. This meant that managers had to start thinking constructively about the future. Equally, they accepted that there is rarely one optimal solution for a decision. There are a large number of feasible solutions and yet a decision on just one must in the end be taken. This must involve choice by the decision-maker, not the planner; but it was found that such a choice is extremely difficult to make, unless the manager has a very clear idea of the purpose of the scheme he is dealing with and how it fits the aims and objectives of his organisation.

It was also found that such changes substantially altered the role of managers by requiring them to be their own planners, and altered the role of the experts who have now to act as advisers rather than makers of decisions. There were also changes in the balance of responsibility and power between the centre and the operating units. These lessons are of such importance that they need further discussion.

(a) Thinking about the future

Although one cannot predict the future, it is possible to achieve an understanding of the forces which will mould it. The decisionmaker has to have such understanding before he can usefully make his decision; he cannot delegate this task to the planner or expert without at the same time delegating away the role of making the decision. But the future is infinite in time and the environment is infinite in space. Therefore, before constructive thinking about the future is possible, one has to limit the range to what is seen as important for the scheme under review.

When planning a new distribution depot, for example, important factors to try and understand could include changes in the area's population, its transport infrastructure, changes in type of demand, local industries, political pressures, the effect of central government policies on the area, etc. World issues, while of interest, are hardly worth studying for such a project. Conversely, development of strategy for a major oil company requires an understanding of world issues, of OPEC politics, of the concerns of non-OPEC producers and of the diverse interests of consuming countries; local problems and pressures are here less important, although they would be vital ingredients in a local energy company's consideration of the future.

Managers are usually far too busy to undertake the work needed to achieve the desire understanding. They need experts to assist them, but not to tell them what to think. One way - with some track record of success - is for the experts, the planners, to develop 'scenarios', defined here as a number of possible futures, each future having consistent assumptions about social, political, economic and technological developments embodied in its description. They are not alternative forecasts of the future,but examinations of the relevant areas of the future. They are designed to stimulate debate between the scenario builder and the manager, thereby cultivating the manager's judgement about possible effects of future events on his project or business.[10)]

The process has to involve the manager from the outset. He has to take part in determining on which areas of the environment the scenarios should concentrate and he should take part in determining on which of the infinite number of possible futures the builders should concentrate. (Experience has shown that more than three scenarios are found to be too confusing.) The end product must stimulate the manager to think deeply about his future environment and how to position himself to take advantage of opportunities and how to guard against dangers. For this, the scenario must be rich in both verbal and numerical description. Here mathematical models can be useful, especially simple on-line ones which the manager and model builder can jointly interrogate.

Initially the manager, accustomed to believe that the future environment is too difficult for him to think about, is suspicious of spending valuable time in debating the future. However, if the scenarios have been well designed, he soon finds the process not just interesting and challenging, but useful in his daily contacts with colleagues, customers or suppliers. He begins to take uncertainty for granted, just like his predecessors of fifty years ago.[11)]

Another benefit of the method is the possibility of bringing the 'unthinkable' into open debate. When deterministic forecasts are used, future dangers can often be ignored because they are assumed to have a low probability of happening. When they come, no one is ready for

---

10) P. Beck, op. cit.

11) P. Wack, "Scenarios: Shooting the Rapids. Harvard Business Review, November-December 1985, p. 139

them. The oil price rise in 1973 and its collapse in 1986 are two good examples. Both were seen as possible, but unlikely and therefore ignored by most policy makers. When alternative scenarios are discussed, such possibilities and their effect can be discussed without giving them exaggerated credibility. Managers, especially top managers, are then far more prepared for the unexpected event and do not resort to panic action quite as readily.

(b) The need for clear aims

If one does not know where one wishes to go, it becomes difficult to decide which way to take at a crossroad. Forecast-based planning implies that the decision-taker is given instructions which road to take on the map of the future environment (also provided). There is therefore no need for him to know the final destination. This can be left to the all-knowing centre. Acceptance of uncertainty implies that no accurate maps can be provided. The road proposed last year may now be blocked. If that happens to a driver who has no idea of his ultimate destination, he is unlikely ever to arrive. As in travel, so in business. Unless the many decision-takers in a company have clear and cohesive views about the aims and objectives of their organisation and of their roles within it, they cannot ever be certain that their decisions are in the interest of their organisation, or that someone else in the firm will not take a line which could nullify the benefits of their own decision. There must therefore be clarity and understanding throughout an organisation about purpose and aim. This can only come from the top management, but at each level in the hierarchy managers have then to translate this message into the aims and objectives of their own unit. To be of use, that can never be a mechanistic translation, but must take into account the forces acting on their particular part; these could well be quite different from those seen as important by the top management of say, an international company.

As an example, a company's objectives may be to provide technologically appropriate services and equipment in the electrical and electronic field to a wide range of users throughout the world and, by doing so successfully, to earn an acceptable return on the capital provided by the shareholders. Before such an objective can become meaningful, the management has to ensure that it is achievable, bearing in mind:

- the environment in which it operates
- the competition it has to contend with
- whether its own strengths and resources are adequate for the task.

The environment to be considered here is the world economy, technological developments, and political factors such as trade restrictions. On the competitive side, one would have to look at similar companies, such as Philips, General Electric, Siemens and Hitachi and compare such organisations with one's own spread of business, R&D capabilities, technological and financial strengths. Only if such an analysis shows that the capabilities of the company are adequate, or can be made to become so, will such objectives make sense; if not, new, less ambitious objectives will have to be developed. Through such a process the centre can provide 'strategic direction' to the whole organisation. Unless such an analysis is done, objectives become 'pipe-dreams' or platitudinal statements which will not command commitment lower down in the organisation.

A subsidiary division of that company, e.g. one dealing with computers in one country, would have to make a similar analysis, this time taking the company's overall aims as given. By looking closely at their more limited environment and their own competitors, which may well be quite different companies from those considered important by the international company, they can determine whether they can meet the company's aims and what resources they would require to achieve them. Then, through debate with the head office, both parties can ensure that the chosen aims of the subsidiary fit the strategy of the company. Having achieved agreement, the subsidiary can provide the necessary strong directions for its staff. In principle, all such analyses could be performed at the centre, but unless the company deals with very few products, head office cannot know the individual businesses in sufficient detail to develop this judgemental feel so essential for setting realistic strategies for the individual businesses. This leads to the difficult question of centralised versus decentralised organisations.

(c) The advantages and dangers of delegation

As already mentioned, forecast-related planning led to organisations with strong - and large - head offices where most of the planning activities were carried out. Peripheral units, such as product divisions, or national operating companies, tended to be responsible for short-term operational planning only. With the re-introduction of judgemental planning this division of responsibilities had to be rethought in many companies.

For a time it was thought that the much-improved methods for collection and processing of data would make it possible to ask for all essential information from the operating units, in order to provide the type of background needed for continuing to develope detailed strategic direction from the centre.

It was found, however, that in businesses which change rapidly, such as those in high technology, some vital information may not reach head office because it had not been asked for while the unit, being largely involved in administration, may not appreciate the importance of such information. When there are large information flows, they can only be handled by being codified; in other words, head office has to tell the operating unit in all detail what it requires. Such instructions can only be based on past experience plus a view of the future. Should this view be wrong, as often happens, the required information flow may not pick up the changing circumstances and strategic policy reaction will be delayed.

Companies in the forefront of technology therefore found that delegation of strategic planning to business divisions and even to business units was necessary if quick reaction to events was essential for success. Companies operating in one type of business only found it possible to plan more centrally - except in fields of high political visibility, such as oil, when it was found that individual country units had to operate, and be seen to operate, in the interest of their host country; such units had to be responsible for most of their own strategy.

The mere decision to delegate, unfortunately, solves little. Delegation is a delicate process which needs trust between the delegator and delegatee. The centre must have the confidence that the managers of the business divisions have the breadth of vision necessary to develop their strategic plans; without such confidence, the centre will try to doubleguess, causing conflict and even greater loss of confidence. The business division, on the other hand, must have the humility not to assume that it - and only it - has all the necessary information. The centre and other divisions are likely to have access to a great deal of useful information and the centre should be seen as the helper in developing the strategic plan. What is here described is a network of interested parties forming a 'learning system', with the centre of the organisation being seen as the facilitator; common interest and trust, as much as shareholding links, holds the system together.

Delegation, in any case, can rarely be total. The centre must keep to itself certain functions; the over-all strategic direction is clearly one, whilst another is control over scarce resources, such as capital or expertise. Control of performance is also essential, as without it the operating units are given power without responsibility.

R&D presents a specially difficult problem. In some well decentralised companies, management of the R&D function is still left to the centre on the assumption that a large diversified laboratory is more effective than a smaller one dedicated to one product field only, and that in this area crossfertilisation is important. Other companies are moving in the opposite direction, having Research departments associated with each business division, plus a central laboratory largely engaged in more long-term work not connected with existing businesses. Allocation of R&D resources, which are usually scarce, is perhaps easier, although more bureaucratic, when the function is run centrally; but it is argued that the inefficiencies of central choice, well away from the ultimate user of the research, eliminates this advantage. There is little doubt that decentralised R&D can be effective, but it probably needs strongly developed networks between the business units, the centre and the research organisations to become so.

(d) Role of the manager

The role of a manager in an effective, diversified company is quite different from that in a centrally directed organisation. In the latter, he is held responsible for the execution of plans given to him; he cannot be held responsible for the quality of the plans. That can make it difficult for him to motivate his staff, should he himself have doubts about the plans. No such problem should arise if the manager is himself responsible for the strategic direction of his unit. Having accepted the over-all strategic aims of the firm, he has the freedom to develop his own plans and can therefore be held responsible for his results. This in turn gives him greater incentive to motivate his staff to achieve the chosen goals.

A manager in this position has to perform two new and vital tasks. Firstly he has to be his own planner. He has to provide the strategic direction for his unit. He must therefore be skilled in considering the future environment of his business and be able to assess his competitive position. Having developed a realistic set of goals, and achieved acceptance for them from his superiors, he has to perform his second task: to lead his staff to those goals. He has to have leadership abilities.

Leadership is sometimes seen as dictatorial behaviour: 'I tell you what to do and you must obey or be punished'. For many social but also technological reasons, such behaviour is more often than not ineffective in fast changing businesses. It causes strife, distrust between managers and staff and therefore resistance to change. In large companies such 'macho-management' style creates the view that individual initiative might be punished and that rigid adherence to strictly codified systems serves an individual manager best. Such a bureaucratic organisation has no future in to-day's fast moving and fast changing business areas.[12] In such areas there is need to harness employee initiative and knowledge down to the shopfloor, research bench and sales counter. That requires a totally different style of leadership - motivational leadership which generates trust and gives people the chance to give their best. Authority is gained more through respect than by job title. Under such leadership, consensus,

---

12) C. Lorenz, "Why 'Terror' is Outmoded", Financial Times, June 25, 1986

rather than conflict, is the way towards decisions; flexible response to change then becomes possible.

In the past, top managements of more simple business organisations could be seen as leaders who imposed their wills on their businesses. Then came 'scientific' management which appeared to require organisational rather than leadership skills. Only recently did it become clear that businesses need leaders, not just at the top, but at every managerial level, just as an army needs leaders right down to platoon level. Thus the modern successful manager has to be a leader, leading his unit towards the chosen goal. He has to be his own planner, developing the vision which enables him to select that goal. It is these two tasks which set the manager apart from the administrator.

(e) Role of the planner

When a manager must develop his own plans, is there still a role for the planner? Yes, there is - indeed two roles. The first is to assist the manager in his planning activities by stimulating thought and debate and by ensuring that the manager cultivates his judgement adequately for the decisions to be taken. He must see himself as the adviser, not as the maker of decisions which he then 'sells' to his manager.

The second role is that of a challenger of 'accepted wisdom'. At any one time there are strongly held beliefs about the future or about worthwhile activities. Examples are the view that oil prices will rise continually for the rest of this century, held strongly in the early 1980s, or the need for companies to diversify, held strongly in the mid-1970s. The planner should seek out alternative views and debate these with his manager to test out the robustness of such commonly held views. He should also question decisions, even if he agrees with them, in order to test their logic with the decision-maker and his commitment to them. In other words, he has to be the resident professional sceptic.

16.5 Conclusions

The idea that planning involves predicting the future, and that decisions about future activities cannot be taken unless such predictions are available, was for too long taken as self-evident. This paper has attempted to show that the future cannot be predicted and yet decisions can be reached and companies can thrive.

Those companies which have shown that they can live with uncertainty as well as with to-day's complexity show many similar characteristics:[13)]

- There is a clear understanding throughout the company about its aims and objectives;
- Managers at all levels see themselves as responsible for developing their own forward plans and, having gained acceptance to them from their superiors, they have to gain commitment from their staff;
- Substantial effort is spent in generating trust between staff and management and in achieving consensus;
- There is considerable delegation of powers for taking decisions, but with strict monitoring of results;
- The concepts of leadership and of excellence are fostered and woven into the culture of the organisation.

It appears that many major Japanese companies and to a lesser extent some West German companies followed such policies and were never seduced by forecast-based planning. This may partly explain their success as agents and beneficiaries of change. By the early 1980s a number of organisations either in high technological fields or in politically sensitive fields started moving in that direction. As complexity and the speed of change accelerated, more companies found such moves essential to become sufficiently flexible, and rapid in response, to remain competitive.[14)]
Other firms tried to respond by improving efficiency and cutting costs without fundamentally changing their managerial style. Even if they have survived so far, it must be doubted whether they can be long-term survivors. It is time that they learn the lesson already absorbed by the successful firms: however hard one tries, the future remains unpredictable.

In the words of Confucius:

"It is impossible to be wise without being aware not only what you do know but also what you don't know."

---

13) T.J. Peters & R.H. Waterman, In Search of Excellence, New York, Harper & Row, 1982

14) Dekker, "Managing a Global Electronics Company in Tomorrow's World", Long Range Planning, April 1986, Vol. 19, p. 31

Chapter 17

STRATEGIC PLANNING IN A CHANGING COMPETITIVE ENVIRONMENT

Wilhelm Rall[1]

17.1 Strategic planning: focus, process, tools

Strategic planning in many companies has been navigating in troubled waters over the last decade. The planning processes and methods developed and successfully applied in the relative economic stability of the 1960s and early 1970s proved to be - at best - of little assistance in dealing with rapid change; in quite a few cases they were misleading and dangerous. Corporations are having to learn the art of coping with uncertainty and instability in the external parameters for their decision-making, i.e., in industry trends and socio-political developments.

- Ever since the breakdown of the Bretton Woods system and the first oil crisis, exchange rates and raw material/energy prices have been fluctuating violently, thus destabilising an important basis for traditional long-range planning on the micro-level. Strategy development has to take these influences into account.
- Industrial structures and dynamics have been changing very rapidly. The familiar maturing process of traditional industries has accelerated. In addition, a whole new group of businesses and industries has emerged in little more than ten to fifteen years. With the development of microelectronics, ordinary products like typewriters and cash registers have been revolutionised, and hordes of new products and applications have been launched, many of them completely upsetting production methods and the key factors for success in the business concerned (for example, factory automation devices). More recently, the evolution of biotechnology has not only revolutionised the production of enzymes and hormones but also provided new substances. Moreover, many traditional and new businesses have entered the stage of global competition, enlarging competitive arenas and requiring a new quality of strategic planning.
- Economic disruptions have been creating socio-political responses, setting new business patterns. For example the GATT rules opened markets by removing tariff barriers, but with more intense global competition governments have tended to react with neo-protectionist instruments much more difficult to overcome than the traditional

1) McKinsey & Co. Inc. Stuttgart, FRG

tariffs. (For example, more than 50 per cent of all foreign trade in automobiles is subject to such barriers today.)

This highly dynamic environment requires new approaches to strategic planning. "In the turbulent cross-currents of the 1980s, a company's skill at *responding* strategically to change is no key to competitive success or even survival. Strategies must, in a sense, unlearn the art of adaptation and begin instead to aggressively *anticipate, seize and exploit* change"[2]. This means a new focus, a new process and also new tools in strategic planning.

Let there be no misunderstanding here: this shift does not mean that gut feeling should replace systematic approaches. But routine procedures, sometimes amounting to bureaucracy, must be overcome; strategic thinking must be given a broader context.

External orientation

Most companies now understand that strategic planning no longer means thorough longer-term budgeting, or advanced quantitative forecasting of their own business trends. Instead, they have to enter at least Phase Three of strategic management[3], in which the focus is clearly externally oriented (*Chart 17.1*). The planning process has to forecast discontinuities in demand or technology, anticipate competitors' moves, and carefully monitor the dynamics of the business. This very intense, complex approach may in rare cases lead to an extrapolation of the past activities of a corporation, but its main purpose is to detect untapped business opportunities or potential threats from competitors' actions. The objectives might best be described as reduction of, and preparation for, uncertainty, enabling a company to anticipate or create changes rather than adapting after the fact to alterations in the environment. Consequently, the result of strategic planning will not be a single linear long-term plan with clearly defined allocation of resources for the whole planning period, but typically a set of alternatives, spreading out the future range of options. In other words, planning will not provide a rigid course of action for the time ahead: the plan has to remain flexible in a volatile environment. A strategy for our times has to define and structure the company's own game board, so that it can respond quickly and effectively when an opportunity or a threat is sensed.

---

2) Frederick W. Gluck, "Strategic Management for the Eighties", The McKinsey Quarterly, Summer 1983, p. 2.

3) See Frederich W. Gluck, Stephen Kaufmann, A. Steven Walleck, "The Four Phases of Strategic Management", Journal of Business Strategy, Winter 1982, volume II/3, p. 9.

Chart 17.1

Phases in the evolution of strategic decision-making

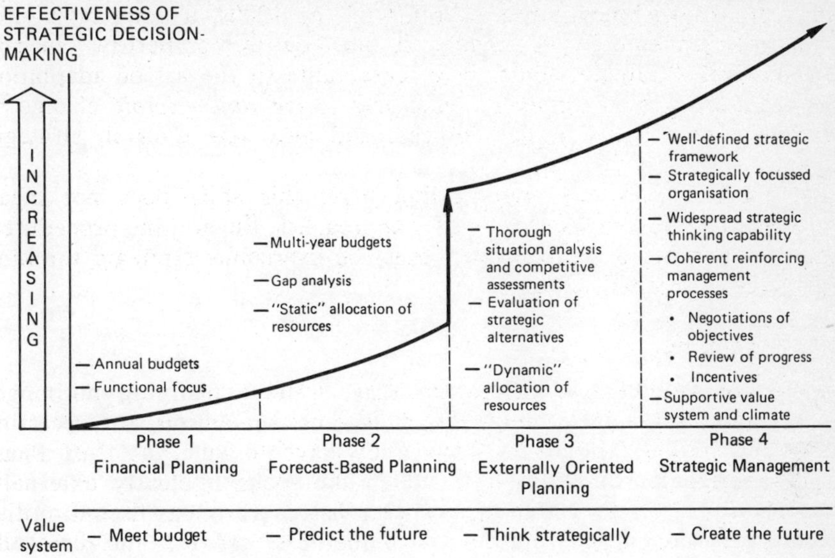

Source: Frederich W. Gluck, Stephan Kaufmann, A. Steven Walleck, "The Four Phases of Strategic Management", Journal of Business Strategy, Winter 1982, p. 11

Line management-oriented process

In many companies, today's strategic planning process is governed by two principles: the prime responsibility lies with the line managers; and the time spans are flexible, determined solely by the requirements of the business and not by the fixed schedule of a planning calendar.

- Decisions on overall corporate strategy have always been the prerogative of top management. This still applies, but the actual process of planning has changed. Whereas in the 1960s and early 1970s the actual planning was done by the corporate planning staff and the process was very much top-down, there has been a strong tendency in the last decade to distribute responsibility for strategic planning to line managers on the business unit level. The old pattern whereby corporate staff thought and planned strategically, while line managers executed, is out of date. More and more corporations believe "that the planning needs to be done by operating people who understand clearly who their customers are, what they can bring to these customers, what they want to do with their talent, and what their own understanding of the future is"[4]. Corporate planning departments still have an important role in this process; they provide a perspective on the development of the business environment, offer additional information, and act as catalysts by challenging line managers' thinking and provoking responses to new trends in the environment. The planning process thus has a strong bottom-up component and increasingly takes the form of a dialogue. The new role of the corporate planning staff is underlined by the fact that some of the staff positions are filled with managers with substantial line experience. Some of the better planning staffs I know in German industry are led by successful former division heads; they have already proved that they can run a business, and their strategic views are well regarded by their former colleagues. For these people, such a staff position is typically a career step towards executive tasks.

The time scope of a strategy depends on the time needed to implement a strategic programme and on the stability of the business environment. The old rule-of-thumb of having a five to seven years' strategic plan as a uniform pattern for all businesses emphatically does not fit the bill. These standard periods are either too short, e.g., in strategic product planning for the automobile industry, or too long, as in consumer electronics. What is required is strategic plans for each business, with business-specific time periods, and periodic annual or bi-annual monitoring enabling the company to redirect the plans if necessary or to put them on a revolving basis. This understanding of strategic planning is not as "neat" as the budgeting-type processes, but it is more problem- and action-oriented and avoids the unproductive bureaucracy observed in earlier decades. Of course, there have to be formal longer term business and financial plans for aggregation and consolidation on the corporate level, but they are an outflow of the planning process rather than its subject, and absorb only a minor share of line and staff planning time.

Action-oriented tools

The tools applied in strategic planning have to provide the information and programme modules necessary for such a detailed and sophisticated process. Methods for forecasting internal variables and mechanisms for

---

4) Ruth Gilbert-Schaeffer, "Developing Strategic Leadership", US National Industrial Conference Board, Research Report Number 847, July 1984, p. 8.

developing a consistent business plan still form part of the tool kit, but much more is needed including:

- Analytical tools for understanding the structure and the dynamics of a business. These are all instruments familiar to trained and experienced planners, comprising, e.g., the logic of basic industry structure analysis, portfolio analysis, business system (or value chain) analysis, or specific approaches such as industry cost curves or experience curves[5].
- Diagnostic indicators allowing a manager to sense potential discontinuities in his business. There are some general sets of indicators for important business developments, such as globalisation, but in most cases they have to be supplemented or modified by business-specific points to watch.
- Game boards and strategy modules that can be used as a framework for specific strategic plans. There is definitely no stereotyped answer to strategic problems, as some devotees of tools like portfolio matrices or experience curves suggest. But it is crucial to understand the generic alternatives and levers for making a company's own programme development effective.

* * *

The following two examples of strategic planning are situation-specific approaches applied by a Western European car producer and by a supplier of factory automation equipment. The cases are primarily intended to illustrate specific tasks and procedures, but also to highlight the variety of approaches used in today's strategic planning.

17.2 Strategic planning in mature markets: an automobile company

Automobile companies are industrial giants with only one or very few businesses. Unlike other large corporations (for example in the chemical or electrical/electronic industries), they depend on one product group. This, or course, has to be reflected in a thorough and sophisticated strategy formulation.

Industry situation: Intensifying competition

Automobiles are a mature industry with only moderate medium-term growth rates in the major markets, but highly cyclical behaviour. More

---

5) For a detailed survey of these analytical tools see Michael E. Porter, Competitive Strategy, Techniques for Analyzing Industries and Competitors. New York and London 1980, Chapters I, III, IV and VII. Michael E. Porter, "Competitive Advantage, Creating and Sustaining Superior Performance", New York and London, 1985, Chapters I and II.

than 80 per cent of total world demand is concentrated in the industrialised market economies, a situation that will not change too much in the next decade. Since the early 1970s, the world market has developed into an integrated competitive arena, with the Japanese companies as a major driving force behind this process; formerly Western Europe, the US, and Japan were very much separate markets. The supply side is oligopolistic, with most of the large companies participating in, or integrating into, at least two of the three major regions.

In the course of this process, competition has heightened considerably. Companies in the industry are confronted with two apparently conflicting challenges:

- The increasing saturation of markets requires a more differentiated approach. Model proliferation can be observed throughout the industry and shorter model life-cycles are expected for the future.
- Cost competitiveness measured against world standards is a *sine qua non* for long-term survival. Only very few high-prestige producers can successfully go for value instead of price competition for their entire model range.

To meet these challenges, the leading companies are rethinking their strategic approaches in terms of products, market penetration, and configuration/management of their business systems. Some of their moves are visible even to the general public, particularly the mergers and cooperations, e.g., General Motors-Volvo, Ford-Alfa, Volkswagen-SEAT, General Motors-Toyota.

Exploiting market potential

Strategic planning has to be clearly problem-oriented, i.e., it has to mirror the critical decisions facing a company. A planning process geared exclusively to financial performance or volume will not meet the challenge. The three dimensions of product, market, and business system have to be covered simultaneously, but treated with differing time horizons (*Chart 17.2*).

In each of the dimensions, creative approaches are needed. The *product strategy* has to anticipate changes in the market (segmentation, trends and fashions in car features, etc.) generated by socio-economic developments, competitors' moves and political actions, but it also has to try to influence these same processes. The most successful product strategy is the one that creates markets instead of merely tailoring the product offering to the present and forecast requirements of given segments. (Although even the latter task seems difficult enough, considering the numerous flops in the last decade.) The creation of the "small sporty" segment by the VW Golf GTI, the remarkable expansion and re-formation

Chart 17.2

Dimensions of strategic planning in the automobile industry

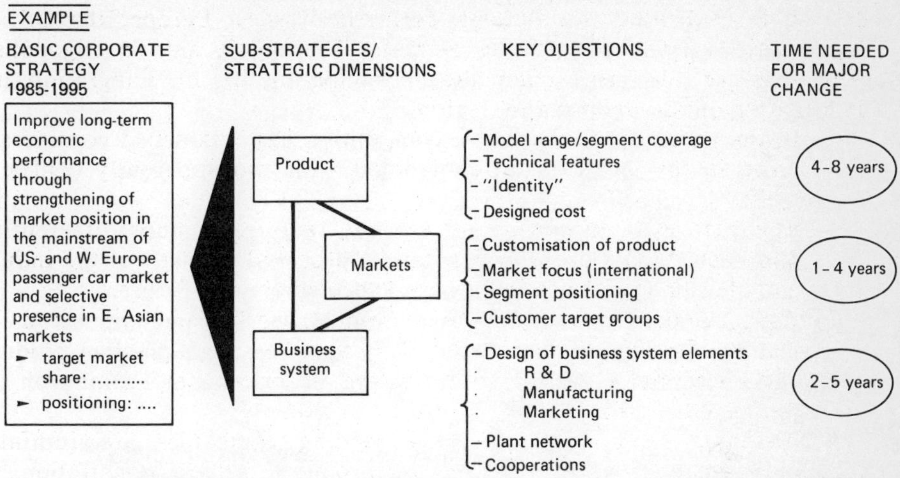

of the "medium-sized sporty" segment by the Daimler-Benz 190 series, and the establishment of the mini-van segment in the US by Japanese companies and Crysler, are the most prominent examples, but there are many others. The *business system strategy* is probably the most challenging part today, because its role and impact have been rapidly increasing over the last few years. The old tenets about the right level of vertical integration no longer apply. Management thinking is governed by joint ventures, at least in certain stages of the manufacturing process, by new forms of cooperation between suppliers and car makers, more effective development processes, and new generations of factory automation. In *market strategy*, slow growth and market saturation require more sophisticated pull-strategies, and selective application of additional push elements. This new generation of market strategies builds on highly sophisticated planning tools and procedures. To illustrate this, as *pars pro toto*, the process is described here in somewhat more detail.

For the sake of simplicity, we will assume that the model range is defined for the medium-term and that the business system needs no major adaptation. This is a fairly realistic case for a one- to five-year strategic plan, since all models available in this period either have already been launched or are well established, since it takes three to five years to develop a completely new car. In such a situation, the primary objective is often to increase market share in the interesting segments by exploiting existing market potential. Development of a strategic plan for a specific country market can be described in five steps.

(i) Understanding market structure and dynamics. This starts with understanding the trend and cycles of the total market, but an even more important factor is segmentation by customers. The significance of segmentation should not be underestimated (experience shows, for example, that none of the technical dimensions, such as length or engine size, sufficiently explains the segments of the market): it is one of the primary arts applied in strategy development. A sophisticated segmentation provides not only a precise description of the competitive environment of a particular car model, it also allows focussed comparisons between true competitors. When the criteria of homogeneous behaviour of customer groups are added, a micro-segmentation is obtained which enables a company to understand every detail of the market's structure and its own position. A matrix such as that shown in *Chart 17.3*, dynamically interpreted, forms an important basis for a market strategy.

Chart 17.3

Segmentation matrix as basis for strategy development

Model segment \ Sociodemographic group	Aa*	Ab	Ac	Ba	Bb	C
Luxury	10 / –	25 / –	50 / –	5 / –	8 / –	12 / –
Large	30 / 15	45 / 10	140 / 5	5 / 20	30 / 12	6 / 8
Medium sporty/ prestige	110 / 3	45	70	40	45 / 6	20
Medium	80 / 16	11	25	18	75 / 16	
Small sporty	xx / xx	xx / xx	xx / xx	xx / xx	xx	
Small	xx / xx	xx / xx	xx			
Mini	xx / xx	xx				
Super-Mini	xx / xx					

Total number of cars in micro-segment (upper figure); Segment share of own company (lower figure)

*Example: Male, higher education age > 20- <40, not married

(ii) Understanding competitors' positions and moves. Thorough analysis of competitors' strengths and weaknesses over products, segments, and various functions in the business system is required here. Issues such as relative performance of the distribution system in a specific market, or basic indicators like brand loyalty rate, are included in this step, as well as a synopsis of all available information on competitors' expected moves.

(iii) Positioning the company's own make and individual models. Success depends crucially on the make having a clear identity and models being differentiated vis-à-vis their competitors, building upon the (perceived) strengths of the cars (*Chart 17.4*). Not all of the model segments have to be covered in each market; it might be wise to avoid competition in the main stream and to focus on up-market models in a situation where strong low-cost competitors are in

Chart 17.4

Differentiating the automobile model profile

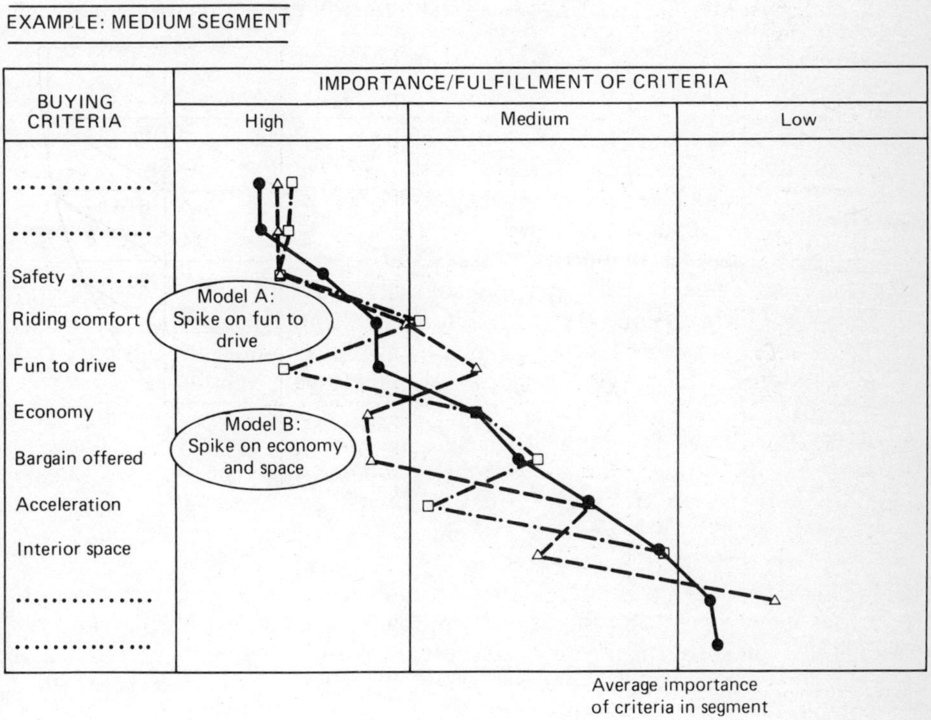

place. Parallel to the product positioning, the socio-demographic target groups have to be defined. If we take, for example, the US market: imported cars are strongly preferred by the "baby-boom" generation, especially in the more highly educated groups. Why not exploit all the opportunities in these socio-demographic groups and forget the others? Typically, strategic positioning is quantified by target shares in the respective segments.

(iv) On the basis of this positioning, the implementation programme is then developed. In this step, strategic planning has to complete detailed designs for all the individual modules which together form the strategic programme, such as specific product features, marketing programmes, promotions, dealer training and control as well as organisational adjustments.

(v) The last step is the traditional strategic plan, which sums up all the implications for financial performance and resources. It is important to remember that this step is not based on financial planning procedures but on detailed strategy work, with the formal financial plan acting only as the keystone. Of course, the financial plan may lead to a revision of the process if the results do not meet the company's financial requirements.

An interactive process

A market-specific strategic plan of this type is no task for staff functions alone: it is the result of very close interaction between line managers at headquarters, line managers in the respective countries, and corporate staff or external experts. Typically, such a process takes several months, with a clear distribution of tasks and roles:

- Line managers in each country take the lead, provide the necessary market information (in the automobile industry market research data are available in abundance), assess positioning options and programme alternatives, and propose the strategic plan to the executive board.
- The line managers at headquarters define the degrees of freedom, for example for customising models or diverging from the worldwide brand identity. In general, they also set the financial targets, and assess implications for the corporation's business system and for performance in other markets.
- The corporate planning department, or external experts, support line management by supplying approaches, methods, and manpower skilled in analytical and conceptual tasks. Challenging traditional views on the market and offering strategic alternatives is another important function of this group.

Of course, this process is not repeated every year, but the results and the validity of the assumptions are closely monitored in a fixed planning cycle to secure active country management.

17.3 Exploiting innovation: factory automation products

This is a fast-growing industry - entirely different from the automobile industry, and thus calling for a completely different approach.

High innovation, rapid growth

Modern factory automation is part of the electronic revolution. The availability of high-performance electronic components and the increase of control know-how has led to products like CNCs, PLCs or process computers and systems, that have meant radical change for production processes. Markets for these products are currently generally less than ten years old, and two-digit growth rates have been the normal pattern. The rate of innovation is also high and, accordingly, so is the R&D cost per unit sold. Product life-cycles are longer than for some other electronic products, but still very short compared with traditional capital goods.

For most of the product groups in this area, a fairly small group of suppliers generally dominates the markets of the industrialised countries, often accompanied by a number of mainly national suppliers that survive under government protection or in market niches. Due to their economics and the high level of know-how and resources required, these businesses are either born global or globalise early in their life-cycle[6]. Successful participants have to take a leading or, at least, an early follower role. Capturing a fair share of a rapidly emerging market is the key not merely to success but to survival.

Planning for globalisation

Strategic planning in such businesses, then, implies planning for change - preparing for opportunities to exploit globalisation potential; the approaches applied have to reflect this. Implementing a globalisation concept makes sense only if inherent factors such as homogeneity of demand or economies of scale are driving a business towards worldwide

---

6) The globalisation of businesses is a development widely discussed in recent years. See, e.g.: A.D. Day, "Competition and Global Industries", HPS bulletin, December 1984; Th. Levitt,"The Globalization of Markets", Harvard Business Review, May/June 1983; K. Ohmae, "A New Worldwide Strategy for New Worldwide Markets", Electronic Business, February 1983; H. Henzler/W. Rall, "Facing up to the Globalization Challenge", The McKinsey Quarterly, Winter 1986.

integration, and if a company's starting position offers the opportunity to achieve a sustainable competitive advantage. Planning, therefore, typically follows a three-step logical process (*Chart 17.5*).

(i) The first question is always whether a business shows inherent globalisation trends. The answer requires an in-depth analysis of the economics of the business with special consideration of discontinuities created by governments (e.g., the stepwise deregulation of the telecommunications market), by changes in customer structure, or by product/production technology. For factory automation devices, such as machine tools with computer numerical control (CNCs), the rapid worldwide restructuring of the machine tool industry was an instrumental driving force in globalisation. And a once for all analysis is not enough; constant monitoring is needed to detect changes in the environment in good time.

(ii) If globalisation potential exists in the business in general, the crucial question remains whether the company under discussion will be able to build a sustainable competitive advantage by exploiting this potential. The first condition for a positive answer is the availability of products that are at least on a level with those of leading competitors. If this is not met, rapid redirection of product strategy and development is necessary. Furthermore, a

Chart 17.5

Strategic plan: Preparing for change

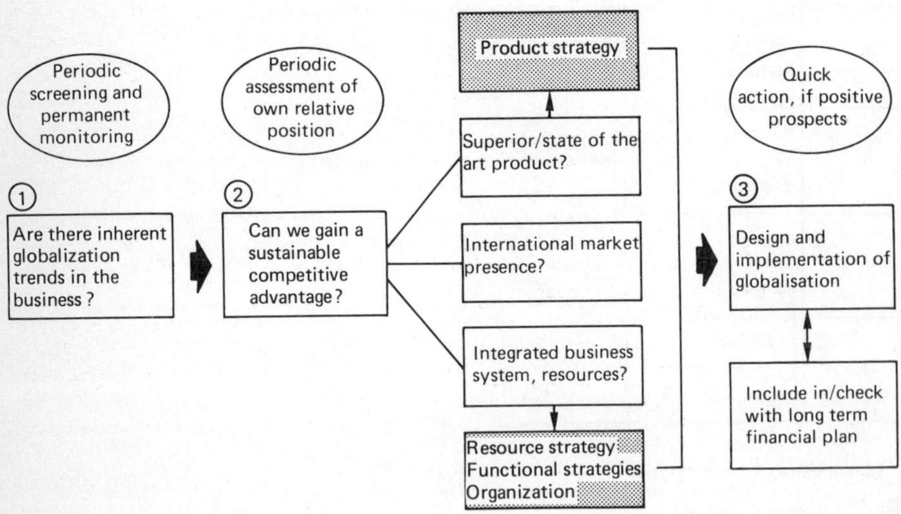

realistic view of the company's own competitive position is needed. *Chart 17.6* is an example of what can emerge from such an assessment of both business trends and the company's own relative position. Whereas product lines B and C are in a clear "go" situation, D definitely is not, because of the company's poor starting position. The feasibility of catching up is questionable; the clever move might rather be to close the business. Especially where highly interesting situations like C are identified, the remaining issue is the adaptability of the company's business system and the availability of funds and management capacity to play a global game. In such cases, companies are often obliged to enforce priorities in the allocation of funds to businesses much more rigorously than in the 1960s and early 1970s.

(iii) The steps mentioned so far have been by way of preparing the ground. Only if we can answer "yes" to the first two questions

Chart 17.6

In depth and realistic analysis of business trend and own starting point

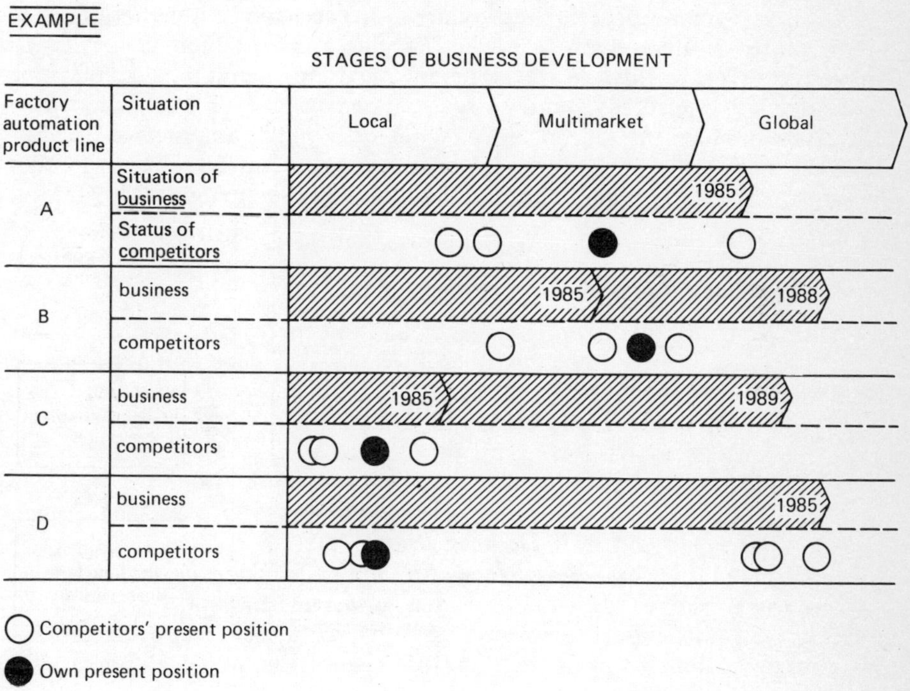

- and it might well take two to three years after the first planning steps to make sure that all the internal requirements are met- will the globalisation program be implemented, i.e., new products will be launched on all major markets in parallel, the worldwide business will be run integratively, worldwide service will be offered, etc.

It goes without saying that here, too, a traditional financial plan has to be set up at the end of the strategic planning process to show the outcome in terms of profit and loss, and to develop yardsticks for control of its implementation.

More than interactive planning required

As in the example of cars, the strategic plan should be designed in an interactive process, with all the international branches of the company heavily involved. But the organisation dynamics of a globalisation programme typically have to go beyond this. Successful implementation often depends on new modes of collaboration between headquarters and subsidiary. Thus, a close link between strategy and organisation development is the key in a globalisation concept. Subsidiaries have to be involved early in the product development process - providing information, discussing features and committing themselves to accepting the new product. Some of the responsibility for worldwide development and implementation of the plans can be taken by selected country organisations instead of by headquarters, i.e., central tasks can be deconcentrated regionally. The interactive planning processes themselves have proved to be an important step towards these new modes of collaboration, thus making a two-fold contribution to strategic success.

17.4 From strategic planning to strategic management

The problems and processes sketched in these two examples mark the transition from periodic, sometimes bureaucratic, plans to more problem- and action-oriented strategic thinking. In other word, the traditional planning procedures still have an important part to play as reporting or documentation tools. But strategy has to play a much greater role; it has to become part of line management's thinking. In the strategically managed company, change becomes the central focus of line management. The role of the planning staff changes accordingly.

"The planner becomes an *alter ego* to the line manager - constantly prodding him to develop a deeper understanding of forces at work in the industry, providing him with fast feedback on new developments in the marketplace, catalyzing the development

> of new alternatives to seize competitive advantage, ruthlessly pointing out the futility of investing in businesses without a winning strategy, and in general getting him obsessed with the idea of being the first in the industry to recognize change and turn it to competitive advantage".
>
> "Some aspects of this new role will be familiar to the planner: analyzing and testing the financial impact of alternative strategies, examining the organizational implications, commissioning special studies, creating short-term task forces and using pilot projects to recruit believers in the need to change. But more time will be spent in orchestrating action. Planners will need to become better at working with line managers to sketch out alternative strategies and to test their appeal against a variety of competitive responses. ... They will need to encourage experimentation".[7)]

In a strategically managed company, strategic planning and managerial decision-making are integrated. Thus the company develops an ability to induce change.

---

7) Frederick W. Gluck, "Strategic Management for the Eighties", McKinsey Quarterly, Summer 1983, p. 15.

COMMENTS ON PART IV - ENTERPRISE STRATEGIES

Josef Kreuter[1)]

It is difficult to deal *en bloc* with several papers about the behaviour of large enterprises in two different worlds - in the world of developed market economies and in the world of the socialist economies. Nevertheless, besides clear differences (which I will come to later) there are also some similarities which could be important.

In my opinion, these similarities in the behaviour of enterprises, in their perceptions of the task of strategic planning, arise primarily because all these enterprises are operating in the world of uncertainty. So the notion of uncertainty becomes a central issue in all the papers. Strategic planning on the enterprise level, as a way of mastering the problems of complexity and uncertainty, is the explicit subject of *Beck* (Ch. 16).

Planning in capitalist corporations

I would first like to express appreciation of the high culture of *Beck*'s contribution, which displays the whole problem in historical perspective, in different stages of prewar and postwar real world development. It is useful also to present this development in relation to the changing external environment, to the new tasks and expectations laid on the planning process, and also - which is very important - in relation to the changing illusions, and disillusions, about the possibilities and realistic limits of planning.

A main theme of *Beck's* argument, as I see it, is his conviction that strategic planning before the 1980s was regarded as a way of eliminating personal judgement about the future from the decision-making process. He shows very convincingly that the uncertain future cannot be forecast, that we can only try to understand the motive forces of the future and that personal judgement is a necessary element in this understanding.

I share the author's conviction that the future calls for mastering the process of flexible planning, for a certain kind of "global" thinking and for delegation and decentralising planning and decision-making power. In my opinion, this analysis is most valuable, not only for enterprise planning but also for planning at the national level.

---

1) Kabinet Prognoz, CSAV (Institute for Forecasting), Czechoslovak Academy of Sciences, Prague.

Rall (Ch. 17), also dealing with strategic planning on the enterprise level, seems to present much the same line of thinking and argumentation. But there are also some differences in accent. From a brief comparison I think that the main message of *Beck's* paper says: the future always was, and remains, inherently uncertain and business always had to take risks; there is a danger that if we fail to adapt flexibly and continuously, we could incur substantial losses. On the other hand, *Rall's* message seems to say: the future is inherently uncertain and risky; but it is not enough just to make flexible adjustments to changing circumstances; we must instead create the changes ourselves and then the future could be profitable. In this sense *Rall* goes further than *Beck*.

Nevertheless, it is a pity that on the practical level - for example, in his account of strategic reasoning in the automobile industry - *Rall's* strategic planning proposal is by definition limited to the medium-term. The medium-term does not seem to allow the type of strategic thinking which was proposed in the first, theoretical part of *Rall's* paper. His strategic blueprint for the mature automobile industry concentrates on the need to find a "free" market segment; that is essentially a passive adjustment strategy, not a creative one. For the long-run horizon (which is not considered in the practical part of the paper) an active, creative strategy, consistent with the main message of the theoretical part of the paper, should also utilise the findings of sociology, mass psychology, urbanism and so on. In this respect, global thinking about the future, on a broader than economic basis (as is proposed by *Beck*), could be relevant for the "creative" long-run strategy.

Another key notion of *Rall's* concept is the word "dialogue" - dialogue between the delegators of decision-making powers and the delegatees. This notion of dialogue is not discussed in detail, but taken only as self-evident. I expect that *Rall* knows how a dialogue between delegators and delegatees is full of problems, contradictory interests, distorted and misleading information. The experience of socialist countries shows very clearly that a main problem of central planning lies exactly in the inherent difficulties of this type of "dialogue".

Central planning in socialist economics

Inspired by these two Western contributions I would like to comment on the problem of uncertainty in a centrally planned economy. It should be said that the problems are rather like those for the capitalist enterprise.

The special conditions of the world economy in the 1950s and 1960s - stable price and costs relations, known technologies, a foreseeable production mix and demand trend, stable exchange rates and easily accessible energy - all this created for the centrally planned economies, as for other economies, a "world of certainty". The special features of the socialist economies (relatively smaller dependence on foreign trade, relative neglect of comparative advantages) reinforced the belief that what was in reality an uncertain future could in fact be foreseen with confidence.

On this basis, the central planning system adopted this supposed certainty within the functionally closed national economy, in the form of the mandatory central plan. Thus a world of nearly absolute certainty was created for the individual producers and the burden of adjusting to uncertainty fell on the shoulders of the central planners.

The outside world changed irreversibly with the 1970s. Essentially, this change was twofold: on the one hand, some long-established parameters (the world price structure) collapsed; on the other, the pattern of overall development, previously latent and slow, began to accelerate. This second type of change, related to the dynamics and structure of demand, to the international comparative advantages, to capital flows and exchange rate fluctuations, and to the acceleration of technical progress - increased uncertainty and complicated allocative decision-making.

The impact on Czechoslovakia

The centrally planned Czechoslovak economy adjusted relatively very successfully (in terms of external balance, internal equilibrium, employment and conventionally measured real economic growth) to the first type of change - to new energy prices and to new terms of trade. This adjustment was effected, at first, by changes in the allocation of increments of national product - strengthening the external balance - and, later, by expanding productive investment at the cost of blocking growth of domestic final consumption and by reducing nonproductive investment. The changes of the geographical structure of foreign trade - increasing the part of socialist countries in the volume of both exports and imports- was also an element of the adjustment.

All this process could be seen in important shifts between the different types of markets for Czechoslovak production. Change plus adjustment in reality shifted the structure of demand faced by the largely unchanged productive structure of the Czechoslovak economy, enlarging the part of the relatively "soft markets" markets (goods for domestic final consumption) and of the very "hard" capitalist market. This shift was first effected through the increments of production; but its direction probably shifted the economy from a path leading to more and more uncertain demand conditions, to markets which were, until the early 1980s, marked by certainty and predictability. So, paradoxically, the changes which led to more uncertainty in the world economy, in this special case of Czechoslovakia led to more certainty for the central plan as well as for the individual producers.

Nevertheless it has become clear since the mid-1980s, especially with the rebuilding of the Soviet economy, that this period of "prolonged certainty" was only temporary in character.

Planning in a socialist enterprise

I turn now to the strategic thinking in a large socialist enterprise, as described by *Horváth* (Ch. 15) for a large Hungarian firm. Comparison with the approach of major western firms, as described by *Rall* or *Beck*, brings out some striking similarities; but some distinctive features of the large socialist enterprise's planning can be attributed to the basically different conditions under which it operates. More precisely, it seems that such an enterprise, even in the market-oriented Hungarian economy, confronts the problem of the future and its inherent uncertainty in a specific and - from the enterprise's viewpoint rather more advantageous - position. The problem of future uncertainty seems to be more manageable than it is for a Western company. I would not like to evaluate the real macro-economic consequences of such microeconomic advantages; they are not necessarily self-evident and can be subject to serious doubts.

From *Horváth's* description of the strategy, which is impressive and shows many resemblances with the flexible strategic planning of the Western firms, some features, in my opinion, deserve stressing for comparison:

- the strong degree of certainty in the socialist enterprise's strategy derives from knowledge of the main lines of the national macro-economic plan. How far the projections of the national plan, with its horizon of the year 2000, can be relied upon remains an open question.
- a whole set of strategic goals is formulated, from the "market position" to the "good atmosphere in the plant". It seems that the freedom of the enterprise to set and achieve such goals - in many respects conflicting - must be greater than in a comparable western company.
- the basis of the strategy is a projection of the future trend of domestic demand for the main products. The alternative scenario differs mainly in respect of the expected trend of demand, in Hungary and on the international socialist market.

These features, if I interpret *Horváth* correctly, suggest that the enterprise operates in a rather protected environment and in a rather privileged position; it does not need to solve some hard decision-making problems concerning, for example, its share of the home market in face of foreign competition or of new entrants on its market. This applies conspicuously to the production of tyres.

If this is true, then the degree of certainty for this Hungarian enterprise is much greater than for a Western firm.

On the other hand, the strategy for the speciality production group - covered by international patents, with very high added value and strong export potential - consistently combines marketing and innovation elements and seems very flexible and well-adapted to the uncertainties of the external world. It could also promote the continuing and efficient reconstruction of the whole progressive product mix of the firm.

The "rather certain" case of tyre production seems to me to suggest, that in this area microeconomic "certainty" can lead - this is just my feeling - into macroeconomic inefficiency. The information in *Horváth's* paper, indicating the formidable lag of this Hungarian production behind world levels in productivity, technology, relative energy consumption etc. gives rise to the suspicion that in a Western company such "certain" production could be in serious doubt.

The Polish problems

Lipiński's comprehensive paper (Ch. 12) is a detailed and very serious analysis of problems which are rather familiar to many centrally planned economies, but which nowhere arise so acutely as in contemporary Poland. The author assesses the situation very realistically, with all its constraints, and tries to find solutions for an economy deeply marked by chronic excess demand and by an imperfect and unfinished socialist market mechanism coexisting with a whole array of state regulatory instruments and allocation priorities.

The conclusions of this valuable analysis seem rather pessimistic. Balancing the different markets, rationalising resource allocation both in protected and in unprotected areas and between them, making supply more flexible, changing the conservative behaviour of enterprises and mastering the wage-price spiral - seem to be nearly intractable tasks, because they are in fact mutually conditioned and interdependent. The problems seem to create vicious spirals which are very difficult to break:

- excess demand cannot be solved by price increases because of the wage-price spiral effect, nor by increasing supply in the short-run;
- inelasticity and insufficiency of supply are conditioned by shortage of inputs and by the conservative, "satisficing" aims of the firms;
- this kind of managerial behaviour is itself strongly influenced by permanent excess demand and at the same time constrains the efficiency of central resource allocation as well as the market allocation mechanism.

To go further, scarce resources are locked in the continuing wasteful behaviour of enterprises; and so on.

I would like to underline that this notion of interdependence of problems and interdependence of constraints, though not always explicitly stated in the paper, is a very valuable feature of the analysis. In spite of my limited knowledge of Polish economic reality, I share *Lipiński's* conviction, that the mutually independent, separate regulatory measures aimed at improving the situation on different markets individually, are mere palliatives, with very limited efficiency.

So it seems to me that underlying this paper, if I interpret its message correctly, is the idea that only a consistent strategy, dealing with all these constraints *en bloc*, could be feasible and in the long-term successful. I cannot claim to outline such a strategy; nevertheless, I would like to consider one approach which might help.

One of the crucial starting points for mastering the interdependent vicious spirals can be the problem of scarce resources - resources wasted, underutilised, or misallocated, but which nevertheless exist within the present economy. Their shortage must not be considered strictly as absolute (with the possible exception of foreign currency), but as relative. One of these scarce resources is manpower, which is largely responsible for the wage-drift process and reinforces the wage-price spiral.

I would like to stress the fact that many resources are wasted not merely as a consequence of the behaviour of enterprises, as the author suggests, but because they are hidden in various production activities which should not exist (at least not in such volume), but which were created by the central allocative decisions. These resources cannot be liberated merely by changing enterprise behaviour. On the contrary, only a central decision, a consistent central industrial policy, can free them for more effective use according to objective criteria of efficiency. So, in my opinion, the hard core of the inflationary situation in Poland lies not exclusively in demand on the consumer market, as the author suggests, but also in the central allocative operations - and, I may suppose, in the so-called protected area which consumes, and wastes, inputs. To free resources at this level could be one of the main steps in a consistent strategy for the Polish economy.

I do not underestimate the practical difficulties, which must be formidable. Nevertheless, it can be one step towards alleviating some of the other constraints, for example, the labour market tensions, the scarcity of raw materials, energy and intermediate products; it could improve elasticity of supply and moderate the wage-price spiral. It is evident that this step, by itself, solves nothing. So it should be taken as part of a comprehensive consistent and very sophisticated strategy covering not only industrial policy, but the economic mechanism, market structure, price structure, central monetary policy, social policy and so on.

The Yugoslav experience

The value of the paper presented by *Bendeković* and *Teodorović* (Ch. 13) lies in its instructive analysis of the past and present of the Yugoslav investment decision-making system. I welcome the historical perspective and the background information about the macroeconomic consequences of the changes in the system and regulation of investment decisions. This macroeconomic background is reflected in the high Yugoslav investment rate, its fluctuations, the changes in the investment structure, the changing efficiency of the investment process, as well as in the continuing inflationary pressures. The analysis suggests that the core of the problem is twofold:

- securing allocative efficiency on the one hand; and strengthening the discipline of investment activity and suppressing its inflationary impact on the other. As I understand it, the origin and permanent existence of these two aspects of the problem lie partly in the imperfect market mechanism with its distorted criteria and behaviour patterns, and partly in the socio-political mechanism and the interventions of non-market forces and interests.

From the paper itself, it is difficult to deduce which bears the larger responsibility. In this respect, the data in Table 13.2 are rather instructive. Changes in the industry structure of fixed investment in the investment boom of the later 1970s show that this boom was strongly propelled by investments in the infrastructure - transport, communications, water etc. - which, I assume, are the area of non-market investment decisions.

It is possible to draw another simplified conclusion from the analysis of past development: soft financing and relatively easy accessibility to funds could also be a main sources of problems. The measures recently introduced in the area of investment decision-making, described by the authors, indicate that the whole problem was so perceived by the Yugoslav authorities. I venture to express the opinion that among the new measures mentioned in the paper those which deal with better professionalism and rationality in investment decisions are probably of minor importance, compared with the measures directed towards the tightening of the financial constraints. Nevertheless, to be successful, the normative measures concerning capital formation in enterprises and the new role of the banks should be complemented by consistent and rather rigorous central monetary policy. In reality, the role of monetary policy, on the macroeconomic level, could be of crucial importance. I am sorry that the authors could not deal with this aspect.

Hans-Jürgen Wagener[1]

1. Planning enterprise strategies in East and West: a comparison

> "Men as individuals, and as groups, have to live largely by a mixture of two ultimately irrational faiths, the faith in reason, which we know is fallible, and the faith in inspiration, which we know is arbitrary."
>
> Frank H. Knight

Strategic planning of individual economic processes is a functional task which should be independent of the economic system. Systems indeed differ

- in the extent of *ex ante* coordination of individual strategic plans,
- in the roles which the enterprise and the central authority play in drafting the plans.

From this we might conclude that strategic planning at the enterprise level exhibits significant differences in scope and method between planned systems in the East and market systems in the West.

So it is quite a provocative hypothesis when *Horváth* writes (Ch. 15) "there is no unbridgeable gap between western companies and socialist state-owned enterprises as regards the content of strategic planning; they differ in their methods only". To test this hypothesis I first turn to the general discussion of the planning idea and then deal with the scope of strategic planning at the enterprise level as presented by *Beck* (Ch. 16) and *Rall* (Ch. 17) for capitalist firms and by *Horváth* and *Kraus* (Ch. 14) for socialist enterprises.

From science to gaming?

I understand by a plan a set of targets (intended future states of the system involved) and a set of policies or actions to be taken to hit the targets. Since in almost all systems of human action the outcome is influenced by external factors, the planning situation cannot be fully described apart from its environment. Defined in such a general way, all decision-making is planning.

The central question is, however: can planning be routinised, bureaucratised; is it contingent upon individuals, or is there a scientific approach to planning? A positive answer to this question facilitates the separation of planning from management, or of strategic planning from operational

---

1) Professor, Rijksuniversiteit Groningen.

planning. Organisationally, this was reflected in the creation of huge central planning staffs in Western corporations and in Eastern economic systems - staff organs which fulfil the planning task on behalf of line management.

The answer to the question of whether planning can be made scientific and routinised depends largely upon the outlook on the world. And the economics profession happens to comprise a number of quite different outlooks:

- one group (neo-classical and new classical economists) sees a world of rationality or rational expectations which allows for a scientific approach and planning in the narrow sense;
- another group (neo-Austrian and post-Keynesian economists) sees a world full of uncertainty and subjective expectations which calls for a person with vision, courage and judgement - called the entrepreneur - whose judgement cannot be bureaucratised;
- a third group (marxist economists) considers uncertainty to be contingent upon the market system of coordination, while in general sharing the rationality optimism of the neo-classical school;
- finally, there are some social scientists, like Weber and Schumpeter who thought that the world is moving from uncertainty to rationality, which implies that bureaucratisation of the control of the economic system will increase in the course of time.

In fact, this last view prevailed in the West among academics and the business world during the 1950s and 1960s. The outlook changed during the 1970s and the possibilities of scientific planning or rational decision-making are now viewed less optimistically. What has changed: insights or ideologies; or objective conditions?

Of course, intellectual modes or ideologies do exist and they exhibit a cyclical pattern: after a period of planning euphoria, the entrepreneur was bound to make his reappearance. But there is more to it than that. *Rall* holds that the change in planning habits is due to increasing uncertainty about external parameters, industry trends and the socio-political environment. *Beck* argues "that it is not uncertainty but complexity which has increased". The contradiction is more apparent than real. By uncertainty *Beck* seems to refer to uncertainties of the natural environment which should have remained stable for the last thousand years or so. Complexity in itself, on the other hand, ought in principle to be no impediment to planning. The collection of information and its treatment may be a problem. But modern communication and computation facilities offered a solution. And the confidence in their capacities and in the rationality of the world gave rise to huge complex models - the world of "computopia" as E. Neuberger has called it - which have now fallen into discredit on the national as well as on the micro level. Only when increasing complexity means increasing dependence upon uncertain developments, natural and decisional, will uncertainty be compounded. So it is very well conceivable "that to-day's uncertainties are greater than those of a thousand years ago".

It would be rash, in my view, to conclude that future states of the world are completely unpredictable. It is correct, of course, that the possibility of forecasting is essential for scientific planning approaches. However, the (im-)possibility of forecasting is no natural predicament. *"Il faut savoir pour prévoir et prévoir pour pouvoir"* (Comte). The real question is: how much can we know, and how much do we know already? The present distrust of scientific planning reflects the insight that our present knowledge, our science of human activities, is rather limited. But any improvement of this knowledge implies an improvement of planning possibilities. Whether this will ever replace discretionary judgement, and make redundant the entrepreneur, is a different question.

It is not only the planning philosophies that have changed somewhat during the 1970s, but also the economic realities. An interesting question, then, is: does strategic planning depend upon the long-run business cycle situation? *Beck's* answer, somewhat oversimplified seems to read: No: strategic planning, as practised in the 1960s, is of no avail, although in times of steady growth it can do little harm. The answer of *Rall* reads: Yes - in times of relative economic stability the methods of the 1960s were appropriate and successful. Again, the contradiction is less real than it appears. The problem, however, is crucial. For under socialism the state tries to create a situation of relative economic and socio-political stability in which planning and rationality ought to flourish and yield optimal results. It may very well be the case that strategic planning and steady growth complement each other, but in the process of evolution they favour incrementalism and proportionalism and impede necessary structural changes. Then the resulting crisis is caused by the cure which was meant to prevent it.

Corporate planning, indeed, could do little harm in the 1960s, in the sense that it was very likely to yield satisfactory results. The principal objective of a firm is growth - growth of value measured in stock price and dividend. If the expected growth rate of the firm happens to coincide with the average growth rate of the industry, the objective can be reached by keeping a constant market share. And if most firms adhere to such a satisficing policy, the individual plan will be little challenged by external forces. The strategic plan can be a long-run forecast of one's own business trends and a single programme for the firm's activities will suffice. Of course, any firm could have done better than successful satisficing, without achieving optimal results. But who cares, in boom times?

Obviously, in a situation of low growth, stagnation, or depression this is no longer possible unless the firm has reduced its growth expectations. That is what changed in the 1970s: the situation of straightforward decision-making and planning moved into a situation of gaming. Satisfactory growth of the firm does not fall out of the air but has to be plucked from other firms' results - market shares get contested, productivity gains have to be relative, innovation must be exclusive. Successful firms cannot just adapt to economic conditions any more; they have to create economic conditions themselves. It is not by chance that indicative planning (of the French type), which is the national planning complement to adaptive corporate planning, is said to have been successful in the 1950s and 1960s but little is heard of it thereafter.

So my conclusion about why strategic planning at the central level is less in vogue than it was would be:

- it lacks the attractiveness of novelty;
- it has to cope with the insight that our present knowledge of economic processes is rather limited;
- it is deemed unsuccessful in the present conditions of great market uncertainty.

This does not mean that strategic planning has been totally abandoned. On the contrary, consultancy is a flourishing business, for instance. Planning has adapted its scope and method to the new situation. In its new form it could be called interactive planning. Part of decision-making has been decentralised to line management; the planning staff at the centre and at lower échelons has been cut, but it is still in existence. The questions now are: why is the line manager considered to be more important than the planner? What makes managers' views more pertinent than planners' views? The reasons lie in the changed situation.

Business success in highly contested markets depends mainly on adequately coping with competitive forces. And competition is a multidimensional conflict: not only the direct competitors in one's own industry have to be considered, but potential market entrants, potential substitutes, and the bargaining power and expectations of buyers as well as of suppliers. All that requires close acquaintance with the respective markets - which is likely to be found on lower rather than central levels.

This does not make the planner redundant. In the first place he has to provide for the long-run perspective and for the holistic views. Secondly, he develops new ideas in a dialogue with the managers. That is why we name the new practice interactive planning: the manager brings in his detailed knowledge and his judgement, the planner brings in his overview and his methodology. The programme of interactive planning sounds quite convincing. It should be clear, however, that it cannot be routinised or bureaucratised. It uses scientific tools, but at the same time depends upon discretionary judgement. Successful strategies can be identified only *ex post*. For iterative n-person games with many strategic variables are difficult to model and to predict. It then becomes of utmost importance to select an able team of good players. This selection process also seems to be hard to routinise and is rather a problem of good judgement.

Enterprise planning in socialist systems

If we now turn to socialist enterprises, as presented by *Horváth* and *Kraus*, it is quite obvious that strategic planning still has the meaning which it had in the West during the 1960s and early 1970s: a consistent concept to cover a long period, which prepares the enterprise to cope with the foreseeable future events. A strategic plan is a long-term programme of the enterprise's activities, to be implemented by operational planning. The novelty about it is that, according to the reformers' intentions, this plan is set up by the enterprise and no longer by a central authority. Apparently, decentralisation is on the agenda here, too, although it happens to occur on a higher hierarchical level than in a western corporation. So what was said about central planning and line management in a capitalist corporation can be translated into the situation of socialist economies, now referring to central planning on the national level and to strategic planning at the enterprise level.

In both systems, the relation between centre and operating unit is very delicate. And before we can discuss strategic planning at the lower level, we have to deal with some problems in this context. The first, in my eyes, is the problem of property rights. *Horváth* very decidedly stated that an indispensable precondition of enterprise planning is autonomy. Autonomy in economic terms would also imply self-reliance on hard budget constraints. The question, then, is: who bears the risk of business failure?

In the capitalist corporation this is not the decentralised strategic business unit, but the owner, represented by the executives at the centre. In socialist economies, I have the impression, the risk still rests with the state as owner. In both cases, this implies that the centre has certain responsibilities and will keep certain decision-making powers. I cannot yet see a new structure of property rights, under socialism of the Hungarian type, which would yield full enterprise autonomy. The Yugoslav situation is less clear to me. Workers seem to bear a great part of the enterprise's risk. But we learn from the contribution of *Bendeković* and *Teodorović* (Ch. 13) that the role of the state in investment decision-making is still sizeable. We conclude that the socialist firm is in a different position from the capitalist firm since the former has a superior authority above it.

A second problem in the delicate relation between centre and unit is to determine the appropriate enterprise unit. Which business unit will get autonomy or quasi-autonomy? There is a parallel to this problem in corporate planning: namely, the choice of the appropriate strategic business unit. A strategic business unit (socialist firm) has to appear and act like an independent firm. Decentralisation creates a tradeoff problem: arguments about optimal firm size are met by arguments about optimal span of control. If the strategic business units (socialist firms) are designed around well-defined markets, their number may become unmanageable for the central authority; if their number is restricted to a manageable size, they are active in too many businesses to have a unique and controllable mission. The problem of the socialist system-designer is even compounded. For together with the determination of the correct business unit he also determines the structure of the respective markets. Here, considerations of competition and of scale play a major role. Socialists are traditionally inclined to think that "big is beautiful". Since their internal markets are well protected by the foreign trade monopoly of the state, competition is rather limited. Apart from efficiency, this preference for large-scale units will have consequences for enterprises strategic planning.

I now turn to planning at the enterprise level and to *Horváth's* hypothesis that it hardly differs in content from corporate planning under capitalism. I wonder whether such a hypothesis is tenable in the light of empirical evidence. It is true that the list of goals which are considered strategic by *Horváth* can also be found in the plans of capitalist enterprises. But there, everything hinges upon market position. I think there is a decisive difference in the environments of the two kinds of enterprise.

As a rule, the socialist enterprise operates in a sellers' market which is hardly contested, while the capitalist firm is operating in a buyers' market which is more strongly contested. The difference must result in competition-oriented strategies in the capitalist firms and strategies which have more slack and are input-oriented in socialist firms. Also the degree of rent-seeking will differ considerably. The Yugoslav enterprise must be sought somewhere in between.

The only obvious exception is the export position of socialist firms in Western markets which, as a consequence, is rather difficult. For socialist firms have to live in an unfamiliar environment there. Rather typical of the different environment are the following characteristics of a socialist enterprise (e.g. the Taurus corporation described by *Horváth):*

- CMEA exports are contracted for long periods in advance,
- the Soviet market, in particular, is a safe background which in some cases, as we are told, more than covers development costs,

- the foreign trade organisation and development centre serving a big enterprise will, in most cases, serve the entire industry.

Looked at more closely, the strategy of the Taurus group is plainly a strategic plan for the whole rubber industry. Taurus seems to have taken over the former task of the central planner. This is a typical example of adaptive, forecast-based planning by a market leader. If we compare it with the examples of positioning analysis in *Rall's* paper, the difference should be evident. On the other hand, the difference between a market-leading Hungarian firm and a GDR Kombinat appears to be rather marginal.

The Yugoslav Metalservis described by *Kraus* seems also to have been able to live a quiet life without competitive challenges. (Of course, the firm itself is not to blame. Any capitalist enterprise would love to be in a similar position; but its markets are generally less protected against internal, external, and potential competitors.) Metalservis's strategy to conquer and develop the market, and to diversify, sounds rather familiar to Western business. But this apparently happens in an environment which *Kraus* describes as a "consensus economy" and in which such a strategy is not suspiciously observed by anti-trust or fair trade administrations or by actual competitors. We do not want to dispute the economic rationale of the situation, for instance from a development point of view. One of the necessary consequences is that economic efficiency is not forced upon the enterprise by external factors but, if at all, has to be produced internally. It is no wonder that we learn about the great inertness and relatively quiet life which previously existed in Metalservis.

This situation begs the question of why workers, who formally have extensive property rights and ought to approve the firm's strategic plans, abandon the quiet life if that is, next to money income, an element in their utility function and if there are few external forces imposing higher work intensity upon them. *Kraus* mentions efforts to get rid of Metalservis management at one time. Are such attempts to be seen in this context? Did the managers try to force upon the worker-owners a strategy which did not conform to their utility function? Evidently strategic planning under workers' self-management has to take account of the workers' interests - probably more so than a capitalist firm.

It becomes clear, in my eyes, that strategic plans are determined by the property rights arrangements and the market situation of the firm concerned. Eastern and Western enterprises differ significantly in both respects. The pressure for structural change and innovation is still rather weak in the socialist economies, as it was under capitalism during the 1950s and 1960s (although innovation and structural change did happen there). Strategic plans in the East, therefore, are still oriented to adaptive growth and result in incrementalism and proportionalism. This may also be due to the important role of the central authorities.

To conclude, let me return to the delicate relation between central and enterprise planning. The authors are amazingly reticent about the central planner although he exists in both economic systems. What is his concrete role and what is his impact upon enterprise strategic plans? If the central planner has allocative or redistributive functions - for instance with respect to imports, foreign exchange, capital - or if he has discretionary fiscal powers, it would be quite natural to expect that firms' strategies would be directed in part towards obtaining favours from the centre (rent-seeking). The close association between economic and political power will make it difficult for the central planner to deviate in conferring his favours from the political power structure which reinforces incrementalism.

Suppose now that the central planner withdrew from direct participation in enterprise decision making. Then, the interesting question is whether the central planner, by means of coordination, could create an environment in which enterprise strategic planning is facilitated. Or to put the question more precisely: is central planning able to create a stable environment in which independent enterprises can formulate and execute rational strategic plans?

2. Planning and stability lessons from Yugoslavia and Poland

It has been a fundamental claim in favour of planned economies that they are able to guarantee rapid and stable economic development. This claim has lost some of its apparent persuasiveness, since growth rates in Eastern Europe have dropped to rather modest levels and some countries exhibit features of serious disequilibrium: Poland and Yugoslavia are the most prominent examples.

The economic systems of the two countries are quite different, of course. The simultaneous reliance in Yugoslavia on the market mechanism and a system of planning is accompanied by such system-specific contradictions as, for instance, the chronic unemployment. *Bendeković* and *Teodorović* (Ch. 13) make it clear that in Yugoslavia a lot of non-market allocation and administrative controls have developed during the last decade or so while Poland in its reforms tried to decentralise decision-making. Apart from the economic system, it is economic policy which determines the actual outcome. And here, too, similarities can be detected. So, a comparison of the two can be quite meaningful.

The Yugoslav economy is depicted as a multi-layer system of decision-making, a system which the Polish reformers have probably had in mind although perhaps they would lay more stress on the central planning element. It becomes evident from the recent economic history of both countries that the coordination of plans on the different decision-making levels seems to be a major problem. The high inflation which both countries experienced in the 1980s may be attributed to such a coordination problem.

Market disequilibria can also be analysed in connection with economic strategy which, of course, is not completely separated from the decision-making structure. Both countries - Poland in the first half and Yugoslavia in the second half of the 1970s - went through a period of overinvestment with investment rates reaching 40 per cent of GDP. That the concomitant savings decisions have been enforced *ex post* by inflation is, then, a plausible hypothesis. The two contributions by *Lipiński* (Ch. 12) and by *Bendeković* and *Teodorović* (Ch. 13) give valuable insights into the working of the decision-making process which produces the observed instabilities.

Poland: the obstacles to equilibrium

Lipiński treats problems of economic order and decision-making in a situation of excess demand on almost all markets - goods markets, labour markets, and capital markets (or the substitute for a capital market under central planning). This, in fact, is the present situation of the Polish economy. The author gives recommendations on how to cope with it. Similar situations are not unknown in other socialist countries. So the chapter is of fairly general interest.

It should be noted that in the paper, and hence in Poland, all markets are considered to be in excess demand, including the consumer goods market. Quite often this market is treated as conceptually in a macro-equilibrium and only in micro disequilibrium. The first question, quite obviously, should be the reasons for this permanent widespread disequilibrium. My reading of *Lipiński's* paper is the following:

- Enterprises are state owned, but more or less free to decide upon output and wages and - if perhaps to a lesser degree - on prices;
- Because of an excess demand for labour, enterprises accept any wage claim: fiscal or other administrative controls on wage rises prove inefficient;
- Because of monopolistic market structures and excess demand on the goods markets, wage rises can be compensated for by rising prices, i.e. they have no effect upon the demand for labour;
- By the same token, prices not only cover wage rises, but any cost increases incurred by the enterprises. In these conditions prices for producer goods will also have no effect on demand. (I do not understand why the author claims that there are hard financial constraints upon investment expenditures after what has been said about wages and prices.)

Further, we learn that for producer goods there are no real markets; but there still exists a system of administrative allocation - a form of the time-honoured *Gossnab* which, despite *khosraschet* (accountability) and similar rules, is not controlled by economic instruments and thus exhibits its own form of excess demand. My impression, now, is that the present economic system of Poland does not differ in any fundamental aspect from the traditional socialist system which, because of notoriously soft budget constraints, has a tendency to create excess demand, but which is not out of equilibrium in the way that the Polish system is just now. The explanation for this divergence, to my mind, is:

- There are none of those administrative controls on wages which, with excess demand for labour, can control consumer goods markets;
- There is no control of money supply, or perhaps we should more correctly say, on the supply of consumer money.

If workers can set money wages and firms can set prices more or less at their will, and if money supply is extremely elastic, budget constraints is extremely soft and the disequilibrium must be extremely serious. A precondition for bringing the consumer goods market into (macro-) equilibrium is hard budget constraints for enterprises (control of wage funds, for instance) or for consumers (planned nominal incomes). Any attempt to bring the market under control should start from here.

We are told by *Lipiński*, however, that this is impossible in present conditions. Two reasons are given:

(a) Consumers have a kind of money illusion. They prefer disequilibrium consumer goods markets and queues to equilibrated markets. As a motive for this peculiar preference, some kind of egalitarianism may be presumed; on equilibrium markets those who have money can buy and others cannot. On disequilibrium markets everybody has money but nobody can buy unless he hits by chance, or by queuing, upon some goods he wants. This produces a feeling of equality. I think, however, two remarks have to be made:

- If there is no privileged access to the market, and if there are no grey or black markets with equilibrium prices, the result is egalitarian, indeed, and any planned income differences are purely nominal. This contradicts the socialist principle of distribution according to work, and hence privileged access to the market (special shops, *pajok)* and grey or black markets have been tolerated in all socialist countries which were unable to bring their consumer markets into equilibrium;
- I should like to see the empirical evidence for the supposed preference. Labour participation of Polish women is traditionally high, the work week is, on paper at least, some 46 hours, public transport is not very efficient, the number of children is comparatively high - I think these are reasons

enough for not wasting time on troublesome shopping activities. The easiest way out for the individual is to use working time for such activities. This perhaps explains why the actual week worked is estimated to be 28 hours on average.

(b) The second reason is a lack of consensus, or at least confidence, between the system's rulers - be it the State or the Party - and the population. There is no room for economic policy to make rational decisions. Any measures which are not openly in favour of the consumer would be resented by the population and would destabilise the political system. I have no reason to doubt the author's opinion on that point. What remains unclear to me is why is it impossible to convince the public that a change to balanced consumer goods markets is a move to the Pareto-superior situation which it obviously represents.

Once we accept *Lipiński's* analysis and his socio-political constraint on economic policy, his recommendations sound quite reasonable. First of all he proposes: keep down the prices of those basic commodities which induce wage rises, if necessary by subsidies. This makes it possible to curb wage claims and to bring at least the markets for less wage-sensitive consumer goods (let us call them consumer non-basics) into equilibrium. It is an empirical question whether consumers really distinguish between basics and non-basics and hence whether wage claims can be avoided by partitioning the market and keeping prices constant on the allegedly smaller basic part.

If this recommendation were implemented, however, we would be back in the traditional economic system of socialism, the only difference being absence of direct wage controls. And with it would return - or remain - the traditional problems of that system:
- low efficiency,
- no incentive to get rid of excess demand (socialist politicians must envy the EC agricultural subsidy system which elicits huge excess supplies).

What remains of inflation is ascribed to government because of its price policy for raw materials. The author is eager to show that inflation is not caused by enterprises which have been given more decision-making power by the economic reform. Government and wage earners are the bad guys. As far as the immediate cause goes, this, of course, is true. But firms which are unrestricted by any effective budget constraint are a very powerful transmission mechanism for inflationary pressures, (as we can see also from the Yugoslav example). If government is weak and cannot resist excessive claims from the enterprise sector, then it is hard to tell who is to blame for the resulting disequilibrium.

I must confess that the future prospects for the Polish economy which can be derived from the paper are bleak. There are few policy options and those which are said to be open lead backward rather than forward. The major problem seems to be the socio-political constraint. Only if this constraint can be softened, will there be scope for more promising policy alternatives. A government which lacks support from the majority of the population must control everything or it will not be able to control anything.

In the West there is, if not a circulation of élites, at least a circulation of ruling parties in order to regenerate the often rather short-lived confidence of the population. In the East we have the examples of Kadar and Honecker who, apparently in very different ways, succeeded in securing a fair consensus. And, certainly not by chance, Hungary and the GDR, again for quite different reasons, are considered success stories. The Poles, by reason of their very specific history, have a long tradition of dissent from their rulers. Lack of coordination is an impediment to development. They have to live with it, or change the situation.

Yugoslavia: a case of overinvestment

Switching now to Yugoslavia we change the focus of attention from consumer goods markets to investment decision-making. Investment decisions are one of the major tasks of enterprise strategic planning. Under capitalism, it is done by the owner of the firm or his representatives on the central management board. There are no policy instruments by which capitalist governments can coordinate enterprises' investment decisions on the private sector, except monetary and fiscal policy which are anyway not very effective. This state of affairs has been deplored by Keynes and severely criticised by the socialists. However, in a system with fairly hard budget constraints and private property rights there is very little scope for an active government role in investment decisions.

Soviet-type central planning has solved the problem by centralising all financial resources and decision-making power in order to control the size and structure of accumulation. This has led to new problems which I do not want to discuss here. A major stumbling-block for all reforms of the traditional Soviet-type system, besides the pricing mechanism, has been investment decision-making. And Yugoslavia has probably gone furthest into the direction of decentralisation. So it is of utmost interest to learn more about the concrete details and consequences.

Bendeković and *Teodorović* report that investment planning is done on several levels. It remains somewhat unclear, however, who takes the final decision and whether he will also have to bear the risk. Take, for instance, a large corporation consisting of several BOALS (Basic Organisations of Associated Labour). In the system of self-management, the BOAL is the basic unit, the firm in the economic and juridical sense. But the basic strategic unit, the corporation, is a kind of joint venture of several independent BOALs. The contrast to the capitalist corporation should be stressed: a single big capitalist firm is split up into several strategic business units; in Yugoslavia several small firms constitute a unified strategic business unit. Property rights concentrate in the first case on the higher level and in the second case on the lower level. Strategic planning, I would surmise, is done on the corporate level. Still the workers are formally liable for investment decisions. So there seems to be some ambiguity about the division of responsibility between the BOAL and the corporation management in investment decision-making. In passing, I should like to mention a related point: conflicts of interest can be alleviated by a policy of cheap money which makes it possible to postpone the question of how to finance the investment decision.

The next question refers to the relation between the corporation and the state which, however, has three levels: the commune, the republic and the central state. Before 1975 there existed a system of indicative planning, which implies a far-reaching discretion for entrepreneurial decision-making. It resulted, as we are told, in market distortions, probably as seen from the central level. Why did the harmonisation of the market not work? Because of inadequate monetary and fiscal policies? Because of underdeveloped competitive forces? Because of soft budget constraints for the enterprises? Or because the planned strategies of the centre and the units diverged? Some clarification could be helpful.

After 1975, harmonisation took place by means of *ex ante* plan coordination, which means dovetailing central and enterprise strategies. Entrepreneurial discretion was restricted by regulations and direct state intervention - which hardly warrants statements about "a further reduction of the state's role in planning".

The state has a major interest in structural developments and it uses investment decisions as the policy instrument to execute its structural policy. In view of the experience of several Western countries which tried out selective structural policies, it is not much of a surprise that "the priority allocation mechanism had problem(s) of defining and choosing the priorities". Determining priority sectors or priority business, the portfolio decision, is one of the major strategic planning tasks. It depends largely upon the information and interests of the decision-takers.

Not only has the state an interest; on the micro-level, the portfolio decision rests with the enterprise and, formally in the end, with the workers; and they, it is plausible to assume, are in the first instance interested in real incomes. The fact that managers and local and central bureaucrats are mostly interested in investment - although not necessarily in the same projects - may account for the overinvestment tendency.

Unless the state is able to coordinate at least four decision-making levels, of which the state itself is one (or two), the situation is bound to lead to disequilibrium. Unless there is a tight monetary policy, this conflict of interests will result in inflation. For without monetary restrictions or other means of effective plan coordination, each level will be in a position to put its own plans into operation.

Of course, some plans are doomed to be defeated *ex post*. I would suggest that workers' intentions to increase their real wages have always been frustrated *ex post* because, in their eyes, of excessive accumulation and consequent inflation. Trying to resist accumulation, they will increase their nominal claims in the next round. Being the decision-maker and the coordinator at the same time, the state is in a very delicate position with the result that most anti-Keynesians have predicted, namely an ever-increasing inflation. I have the impression that the law of expanded reproduction is, in fact, a law about wages. It tries to put the burden of stabilisation upon the workers. It seems to say nothing about the state's investment activities. Of course, stabilisation is a dire necessity. But so long as no monetary restrictions or budgetary controls are applied, the state is exempted and can go on to enforce an accumulation policy.

The "Federal social compact on economic criteria of investment" is a further step away from entrepreneurial discretion and market coordination. Of course, "investment project evaluation must be done externally". But the question is whether it can be done at all in a satisfactory way *ex ante*, and whether it can be done effectively by any financially uninvolved external organisation. This is, essentially, the problem of the possibility of scientific planning dealt with by *Beck* and *Rall*. They contend that the uncertainties involved make strategic planning a task for vision and entrepreneurial judgement, which objective scientific criteria can do no more than complement. So external project evaluation in a market economy is done *ex ante* by those who risk their capital - or that of their shareholders and creditors - and it definitely takes place *ex post* in the market.

A well-functioning decentralised selection procedure for investment projects presupposes, however, fairly well-functioning markets. Apart from differences in risk aversion, *ex ante* evaluation will be unsatisfactory from a social point of view if the parties involved expect to be able to shift the burden of the risk, and if necessary the cost, to someone else. This is generally the case when soft budget constraints prevail. In such conditions, decentralised decision-making does not work any longer and administrative control or administrative project evaluation will become necessary.

I wonder why the Yugoslav authorities have chosen the way of more administrative control, which seems contrary to the logic of market socialism.

If the market does not do the selection and coordination job satisfactorily, the reason can be either that it fails or that there is not enough market. And the same is true of planning. It is perhaps the dilemma of a mixed order that the opportunities for failure are compounded.

We are told further that at the end of 1985 some new measures were taken. In part they represent harder budget constraints, imposing the obligation to cover the possible losses upon the banks. But other new measures are moves towards more administrative control. Thus a common methodology for comparative investment analysis is necessary only when prices and profitability are not considered good indicators. In this context, one would wish to know more about the impact of frequently revised regulations on enterprise strategic planning. Are not enterprise managers completely frustrated by continuous changes in the systemic framework of their decision-making, or do they react cheerfully and do business as usual?

If for a conclusion we briefly compare the Polish and the Yugoslav cases it is of course clear that the instabilities observed have historically unique causes. However, in both cases the coordination mechanism seems unable to provide an economy-wide consensus about the strategies to be followed. Although the one system relies more on central decision-making and the other more on decentralisation, it is either the weak power position of the state or inadequate policies that make coordination fail. For in both countries the state appears unable to impose upon the system either effective administrative control or effective monetary and budgetary discipline.

Peter Beck

Two phrases seem to have flooded over me - 'high technology' and 'delegation'. Greater use of both, I am told, will, rather like the latest washing powder, wash most economies whiter than white. Perhaps; but I can't help wondering whether either phrase is really understood.

Firstly, 'high technology': this is usually perceived to be the 'microchip' and new industries based on it. In reality, however, it is not the generation of new industries which is the really important use of high technology, but its use in revolutionising existing and old-established industry. The micro-chip has not outdated the machine tool industry, but it has enabled that industry to develop and market far more efficient machines. Equally, shipbuilding is still shipbuilding, but use of 'high technology' has changed the way ships are designed and built. To make effective use of this technology requires old industries to learn new ways and managers and workers to throw away old-established habits. That is difficult, especially as experience has shown that such changes require willing co-operation and understanding from managers and workforce. To accept 'high technology' often means painful change and high motivation; willingness to take risks is a prerequisite for success.

'Delegation' in an organisation is easy to talk about, but again very difficult to apply in practice. Lower level managers often see it as a system whereby they get the blame when things go wrong, but the 'boss' gets the credit when things go right. Real delegation requires trust between the delegator and the delegatee, making it possible to share problems, successes and failures. To establish it where it does not exist needs considerable qualities of leadership. It cannot be established by edict. Many companies which are successful users of high technology have found that they needed to develop a culture where trust between the manager and the managed is high. True delegation then becomes possible, motivation is high and change is accepted as normal. That is the reason for their success. I was most interested in *Lipiński's* paper (Ch. 12). It showed very clearly that Polish managers are as human as British managers. Rather than acting like economic beings, they like a quiet life. Improving efficiency is often hard and unless there is trust between the top management and the line managers, the latter will not take the risk of forcing through unpopular changes in work practice. Attempts to compel action, e.g. by reducing central resources like money, hardly ever have the desired effect; because in to-day's complex world cuts can always be applied where they cause damage or public outcry rather than improvements in efficiency. I can see many of the problems outlined in the paper when I visit my local hospital. Even though the UK government says that it is spending more and more on the Health Service, the visible manifestation of the Government's drive for greater efficiency is closed wards and longer waiting lists. No economic signals will overcome lack of trust and motivation.

László Horváth

A rejoinder to some comments on my paper on Hungary (Ch. 15)

Wagener asks about the extent of enterprises' autonomy in socialist economies. I would point to a fairly new development in Hungary, where property rights are vested in communities - more exactly, in most cases, in the councils of employees. Certainly, in the learning stage, the functioning is not too easy but it is going better than I myself expected. Communities bear the risks.

Contrary to the inclination attributed to socialists to hold that big is beautiful, I must state that small is beautiful - at least in the specific circumstances of Hungary.

I think that the strategic goal always takes into account the environment, and is based on market demands. The enterprise must be very open because this is necessary for elaboration of a plan.

Wagener is right: my account of the Taurus Group serves as an illustration of the whole Hungarian rubber industry, influenced as it is by the world market.

I am grateful to *Kreuter* for the empathy expressed in his interpretation of my paper on enterprise strategy. I think we can agree that we need good, reliable plans on both the macro- and microeconomic levels. The ways to achieve this can differ in some details; the development of socialist countries indeed shows some existing differences. In Hungary, on the basis of our experience, we take the view that in some cases a very complicated, consistent planning system, incorporating planning on both macro- and microeconomic levels, delays decision-making, the correction of mistakes etc.; and that a system can be more flexible if decisions on details are left to local decision-makers with the responsibility for their operations. However I agree with *Beck's* exposition of the respective roles of the leadership and the managers in determining the plan.

Kreuter suggests that Taurus is in a special situation, allowing it to elaborate a strategy in a state of uncertainty.

I can illustrate the real situation of Taurus with some supplementary information.

(a) On the role of the domestic market: to our regret, the first analysis of our activity convinced us that the Hungarian market is not suitable for any strategic decision about, for instance, the strategic products of the future. This can be seen from some figures for the most important products:

	Proportion of domestic demand (%)
Heavy steel radial tyre	30-40
Drilling hose	5
Air springs	25
Camping equipment	8-10
Conveyor belts	80

As my paper emphasised, the present strategy is strongly export-oriented. If the question arises of how we could achieve the desired position on the world market, the answer is simply: by strategy.

(b) The efficiency indicators relate not only to Taurus but to the Hungarian rubber industry. It is relevant that the selected strategic products are competitive in both technology and efficiency.

(c) The strategy of Taurus elaborated in 1970-71 was confirmed as a whole. When revising the strategy in 1981-82, we decided that we had to change the strategic product structure only in two product groups: we completed the list with conveyor belts. We had to eliminate an interesting new product: the rubber sheets used for insulating water channels, basins etc. The reason was the Iran-Irak war.

Kreuter expressed the hope that his interpretation had been correct, which I confirm. The present remarks are needed simply to fill gaps in the information provided in my paper!

Jan Lipiński

A rejoinder to some comments on my paper on Poland (Ch. 12)

The Polish economy badly needed a substantial reform of its system of economic control. It was, however an unfortunate circumstance that the implementation had to be started (in 1982) in a situation of considerable excess demand for commodities and resources. If a similar reform had been started much earlier - for instance, in the late 1950s (after 1956) or in the 1960s - it might have been carried through in a situation of balanced or nearly-balanced markets, and might thus have brought easier and quicker success. A developed draft for such a reform was put forward by a group of Polish economists as early as 1957. Unfortunately, it was set aside (though not overtly rejected) by the Polish political leaders of the time.

A particularly grave obstacle to rapid suppression of excess demand for consumer goods is a factor of socio-economic nature - namely, the typical attitude of an average Polish consumer, which, as I suggested, makes him prefer to queue for a chance of buying a commodity at a price accessible to him, rather than to give up that commodity altogether because of a prohibitive price while people richer than himself could buy it without a queue.

I do not attribute that attitude to a "monetary illusion" as *Wagener* suggests; but regard it as entirely reasonable for an individual household (though not, of course, reasonable for the nation as a whole). It seems to predominate among workers' households in Poland, except the richest. Empirical evidence for this supposition can be found in the long queues observed in front of butchers' shops, formed early in the morning by those who want to get better sorts of meat for their ration cards. These queues appear despite the existence of a parallel, legal free market for meat. I should say that I have myself adopted a similar attitude as a consumer, with regard to some industrial goods.

What I have said, however, is subject to a qualification. Suppose that a household prefers a situation where a commodity is sold at a lower price but there is excess demand for it, to a balanced market at a higher price. Such a preference is not obviously reasonable unless the market-balancing price is prohibitive, or nearly so, for the household. If that is not the case, the preference is likely to depend on the valuation by a household of the income effect of a price rise as against the waste of time standing in queues. But there are many families whose non-employed, retired members are prepared to spend a lot of time in queues.

I tried to describe the typical conditions for financing the activities of a state-owned enterprise in Poland. I pointed out that most of those enterprises enjoy "soft" financing of their current expenditures, while some encounter difficulties in financing their investment projects. *Wagener* is doubtful how the second circumstance can coexist with the first. This, however, can easily be explained by taking into account the different ways of financing current and investment activities of enterprises, and relating them to the present practice of price formation.

Current expenditures of an enterprise constitute elements of cost calculation and thus - in a situation of excess demand - can easily be transferred to prices, without affecting sales. If the price of a product is centrally fixed at a lower level than the production cost, that deficit is covered by a subsidy.

Investment expenditures of enterprises are financed from the following main sources: amortisation of the existing capital equipment and profit. Amortisation constitutes an element of production cost, but the amounts are comparatively stable; besides, a fixed part of it goes to the State budget. As regards profit, the margin adopted in price-setting is normally fixed at a standard level, which is uniform for a large commodity group. Even where prices of commodities can be freely set by enterprise managers, the latter usually refrain from raising the profit margin above the standard level, for they do not want to be blamed by their ministerial or political supervisors or to be criticised by the public. The point is that "excessive" profits normally encounter much more criticism than excessive costs.

Accordingly, both sources of finance for investment by enterprises - amortisation and profit - are subject to constraints which coexist with "soft" financing of current operations. To be sure, those financial constraints on investment may be alleviated by tax reliefs, but these are granted only to some enterprises.

Moreover, when the workers' council of a state-owned enterprise decides on the division of the profit, it normally gives priority to the current material interests of the workers over the development or modernisation of the enterprise. Thus only a residual part of the after-tax profit is available for financing productive investment. In these circumstances, the importance of financial constraints on investment activities differs a great deal between enterprises.

I entirely agree with *Kreuter* that the Polish economy needs substantial changes in its structure and its technical level. I also agree with him that the implementation of those necessary changes calls for coherent state economic policy, based on a central plan. In my opinion, however, the goals of that policy ought to be attained, in the first place, by "economic" instruments (bank credit, taxes), whereas the application of administrative measures should be minimised. Besides, considering the present state of the Polish economy, such a policy would be unlikely to produce its full effect in a period of less than 6-7 years.

In my paper, I put forward some of the measures proposed for the near future. *Wagener* qualifies them as appropriate to a traditional, centralised system of economic control. I cannot accept that appraisal. My proposals for the near future would imply substantial alleviation of the present administrative constraints on the activities of state-owned enterprises. For example, with regard to the prices for manufactured goods, I proposed abolition of administrative intervention in setting prices of individual commodities and replacing it by group price ceilings.

APPENDIX

ECONOMIC TRENDS AND DEFENCE BURDENS IN THE UNITED STATES AND THE SOVIET UNION

Richard F Kaufman[1)]

Definitive conclusions about the defence burdens of the superpowers cannot be made. The principal reason is that not enough is known about the linkages between military spending and economic performance to be sure of how changes in the former affect the latter. It is possible to compare economic trends in the two countries, to consider them in light of military expenditures, and perhaps say something illuminating about defence burden issues.

Economic trends

The Soviet Union has been experiencing a long-term decline in economic growth. The decline is indicated by the following figures:

USSR growth rates

Five-year period	Average annual growth of GNP (%)
1951-1955	5.5
1956-1960	5.9
1961-1965	5.0
1966-1970	5.2
1971-1975	3.7
1976-1980	2.7
1981-1985	2.5

Growth rates in the early 1980s were less than half the rate in the late 1950s. Productivity performance has been even more dismal. Total factor productivity has declined since 1970. Labour productivity growth was 2.9 per cent in the late 1960s. In the early 1970s, it was 2.3 per

1) General Counsel, Joint Economic Committee, United States Congress. The views expressed in this paper are those of the author and not necessarily those of the Joint Economic Committee or the US Congress. The paper is based on The Economic Consequences of Military Spending in the United States and the Soviet Union, a report to a conference sponsored by Cornell University, May 9 and 10, 1986.

cent and has stayed in that range during the past 10 years. The trend in capital productivity is worse.

In the early Khruschev period, Soviet growth was so rapid that fears were widespread that the United States would be overtaken economically, with serious consequences for the military balance. Brezhnev, by the early 1970s, officially acknowledged the seriousness of the slowdown in growth rates and a number of steps were taken to reverse the decline. Gorbachev has called publicly for fundamental reform largely because of this problem.

What are the causes of the slowdown? Most Western experts cite several major factors, as well as the nature of the Soviet system of central planning. The more important factors are the slower growth in labour and capital as well as the rising costs of raw materials. The Soviet leadership would agree with this, and, in fact, this forms the basis for the policy of greater "intensification" in the economy, that is, for the more efficient use of resources. Westerners also emphasise the "systemic" problems. According to this argument, Soviet central planning and management is impractical in such a large and complex economy, and, besides, it retards efficiency and technological advantages.

Some Western analysts, particularly those at the Central Intelligence Agency, maintain that the high level of defence activities has been a drain on the economy and has slowed growth. US intelligence estimates, concurred in by the CIA and the Defence Intelligence Agency, show that the annual rate of growth of Soviet defence spending slowed from four per cent to two per cent, beginning in 1975, and that the growth rate for procurement has been about one per cent. The CIA believes this slowdown has persisted through at least 1984. If the Soviet Union strengthened its military capabilities in the past ten years, as many analysts believe, it did so with a virtual freeze on procurement. Nevertheless, because of slow growth in the economy during this period, the Soviet defence burden did not decline and remains high. The share of Soviet GNP allocated to defence is estimated at 15 to 17 per cent, measured in current roubles.

The military burden, it is pointed out, aside from being high and persistent, is particularly onerous because of the priority given to the military and the uneven effects of military activities on the economy. The military is given priority access to, among other things, the best quality raw materials for defence production, the best industrial workers, and the most advanced machinery. Key industries provide large shares of their production to the defence sector. Twenty-five per cent of machinery production and 20 per cent of metallurgy production supports military procurement. A disproportionate share of research and development is also diverted from civilian purposes.

An interesting question is whether the diversion of resources is, by itself or in combination with other factors mentioned, a major cause of the poor productivity performance and ultimately the slowdown in GNP growth. Depending upon the answer, one might be able to argue that no amount of reform of the economic system will cure what ails the Soviet economy, unless the military burden is sharply reduced for a sustained period.

The prevailing official view from Washington is that the Soviet economy is faltering under an excessively heavy military burden (few realise that the military burden and systemic problem theses may be incompatible), while the US is on the way to solving its economic problems through sustained growth. The record of the past few years provides superficial evidence to support this view. The US has been growing in recovery from the serious recession of 1981-1982, inflation is low, and there have been significant gains in employment.

A close examination reveals a different picture, with startling similarities to the Soviet Union. The slowdown in US economic growth has not been as steep but it has been as persistent as in the Soviet Union. The following figures illustrate the point:

US growth rates

Five-year period	Average annual growth of GNP (%)
1951-1955	4.5
1956-1960	2.2
1961-1965	4.6
1966-1970	3.0
1971-1975	2.2
1976-1980	3.4
1981-1985	2.4

US growth rates averaged 3.8 per cent in the 1950s and 1960s. In the 1970s, they averaged 2.8 per cent and since 1980 they have been only 2.4 per cent. A comparison shows the similarity in US and Soviet growth trends since 1950. Even the peaks and troughs, although more extreme for the US, roughly coincide. The downward trend for both countries is apparent.

Trends in US productivity also show a slowdown. Labour productivity grew at a 3.3 per cent rate from the late 1940s to 1965. During 1965-1973, the rate was 2.4 per cent; during 1973-1978 it was 1.8 per cent; and during 1978-1984, it was less than 1 per cent. The Bureau of Labor Statistics' new series on multifactor productivity shows that is rose at a 2 per cent rate during 1948-1973, but by only a 0.2 per cent rate after 1973. Capacity utilisation has moved downward and unemployment upward during the postwar period.

Not a great amount of thought has been given to explain the long-term decline in the US. Some economists would dispute the fact of the decline, preferring to focus on the business cycle and special factors, such as the 1973 energy crisis. There was a view in the late 1970s, triggered by concern about poor economic performance, that there had been inadequate capital formation, together with low savings and investment rates, as a consequence of too much emphasis on the demand side of the economy. This thinking led to a call for "supply-side" economics to reverse the undesirable results. However, recent revised estimates of capital formation during the 1970s show that it compared favourably with earlier periods. The new estimates raise questions about the premisses of supply-side economics.

Another school of thought correlates the supposed US economic decline with high levels of military spending. Proponents of this view place great weight on comparisons of military spending and economic performance in the non-Communist industrialised nations. They find that the relatively high level of US military spending (at present, 6 per cent of GNP is allocated to defence) has contributed to lower levels of investment and lower productivity growth.

There is, as yet, no conclusive evidence linking the US military burden to specific economic shortfalls, such as the GNP growth decline, the slowing of productivity growth, or the fall-off in international competitiveness. But it should be acknowledged that similar evidence is lacking with regard to the USSR.

Military burden issues

At least three military burden issues should be recognized. One concerns the need to differentiate short-term and long-term effects. In the short term, military spending acts like any other source of fiscal stimulus. The precise economic effects will vary depending upon economic conditions, the level of military spending, and the magnitude of changes in the level of spending. In the past, sharp rises in military spending have been accompanied by higher Federal deficits, increases in inflation, industrial bottlenecks, and other problems. Such short-term effects can usually be offset by other policies. The longer term effects are more difficult to identify. These are the problems of assessing the influence of high levels of defence spending over a sustained period on such measures as growth and productivity.

A second issue concerns measurement of the military burden. The practice is to calculate the share of GNP allocated to the military. There are, of course, direct and indirect categories of military spending. In addition, parts of the military establishment, such as the Army Civil Corps of Engineers, are involved primarily in the civilian sector. More difficult are questions concerning the space programme, interest on the national debt, and the like. Such questions have been raised before, but remain unresolved.

These questions are clearly relevant to comparisons of the US and Soviet military burdens. Obviously, simple comparisons of the size and trend of the burden should be based on the same definition of what goes into the military category. This turns out not to be the case. In estimating the size of the Soviet military burden, the Defence Intelligence Agency includes the Soviet civilian space programme, and the costs of military construction and railroad troops, as well as the internal security forces. As official estimates of the US military burden exclude such activities, US-Soviet comparisons are being made on a somewhat uneven footing.

A more serious measurement issue is raised by those who conclude that the Soviet Union is more militarised than the US, that it is a veritable Sparta, and that efforts to use military expenditures as a measure of the Soviet military burden are misguided. There may be an element of truth to this thesis in that the Soviet military does get preferential treatment and imposes a pervasive influence throughout Soviet society. But much the same can be said about the US military. The difficulty is defining the threshold of military influence where a society becomes "militarised" rather than merely preoccupied with the requirements of national security.

The third issue has to do with projecting the future effects of the military burden. Most research to date has concentrated on the past effect of the military burden. It is also useful to try to anticipate the consequences of present trends. The CIA currently projects a short-term trade-off problem for the Soviets regarding labour and materials used in military and nonmilitary production, and a potentially more serious competition for resources unless economic growth picks up in the next few years.

Some government officials believe the Soviets need an arms agreement in order to alleviate the military burden and provide more time to deal with economic problems. This reads much more into the present state of the art of burden analysis than presently exists and probably exaggerates both the seriousness of the Soviet economic situation and the amount, if any, of relief from the military burden that can be expected from an arms agreement.

LIST OF PARTICIPANTS
in Workshop held in Florence, 22-24 September, 1986

Abbreviations:

WIIW - The Vienna Institute for Comparative Economic Studies (Wiener Institut für Internationale Wirtschaftsvergleiche)

Peter Beck - Chairman, Strategic Planning Society, London

Jadranko Bendeković* - Ekonomski Institut, Zagreb

Mila Biagotti - Foundazione di Ricerche e Studi Internationali, Florence

Carlo Boffito - Consultant, Banca Commerciale Italiana, Milan

József Bognár - Academician; Director, Hungarian Scientific Council for World Economy, Hungarian Academy of Sciences, Budapest

Oleg Bogomolov - Academician; Director, Institute for the Socialist World Economic System, Academy of Sciences of USSR, Moscow

Andrea Boltho - Magdalen College, Oxford

Daniel L. Bond - Wharton Econometric Forecasting Associates, Inc., Washington, DC

Henri Bourguinat	- Faculté de Sciences Economique (LARE) Pessac, France
Fritz Breuss	- Austrian Economic Research Institute (WIFO), Vienna
Ante Čičin-Šain	- Ekonomski Institut, Zagreb
Raimund Dietz	- WIIW, Vienna
Gerhard Fink	- Director, WIIW, Vienna
John P. Hardt	- Senior Specialist Office, Library of Congress, Washington DC
Wolfgang Heinrichs	- Professor, Zentralinstitut für Wirtschaftswissenschaften, Akademie der Wissenschaften der DDR, Berlin, DDR
László Horváth	- Hungarian National Management Centre, Budapest
Richard F Kaufman	- General Counsel of Joint Economic Committee of the Congress, Washington DC
Lawrence R. Klein	- Professor, University of Pennsylvania, Philadelphia
Norbert Kloten	- Board Member of the German Federal Bank, Stuttgart, FRG
Aleksander Kraus	- General-Director "Metalservis", Belgrade
Jósef Kreuter	- Kabinet Prognoz CSAV, Prague
Rikard Lang	- Ekonomski Institut, Zagreb
Friedrich Levcik	- Professor, WIIW, Vienna

Jan Lipiński	- Professor, Central School of Planning and Statistics, Warsaw
Aleksander Lukaszewicz	- Professor of Economics, Warsaw University, Warsaw
Paul Marer	- Professor of Interational Business, Indiana University, Bloomington, USA
Giangiacomo Nardozzi	- Professor, Faculty of Political Science, University of Florence
Domenico Mario Nuti	- Professor, European University Institute Fiesole, Italy
Józef Pajestka	- Professor, Polish Academy of Sciences, Warsaw
Wilhelm Rall	- McKinsey & Company, Stuttgart, FRG
Philipp Rieger	- Creditanstalt-Bankverein, Vienna
Dominick Salvatore	- Professor, Department of Economics, Fordham University, New York
Christopher Saunders	- Science Policy Research Unit, University of Sussex, Brighton, UK
Gerlinde Schöfbeck	- WIIW, Secretariat, Vienna
Hans Seidel	- Professor, Institut für Höhere Studien, Vienna
Peter Sydow*	- Akademie der Wissenschaften der DDR, Forschungsbereich Gesellschaftswissenschaften, Berlin, GDR
Márton Tardos	- Institute of Economics, Hungarian Academy of Sciences, Budapest

Ivan Teodorović - Ekonomski Institut, Zagreb

Sabina Vivarelli - Foundazione di Ricerche e Studi Internazionali, Florence

Dragomir Vojnić, - Professor, Ekonomiski Institut, Zagreb

Hans-Jürgen Wagener - Professor, Rijksuniversiteit Groningen, The Netherlands

Helgard Wienert-Cakim - OECD, Paris

* Author, or part-author but unable to attend the Workshop

INDEX*

Page references in *italics* indicate authorship of papers in this volume.

Africa
  famines, 57
  trade prospects (late 1980s), 43
Agriculture
  German Democratic Republic, 8
    increased production, 118-19
    integration into industrial structure, 118
    trade, 116-20
  nontariff barriers, 158
  oversupply of commodities, 44
  subsidies
    EEC, 177
    USA, 158, 177
  trade between EC and US, 158-9
  Yugoslavia, investment share, 263
Algeria, indebtedness, 25
Antidumping measures, 157, 169
Argentina, indebtedness, 45
Arms control, effect on world economy, 30
Arms race, effect on world economy, 19
  see also Defence spending
Austria
  'Austro-Keynesianism', 6, 91-2, 97, 99, 218
  balance of payments, 94-5
  budget deficits, 96
  Commission for Prices and Wages, 92, 93
  crisis of nationalised industries, 99
  economic growth, 217-18, 221-2
  economic institutional structure, 93
  effect of oil price shock, 91, 92
  effects of international integration, 95
  exchange rate policy, 94
  incomes policy, 92, 98
    results, 92-4
  indebtedness, 94, 97
  industrial structure, 99
  inflation (1973-85), 91
  interest rates, 95
  international standing, 91
  macroeconomic policies, 6-7, 91-9
  monetary policy, 92, 97
  prices, 95, 98
  productivity, 99
  structural adjustment, 98-9
  unemployment, 91, 98, 99, 222
  working week shortened, 97-8, 222
Automobile industry
  cooperative ventures, 320
  exploiting market potential, 320-4
  in socialist countries, 106-7
  Japanese exports, 163-4, 223-4
  market concentration, 320
  nontariff barriers, 160, 162, 316
  strategic planning, 319-25, 331

Baker plan, 24
Balance of payments
  and import substitution, 210
  Austria, 94-5
  socialist countries, 105
Banks
  lending practices, 57
  role in socialist macroeconomic policies, 105-6
  role in Yugoslav investment, 265
Beck, Peter, 15-16, 17, 64, *295-314*, 330, 331, 337-9, *351-2*
Belgrade Institute for Scientific Research, 275
Bendeković, Jadranko, 13, 17, *255-67*, 336, 341, 345, 348
Bognár, Jószef, 7, *101-9*, 225
Bogomolov, Oleg, 2-3, *19-32*, 59-60, 225
Bolivia, indebtedness, 45
Boltho, Andrea, 5, *61-3*
Bond, Daniel L., 2, 3-4, 5, *33-46*, 59, 62, 64, 223
Bond issues, in ECUs (1983-5), 153
Bourguinat, Henri, 8-9, *133-53*, 227
Brazil
  foreign economic strategy, 188-90
  indebtedness, 45
Bretton Woods system, 74, 315
Breuss, Fritz, 11, *223-5*
Budget deficits
  Austria, 96
  West Germany, policies to reduce 78-9
Bulgaria
  foreign direct investment, 198
  indebtedness, 59, 201
Burma, economic strategy, 192
Business cycles, 70
  and strategic planning, 339
  control by fiscal means, 71
  policies related to stabilisation policies, 68
Business management
  accepting uncertainty, 1, 306-313

* Compiled by *Audrey Bamber*

in changing circumstances, 304-6
in uncertainty, 1
motives for actions, in Poland, 233-5
relationships with workers, 234
role of manager, 312-13
role of planner, 313
training, Yugoslav experience, 271-2
see also Decision-making

Canada, reduced inflation, 36
CAP, *see* Common Agricultural Policy (CAP)
Capital
allocation, Yugoslavia, 259-60, 262-5
international flows, 183, 184
role of EMS, 144-5
project evaluation, 297-8
substitution for labour, 168
see also Foreign direct investment
Central control, deficiencies, 101
Centrally planned economies
and autonomy of enterprises, 341
in Poland, 234
constraints on foreign economic strategy choice, 208
convertible-currency imports, 194
expansion drive, 192, 211-12
exports, 198
foreign direct investment, 198-201
foreign economic strategies, 192-203, 228-9
foreign trade policies, 202
imports from West, 194
in circumstances of uncertainty, 331-2
inherent protectionism, 212-13
internal trade instruments, 196-8
international financial integration, 201-3
links with multinational corporations, 203
prices, 198
reform measures required, 213
resource availability constraint, 193
strategic planning, 341
trade negotiations, 198
trade on basis of quotas, 198
Yugoslavia (1947-52), 255
Chile, indebtedness, 45
China
development potential, 30
economic growth rate, 29
economic reforms, 29, 213
foreign direct investment, 198-9
indebtedness, 201
introduction of economic reforms, 102
trade potential, 30
trade prospects (late 1980s), 42
Čičin-Šain, Ante, 11, *225-7*
Clothing, nontariff barriers, 160, 162
Club of Rome, 300
economic projections, 48
CMEA, *see* Council for Mutual Economic Assistance
Commission for Prices and Wages (Austria), 92, 93
Common Agricultural Policy (CAP), 157, 158
Common Currency Union, 141
Communications, Yugoslavia, investment share, 263
Competition
analysis, 323
East and West compared, 342
for resources, in Poland, 238
Hungarian rubber industry, 289
in automobile industry, 320
restricted by protectionism, 210
resulting in nontariff barriers, 163
strategic planning, 340
Conservation programmes, *see* Energy: conservation programmes
Controls, on macroeconomic policy, 80
Council for Mutual Economic Assistance (CMEA), 8, 193
annual growth in GDP (1984-5), 26
annual growth in GNP (1986-90), 29
compared with EEC, 196, 197
Comprehensive programme for .... progress to the year 2000, 124, 131, 219
development tasks, 26
domestic economic requirements, 111
German Democratic Republic's trade with, 115-16
internal foreign direct investment, 200-1
internal integration, 214
internal trade
instruments, 196-8
oil, 38-9
Soviet pressure on Eastern Europe, 41
volume, 197
international economic cooperation, 30
prices, 198
stabilising factors, 26
technological development, 46
effect on trade with West, 31
transferable rouble
'turnkey' projects, 31, 198
see also Centrally planned economies; Socialist countries
Council of Economic Exports (Federal Republic of Germany), 66
Countervailing duties, 157, 169
Credit
and foreign financial integration, 187
policies of socialist countries, 105-6
West German experience, 74

Czechoslovakia
  coping with uncertainty and change, 332
  indebtedness, 201

Debt, 2
  alleviating factors, 45
  Austria, 94, 97
  causes, 57
  causing imbalances in world economy, 45
  convertible-currency, of centrally planned economies, 201, 202
  differences in dependence on external finance, 201
  increases in West Germany, 70, 72
  of developing countries, 22, 23
  resulting from global policies, 57
  Soviet Union and Eastern Europe, 43-4
Decision-making
  based on scenarios, 308
  development as science, 297
  drawbacks of mathematical models, 303
  under uncertainty, 1, 306-7
  see also Business management
Defence spending
  and US indebtedness, 2-3
  measurement of economic burden, 361
  related to decline in economic growth, 359-60
  short- and long-term economic effects, 360
  Soviet Union, 358
  see also Arms race
Delegation in planning, 310-12, 351, 352
Demand
  aim of West German stabilisation programmes, 72
  restraint, in Poland, 242-4
Demand management
  Austria, 96-7
  effect of outside influences, 69
Developing countries
  announcement of NIEO, 53
  effects of loss of macroeconomic control, 211
  effects of protectionism, 23, 178
  effects of worsening terms of trade, 23
  estimates of required external resources, 24
  growth rates, 43
  impact of oil price increases, 60
  import substitution, 205
  increasing indebtedness, 3, 22, 23
  terms of trade, 205
  trade prospects (late 1980s), 42, 45
  ways to economic survival, 22-3
Division of labour, 219
  in CMEA programme, 124
  international, 129
Dollar, *see* US dollar

East-West relations, 57
  in trade, 111
  joint ventures, 46, 291-2, 320-1
  prospects, 36-7
  role in world economy, 30-2
Eastern Europe
  eoonomic growth, 4
  effect of dollar decline, 37
  effect of investment decline, 43
  effect of oil price drop, 41-2
    on export revenues, 38-9
  export promotion, 195
  forecast growth rates, 43
  forecast hard currency exports, 43
  foreign economic strategy, 204
  import substitution, 205
  indebtedness, 43-4, 59
    repayment, 37, 42
  internal integration, 214
  introduction of economic reforms, 102
  joint ventures with West, 46
  loans from Western lenders, 37
  technological exports, 41
  see also Centrally planned economies; Council for Mutual Economic Assistance (CMEA); Socialist countries
Economic growth
  decline in Soviet Union, 357-8
  decline in United States, 359-60
  Eastern Europe, 4
  effects of inflation, 75
  effects of oil price increases, 52
  effects of social consensus, 60
  endogenous factors, 209
  export-led
    in socialist countries, 225-6
    strategies in GDR, 123-31
  future prospects, 59
  in 1950s and 1960s, 155
  influence on choice of foreign economic strategy, 204
  of German-speaking countries, 217
  policy of West German Stability and Growth Act, 67, 68
  recovery in West, 2
  related to strategy formulation, 1
  within market-oriented system, 3, 68
  Yugoslavia, 262
Economic growth rate
  Austria, and effect on debt servicing, 94-5
  China, 29
  CMEA, 29
  EMS countries, 140
  German Democratic Republic, 112, 116
  optimal, for structured economies, 112
  West Germany, decrease, 70

Economy
comparisons of market and centrally-planned, 183
role of governments, 184
see also Foreign economic strategy; Macroeconomic policies
ECU, *see* European Currency Unit
Electronics, nontariff barriers, 160, 162
Employers' associations, wage negotiations, Federal Republic of Germany, 69
Employment
capital substitution, 168
effect of protectionism, 167-8
effects of inflation, 75
in Austria, working week shortened, 97-8, 222
policy of West German Stability and Growth Act, 67
EMS, *see* European Monetary System
Energy
conservation, in finishing processes, 113
conservation programmes, 51, 52, 61, 128
effect of oil price decrease, 25
IIASA study, 302
imports to socialist countries, 106
in Taurus strategic plan, 288
intensification of use in German Democratic Republic, 113, 117
OECD consumption growth, 25
price mechanism, 244
resource limitations, 51, 52, 61
sources in German Democratic Republic, 128, 130
Enterprise size, in strategic planning, 282-3
Escape clause procedures, 169-73, 178, 224
European Currency Unit (ECU), 9, 133
advantages, 141
bank assets and liabilities (1983-5), 153
bond issues (1983-5), 153
development in private financial markets, 140, 141
importance of West Germany, 9, 142, 144, 145
limited official use, 141
private/official link, 141-2
role in an international monetary system, 142-3
European Economic Community
agricultural subsidies, 177
agricultural trade with US, 158-9
Common Agricultural Policy (CAP), 157, 158
compared with CMEA, 196, 197
effect on foreign trade policy, 81
foreign direct investment, 191
foreign economic strategy, 190-1
trade not affected by EMS, 137-8
European Monetary System (EMS), 8-9, 227
aims, 137
and liberalisation of capital movements, 144-5
case for UK entry, 9, 143-4, 145
convergence, 134-7
nominal and real exchange rates, 134-5
real interest and inflation rates, 135-6
early fears, 133
economic growth rates, 140
effect on foreign trade policy, 81
successes, 133
trade imbalances, 136-7
trade not stimulated by, 138-9
Exchange rates
Austrian policy, 94
effects of EMS, 134-5
floating, 74
fluctuations
and demands for protectionism, 173, 224
and nontariff barriers, 179
post-1969, 33
variability in EMS, 147
West German policy, 69
see also European Currency Unit; European Monetary System; International monetary system
Export promotion, 206
by centrally planned economies, 195
characteristics, 185
influence on economic performance, 210
Exports
bank interests in deciding markets, 105
competitive performance, 209
from centrally planned economies, 198
from CMEA to West, 342-3
German Democratic Republic
incentives, 120-2
strategy, 129-30
importance to socialist economic reform, 102-3
institutions established by socialist countries, 104
External balances
effect of international institution membership, 81
policy of West German Stability and Growth Act, 67,69-70

Factory automation, 321
strategic planning by industry, 325-8
Fink, Gerhard, 5, *59-60*
Fiscal policies, for price control in Poland, 249-50
Food supplies, importance to political stability, 117

Forecasts, 79
as basis of planning, 298
factors for consideration, 307
importance of information systems, 295
importance to target achievement, 70-1
in strategic planning, 316
problems confronting, 19
reasons for limited accuracy, 295, 300-1
scientific, 15
types, 299-301
use of mathematical models, 301-3
world trade growth (1986-90), 42
see also Planning
Foreign direct investment, 183, 186-7
between CMEA countries, 200-1
centrally planned economies, 198-201
constraints on profitability, 199-200
European Economic Community, 191
Hong Kong and Singapore, 188
regulation, 186
Foreign economic strategies, 228-9
and instruments, 183-7
Brazil, 188-90
centrally planned economies, 192-203
consequences of choice of alternatives, 208-14
determinants of choice of strategy, 203-8
elements, 184-5
European Economic Community, 190-1
export-orientated, 208
foreign direct investment, 183, 186-7
foreign financial integration, 187
Hong Kong, 188
international financial integration, market economies, 190
Japan, 188-90
market economies, 188-92
outward-orientated, 208, 209-12
Singapore, 188
South Korea, 188-90
Taiwan, 188-90
trade, 185-6
Foreign exchange
dollar-rouble imbalances, 105
equilibrium, 105
see also Exchange rates
Foreign trade participation ratio (FTPR), 185
France, inflation rates, 136
Free trade, compared with nontariff barriers, 167
FRG, *see* Germany, Federal Republic

GATT, *see* General Agreement on Tariffs and Trade (GATT)
General Agreement on Tariffs and Trade (GATT), 9-10, 157, 158, 179, 224-5
bypassed by VERs, 166, 178, 315-16
German Democratic Republic (GDR)
agriculture, 8
traded goods, 116-20
economic growth, 112, 116, 218-19, 219-20
economic reform needs, 111
economic strategy, 111
energy sources, 128, 130
export-led growth strategies, 123-31
export promotion, 113
exports, incentives, 120-2
foreign trade, 111
indebtedness, 201
industry
cooperation with universities, 127
efficiency, 128-9
renewal, 112-13
integration with CMEA, 124
intensive development, 125-7
labour costs, 126
links with Western countries, 111
macroeconomic policies, 7-8
price structure, 120-2
product renewal rate, 127-8
productivity, 113-14
projected national income (1990), 113
trade strategy, 129-31
trade with non-socialist countries, 116
trade with Soviet Union, 115
wages, 126
Germany, Federal Republic (FRG)
central role in future of ECU, 9, 142, 144, 145
Council of Economic Experts, 66, 76
economic growth, 21, 217-18, 220-1
Economic Policy Council, 75
Economic Stability and Growth Act (1967), 65, 66-70
economic statistics, 83-90
failure of economic management (post-1960s), 70-5
free economic order, 65
indebtedness, 70, 72
inflation rates, 136
macroeconomic policies, 5-6
factors influencing, 65
necessary conditions for success, 79-82
monetary policy, 69, 74, 77
shift to monetary management, 75-9
no policy coordination (1950s and 1960s), 65
political differences on economic policy, 65
public sector (continued)
expansion, 70, 72-3, 75, 76, 80-1
Fiscal Planning Council, 75
social market economy, 65-70

Stability and Growth Act, 5, 65, 66-7, 68, 69-70, 220, 221
analysis of outcome, 75
targets, 67, 70-5
taxation, 70, 72-3, 75, 78
trade unions, 69, 73
unemployment, 70
weakened investment, 22
Global balance planning, Yugoslavia (1956-61), 255
Global economy, 4
distinguished from world economy, 47
effect of West's strategy, 124
features of monetary system, 54
influence of policy changes, 55-6
lessons for national policies, 58
logic of change, 61, 62
'partisan global policy', 54-5, 57, 61
process of change, 49-50
projection models, 49
see also World economy
Gold sales, by Soviet Union, 40
Government procurement
nontariff barriers, 157, 158
Poland, 238-9
Governments
political strength, influence on choice of foreign economic strategy, 206
role in economy, 184
role in Yugoslav investment, 265
Grain, price reduction, effect on East-West trade, 36

Heinrichs, Wolfgang, 7-8, *111-22*, 225
Historical factors, influence on choice of foreign economic strategy, 204
Hong Kong
foreign economic strategy, 188, 203
nontariff barriers against, 160, 162
Horváth, László, 14-15, 16, *279-314*, 333-4, 337, 341-2, *353-4*
Hungary
economic reforms, 7, 102, 213
foreign direct investment, 198
foreign economic policy, 211
imports from West, 195
indebtedness, 44, 59, 201
industry, 333-4
introduction of economic reforms, 102
joint companies in other countries, 104
macroeconomic policies, 7
property rights, 353
rubber industry, 284-5
see also Taurus Rubber Works
strategic planning, 279-83
goals, 280, 282-3
time span, 280

IIASA, *see* International Institute for Applied Systems Analysis
IMF, *see* International Monetary Fund
Import substitution
as protectionism, 11
bureaucratic control, 210
by industry in German Democratic Republic, 130
characteristics, 185-6
competition implications, 210
constraints on manufacturing inputs, 209-10
Eastern Europe, 205
in centrally planned economies, 194
in developing countries, 205
in socialist countries, 11
Imports, effect on socialist macroeconomic policy, 106
see also Trade
Income
distribution
effect of oil price increases, 50
global anomalies, 52, 53
substitution, constraints on foreign economic strategy choice, 208
Incomes policy
Austria, 92, 98
results, 92-4
Federal Republic of Germany, 69, 76-7
role in macroeconomic policy formation, 79
Indebtedness, *see* Debt
India, economic strategy, 191-2
Indicative planning, Yugoslavia (1961-75), 255, 256
Indonesia, indebtedness, 25, 33, 45
Industry
aided by implicit nontariff barriers, 157-8
Austria, structure, 99
CMEA, vertical integration within countries, 197
competition, leading to protectionism, 163
cooperation agreements, 187
development for export, in socialist countries, 103-4
effect of targeting, 174
escape clause procedures, 169-73, 178, 224
finishing processes, 113
German Democratic Republic
cooperation with universities, 127
efficiency, 128-9
increased effectiveness, 113-15
intensive development, 125-7
need for renewal, 112-13

markets for socialist countries, 103-4
organisation, resistance to monopoly, 232-3
Poland, demand excess, 232, 236-7
policy, and new protectionism, 173-5
production, in EEC, USA and Japan, 152
structural changes, effects on planning, 315
subsidies, 173, 179, 224
US development bank proposal, 175
Yugoslavia, investment share, 263
see also Factory automation; Joint ventures; Resource allocation
Inflation
Austria, 91
block to target achievement, 67-8
corrected by monetary policy, 75
effects of EMS on rates, 136
expectations of workforce, 62
following oil price increases, 52
reduction, 33
and increased unemployment, 36
correlation with oil price decreases, 34
remaining pockets of high levels, 36
Information systems
application of modelling techniques, 297
complexity, 296
importance in forecasting, 295
role in Yugoslav investment decisions, 266
Interest rates
Austria, 95
effects of EMS, 135-6
increase, leading to indebtedness, 57
international rises, effect on Austria, 95
long-term in European countries (1972-86), 149
reduction, 33, 35-6, 62
effect on debtor countries, 37
effect on East-West trade, 36
short-term in European countries (1972-86), 148
United States, 20
International cooperation, 124
International financial integration, centrally planned economies, 201-3
International Institute for Applied Systems Analysis (IIASA), 302
International Monetary Fund (IMF), 187, 201
advantages for socialist producers, 106
effect on foreign trade policy, 81
membership of centrally planned economies, 201
International monetary system, role of the ECU, 141, 142-3
International Trade Organisation, 156-7
Investment
decline in Eastern Europe, 43
fixed capital, 22
in Soviet technology, 28
in Taurus strategic plan, 288
Poland, 355-6
demand restraint, 242-4
Yugoslavia, 255-67
allocation, 262-5
decision-making, 13, 265-7, 336, 344-5, 348-51
Metalservis experience, 275-6
efficiency decrease, 263
Long-Term Stabilisation Programme, 259
priority system, 258
role of workers in decision-making, 260-1
sources of finance, 264, 265
system after 1974, 257-60
see also Foreign direct investment
Iran, indebtedness, 25
Iraq, indebtedness, 25
Italy, inflation rates, 136

Japan
automobile industry, 223-4, 320
VER on exports, 163-4
foreign economic strategy, 188-90, 203
GDP growth rates (1986), 21
industrial subsidies, 177
international financial integration, 190
nontariff barriers, 159, 161, 223
reduced inflation, 36
steel industry, 174, 224
trade prospects (late 1980s), 42
weakened investment, 22
see also Yen
Joint ventures, 46, 321
automobile industry, 320
with Taurus (Hungary), 291-2

Kaufman, Richard F, 3, *357-61*
Klein, Lawrence R., 2-5, *33-46*, 59, 62, 64, 223
Kloten, Norbert, 5-6, 11, *65-90*, 217, 220-1
Kraus, Aleksander, 14, 17, *269-77*, 337, 341, 343
Kreuter, Josef, 16, *330-6*, 353-4, 356
Labour costs, German Democratic Republic, 126
Latin America
destabilisation threat, 57
export and import volume reductions, 23
foreign economic strategy, 204, 205
indebtedness, 45
trade prospects (late 1980s), 42-3
Leontief, Wassily, 19
economic projections, 48
LINK, *see* Project LINK

Lipiński, Jan, 12-13, 16, 17, *231-53*, 334-5, 345-7, 352,*354-6*
Lukaszewicz, Aleksander, 11, *228-9*

Machine tools, nontariff barriers, 160, 162
Macroeconomic policies
  Austria, *91-9*
  conditions necessary for success, 79-82
  factors influencing, 65
  Federal Republic of Germany, 65-70
    conditions for success, 79-82
    factors influencing, 65
  influencing choice of foreign economic strategy, 205-6
  medium-term strategies, 80
  of socialist countries, interests of individual companies, 104
  transformation and import-saving model, 101-3
Macroeconomic controls, effect on economic performance, 210-11
Management, *see* Business management
Managers
  line, role in strategic planning, 16, 317-18, 324
  role in planning, 312-13
Marer, Paul, 10-11, *183-216*, 228-9
Market economy
  basis of West German Stability and Growth Act, 66
  foreign economic strategies, 188-92
  provision of basic data, 80
Market position, in strategic planning, 280, 282
Marketing, organisation by Taurus (Hungary), 291-2
Markets
  partial, 232
  structural forms, 232-3
  structure and dynamics, 322
Mathematical models, *see* Modelling
Metalservis, 14, 269-77, 343
  current preoccupations, 277
  development, 273-5
  equipment from West, 271
  historical background, 269
  introduction of experts, 270
  links with small enterprises, 274
  new storage constructed, 270-1
  takeover of Belgrade Institute for Scientific Research, 275
Mexico
  economic strategy, 191
  indebtedness, 25, 33, 42-3, 45
  macroeconomic controls, 212
Middle East, trade prospects (late 1980s), 43
Mining, Yugoslavia, investment share, 263
Modelling
  applied to information systems, 297
  of world economy, 48
  use in forecasting, 301-3
  see also Project LINK; Wharton World Model
Monetary policy
  Austria, 92, 97
  Federal Republic of Germany, 69
    Cash Deposit Act (1972), 74
    DM floated, 74
    external influences, 77
    from 1975 on, 77
    limited policy results, 70, 74-5
    targets, 77
  integration through EMS, 145
  role in macroeconomic policy formation, 79
  to correct inflation, 75
Monetary system, after oil price rises, 54
Multi Fibre Arrangements, 162
Multinational corporations
  cooperation with centrally planned economies, 198-9, 203
  in EEC, 191
  links with centrally planned economies, 203
  see also Transnational enterprises
National sovereignty, and foreign direct investment, 186
Natural gas
  price linked with oil, 40
  Soviet trade with West, 40
Natural resources, influence on choice of foreign economic strategy, 203-4
Netherlands, inflation rates, 136
New International Economic Order (NIEO), 54, 55
  failure, 53, 56
Nigeria, indebtedness, 33, 45
Nontariff barriers, 9-10, 155-81
  attacking strategies, 176-7
  causes and effects, 162-9
  compared with free trade, 167
  escape clause petitions, 169-73, 178, 224
  explicit and implicit, 157, 223
  from 1975, 155
  future effects on international trade, 175-8
  Japan, 159, 161
  products affected, 160, 161
  retaliatory action, 156
  share of world trade affected, 159, 161
  United States, 156
Nuti, Domenico Mario, 11, *219-21*

Oil
decreased production, effects, 25
demand from OECD, 25
prices, 3, 4
decrease, 19, 33, 62
effect on East-West trade, 36, 38-42
effect on Eastern Europe, 41-2
effect on Soviet export revenues, 38-40
effect on world economy, 25, 33
fluctuations, 64
future prospects, 59
gas prices linked, 40
increases
effect on Austrian economy, 91, 92
global effects, 50-2
impact on non-OPEC countries, 60
OPEC's lack of control, 64
reactions to, 61
Soviet/OPEC aim to increase, 39
stabilisation efforts, 25
Oil industry
Hungarian hoses, 290
project evaluation, 297-8
Orderly market arrangements, 157, 162
Organisation for Economic Cooperation and Development (OECD)
energy consumption growth, 25
growth of GDP, 223
rise in unemployment, 36
Organisation of Petroleum Exporting Countries (OPEC), 4
debt of poorer countries, 25
fall in export income, 23, 25, 36
global effect of oil price increases, 50-2
price stabilisation efforts, 25
reacting to market forces, 64

Pajestka, Józef, 2, 4, 5, *47-58*, 60, 61-2, 64
Payne, Bruce, 271
Personnel, in strategic planning, 282, 283
Peru, indebtedness, 45
Petrodollar recycling, 57
Philippines, indebtedness, 45
Planning
and complexity, 338-9
as a science, 337-8
centralisation, 298
see also Centrally planned economies
choice of objective function, 303-4
delegated, 310-12, 351, 352
factors for consideration, 307
forecast-based, 298
assumptions examined, 299-304
in changing business environment, 304-6, 331
historical background, 296
in Soviet Union, 28-9
in Western corporations, 330
investment projects, in Yugoslavia, 266-7
nature, 337
need for clear aims, 309-10
Yugoslav strategies (1947 to date), 255-7
see also Forecasts; Strategic planning
Poland, 334-51
behaviour of enterprise managements, 233-5
demand excesses, 232, 235-7, 345, 355
demand restraint, 242-4
demand-supply relationship, 236-7
proposals for future, 251-3
ways to improve, 240-2
economic reforms, 12, 231, 344-5, 354
foreign direct investment, 198
imports from West, 195
increasing efficiency of state-owned enterprises, 252
indebtedness, 37, 44, 45, 59
investment decisions, 242-3, 355-6
macroeconomic controls, 212
obstacles to equilibrium, 345-8
prices, 12, 235, 236, 347
controls, 247-8
fiscal instruments, 249-50
mechanism, 244-9
rises, 241-2
relationship between management and workers, 234
resource allocation
protected zone, 237-9
unprotected zone, 239-40
state-owned enterprises, autonomy, 231, 233
wages, 241
Political factors
in forecasting, 307-8
influence on choice of foreign economic strategy, 205
Prebisch, Raúl, 49, 54, 205
Prices
Austria, 95, 98
changes, EEC, USA and Japan, 150
CMEA, 198
commodity, effect of reductions, 36
fluctuations, 315
German Democratic Republic
ceilings, 120, 121
premiums, 121-2
reductions for outdated products, 121-2
Poland, 12, 235, 236, 347
controls, 247-8
mechanism, 244-9
rises, 241-2
West German Stability and Growth Act, 67

Product renewal rate, German Democratic Republic, 127-8
Production potential, as economic indicator, 80
Productivity
  Austria, 99
  German Democratic Republic, 113-14
Project evaluation, 297-8
  in uncertainty, 304, 306
Project LINK, 3, 48
  dollar depreciation effects, 34
  oil price decrease effects, 33
Protectionism
  and import substitution, 185-6
  and industrial policy, 173-5
  effect on developing countries, 23, 178
  effect on employment, 167-8
  effect on world economic development, 124
  escape clause procedures, 169-73, 178, 224
  in centrally planned economies, 194
  in light of other macroeconomic policies, 168
  inherent in centrally planned economies, 212-13
  Japan, 189
  nontariff barriers, 9-10
  restricting competition, 210
  South Korea, 189
  strategies to reverse trend, 179
  Taiwan, 189
  United States, 23, 45
  use as political lever, 24
  see also Nontariff barriers; Tariff barriers
Public sector
  role in macroeconomic policy formation, 79
  West German expansion, 70, 80-1
    Fiscal Planning Council, 75
    increased public employment, 72, 73
    policy changes, 77-8
    restructuring expenditure, 76
Purchasing power parities, EMS currencies, 135

Quotas, 157

Rall, Wilhelm, 15-16, *315-29*, 331, 337, 338, 339, 343
Raw materials
  imports to socialist countries, 106
  intensification of use in German Democratic Republic, 113, 117
  price mechanism, in Poland, 244-5
Recession
  of 1975, 155
  leading to indebtedness, 57
  policy aim, 61
  reaction to OPEC price increases, 56-7
  social repercussions, 52
Resource allocation
  and wastage, 335
  Poland
    protected zone, 237-9
    unprotected zone, 239-40
  use of forecasts, 298
Romania
  foreign direct investment, 198
  imports from West, 195
  indebtedness, 59, 201
Rubber industry (Hungary)
  consumption, 284
  development alternatives, 285-6
  foreign trade, 284-5
  international trade, 289
  labour productivity, 285, 288
  role in economy, 284
  structure, 285
  see also Taurus Rubber Works

Salvatore, Dominick, 9-10, 11, *155-81*, 223-4
Saudi Arabia, oil supply/demand balance, 64
Saunders, Christopher, *1-17*
Scenario development, 308
Schumacher, Frederick, 303
SDI, *see* Strategic Defence Initiative
Seidel, Hans, 6, *91-9*, 217, 218, 221-2
Self-management planning, 341-2
  Yugoslavia (1975 to date), basic features, 255, 256-7, 270
    role of workers in decision-making ,260-1
Singapore
  foreign economic strategy, 188, 203
  nontariff barriers against, 160, 162
Social factors, linked with economic strategies, 123, 126
Social security contributions, increases in West Germany, 70, 75, 78
Socialist countries
  contribution to world economic development, 26
  cut off from international progress, 124
  economic instruments, 107
  effect of changes in international monetary system, 55
  export-orientated industries, 104
  external economics, government decision-making involvement,107-8
  financial system interests, 105-6
  foreign economic strategies, of centrally planned economies, 192-203
  foreign trade policies, 101-3
  import policies, 106-8
  import substitution, 11

importance of external economic factor, 102
introduction of economic reforms, reconciling interests, 103-5
macroeconomic policies, government tasks, 1, 108-9
outward oriented policies, 225-7
structure of economic decision-making, 101-9
see also Council for Mutual Economic Assistance (CMEA)
South Korea
foreign economic strategy, 188-90, 203
international financial integration, 190
nontariff barriers against, 160, 162
Soviet Union
decline in economic growth, 357-8
defence spending, 358, 361
effect on economic performance, 359
economic reforms, 59-60
economic strategy, 26-7
effect of oil price decreases, 36-7
on export revenues, 38-40
energy and raw material exports, 197
forecast growth rates, 43
forecast hard currency exports, 43
foreign direct investment, 198
gold sales, 40
import substitution, 41
indebtedness, 43-4, 201
loans from West, 40
natural gas sales to West, 40
new economic mechanism, 28-9
planning, 28-9
reform of social relations, 29
repayment of debts by east European countries, 37
technological development, 27-8
technological imports, 41
trade with German Democratic Republic, 115
Sri Lanka, economic strategy, 192
Stagflation, 60, 61
counterreaction to oil price increases, 51-2
State-owned enterprises, *see* Poland, state-owned enterprises
Steel industry
Japan, 174, 224
nontariff barriers, 160, 162
Sterling
as EMS reserve currency, 143
volatility compared with EMS currencies, 134-5
Strategic Defence Initiative, projected costs, 19
Strategic planning
aims, 279
and business cycles, 339
centralised, 340
East and West compared, 337
external orientation, 316
goals, 280, 282-3
Hungary, 279-83
in automobile industry, 331
in centrally planned economies, 341
in circumstances of uncertainty, 1, 15-16, 315
in factory automation industry, 325-8
in mature markets: case study, 319-25
in new markets, globalisation, 325, 326-8
interaction of personnel, 324-5, 328, 331, 340
leading to strategic management, 328-9
principles, 15
role of central planner, 344
role of line management, 16, 317-18, 324, 340
time span, 318
tools, 318-19
Strikes, in Austria, 93
Subsidies
agricultural, 177
and price control in Poland, 250
industrial, in USA, 177
Sydow, Peter, 7-8, *123-31*, 217, 219-20, 255

Taiwan
foreign economic strategy, 188-90, 203
international financial integration, 190
nontariff barriers against, 160, 162
Tardos, Márton, 11, *217-19*
Target achievement
and planning, 309-10
importance of excellent forecasting, 70-1
policy of West German Stability and Growth Act, 67
shortfall, 70-5
Tariff barriers, 157
Taurus Rubber Works, 14-15, 16, 333-4, 342-3, 353-4
capital investment, 288
marketing, 288-90
innovation link, 290-1
organisation, 291-2
product structure, 287
strategy formation, 283-8
Taxation in West Germany
consolidation policy, 78
increases, 70, 75, 78
repayable anticyclical surtax, 72
used as vote-attracting method, 73
Technological development
attendant risks, 45
Belgrade Institute for Scientific Research, 275

in CMEA countries, 46
in Hungarian rubber industry, 290-1
in strategic planning, 282
use of 'high technology', 351-2
see also Metalservis
Technology transfer, 46
German Democratic Republic, 111
Teodorovič, Ivan, 13, 17, *255-67*, 336, 341, 345, 348
Terms of trade, of developing countries, 205
Textiles
capital-labour ratio, 168
nontariff barriers, 160, 162
Thurow, Lester C., 21
Trade
balance, changes in EEC, USA and Japan, 151
CMEA with West (1970s and 1980s), 30
volume, 26
controls in centrally planned economies, 194
exchanges, commodity structure, 30-1
export-led, 226
foreign economic strategy, 185-6
future effects of nontariff barriers, 175-8
German Democratic Republic, 111, 116, 129-31
growth, effect on East-West trade, 36
imbalances in EMS countries, 136-7
in 1950s and 1960s, 155
international cooperation, 31-2
liberalisation, 155, 223
policies of centrally planned economies, 202
policies of socialist countries, 101-3
strategies, 10-11
volume, 1975-9 and 1980-5 compared, 156
worldwide restrictions, 24
Yugoslavia, 273
see also Nontariff barriers; Tariff barriers; World trade
Trade unions, 62
in Federal Republic of Germany
reaction to economic programmes, 73
wage negotiations, 69
Transformation and import-saving model, 101-3
Transnational enterprises
importance in global economy, 54
US dominance, 55
see also Multinational corporations
Transport in Yugoslavia
investment share, 263
Metalservis distribution network, 273-4
'Turnkey' projects, 31, 198
Uncertainty
and business management, 306-313
and planning, 1, 15-16, 315, 339
Unemployment, 1
Austria, 91, 98, 99, 222
effect of protectionism, 167-8
following oil price increases, 52
implications, 44
in OECD countries, 36
in West Germany, 70
leading to protectionism, 163
United Kingdom
case for joining European Monetary System, 9, 143-4, 145
interest rates, compared with EMS currencies, 135
United Nations
announcement of NIEO, 53
Development Decades, 48, 55
Development Planning Committee, 24
United States
agricultural subsidies, 158, 177
agricultural trade with Europe, 158-9
as debtor nation, 21, 35
automobile imports from Japan, 163-4, 223-4
budget deficit, 20, 63
arms costs, 20
financing, 20, 34
longer-term problems, 45
capital flight scenario, 34-5
decline in economic growth, 359-60
related to defence spending, 360
development bank proposal, 175
dominance of transnational corporations, 55
effect of recovery on Europe, 21
effects of borrowing on world economy, 19-22
equipment supplied to Yugoslavia, 271
escape clause procedures, 169-73, 178, 224
foreign capital flows, 20-1
GDP growth rates (1986), 21
indebtedness, 2-3
industrial subsidies, 177
interest rates, 20
multinational companies in EEC, 191
nontariff barriers, 156, 223
protectionism, 23, 45
reduced inflation, 36
relinquishing economic leadership role, 21-2
Tariff Commission, 169
Trade Act (1974), 170-1
trade deficits, 21
Trade Expansion Act (1962), 170-1

US dollar
appreciation, leading to indebtedness, 57
depreciation, 19, 33, 62
effects, 34-6
exchange rate fluctuations, 20
future prospects, 59
role in an international monetary system, 142
volatility compared with EMS currencies, 134-5

Venezuela, indebtedness, 33, 45
Voluntary export restraints (VERs), 10, 157, 162, 163, 178, 223
causes and effects, 164-6
Japanese automobile exports, 163-4

Wagener, Hans-Jürgen, 16, 17, *337-51*, 353, 355, 356
Wages
Austria
and international competitiveness, 94
flexibility, 93-4
German Democratic Republic, increases, 126
Poland, 241
increases, 234, 236
role in macroeconomic policy formation, 79
Western Europe
annual growth in GDP (1984-5), 26
joint ventures with East, 46
natural gas from Soviet Union, 40
reduced inflation, 36
supplying equipment to Yugoslavia, 271
trade with socialist countries, 26
Wharton World Model, 3
dollar depreciation effects, 34
oil prices, 33, 38, 39, 64
World Bank,187, 201
advantages for socialist producers, 106
membership of centrally planned economies, 201
World economy
analytical methods, 47-8
areas needing stimulation, 24
distinguished from global economy, 47
effect of 1986 events, 62
expansion, reducing protectionism, 176
favourable factors, 33
imbalances caused by indebtedness, 45
recession avoided in 1985, 44
see also Global economy
World trade
forecast growth rate (1986-90), 42
slump in mid-1980s, 42

Yen
role in an international monetary system, 142
volatility compared with EMS currencies, 134-5
Yugoslavia
Associated Labour Act, 269
economic reforms, 102, 213
foreign trade, 273
indebtedness, 44, 59
investment, Long Term Stabilisation Programme, 259
investment decision-making, 13, 255-67, 336, 344-5, 348-51
new developments, 265-7
role of workers, 260
planning strategies, 255
strategies planning, 341-2
see also Metalservis